CONTENTS

D1407606

volume **9** number **3** december **2004**

ANGELAKI
journal of the theoretical humanities

general issue **2004**

issue editor: **pelagia goulimari**

ANGELAKI

journal of the theoretical humanities

Subscription Information:

Angelaki: journal of the theoretical humanities is a peer-reviewed journal published three times a year (April, August and December), by Routledge Journals, an imprint of Taylor & Francis Ltd, 4 Park Square, Milton Park, Abingdon, Oxfordshire OX14 4RN, UK.

Annual Subscription, Volume 10, 2005 (Print ISSN 0969-725X)

US$318 £194   Individual US$74 £46

An institutional subscription to the print edition includes free access for any number of concurrent users across a local area network to the online edition, ISSN 1469–2899.

For more information, visit our website: http://www.tandf.co.uk/journals

For a complete and up-to-date guide to Taylor & Francis Group's journals and books publishing programmes, and details of advertising in our journals, visit our website: http://www.tandf.co.uk/journals

Dollar rates apply to subscribers in all countries except the UK and the Republic of Ireland where the pound sterling price applies. All subscriptions are payable in advance and all rates include postage. Journals are sent by air to the USA, Canada, Mexico, India, Japan and Australasia. Subscriptions are entered on an annual basis, i.e. January to December. Payment may be made by sterling cheque, dollar cheque, international money order, National Giro, or credit card (Amex, Visa, Mastercard).

Ordering information:

USA/Canada: Taylor & Francis Inc., Journals Department, 325 Chestnut Street, 8th Floor, Philadelphia, PA 19106, USA. UK/Europe/Rest of World: Taylor & Francis Ltd, Rankine Road, Basingstoke, Hampshire RG24 8PR, UK.

Advertising enquiries to:

USA/Canada: The Advertising Manager, Taylor & Francis Inc., 325 Chestnut Street, 8th Floor, Philadelphia, PA 19106, USA. Tel: +1 (215) 625 8900. Fax: +1 (215) 625 2240.

EU/RoW: The Advertising Manager, Taylor & Francis Ltd, 4 Park Square, Milton Park, Abingdon, Oxfordshire OX14 4RN, UK. Tel: +44 (0)1235 828600. Fax: +44 (0)1235 829000.

The print edition of this journal is typeset by Infotype Ltd, Eynsham, Oxfordshire, UK and printed on ANSI conforming acid free paper by Alden Press, Oxford, UK. The online edition of this journal is hosted by Metapress at http://www.journalsonline.tandf.co.uk

journal of the theoretical humanities
volume 9 number 3 december 2004

Angelaki publishes three issues per year: two special issues followed by one general issue. Our 2005 special issues, edited by Damian Veal, are both devoted to Continental philosophy of science and are closed to submissions. The 2005 general issue will remain open until the end of February 2005. The first special issue of 2006, *Creative Philosophy: Theory and Praxis*, is being edited by Felicity J. Colman and Charles J. Stivale. For a Call for Papers, please write to fcolman@unimelb.edu.au or c_stivale @wayne.edu. Abstracts of 500–750 words should be submitted electronically by 15 February 2005.

The journal invites proposals for special issues for publication in 2006 onwards. Please write to me (see below) with a brief outline of your collection idea. *Angelaki* collections are normally around eighty thousand words and include ten to fourteen essays. The journal does not publish proceedings, though edited collections to be developed from conferences will be considered.

in theory, 1993–2004

The year 2003 saw ten years of *Angelaki*. The journal was established in September 1993 to provide an international forum for vanguard work in the theoretical humanities, identified as the productive nexus of work in the disciplinary fields of philosophy, literary criticism and cultural studies. It has now published over four hundred pieces of work. *Angelaki*'s sustained volume and quality of publishing over a decade has established it as one of the leading interdisciplinary humanities journals in the world. We have made a selection of one hundred articles from our output since 1993 and the list can be found at the URL below. Please take a look, and if your library is not yet subscribing we would

EDITORIAL INTRODUCTION

pelagia goulimari

GENERAL ISSUE 2004

be very grateful if you would direct departmental decision makers to the site. The journal is now included in *Arts and Humanities Citation Index* and *Current Contents Arts and Humanities*. http://www.tandf.co.uk/journals/titles/rangintheory.asp

debate

We encourage the submission of responses to work published in the journal. These will be considered for publication in the Debate section of general issues.

angelaki humanities book series

The fifth book in the series, *Subversive Spinoza: (Un)Contemporary Variations*, a collection of

ISSN 0969-725X print/ISSN 1469-2899 online/04/030001–02 © 2004 Taylor & Francis Ltd and the Editors of *Angelaki*
DOI: 10.1080/0969725042000307574

editorial introduction

essays by Antonio Negri, edited by Timothy S. Murphy, was published in August of this year. The sixth volume, *Late Modernist Poetics: From Pound to Prynne*, by Anthony Mellors, will be published before the end of the year. The year 2006 should see the reissue of Michèle Le Doeuff's *Hipparchia's Choice: An Essay Concerning Women, Philosophy, Etc.* and also *Postmodernism: What Moment?*, a collection edited by Pelagia Goulimari.

acknowledgements

I am most grateful to the following for peer reviewing: Gary Banham, Jon Beasley-Murray, Charlie Blake, Leslie Anne Boldt-Irons, Zachary J. Braiterman, Mark Cauchi, Melinda Cooper, Simon Critchley, David Cunningham, Samir Dayal, Simon Duffy, Alexander García Düttmann, Diane Elam, Aden Evens, Moira Gatens, Philip Goodchild, Andrew Haas, Peter Hallward, Antoine Hatzenberger, Joanna Hodge, Lars Iyer, Nikolas Kompridis, Gray Kochhar-Lindgren, Filip Kovacevic, William Large, Diane Morgan, Forbes Morlock, Warwick Mules, John Mullarkey, Timothy S. Murphy, Saul Ostrow, Thomas Anthony Reynolds, Daniel W. Smith, Robert Smith, Charles J. Stivale, Barry Stocker, Cornelia Tsakiridou, David Webb, Shane Weller, Rob White, and Sarah Wood.

jacques derrida, 1930–2004

The editors of *Angelaki* salute the memory of Jacques Derrida.

Pelagia Goulimari
General Editor
Angelaki
36A Norham Road
Oxford OX2 6SQ
UK
E-mail: goulimari@angelaki1.demon.co.uk
http://www.tandf.co.uk/journals/titles/
0969725X.asp

ANGELAKI
journal of the theoretical humanities
volume 9 number 3 december 2004

I am not a "political philosopher." I do not believe generally in the "divisions" of philosophy. Nor do I believe in localising philosophy within some division of knowledges and discourses. For me, philosophy consists of singular nodes of thought which are opened by undoing the established divisions between disciplines. Indeed, against these divisions, I have continued to wander into literature, social history, politics, and aesthetics. And I have continued to do so because of problems and objects of thought thrown up by "non-philosophical" events.

So, in the wake of '68 and the thwarting of the hoped-for union of students' and workers' movements, I set out to reconsider the history of relations between workers' movements and utopias or theories of social transformation. I tried to understand the history of workers' emancipation from its beginning, to show its originary complexity, and the complexity of its relations with those utopias and theories.

Later, in response to developments in the 1990s, I tried to elaborate a theoretical framework for a new reflection on politics. The situation in the 1990s was one of surprises, surprises which required a rethinking of the notion of democracy and, indeed, the idea of politics itself.

In the first instance, the collapse of the Soviet system had an effect *à double détente*. It seemed to spell the death of the old opposition between formal and real democracy and, therefore, to herald the triumph of the values of so-called formal democracy. That is, it seemed to allow the values of democratic debate to be identified with those of the liberal economy and the state of right. We then experienced a flourish of assertions of the return of politics in different forms: some, following Leo Strauss, celebrated the return to the original values of politics,

jacques rancière

translated by steven corcoran

INTRODUCING DISAGREEMENT[1]

understood as the search for the common good; others rediscovered the Arendtian vision, opposing political action to the empire of social necessity; still others put forward the Rawlsian theory of justice as equity and the Habermasian conception of communicative action as models of democracy.

What the collapse of the Soviet system soon betrayed, however, was an internal weakening of the very democracy that was assumed to have triumphed. For the moment, I am not speaking of problems in the former communist countries. The identification of formal democracy with the liberal economy in fact manifested itself more and more in the so-called democratic regimes. It appeared as the internal exhaustion of democratic debate. The end of the socialist alterna-

ISSN 0969-725X print/ISSN 1469-2899 online/04/030003-07 © 2004 Taylor & Francis Ltd and the Editors of *Angelaki*
DOI: 10.1080/0969725042000307583

tive, then, did not signify any renewal of democratic debate. Instead, it signified the reduction of democratic life to the management of the local consequences of global economic necessity. The latter, in fact, was posited as a common condition which imposed the same solutions on both left and right. Consensus around these solutions became the supreme democratic value.

What thus accompanied the routing of Marxist regimes was the triumph of a certain Marxism, one which turned political forms into instruments of economic interests and necessities. At the same time, theories of the "return of politics," the common good, etc. became ideal justifications of the consensual order. Assertions of the primacy of the political over the "social" could be heard everywhere. What these assertions served to do in reality, however, was to stigmatise the social movements fighting against the identification of democracy with the state administration of economic necessity.[2] The apparent return of politics was, in fact, its liquidation. That liquidation in turn required nothing less than a rethinking of the following questions. What is the specificity of democracy? What is the specificity of politics as a form of common action? And what does this "common" consist of?

This reflection became all the more necessary as the triumph of consensual democracy brought with it some strange counter-effects. "Consensus" was presented as the pacification of conflicts that arose from ideologies of social struggle, and yet it brought about anything but peace. Not only have a number of states liberated from the Soviet system fallen prey to ethnic and religious conflicts – occasionally in radical forms – but a number of consensual-democratic states have also witnessed the re-emergence and success of racist and xenophobic movements.

At the time, these new forms of violence disturbing the consensual idyll were seen in two ways. First, they were thought from within the logic of consensus. That is, they were understood as exceptions to the consensus and, as exceptions, they were presented as remnants of the past or temporary regressions. The success of the extreme right in France and then in other European countries was accordingly explained away as the reaction of social strata threatened by modernisation.

My thinking took the reverse tack: these phenomena had to be thought not as exceptions to but as consequences of the logic of consensus. They had to be thought as effects not of economic and sociological causes but of the erasure of democracy and politics constitutive of the logic of consensus. Politics, in other words, had to be thought as something denied by identity politics, because it had already been denied by the logic of consensus. Politics had also to be thought as something radically heterogeneous to the tradition of political philosophy. That is what determined the re-reading of the political-philosophical tradition I undertook in *Disagreement*.

This tradition considers politics to be the result of an anthropological invariant. The invariant may be the fear that compels individuals to unite. Or it may be the possession of language that permits discussion. In the return to political philosophy much has been made of this linguistic power of the human animal, with reference either to the Aristotelian definition of man as an animal endowed with logos or to the pragmatics of language found in Habermas. In both cases, the definition of political citizenship seems to follow logically from the definition of the human animal as an animal endowed with language. Aristotle says in essence: man is a political animal – he can be recognised by his possession of logos, which is what enables him to discuss the just and the unjust, while animals have a voice only to express pleasure and pain (*Politics* 1253a). Elsewhere he adds that a citizen is one who participates in the fact of governing and being governed. Deducing the second proposition from the first is apparently simple, as is founding the reciprocity that characterises politics and democracy in general on the shared human privilege of language. In the same way, Habermas shows that entering into an interlocutory relation in order to defend certain interests or values requires submitting assertions to objective criteria of validity, on pain of performative contradiction. It seems that the fact of giving one's word to be understood implies an immanent telos of inter-comprehension as the basis of rational community.

There is, of course, no evidence for this kind of conclusion. Indeed, immediately after positing the essence of the political animal, Aristotle makes a distinction between those who possess language and those, like slaves, who can only understand it. This is because the possession of language is not a physical capacity. It is a symbolic division, that is, a symbolic determination of the relation between the order of speech and that of bodies — which is why the very distinction between human speech and an animal's voice is problematic. Traditionally, it had been enough not to hear what came out of the mouths of the majority of human beings — slaves, women, workers, colonised peoples, etc. — as language, and instead to hear only cries of hunger, rage, or hysteria, in order to deny them the quality of being political animals. It was in just such terms around 1830 that the French thinker Ballanche rewrote the apologia of the plebeian secession on the Aventine Hill in ancient Rome. The conflict was, above all, one over what it was to speak. Plebeians, gathered on the Aventine Hill, demanded a treaty with the patricians. The patricians responded that this was impossible, because to make a treaty meant giving one's word: since the plebeians did not have human speech, they could not give what they did not have. They possessed only a "sort of bellowing which was a sign of need and not a manifestation of intelligence." In order to understand what the plebeians said, then, it had first to be admitted that they spoke. And this required a novel perceptual universe, one where — contrary to all perceptible evidence — those who worked for a living had affairs in common with free men and a voice to designate and argue these common affairs.

This is what "disagreement [*mésentente*]" means. It cannot be deduced from the anthropological fact of language. Nothing can be deduced from some anthropological property common to humanity in general, because the "common" is always contested at the most immediate level: the fact of living in the same world, with the same senses [*sens*], and the same powers of holding something in common. Deducing the existence of a common political world from the comprehension of language can never be natural when that world presupposes a quarrel over what is common. *Mésentente* — a term untranslatable into English — indicates this node in between two things. It means both "the fact of not hearing, of not understanding" and "quarrel, disagreement." Combining both meanings yields only this: the fact of hearing and understanding language does not in itself produce any of the effects of an egalitarian community. Egalitarian effects occur only through a forcing, that is, the instituting of a quarrel that challenges the incorporated, perceptible evidence of an inegalitarian logic. This quarrel is politics.

Indeed, that is what is implied by the word "democracy." The name needs to retain all its polemical force. It was invented not by democrats as a rallying cry but by their adversaries as a term of abuse. Democracy meant the power of the people with nothing, the speech of those who should not be speaking, those who were not really speaking beings. The first significant occurrences of the term "demos" are to be found in Homer and always appear in speech situations. Greek and Trojan leaders alike denounced the same scandal: that men of the demos — men who were part of the indistinct collection of people "beyond count" — took the liberty of speaking.

The word "demos" does not designate the poor or suffering part of the population. Properly it designates those who are outside the count, those who can assert no particular title over common affairs. In *The Laws*, Plato enumerates all the titles — age, birth, virtue, knowledge, strength, etc. — to exercising power, titles which give some the right to govern others — who are, conversely, young, of low birth, ignorant, etc. Right at the end of the list, though, is a title which is not one: God's part, as he ironically puts it, that is, the lot of fate, chance, or, simply, democracy.

Democracy, then, is the specific power of those who have no common title to exercise power, except that of not being entitled to its exercise. Democracy is the disrupting of all logics that purport to found domination on some entitlement to dominate. There are many such

5

logics, but through various mediations they can be reduced to two: those of birth and wealth. By contrast, the power of those without title is the accident that interrupts the play of these logics, and with it the dominant movement that leads from the archaic power of birth to the modern power of wealth. It is this accident which allows politics as such to exist. Politics is not the general art of governing human assemblies by virtue of some principle inherent in the definition of a human being. It is the accident that interrupts the logic by which those who have a title to govern dominate – a title confirmed only by the fact that they do dominate. Human government is not the putting into practice of some "political virtue" native to the human animal. Instead, all that exists are the contingency of domination founded on itself and the contingency of equality which suspends it.

Between the general human capacity for speech and the definition of "citizenship" as the capacity to govern and be governed lies "disagreement," which opens the sphere of politics as a suspension of all logics that would ground domination in some specific virtue. Here lies the power of the demos, understood as the collection of those with no title to dominate or be dominated. Democracy, in this sense, is not one political regime within a classification of different forms of government. Nor is it a form of social life, as the Tocquevillean tradition would have it. Rather, democracy is the institution of politics itself as the aberrant form of government.

The term "demos," as the very subject of politics, sums up the aberrant, anarchic nature of politics. The demos is not the real totality or ideal totalisation of a human collectivity. Neither is it the masses as opposed to the elite. The demos is, instead, an abstract separation of a population from itself. It is a supplementary part over and above the sum of a population's parts. Political subjects are, thus, not representatives of parts of the population but processes of subjectivation which introduce a disagreement, a dissensus. And political dissensus is not simply a conflict of interests, opinions, or values. It is a conflict over the common itself. It is not a quarrel over which solutions to apply to a situ-

ation but a dispute over the situation itself, a dispute over what is visible as an element of a situation, over which visible elements belong to what is common, over the capacity of subjects to designate this common and argue for it. Political dissensus is the division of perceptible givens themselves.

This presupposes the introduction of a dividing line in what is generally designated as the political sphere. Politics is not primarily the exercise of power or the deciding of common affairs. Every decision on common affairs requires the prior existence of the common, that is, a form of symbolising the common. There are two broad forms of this symbolisation of the common. The first symbolises the community as an ensemble of well-defined parts, places and functions, and of the properties and capabilities linked to them, all of which presupposes a fixed distribution of things into common and private – a distinction which itself depends on an ordered distribution of the visible and the invisible, noise and speech, etc. This type of distribution can take on more or less archaic or modern forms. It stretches from the patricians' not hearing the plebeians speak to modern statistics, where opinions are distributed as functions of parts of the population, such as socio-economic or age groups. Archaic or modern, the way of counting parts, places, and functions remains the same. This way of counting simultaneously defines the ways of being, doing, and saying appropriate to these places. I call this form of symbolising the common, that is, the principle of distribution and completeness that leaves no space for a supplement, the police [*police*].

And I reserve the name of politics [*politique*] for another, second form of symbolising the common, one which calls into question the divisions of common and private, visible and invisible, audible and inaudible. This calling into question presupposes the action of supplementary subjects, subjects that are not reducible to social groups or identities but are, rather, collectives of enunciation and demonstration surplus to the count of social groups. The young Marx in a famous formula speaks of the proletariat as a "social class which is not a social class but the dissolution of all classes." I've twisted this phrase from the meaning Marx gave it to turn it into a definition of political subjects in general, since, even when they bear the same name as social groups, political subjects are supernumerary collectives which call into question the counting of the community's parts and the relations of inclusion and exclusion which define that count. Thus, "workers" or "proletarians" were subjects who instituted a quarrel over the character (private or common?) of the world of work. Their actions brought a universe previously thought of as domestic into public visibility. It made the inhabitants of that world visible as beings belonging to the same (public) world to which others belonged, that is, as beings capable of common speech and thought. Such a demonstration could occur only in the form of a dissensus, as was the case at another moment with the demonstration of women's capabilities. On each occasion, what mattered was challenging the accepted perceptible givens, and transforming one world into another. What we have here, though, is not merely the historical form of the excluded group's entry into public view. All political action presupposes the refutation of a situation's given assumptions, the introduction of previously uncounted objects and subjects.

This is why a vicious circle emerges in the opposition between the political and the social as maintained by a certain reading (Strauss, Arendt) of ancient philosophy. This tradition seeks to purify politics from the impingements of the social, but the effect of this purification is to reduce politics to the state, and thereby reserve politics for those with a "title" to exercise it. Politics, however, consists of calling the social/political, private/public divide into question. Habermas's pragmatic logic contains the same kind of vicious circle. "Performative contradiction" only functions if a speech situation with its partners and rules already constituted is assumed. Political interlocution, though, is deployed precisely in situations where no prior scenario to regulate the objects or partners of the common exists. In politics, subjects act to create a stage on which problems can be made visible – a scene with subjects and objects, in full view of a "partner" who does not "see" them.

This means that politics is not a permanent given of human societies. There are always forms of power, but that does not mean that there is always politics. Politics occurs only when political subjects initiate a quarrel over the perceptible givens of common life. This difference is always precarious, as political subjects are operations [dispositifs] of enunciation supernumerary to the parts of society or collective identities. They are always on the verge of disappearing, either through simply fading away or, more often than not, through their re-incorporation, their identification with social groups or imaginary bodies: "workers" and "proletarians" were once exemplary subjects, before their incorporation as a part of society or the glorious body of a new community.

The identification of democracy with consensus is the current form of this evanescence. Consensus does not mean simply the erasure of conflicts for the benefit of common interests. Consensus means erasing the contestatory, conflictual nature of the very givens of common life. It reduces political difference to police-like homogeneity. Consensus knows only: real parts of the community, problems around the redistribution of powers and wealth among these parts, expert calculations over the possible forms of such redistribution, and negotiations between the representatives of these various parts. In other words, the consensual state props itself up on global economic necessity presented as an intangible given, in order to transform conflicts over what is common into the internal problems of a community. All of which assumes that a whole objectivation of the problems and parts of the community is possible. Consensus, then, is actually the modern form of reducing politics to the police. And the philosophies of the return of the political and the return to politics are the ideological coronation of this effective depoliticisation.

From here it is possible to understand how consensus is able to engender new forms of identitarian passion. The core of consensus lies in suppressing supernumerary political subjects, the people surplus to the breaking down of the population into parts, the subjectivations of class conflict superimposed onto conflicts of interest between parts of the population. At the core of consensus is the dream of an administration of affairs in which all forms of symbolising the common, and thus all conflicts over that symbolisation, have been liquidated as ideological spectres.

Of course, there is no such thing as the simple management of common interests or the zero symbolisation of the community. Whenever the paradoxical power of those without title vanishes, there remains the conflict between the two great titles, the powers of wealth and birth. Whenever the people *en trop* of democracy disappears, another people appears: namely, the corps of those with the same blood, ancestors, or identity. And whenever the worker or proletarian disappears as a figure of political alterity, the migrant remains as a naked, unsymbolisable figure of the other. This other can no longer be counted, even in the name of the uncounted. It can only appear as that which is to be excluded, visibly in excess of any relation to the community. On the one hand, identitarian extremism carries the consensual logic of suppressing surplus subjects to its logical conclusion; and, on the other, it presents itself as the sole alternative to consensus, the only force to refuse the law of economic or sociological necessity and thus reinstate alternative and conflict. In effect, identitarian extremism restages the archaic power of birth as the only alternative exactly when democracy is reduced in the name of consensus to the simple power of wealth.

The concepts offered in *Disagreement* attempt to provide tools for thinking through the singular historical situation of the eclipse of politics. They seek to draw reflections on our situation away from those grand narratives and prophecies of the "end" which work to transform the eclipse of politics into some final realisation of a great historical destiny. These teleologies take several forms. First, there is the vision of the "end of utopias," the celebration of the return of reasonable politics. In reality, however, this reasonable politics is nothing but the disappearance of politics in favour of management. Second, there is the sociological vision of the end of politics which identifies democracy in its terminal state with the self-management or

peaceful interaction of the interests and affects pertaining to the "democratic mass individual." Democracy, though, is not a state of the social, it is a division of society. And the people of politics never disappears into some simple coexistence of individuals and social groups without remainder, it is always replaced by another people. Finally, there is the thematic of the "end of history," understood as the end of the era of conflicts and the passage into a post-historical, pacified world. All this while in our world double the number of conflicts and massacres is conducted in the name of God or race. Ours is a world dominated by a power that can only pacify conflicts – here and there – through recourse to an armed violence identified with the battle without limits of God or of good against infinite evil. Some find the archaic, ethico-religious rhetoric used by George W. Bush amusing. Others see in it the height of cynicism. I don't think it is either. What we have here is simply the extreme limit of the logic of consensus, that is, the dissolution of all political differences and juridical distinctions into the indistinct and totalising domain of ethics.

I have no pretensions to offering remedies to the various forms of this eclipse of politics. It does seem at least possible, however, to identify these forms. And it seems necessary to distinguish such research from prophecies of catastrophe. Against thoughts of the end and catastrophe, I believe it is possible and necessary to oppose a thought of political precariousness. Politics is not some age of humanity which is to have been realised today. Politics is a local, precarious, contingent activity – an activity which is always on the point of disappearing, and thus perhaps also on the point of reappearing.

notes

I This paper was delivered by Jacques Rancière at the Institut Français, Berlin, 4 June 2003. It addresses the reasons why he was prompted to reconsider the tradition of political philosophy and its thinking of politics in his book *La Mésen-*

tente: Politique et philosophie (Paris: Galilée, 1995), translated by Julie Rose as *Disagreement: Politics and Philosophy* (Minneapolis: U of Minnesota P, 1999). I would like to thank my reader at *Angelaki*, Forbes Morlock, for his extensive suggestions and comments on two earlier drafts of this translation. I would also like to thank Gene Ray and Jasmin Mersmann for their comments on an earlier draft of this translation. [Translator's note.]

2 For example, the massive strikes in the winter of 1995 in France against plans by the Juppé government to move France's social security and health system closer to an American-style system were condemned by the usual figures who constitute the service intelligentsia as being out of step with the rigours of "economic imperatives." Many of these "unsentimental" intellectuals, having willingly shed all their radical positions and become cognisant of economic activity, openly supported this government's "fundamental reform" in a letter to *Le Monde.* The popular mass uprisings were denounced as "archaic," "corporatist," "classist," in sum, no more than a tide of egalitarian nostalgia holding back the progress of modern, consensual, democratic France. On this point see Kristin Ross's *May '68 and its Afterlives* (Chicago: U of Chicago P, 2002) 208–15. [Translator's note.]

Jacques Rancière
c/o Éditions Galilée
9, rue Linné
75005 Paris
France
E-mail: ranciere@club-internet.fr

Steven Corcoran
Wichertstrasse 52
10439 Berlin
Germany
E-mail: eyed_awry@yahoo.com.au

Routledge
Taylor & Francis Group

 ANGELAKI
journal of the theoretical humanities
volume 9 number 3 december 2004

Today the values and attitudes that come together under the word individualism are marked by a serious ambiguity that saps contemporary political thought and blocks the moral resources of democratic regimes. Is the analysis and critique of contemporary individualism perhaps a precondition for coming out of the profound malaise that affects our civilisation?

The term individualism was introduced into French philosophical vocabulary as late as 1825 to refer to the theory that sees the individual as the supreme value in the political, economic or moral domain. It very quickly entered into everyday language, indicating in a positive sense the attitude of mind which favours individual initiative and reflection, though from 1834 Balzac depicts individualism pejoratively, detecting in it a tendency to egoism.

This word is one of very few "isms" that in their popular use manifest the active presence of philosophical categories in our world – along with, for example, scepticism, stoicism, idealism. It is hardly fortuitous that it was coined at the beginning of the nineteenth century. It is in fact a response to the expansion of an individual mode of being which then seeks to assert itself thanks to the ebb of the radical version of the ideals of the French Revolution.

Picking up on this point from the humanists of the Renaissance, the thinkers of the seventeenth century conceived of the human individual as a principle, inasmuch as he appears as the being that distinguishes himself from all community, from all tradition in effect. But, unlike their predecessors, they saw the individual not as a being whose full richness would reside in particularity or singularity but, on the contrary, as an agent of universality. The figure of the honest man sufficiently summarises this "classical" quest for universality in the individual. The honest man

dominique lecourt

translated by sean gaston

ON INDIVIDUALISM[1]

does not seek to singularise himself. This would be a failure of universality.

In the major works of the philosophers of the Enlightenment, the individual becomes an elementary isolated being joined with others to form the "body politic" according to an interaction of forces favouring equilibrium. The model of Newtonian mechanics is a powerful inspiration for these works. Of course, the thinkers of this time were striving to give a positive and concrete content to the political systems that they derived from this model. But, ultimately, the theoretical constructions of the "social contract" that put into play this "social atom" do not have a purely descriptive purpose; they aimed to free the mind of theologico-political conceptions that had prevailed since the time of feudalism. It is a question of undoing in the

ISSN 0969-725X print/ISSN 1469-2899 online/04/030011–05 © 2004 Taylor & Francis Ltd and the Editors of *Angelaki*
DOI: 10.1080/0969725042000307592

abstract the ties between law, politics and religion. Some did this in favour of absolute monarchy (Hobbes), others against it (Rousseau). The political stakes of these philosophical elaborations appear very clear in the eyes of contemporaries.

This individual social atom plays an analogous role in political thought to that of the corpuscle in Newtonian mechanics, but in order to appear as a stakeholder [*partie prenante*] in a transaction that is very different from that of a physical interaction, namely a contract that when transferred from the realm of law to that of politics is supposed to guarantee the foundations of society as such, instead of God.

Auguste Comte, writing after the Hundred Days, made no such mistake: he castigated this conception of the individual as a metaphysical abstraction and made a point of denouncing its destructive character for all social order. The author of *System of Positive Polity* firmly stated his opposition to individualism in this sense: the classical conception of the individual, he asserted, had had its time, had fulfilled its historical role in destroying the old order. It is a perilous illusion to want to build a new organic unity, a stable and harmonious society, on individualism. It is to risk spreading and aggravating the intellectual and moral anarchy that has threatened Europe since the end of the French Revolution. Comte's criticism is aimed at the philosophical (he says "metaphysical") presuppositions of political economy. It leads him to advocate the religion of Humanity as the first demonstrated religion to be adapted to the positive state of knowledge and society. He is then close to the positions of the traditionalists (Joseph de Maistre, L.G.A. Bonald), which Charles Maurras and the *Action Française* will use later for their own purposes.

During this same period, other less renowned but without doubt more effective theorists set out the basis for a thought on the individual that has very concretely shaped our world in aiming to establish – today at a cost to the planet – a social atomisation that responds to the demands of the market. On this subject, Georges Canguilhem always referred to the texts of the Belgian mathematician, statistician and astronomer Lambert Adolphe Quêtelet (1796–1874), author of a

theory of the "average man [*homme moyen*]" as the subject of what he calls the "moral statistic": the wise man is one whose free will acts as a motivating force oscillating around an average reasonable state. "Whatever the circumstances in which he finds himself, the wise man diverges very little from the average state which he believes he must stay close to ... Social phenomena, influenced by the wise man's free will, proceed, year in and year out, with more consistency than the phenomena influenced purely by material and accidental causes."[2]

But politically this atomisation corresponds to an apathy that can only benefit democracy in the framework of *a mass individualism* [*un individualisme de masse*]. John Stuart Mill, the English friend of August Comte, highlighted this in *On Liberty* (1859) as one of the essential motivating forces: "In our time, from the highest to the lowest class of society, everyone lives as if under the gaze of a hostile and feared censor ... [E]ven in what people do for pleasure, conformity is the first thing that they consider; they like *en masse*; they limit their choices to things that they can do commonly; they avoid as a crime all singularity in taste."[3]

The mathematician and philosopher Gilles Châtelet shows in scathing terms how this mass individualism finds itself directly linked to the current political alignment on the economy. He summarises in one sentence the lesson to be drawn from an astonishing passage in John M. Keynes' celebrated *General Theory of Employment, Interest and Money*. The whole problem rests on anticipating the anticipations of others, *singularising oneself by imitating the world before everyone else*, predicting the sudden "balances" [*équilibres*] of the cyber-psychodramas played out on a world scale. Keynes himself compares the technique of investment to "those competitions organised by the newspapers where the participants have to chose the six prettiest faces from a hundred photographs, the prize being awarded to the one whose preferences come the closest to the average selection made by the group of candidates."[4] "Each candidate," the renowned economist notes, "must choose not the faces that he himself judges the prettiest, but those that he estimates the most likely to get the votes of other candidates."

Châtelet harshly concludes: "the rational attitude is no longer that of a clear-headed discipline that requires complete autoregulation" – "to buy when everyone sells and to sell when everyone buys" – "but that which rewards the servile opportunism of the acrobat of 'speculative bubbles.'"

The American linguist Noam Chomsky speaks on his part of "the profitable industry of consensus" systematically implemented by social engineers, those perpetual inventors of "scapegoats" ["*bêtes noires*"] and "great causes" that one sees so clearly in the USA. There is a good analysis in his book *Pirates and Emperors* (1986) of what has lately been called "trial by media" [*lynchage médiatique*].

The human disaster produced by this mass individualism can be seen today. Some symbolic figures summarise the essence of this disaster, particularly the motorist in a traffic jam, the incarnation of a visceral aggression and hysteria that can seize these "elemental particles" which make such sad novels.[5] "Units of distress," "balls of anguish," the human beings shaped by mass individualism seem to have radically lost any passion for humanity which is not driven by a death wish [*mortifère*]. The multinationals of sentiment [*les multinationales du sentiment*] appeal to the "pure sensation" of these beings deprived of belonging. In reality, the secret of this disaster is not difficult to decipher. The concept of the individual which, in the name of globalisation [*la mondialisation*], seems in the process of taking over the entire planet has in reality been dictated by the economists. Witness, for example, this pronouncement by 1992 Noble Prize winner Gary Becker, who explains that all human life is only the optimal management by a *rational egoism* of a drive to survive in a world subject to scarcity: "We optimise as others breathe! We are the first generation to 'internalise' all the attitudes of scarcity with such perfection," he writes, before using the example of a couple: "Isn't getting married facing a market of specific goods and services, with its rules, its investments – the children – and its conception for [the acquisition of] some rare resources – IQ, education, fortune?" And he ends with a disarming rhetorical question: "Is a couple sustainable if it does not succeed in increasing the useful function of each partner?" The whole symbolic dimension of marriage and human filiation is negated by this distinctive – and at the very least imperious, if not tyrannical – rationality. Pierre Legendre has shown that one can easily add to this instrumental rationality a butcher's idea of sexuality, a conception which molecular biologists and doctors embrace far too often (*Leçons IV: L'Inestimable objet de la transmission*). In these circumstances, it is no surprise that the sects are the winners. The market of anguish is flourishing today. These are the sad [*triste*] passions that dominate the world today, as Spinoza would say. These passions reveal a great ferocity, always ready to revive the cruellest "theological hatreds" driving men against each other. Mass individualism nourishes in reaction the most alienating forms of communitarianism, which, by various other methods, annihilates the capacity of the human being to be an individual.

This is a very gloomy picture, you will say. Without any doubt.

But the history of Western thought actually harbours another conception of the individual, whose resources can assist in rethinking ethics and politics and emancipate us from the caricatures that currently dominate them.

One of the best French philosophers of his generation – and one of the least known – Gilbert Simondon has masterfully applied himself to demonstrating that the notion of the individual related to the human being cannot be reduced to a social atom.

But if you will allow me, I can back this up with the most classical of philosophers whose name I often brandish: Denis Diderot. His most traditionally "philosophical" texts (*Le Rêve de D'Alembert*), as his other more literary works (*Le Neveu de Rameau* or *Jacques le fataliste*), aim to demonstrate that individuality cannot be regarded as either a last or an absolute reality and that it is best to think of all singular human beings by abandoning a substantialist view of the individual. Diderot makes the individual a being that is always evolving, relative to the evolution of the world and to human realities.

Epicurus, Spinoza or Goethe equally raise the

question that modern individualism wants to avoid: the individuation or individualisation of human beings. As soon as it is formulated, this question clearly indicates what is important: the process without end which means that a human individual has never been and will never be identifiable with or reducible to this other type of individual, the billiard ball. We continuously construct ourselves, form, reform and deform ourselves. The individual literally shapes himself, situating himself in relation to the field of forces in which he is placed by his becoming [*devenir*] and that he helps to modify.

The human individual constantly individualises himself, on condition that he controls it by thinking of this process that always puts others into play, not externally but transindividually. Joy is the feeling that comes to each person from any increase in his capacity to act and any development of his thought. But this growth and this development can take place only with and through others. Democracy, Spinoza dared to write, is the most natural form of government! It does not in fact depend on any sad passions. And above all not on fear. The mass individualism that locks individuals into a ready-made "self" [*un "eux mêmes" de confection*], and makes them enter into a relation of universal rivalry, is in itself violent. It is high time that we finish with the pathetic narcissism that has imposed itself on the Western world for some decades to adapt to the tyranny of the market. One day, we will again have to take up the path of an inventive political thought that will devote itself to the task of making solidarity the basis for controlling – always through a common effort – the natural necessities as much as the imperatives of a social life, which does not come down to good management.

The universal electronic communication from London to Tokyo, from Paris to Honolulu, and the airport cosmopolitanism of linked-up spaces do not constitute such an opening: the illusion of complete power and omniscience has never broken any isolation, it leads instead to madness. And there is a certain transcontinental way of remaining at home [*chez soi*] and in one's self [*entre soi*] which is a denial of the passion for humanity that is found in the beautiful name of cosmopolitanism.

The twentieth century will have finally seen, until further notice, the triumph of individualism accompanied by the debasement of politics into management that, with the help of the media, subjects the atomised masses to continuous opinion polls. This deplorable victory is no doubt due to our only having for a long time known to oppose it to an egalitarian philosophy which, under the name of communism, ultimately aims at the same mass conformity, through other, less subtle and often more brutal means.

The real challenge for tomorrow will be to invent a thought of the becoming-citizen [*devenir-citoyen*] relying on our essential solidarity to take control of our destiny. This will first involve a real critical overhaul of the human and social sciences which, after having conformed to an organicism (or, as one says since Hayek and Popper, to "holism"), give way to the real vice of thought that we have nobly baptised "methodological individualism." To start with the individual already formed with his knowledge, his beliefs as a basic unit to understand social life, is to give in to a Robinson Crusoe world [*robinsonade*] that no longer has the emancipatory freshness of Daniel Defoe. Let us stop privileging particularisation to the detriment of the individuation that alone can account for the ever-present possibility of the individual exceeding himself.

notes

1 This text is a revised version of an article that first appeared in *Actuel Marx* 28 (2000). All words and phrases in square brackets in the text have been added by the translator. [Translator's note.]

2 This quotation probably comes from Quêtelet's *Sur l'homme et le développement de ses facultés ou Essai de physique sociale*. [Translator's note.]

3 The quote from *On Liberty* is taken from the French translation of Mill's text. [Translator's note.]

4 Lecourt quotes from the French translation: Keynes, *Théorie générale de l'emploi et de la monnaie* 171.

5 Lecourt is most likely referring to *Les Particules élémentaires*, a recent novel by Michel Houellebec. [Translator's note.]

bibliography

Châtelet, Gilles. *Vivre et penser comme des porcs. De l'incitation à l'envie et à l'ennui dans les démocraties-marchés.* Paris: Exils, 1998.

Chomsky, Noam. *Pirates and Emperors, Old and New: International Terrorism in the Real World* [1986]. London: Pluto, 2002.

Comte, Auguste. *System of Positive Polity.* Trans. John Henry. 4 vols. Bristol: Thoemmes, 2001.

Keynes, John Maynard. *Théorie générale de l'emploi et de la monnaie.* Paris: Payot, 1968.

Legendre, Pierre. *Leçons IV: L'Inestimable objet de la transmission – étude sur le principe généalogique en Occident.* Paris: Fayard, 1985.

Mill, John Stuart. *On Liberty and other Essays.* Ed. John Gray. Oxford: Oxford UP, 1991.

Quêtelet, Lambert Adolphe. *Sur l'homme et le développement de ses facultés ou Essai de physique sociale.* 2 vols. Paris: [n.p.], 1835.

Simondon, Gilbert. *L'Individu et sa genèse physico-biologique.* Paris: PUF, 1964.

Simondon, Gilbert. *L'Individuation psychique et collective.* Paris: Aubier, 1989.

Simondon, Gilbert. *Du mode d'existence des objets techniques.* Paris: Aubier, 1958.

Dominique Lecourt
Centre Georges Canguilhem
Université Paris 7 – Denis Diderot
Case courrier 7041
2, Place Jussieu
75251
Paris cedex 05
France
E-mail: diderot@club-internet.fr

Sean Gaston
81 Godstow Road
Wolvercote
Oxford OX2 8PE
UK
E-mail: elan-gaston@carsean.demon.co.uk

Routledge
Taylor & Francis Group

ANGELAKI
journal of the theoretical humanities
volume 9 number 3 december 2004

In the history of German idealism, Hegel is often portrayed as the philosopher who, better than anyone else, captures the tensions of modern life, the way in which our search for autonomy and self-determination is linked up with the threat of alienation and homelessness. Herder, by contrast, is hardly known for his views on modernity. Instead, he is frequently portrayed as a thinker who prides himself on avoiding the problem of modernity altogether. "Community" and "belonging" are terms often used in discussions of Herder's work; the rhetoric of the fatherland and the mother tongue is never far away. Even the most charitable readers of Herder's work, such as Isaiah Berlin and Charles Taylor, are not usually in the habit of promoting him as a great philosopher of modernity. Herder, one might think, offers intriguing insights about the intertwining of thought and language, about history and the challenge of cultural differences. Yet it is Hegel, not Herder, who presents us with the true dilemmas of modern life.

This picture of Herder, I want to argue, is not entirely just. For although Herder does not engage in any straightforward discussion of modernity, this does not mean that he ignores the issue altogether. In order to see this, however, one cannot simply focus on the later Herder's discussion of cultural identity and belonging. Rather, one ought to consider the early Herder's reflections on art and history, and in particular his work on Shakespeare. Here, Herder focuses on the epistemic conditions of historical research and literary interpretation. This area was surely not alien to Hegel either. However, Hegel's major contribution to this field is the idea of an all-comprehensive, continuous *Geist* in light of which past life forms present themselves to the hermeneutic mind as princi-

kristin gjesdal

READING SHAKESPEARE – READING MODERNITY

pally intelligible. Herder, by contrast, undermines this hermeneutic holism by emphasizing how past and distant civilizations, in their alterity, beg a conception of history that also takes into account the untranslatablility of the experiences that they convey. It is this aspect of his thinking – the deep-seated hermeneutic pluralism that he defends – that makes Herder a significant philosopher of modernity.

I shall explore these notions of modernity – Hegel's and Herder's – by, first, looking into Hegel's conception of reason in modernity, his discussion of Descartes and the predicament of post-Cartesian philosophy. I then go on to show how, according to Hegel, this predicament gets reflected within the framework of Shakespearean drama and how he claims that the tensions of early modernity are elevated into a higher unity

ISSN 0969-725X print/ISSN 1469-2899 online/04/030017–15 © 2004 Taylor & Francis Ltd and the Editors of *Angelaki*
DOI: 10.1080/0969725042000307600

by the coming to the fore of absolute knowledge. At this point Herder's philosophy of art and history offers an important alternative. Stepping back a good sixty years prior to Hegel's lectures on aesthetics, I explore the initial debate about Shakespeare in Germany, as well as the three different versions of Herder's essay "Shakespear." Finally, I conclude by sketching out the basic structure of Herder's hermeneutics and by suggesting how his theory of understanding fundamentally challenges the Hegelian tenors of later hermeneutic philosophers such as Hans-Georg Gadamer.

I

According to Hegel, no historical period can be understood in isolation. History, he argues, is a totality, an organic totality even. "The True," as he famously puts it, "is the whole."[1] Any particular culture, any particular period of time, gains significance in terms of the larger, world-historical unity. Ultimately, this unity is conceptualized as the absolute, the unity of spirit, whose phenomenological journey through history culminates in the luminous transparency of speculative logic. Hence, in Hegel's view, the absolute "is essentially a *result*, [...] only in the *end* is it what it truly is."[2]

Modernity is also inscribed within this grandiose Hegelian narrative. Like any other stage along spirit's path towards self-knowledge, modernity gains meaning and identity from previous times and periods. Yet in the story Hegel tells, modernity also emerges as something special. "A new epoch has arisen in the world," Hegel declares upon addressing the intellectual framework of his own period.[3] Modernity is our era, the point at which philosophy consciously retrieves the achievements of world-historical spirit. As such, it is the era of a reason that has grown up and matured.[4] Epistemologically speaking, this means that reason not only knows a number of things about the world, but also possesses a second-order knowledge of what knowledge is.[5] In this sense, modernity is the period when spirit has left the ontological level of a *being-in-itself* in favor of a dialectically

mediated *being-for-itself* – the period of absolute spirit, the position in light of which previous philosophical conceptions of knowledge, culture, and morality gain their ultimate meaning.[6] In short, on Hegel's understanding, modernity is the period of self-reflection.

Self-reflection amounts to self-determination, Hegel thinks, and self-determination is tantamount to freedom. In post-revolutionary Europe, we encounter, for the first time, the idea of emancipation not just for a privileged minority but for all. Freedom is no longer an abstract principle. It is embodied, realized, and built into the teleology of our civil institutions. Because Hegel supports freedom, he supports modernity. Modernity is the highest stage of self-realizing spirit, and as such modernity is good.

However, for a dialectical thinker such as Hegel, no truth can be as plain and simple as that. If modernity comes across as a gain, this gain is the result of a painful and laborious *Bildung* in history. Knowledge and freedom are won through hardship and suffering.[7] Furthermore, having reached the level of absolute knowledge, spirit realizes that no progress is made without the tragic parting with times and life-forms past. Gaining something also means leaving something behind. Reflection on the development of spirit includes a dimension of lament and mourning – neither of static melancholy nor of petrifying obsession with the past, but of coming to terms with the ruination that is integral to the idea of the advancement of spirit as an advancement in history. This understanding of the history of spirit is reflected in Hegel's discussion of early modernity, and in particular in his reading of Descartes, the philosopher who came to initiate the paradigm of modern thinking.

II

Traveling through a terrain that is basically unified, Hegel's world-historical spirit presents itself through a number of different characters and in different guises – "a gallery of images," as Hegel puts it towards the closing of the *Phenomenology*.[8] Its *modus* is that of "a self-originating, self-differentiating wealth of shapes";[9] it is always the same, yet always different. This, however, does not mean that each historical constellation, each historical character, emerges as equally important. Hegel was no democrat in this sense of the term. Some figures, Hegel argues, articulate the intellectual watersheds, the junctions of history, in ways more apt than others. Within Hegel's retrieval of ancient Greek culture, Antigone and Socrates work as such emblematic figures. When Hegel turns to his own field – that of modern philosophy – it is Descartes who stands out as the most significant voice. With Descartes, Hegel argues, reason is brought to consciousness of itself. This is the point at which spirit as we know it reaches familiar coasts.[10]

Descartes, Hegel claims, liberated philosophy from theology.[11] In so doing, he did for philosophy what Luther did for religion.[12] Thinking was freed from the stifling grasp of tradition, and, in particular, from the doctrines of medieval Scholasticism. One cannot, Hegel remarks, but admire the boldness of this maneuver. For the first time in history, individual thought made good on its own validity, and did so more or less from scratch. The ultimate touchstone is now "my own free thought."[13] Philosophy emerges as responsible in a deeper sense than before.

Self-grounding is an a priori of modern thinking, an enabling condition, and to the extent that Descartes is the first to articulate this philosophically he is championed by Hegel as a hero of world-historical importance.

But if Descartes is championed as a hero of world history, he is nevertheless a hero of the past. Writing at the beginning of modernity, rather than at its end, Descartes could not possibly have reached the highest point of reflection, the maturity that Hegel found characteristic of his own time. Descartes's notion of self-grounding therefore cannot be ours, even if self-grounding in general is a principle that we adopt. What, then, hampers the Cartesian notion of self-grounding? According to Hegel, it is this: Descartes arrives at his famous cogito argument by hypostatizing the division between the freely determined scope of theoretical subjectivity and the causally determined realm of the material world. Descartes, Hegel finds, does not see that thought and reality are intertwined and thus ends up defending what Hegel takes to be an untenable form of philosophical idealism.[14]

Modern philosophy is haunted by this idealism. After Descartes, Hegel argues, philosophy inevitably has something abstract about it.[15] When spirit is seen as completely free and the world is understood in terms of causal laws, then mind is no longer able to recognize itself in its surroundings.[16] Hence the problem of Cartesianism is the problem of alienation. It is the problem of a mind that no longer belongs in the world, the problem of homelessness.

Now, it is one thing to attribute to modern philosophy – post festum, so to speak – the problem of homelessness and alienation. It is something quite different, however, to show that the feeling of alienation gets reflected, on a deeper level, within early modern culture itself. If philosophy, as Hegel argues, is but a conceptual articulation of a pre-conceptual, perhaps even pre-reflective, horizon of practice and understanding, then Hegel's case would be considerably stronger were he able to trace this problem back to Descartes's own time. This is the task that Hegel sets himself in his interpretation of Shakespeare.

III

Hegel did not lecture extensively on art and aesthetic experience until the 1820s. Shakespeare's work, however, had been with him for almost a lifetime.[17] The 1820 lectures, given at the University of Berlin, address both the comedies and the historical dramas: among them *Anthony and Cleopatra*, *As You Like It*, *Henry V*, *Julius Caesar*, *Richard III*, *Romeo and Juliet*, and *The Tempest*. Yet one cannot help noticing that it is the great tragedies – *King Lear*, *Macbeth*, *Othello*, and *Hamlet* – that draw most of Hegel's attention. It is here, Hegel seems to imply, that the modernity of Shakespearean drama crystallizes in its clearest and most palpable form.

Because he focuses on Shakespeare's modernity, one would perhaps think that Hegel simply brackets the English playwright's indebtedness to the past. This, however, is not the case. Hegel repeatedly emphasizes how Shakespeare borrows his material from "sagas, old ballads, tales, chronicles."[18] Shakespeare's modernity does not, in other words, rest with the mere content or material of his theatre, but rather with the way in which this content gets shaped. According to Hegel, it is Shakespeare's accomplishment to change the past tragedy of society and trans-individual world-views into a tragedy of subjectivity itself.

In Hegel's aesthetics, pre-Shakespearean drama is identified predominantly with Greek tragedy, and no Greek tragedy has been subject to closer philosophical examination than Sophocles' *Antigone*. *Antigone*, Hegel claims, presents us with the artistic core of tragedy. Here we face two different views of the world – each one of them perfectly coherent, each one of them perfectly justifiable in its own terms – in unrelenting conflict. Mediation is not an option here; nor is passive co-existence. As represented by Creon, the abstract justice of the gods crudely opposes the ethical message of family, kinship, and care that Antigone brings forth. This is not contingently so. It is a matter of strict necessity. In Hegel's interpretation, the characters of Greek drama personalize an ethical paradigm that is larger than themselves and through which their lives gain meaning and direction. Greek drama is populated by characters who, speculatively speaking, *are* their own absolutes.

This is not so, however, with Shakespeare's characters. Take, for example, the figure of Hamlet, the Prince of Denmark. As opposed to Antigone and Creon, Hamlet incarnates no higher principles. Nor do the other characters in the play. Neither does Claudius, the brains behind the murder of the king and the target of Hamlet's fury, emerge as a person of principles. Draped in his new-won regality, Claudius does not, unlike Creon, deserve respect or obedience.[19] In fact, he is not even deserving of a gruesome and well-plotted death, as in the old revenge dramas such as Kyd's *Spanish Tragedy* or the epic of *Amleth*. The new king, whose presence, *via negativa*, determined the older Amleth's actions, is in Shakespeare's play a creature inviting unanimous contempt. In Shakespeare's version, the drama is not really between Hamlet and the new king. It is between Hamlet and Hamlet. This, Hegel argues, is something entirely new.

What kind of explanation does Hegel offer here? How does he account for this turn of Shakespearean drama? Hamlet, Hegel explains, is "full of disgust with the world and life."[20] Nothing in this world, not even the presence of fair Ophelia, may temper his disgust or subject it to dramatic reparation. Denmark is rotten to the very core. Deprived no less of someone to love than of someone to hate, Hamlet has only himself to lean on. This, one may note, is a condition he shares with the Cartesian philosopher, as Hegel portrays him. Hamlet, however, has no share in the Cartesian confidence. The solid ground of clay and stone that Descartes, turning towards the thinking cogito, claims to have uncovered, is for Hamlet beyond reach. No remedy is powerful enough to put an end to his torturing doubts. Even a message as stark as the one brought forth by his father's ghost appears in a dubious light, and, as if that were not enough, Hamlet is not even convinced that the ghost was really present in the first place.[21]

On Hegel's reading, a life of such uncertainties is not a life worth living. Yet it is also a life in which death is deprived of meaning. Antigone could punish Creon by taking her own life. Hamlet is left no such alternative. When death comes to Hamlet, it is stripped of pathos-filled splendor. Death arrives as an accident, a simple, almost trivial mistake (the swapping of swords). This is not the death of a man of honor. It is the death of a man of doubt, a death that provides no consolation, neither to Hamlet nor to us, the spectators and readers of Shakespeare's drama. Hamlet's death solves no problems and promises no future redemption. To a life absorbed in self-ransacking and uncompromising questioning, death comes as the ultimate confirmation of the meaninglessness of it all. But precisely for all his anti-heroic qualities, his despair and exasperation, does Hamlet appear to Hegel as a hero of modern life.

IV

Two very different personalities – Descartes and Hamlet – mark the beginning of Hegel's reconstruction of spirit's travel through modernity. By the looks of it, these personalities could hardly be more different. On the one hand, Descartes, who, although adopting the idea of a methodological doubt, believes that thought's reflective turn towards itself leads to a certainty so solid as to withstand the pressure of any skeptical objections. On the other, Hamlet, who could not possibly have dug himself deeper into doubt, self-hatred, and merciless agonizing. If Descartes embodies the philosophical nerve and cultural optimism of modernity, Hamlet emerges as the incarnation of dark melancholy and existential gloom.

How, then, can these two images of modernity be brought together? Can they be joined in any way? Or must we speak of two incompatible aspects of the same intellectual era? At least in Hegel's mind, this is not the situation. Rather, he suggests that the character of Hamlet exhibits the existential flipside of the modern (Cartesian) search for freedom and self-determination through a turn towards subjectivity. In modernity, self-determination is not a matter of opinion. It is a condition into which we are born. Even to eschew the path of self-determination is a self-determined choice. In such a predicament, individuals appear almost like "free artists of their own selves."[22] The modern self does not, like previous Creons and Antigones, possess a set of ethical principles with which it may identify wholeheartedly,[23] but appears, rather, as a creation – a work of art, as Hegel puts it.[24]

However, in order to be fully self-responsible, spontaneous self-creation is not enough. The individual must also objectify herself, perceive herself from the outside. This generates a split mind, one of the judge and the judged, the reflecting and the reflected. Shakespeare, Hegel claims, presents us with an image of this predicament. He gives us a set of characters who, like Hamlet, are "inwardly divided against themselves."[25] There are no absolutes in Shakespeare's universe, no transcendent God or principles that may, once and for all, put an end to this alienation. Self-determination, he shows us, means a condition in which no peace is on offer, one in which the modern individual is left to "endure the fate of finitude."[26] This, in turn, means to endure the fact that our death, no less than Hamlet's, will have no greater meaning; it means to endure a condition in which we can find no consolation in the world, yet are deprived of the hope of a world beyond this one. Subjectivity has taken on too many God-like powers, as it were. Hence it must bear responsibilities of God-like proportions: the responsibility of healing alienation and division, the responsibility of finding meaning in life. In this sense, Hamlet's tragedy is the tragedy of a life that is led in the spirit of Cartesian philosophy – a spirit which Hegel, to be sure, felt like celebrating, but which he could still not see as an achievement worth celebrating on its own merits.

V

However compelling and influential, Hegel's analysis of nihilism and alienation does not conclude his narrative about spirit's passage through modernity. The Cartesian spirit initiates modernity, but does not make up the final chapter of Hegel's retrieval of modern life. Through the movements of progressive history, spirit moves beyond the drama of early modernity. Division and alienation are overcome. Having taken subjectivism to a point at which it has exhausted its uttermost possibilities – where it embodies in its shape "as much of its entire content as that shape was capable of holding"[27] – modern subjectivity no longer has to negotiate the dilemma of values and normativity being *either* bestowed from a trans-subjective beyond *or* being an outcome of its own creation. Intersubjectivity has taken over the perspective of subjective idealism, and the "I" recognizes itself as situated within a dialectics of mutual recognition. The field of intersubjectivity is the realm of a higher autonomy: through the civic institutions of family, law, and government, the modern self takes on a shared responsibility for its own condition. In ethics, art, and epistemology, the transition from subjective idealism to that of intersubjectivity announces the beginning of absolute knowing, the epistemic point of view that, ultimately, constitutes the condition of possibility for Hegel's phenomenological retrieval of the history of spirit.

Absolute knowing, however, demands not only a responsible and secularized conception of who we, as members of a given society, are and want to be, but also a notion of how we have become the ones we are – i.e., a reconstruction of spirit's way through history. In Hegel's opinion, this reconstruction, dialectically teasing out the various conjugations of spirit's development, is, as I have mentioned, a task of unification. The agony, doubt, and existential bewilderment that had been haunting Hamlet (as an emblem of early modern culture) is replaced by the tranquility of a fully perspicuous philosophical overview. Previous suffering – the intrinsic brutality of history – gets justified in light of a larger teleological meaning: the self-identity of absolute spirit.

It is at this point that the young Herder's studies of art and history offer an alternative to the Hegelian narrative, a conception that, many years prior to Hegel's *Phenomenology* and his *Lectures on Fine Art*, questions the idea of an overreaching, continuous reason in history. In Herder's work, the self-responsibility of reason is connected with the challenge of philological rigor and respect for the alterity of cultures that are historically or geographically distant from ours. This becomes particularly clear on comparing Hegel's reading of *Hamlet* with Herder's discussion of Shakespeare's work and literary style – or rather, his defense of the idea that Shakespeare had a literary style worth mentioning in the first place.

VI

In the 1820s, when Hegel first drafted his Berlin lectures, Shakespeare's reputation in Germany had reached almost stellar levels. Shakespeare was seen as the bard of the North, and since every culture needs a bard, a life without Shakespeare was, in Goethe's phrasing, barely a life at all.[28] Hegel, in other words, could well afford expounding on Shakespeare's philosophical insights, rich and compelling as they were. Herder, addressing Shakespeare's work about sixty years earlier, knew no such luxury. For in order to arrive at a point where such a contemplation was possible, an intellectual atmosphere would have to be created in which Shakespeare's drama could be appreciated as art. That turned out to be easier said than done.

When Herder published his most famous piece on Shakespeare in 1773, the essay had been rewritten twice. The first version of the essay was finished in 1771, the second a year later. These two drafts provide a glimpse into the development of Herder's understanding of Shakespeare – how his perspective changes and how he, year by year, obtains a firmer grasp of the real philosophical problems behind the Shakespeare debate in Germany.

Within the context of German aesthetics, this debate stretched back to 1740, when *Julius Caesar* was made available in C.W. von Borcke's translation. Having spent three years as an ambassador in London, von Borcke thought it was high time the German audience got acquainted with the English poet. Presenting Shakespeare in a free, Shakespearean prose, however, would be going a step too far. Alexandrines it had to be, or nothing at all. In this sense, von Borcke, although appreciative of Shakespearean drama, was still under the sway of classicist aesthetics – which now appears as something of a paradox, considering how the debate that was to follow his translation was driven extensively by classicist worries.

Critical voices emerged as soon as von Borcke's translation was published. Among the most powerful of these was that of Christian Gottsched. Gottsched immediately sensed the threat of Shakespearean drama. This was a kind of drama, he feared, that would bring about a questioning of the ideals that he, as a poet as well as a theoretician, had vindicated with all his strength and energy. Thus he braced himself for a fight. Two arguments fueled Gottsched's crusade against Shakespeare, and one cannot help noticing the obvious tension between the two.

First, Gottsched found it necessary to remind

the critical audience that Shakespeare was not German.[29] That, he thought, was a point to be used against him. Shakespeare's tradition was different from their own; his way of thinking was not natural to the Germans. This was a playwright who brought the lowly classes to the scene. The characters spoke with unsuitable accents. Princes socialized with peasants and gravediggers. As if that was not enough, Shakespearean tragedy inclined towards the supernatural. Ghosts and witches were not alien to this playwright, nor were fairies, spirits, and sinister elves. This was not the world as Gottsched knew it. And it was not a world that had anything in common with art as he knew it, either.

Art, as Gottsched knew it, was built on the ideals of a past long gone, the golden age of the Greek tragedies, whose aesthetic premises were laid out in Aristotle's *Poetics* and brought to life again in the work of Corneille, Racine, or, in a German context, his own dramatic writings. This gave rise to a second line of criticism. Despite the blatant nationalism that seems to drive his first objection, Gottsched now claimed that Shakespeare had missed out on the rules provided by the French. By these rules, he thought, German art ought to be guided. They were not expressive of a certain view of art, but of art as such. Order was required. There had to be a clear and well-organized plot. A firm and stable unity of time and place was a condition beyond questioning.

Neither of these requirements was heeded by Shakespeare.[30] Worse still, if Shakespeare broke the rules of French classicism, he did not care to do this with the rigor and consistency that ought to characterize the introduction of a new aesthetic regime. Shakespeare went against the rules of French classicism without even trying to offer another, alternative set of guidelines, or at least not anything Gottsched was able to recognize as a normative foundation for the new dramatic arts. Shakespeare was somewhat of an aesthetic anarchist, and from Gottsched's perspective that was an offense beyond redemption.

The second objection carries the burden of Gottsched's attack. For, as it is, Gottsched's nationalism did not go very deep. Neither did he reject the force of French drama, nor was he,

generally speaking, opposed to the influence of English culture. He quoted Shaftesbury and Addison and is, indeed, known to have imitated the latter's polemical prose.[31] It is the question of breaking the rules of the classicist dogma in modern theater that emerges as the burning issue for Gottsched, and hence also for the writers rushing to defend Shakespearean drama against his virulent criticism.

Gottsched's writing proves a foil for Herder's essays. But so, one must add, do the texts that came to Shakespeare's aid. Important here is Johann Elias Schlegel's comparison between Shakespeare and Andreas Gryph (1742), but also, later on, essays by Lessing and Mendelssohn. More than anything else, however, it was Heinrich Wilhelm von Gerstenberg's *Briefe über Merkwürdigkeiten in der Litteratur* (1766) that would trigger Herder's curiosity and provoke his critical reaction.

Occasioned by Christoph Martin Wieland's Shakespeare translation – by which von Gerstenberg was not visibly impressed[32] – von Gerstenberg's essay voices the growing will to defend Shakespearean drama, although he is by no means ready to go all the way with the English playwright. Shakespeare, von Gerstenberg claims, had so far been judged by the wrong criteria. By and large, he had been judged by the standards of French tragedy. Yet French drama does not exhaust the resources of Greek poetics. Greek art is not just about rule-following and formal constraints, at least not if we follow Aristotle and his emphasis on passion and empathy.[33]

If Shakespeare does not follow Aristotle in a way that can be recognized through the optics of a Francophile taste, this does not mean that he does not relate to Aristotle altogether. As opposed to previous drama, Shakespeare creates a new *historical* plot, von Gerstenberg claims, referring to the Scottish philosopher Henry Home. This turn towards history allows for a certain dramatic beauty, which very well complies with Aristotelian poetics.[34] Keen to defend the originality of Shakespearean drama, ultimately von Gerstenberg sympathizes with the well-known paradigm of the ancient Greeks. This is precisely what worries Herder, and what turns out to be his major concern in the first draft of the "Shakespear" essay.

VII

Herder's first draft is composed as a letter to von Gerstenberg. Starting out in highly appreciative wording, the tone soon takes a more acrimonious twist. Von Gerstenberg, Herder acknowledges, defends Shakespeare by (indirect) reference to Aristotle. Yet the Aristotle to whom von Gerstenberg refers is a philosopher dressed up beyond Herder's recognition.[35] It is an Aristotle who has little in common with the teacher of Alexander the Great, i.e., the Greek philosopher as most of us would know him. Thus, in Herder's view, von Gerstenberg's mistake is twofold. First, von Gerstenberg thinks that Shakespearean drama is defensible only to the extent that it complies with the normative grid of Aristotle's poetics. Second, he stretches the scope of Aristotelian poetics so as to accommodate a drama whose complexity would be way beyond the reach of the ancient Greek imagination.

Shakespeare's theater, Herder argues, could hardly diverge more drastically from the drama that Aristotle had in mind. Take the issue of character. The famous Aristotelian hero was as grand as he was decisive. His fatal flaw – the flaw that would eventually bring him down – was one of which he was unaware and which therefore had the power to determine his actions. Shakespeare generates no heroes of this kind. Drowning in doubt and existential insecurity, Hamlet, for instance, is no man of action. In fact, according to Herder, Hamlet's pensive character makes one ask whether the plot would develop at all without the aid of the king, the queen, Polonius, Laertes, and Ophelia.[36] If Hamlet is the main character of Shakespeare's drama, he is, at the same time, a deeply impoverished main character: not a hero who carries the dramatic development on his shoulders, but one who sinks into a potentially un-dramatic agonizing.

Likewise with the question of dramatic genre. With Shakespeare, this problem emerges as much more pressing than in the case of the Sophoclean drama to which Aristotle refers. Drama, Aristotle claimed, is either tragedy or comedy. Yet Shakespearean drama is often difficult to classify. Shakespeare, in fact, makes this an explicit point in *Hamlet*. When Hamlet, in Act Two, stages the play within the play, we immediately encounter, along with tragedy, comedy, history, and pastoral, the register of the pastoral-comical, the historical-pastoral, the tragic-historical, and the tragic-comical-historical-pastoral. Ultimately, Herder notes, it does not really make sense to speak of genre in a context like Shakespeare's. Every play will have to give itself its own genre, a name of its own,[37] and in giving itself its own name it also gives itself its own standard of dramatic imperatives and prohibitions.

To his points about character and genre, Herder now adds a third, namely the idea that Shakespearean drama is not really drama but, as he puts it, *Geschichte* (history).[38] As we have seen, this point, first developed by Home, had already been explored by von Gerstenberg. According to Herder, however, it was not given the appropriate weight. In Shakespearean drama, Herder claims, the theatrical simply vanishes and so do scenery, imitation, and declamation. Shakespeare does not present us with theatre in the old-fashioned meaning of the term. He presents us with the world, people, passions, and truth.[39]

Herder, in this context, mentions no names, but the argument draws not only on Home but also on the British poet Edward Young, whose *Conjectures on Original Composition* was translated into German in 1760, just a year after its first appearance in English. Shakespeare, Herder claims – reciting Young's argument (and completely neglecting the influence of Shakespeare's contemporaries) – is original. He gives voice to a natural drive, and does not imitate at all. The French classicists, by contrast, did precisely that. They looked at previous literature, i.e., Greek drama, and held it forth as an aesthetic ideal directly applicable to their own time. Hence they forgot about the relationship between art and world. Ultimately, Herder argues, the fact that Shakespeare, in his originality, produces *Geschichte* rather than drama means that he needs to be freed from the normative yolk of previous literature and poetics. Against von Gerstenberg's attempts at defending Shakespeare with reference to Aristotle, Herder finds Shakespearean drama too different to benefit from such a comparison.

With this argumentative gesture, the critical gist of the German Shakespeare debate is elevated to a new, philosophical level. It shifts from the simple options of pros and cons to a discussion of the validity of ahistorical aesthetic norms in a historically developing art world.

VIII

Herder's second draft, written about a year later, carries this train of thought a good step further, but also adds to it in terms of argumentative richness and sophistication. Whereas in the first draft Herder is happy merely to point out the originality of Shakespeare's plays, he now faces the deeper, philosophical conclusions to be drawn from this originality.

If every Shakespeare play is original and unique, Herder argues, then this must be reflected in our conception of art. The uniqueness of a play cannot be justified with reference to universal definitions or criteria. This, in turn, means that in the case of a drama like Shakespeare's, the work *itself* is forced to carry the responsibility of justifying its own existence.[40] Without the aid of aesthetic imperatives, every work is required to answer the question as to why it is a work of art – and to do so in an original and non-imitative way. For us, having been through the aesthetic paradigms of romanticism and the avant-gardes of the twentieth century, the idea might be familiar. To Herder's audience, however, it was not.

Eager to explore the implications of Shakespeare's modernity, Herder raises a question that had so far been left out of the debate: could Greek poetics be at all normatively binding for Shakespeare? And, furthermore, can it be at all binding for us?[41] Herder, once more, emphasizes the co-belonging of work and world. History develops continuously. Because history is always underway, so also is art. What Sophocles could

take for granted, Shakespeare could not. Sophocles, Herder thought, could write tragedies that were predicated upon an overreaching social unity. His was a relatively homogeneous world.[42] Elizabethan England, by contrast, knew no such homogeneity. Hence, Shakespeare would be unfaithful to his world were he to present it as homogeneous and unified. He simply could not place before us an action that was self-contained in the sense of providing a classic, dramatic unity: one time, one place, and one tragic hero. Instead, he must reflect the world as fragmented and divided. Whereas Sophocles, in making his characters stick unwaveringly to one, and only one, belief-system, writes tragedies that resemble "a beautiful painting," Shakespearean drama is like an entire magic lantern.[43] But precisely in presenting us with the images of a magic lantern, jittery and ephemeral as they are, he also presents us with the unavoidable conditions of our art, of what we, with Hegel, may address as the art of modernity.

In other words, the form of Greek drama was not available to Shakespeare. Nor is it available to us. Modern drama cannot be measured by Aristotelian standards. Shakespeare, to stay with Herder's example, does not need Aristotle. Or rather, as Herder now suggests, if he needs an Aristotle it must be his *own* Aristotle.[44] But this Shakespearean Aristotle must be one who is not geared towards the production of universal aesthetic norms. He must be one who aspires to a skillful reading of the particular works and passages, thus indirectly reminding us that within the area of art and aesthetic expression there is no such thing as a finite set of general rules or criteria.

IX

Transcending the framework of the previous Shakespeare debate – the option of either scorning Shakespeare because he fails to comply with Aristotle, or stretching the boundaries of Aristotle's poetics so as to include Shakespearean drama – Herder, in the second draft, keeps open the possibility that an Aristotle of our time does in fact exist. Not surprisingly, the critic he is thinking of is, again, Home. According to Herder, Home had presented himself as an advocate of cultural diversity and the relativity of taste.[45] Influenced by G.L.L. Buffon's notion of a natural history (and his understanding of the meaning of species as logical rather than real), he had attempted to ground a science of man in the historical description of various cultures and life-forms.[46] Rather than proposing a set of new normative guidelines in aesthetics, he questioned the relevance of trans-cultural, trans-historical guidelines for our understanding of art and culture.

The third and final version of the Shakespeare essay no longer appears to contain any notion of a Shakespearean Aristotle. It seems that Herder has changed his opinions about the normativity of the Greeks. What he now senses is that as soon as one leaves behind the mindset of French classicism, there is no real contradiction between Aristotle, on the one hand, and the call for a new poetics, on the other. Aristotle, he now finds, does not really speak out against the plea for a pluralistic aesthetics and art criticism. On the contrary, Aristotle's point of view may turn out to *support* such a position. The argument, one quickly realizes, is a version of that first developed by von Gerstenberg, although in Herder's essay it is given a philosophical emphasis and direction that could not have been envisaged by von Gerstenberg.

Needless to say, the strategy could hardly be slyer. Joining forces with Aristotle, Herder deprives his opponents of their chief witness in the case against Shakespeare and the new, non-classicist art. It is no surprise, then, that the third and final version of the essay sports a tone of triumph and victory.

In the first two drafts, Herder had sought to undermine the case of Shakespeare's critics as well as those who uncritically celebrated his work. Now his confidence has grown and he decides to address an even more comprehensive problem. Although it is not explicitly brought to the fore, the third version of the essay raises a question of the most universal nature: not just what makes Shakespeare's art modern, but what makes art art. What conception of art can we entertain if both Sophocles and Shakespeare lay

equally justifiable claims to the terms "art" and "literature"?

The classicist paradigm maintained that the qualities of Sophoclean drama may be expressed in the form of aesthetic rules and guidelines, but Herder is not convinced. Is the greatness of Sophocles really to be found in his "rules"? No, he claims, it is not. Modern society with its "History, traditions, customs, religion, the spirit of the time, of the nation, of emotion, of language – [is] so far from Greece!"[47] Hence Greek sculpture and drama cannot be understood in terms of our point of view. As far as possible, Greek art should be understood in terms of itself. According to Herder, "Anyone who reads [Sophocles] with clear eyes and from the point of view of Sophocles' own time will [...] realize that everything he says was virtually the opposite of what modern times have been pleased to make of it."[48] Sophocles lends voice to his world – the joys of his fellow citizens and the worries that plague them. Hence his genius does not consist in presenting a set of eternal aesthetic norms. Rather, his drama expresses the wider horizon of his culture, the ethical and political parameters of the society to which he belongs.

World and work are related – this, Herder now claims, is the lesson to be learned from the ancient Greeks. Grasping the close-knit relationship between work and world not only changes our approach to Greek tragedy but also our conception of Shakespeare. If Shakespeare is to match the genius of the Greek playwright, he cannot simply imitate the way Sophocles lent voice to his world but must lend voice to his own world, that of Elizabethan England. Only thus may he "imitate" the spirit which made Sophocles' tragedies the great works they were; only by being distinctly unlike Sophocles may he be his equal. By adopting Sophocles' "rules," Shakespeare would simply miss out on the genius of the ancient tragedian. What we perceive as Sophocles' "rules" were not rules to him, and this applies to the other tragedians as well. "The artificiality of their rules," Herder claims, "was – not artifice at all! It was Nature."[49] Only to us may these dramas appear as rule-bound, as artifice properly speaking; to the Greeks these "rules" were non-formalized, tacit aspects of tragedy-production and culture at large. In order to do what Aeschylus, Sophocles, or Euripides did, Shakespeare would have to let himself be guided by equally tacit and non-formalized sensibilities. This is the point promoted by the third and argumentatively most mature version of Herder's essay on Shakespeare: that Shakespeare, as Herder puts it with a phrase he borrows from Young, "is Sophocles' brother, precisely where he seems to be so dissimilar, and inwardly he is wholly like him."[50]

X

On the very face of it, Herder's idea of Shakespeare being Sophocles' brother despite the obvious differences between the two – or, stronger still, precisely because of the differences between the two, differences which, in turn, point to deeper similarities, namely the capacity to express the spirit of their age – seems like an early version of the idea, later to be associated with Kant and the romantics, that the work of art is by definition the work of genius; that there is, within the realm of art, no room for imitation and that genius speaks with the free and unhampered voice of nature. One can never learn how to be a genius, the romantics had claimed. Genius is a gift, the gift to produce works whose originality is recognized by the community of qualified judges of taste.[51]

Such a conception, one may easily object, has little to say about pre-modern works, which were often produced with reference to traditional knowledge and craftsmanship. However, Herder is not claiming that every work of art is individual in this radical, romantic sense. In his view, such a model would not even provide us with an adequate description of modern art. Modern art is not brought forth in a creative vacuum. It is not the work of an isolated, individual genius. Rather, every work of art lends voice to the pre-reflective horizon that prevails in the community in which it was created. The work may well transcend the aesthetic resources available to this community, but it is not independent of them. An artwork is neither a purely individual expression nor an expression that may be ade-

quately accounted for in terms of the already prevalent symbolic language of a given community. It is between these two extremes – that of individuality and that of shared symbolic resources – that a work of art, like all communication, is positioned. An ancient work may inhabit this field in a way that differs from a modern work. It cannot, however, transcend this area altogether. Nor is this an option open to the modern artistic mind.[52] However, if every work is unique in this way, understanding becomes a problem. This, one would assume, is even more so when relating to works that are historically or culturally distant.

The problems of historiography and understanding constitute a field in which Herder, in the early 1770s, had already been working for some time. In an early version of the *Critical Forests*, the *Older Critical Forestlet* (1767–68), written just three years before his first Shakespeare essay, Herder had been discussing a number of different historical models, but in particular the idea of a continuous, historical narrative or doctrinal structure (*Lehrgebäude*). Johann Joachim Winckelmann – the "best historian of the art of antiquity,"[53] as Herder was later to put it in *This Too a Philosophy of History* – had been defending such a model. However, in Herder's opinion, a full teleology or system of history would require the recounting of every stage in history to be *"whole*, exhaust the subject, show it to us from all sides."[54] If such an account existed, Herder says, he would praise its author as "the first, the greatest."[55] Yet such an account remains utopian, beyond the reach for "us one-sidedly seeing human beings."[56] Hence, realizing that the turn towards a systematic account of history is the point where "historical seeing stops and prophecy begins,"[57] Herder remarks laconically that he would "prefer to think,"[58] i.e., to turn hermeneutics and the epistemological problems of history into a subject of philosophical scrutiny and discussion.

As expounded in the Shakespeare essay – both in Herder's hands-on engagement with Shakespeare's work and in his theoretical reflections on interpretation – the capacity to overcome historical (or cultural) distance is not something that we can take for granted. Rather, it poses a problem for the interpreter. A work of art cannot be understood merely in terms of its effective history, the way in which its meaning gets elaborated through the gradually richer fabric of spirit's self-interpretation. This does not mean that we have no access to historical texts at all, i.e., that they are bound to remain alien. What it means is that the finely tuned historical mind must be suspicious of over-generalized models, and turn, rather, towards philological work. This is an idea which gradually matures and gets clearer throughout the three editions of Herder's essay on Shakespeare, as it moves from a defense of Shakespeare against those who, with reference to Aristotle, either reject or excuse his work, to a full-fledged discussion of the prejudices with which we perceive Aristotle as well as Shakespeare.

XI

Why, then, does this imply a call for a genuinely modern hermeneutics? In order to see why this is so, it might, again, be useful to turn to Hegel and the way in which his understanding of tradition and history has influenced the direction of later hermeneutics. In this context, one cannot miss noting how Hegel has been particularly important for Hans-Georg Gadamer's *Truth and Method*, the work which more or less coined the current use of the term hermeneutics. Hegel, Gadamer claims, came to determine the direction of his attempt to liberate himself from what he, rightly or not, takes to be the subjectivist legacy of Friedrich Schleiermacher's and Wilhelm Dilthey's notions of a critical method in understanding. By emphasizing how the past presents itself to us against a background of continuous historical mediation, Hegel paves the way for his own conception of the productivity of tradition.[59] Gadamer, however, does not go all the way with Hegel. In particular, he is worried that Hegel's notion of absolute spirit testifies to a problematic idealism. As far as Gadamer is concerned, there is no end to philosophy, no point at which phenomenology may culminate in the lucidity of a grand logical system.[60]

Hegel's idea of reason being able fully to account for its own historical development is, as we have seen, part of his attempt critically to carry on the legacy of early modern philosophy: the turn towards the self-grounding of thought and, furthermore, the connection between the autonomy of reason and its capacity for self-reflection. This is another point at which Gadamer hesitates. In his view, reason is not autonomous in the way the idealist tradition took it to be. Being historically situated, reason is always conditioned by a set of prejudices and assumptions which it cannot scrutinize *in toto*. Through its dialogical interaction with texts and expressions of the past, reason may well expand its horizon, but this, in Gadamer's view, is an ongoing process, not the final outcome of spirit's journey through history. A point of full self-understanding is not within the reach of final reason, not even reason as it develops towards the phases of late modernity.

At this point, Herder offers a third possibility.[61] A modern hermeneutics, he suggests, cannot be grounded in the idea of a continuous, all-embracing tradition. Indeed, in his view, such an idea would not really live up to the challenges of a self-responsive reason. Like Gadamer, Herder is cautious to stress the limitations of historical reason, but unlike Gadamer he finds this incompatible with the idea of an all-encompassing, continuous tradition. History, Herder emphasizes, is marked by "leaps and gaps and sudden transitions."[62] Within this field, "every *general image*, every *general concept*, is only an *abstraction*."[63] Hence, what is needed is not an all-encompassing synthesis-formation (in the form of a speculative logic or a continuous *Wirkungsgeschichte* [effective history]) but the willingness to approach historical works on their own terms. Self-authentication, on this model, is precisely not to act on the notion of an unbroken tradition, be it in the Hegelian or the Gadamerian version, but to realize that the historicity of reason compels us to reflect on our own limitations in the encounter with culturally distant life-forms.[64]

Admittedly, it would not be right to claim that such an insight is completely absent in the work of Hegel and Gadamer. Still, as I have been trying to show, the concern for the alterity of past cultures, even the cultures of our own tradition, is given a different twist, a much clearer emphasis, in Herder's writings on art and history, and in particular in his work on Shakespeare. According to Herder, however, the limitations of historical reason do not imply that we are boxed within our own culture, but beg the kind of intellectual cosmopolitanism that comes only from the study of other cultures. Hence, what makes Herder's hermeneutics, as it develops throughout his early years, genuinely modern, is the suggestion, to be developed further in works such as *Ideen zur Philosophie der Geschichte der Menschheit* (1784–91), that the historian should not strive towards grand historical syntheses, but rather, taking differences, leaps, and discontinuities into account, plead for tolerance and cultural understanding. This – the idea that a modern hermeneutic mind is in this sense responsible for its own interpretative endeavors – is the hermeneutic challenge that opens up in the wake of Herder's engagement with early modern literature and thinking.

notes

I would like to thank the two anonymous *Angelaki* reviewers for their sharp and thoughtful suggestions, and Michael Forster for his many helpful comments on an earlier version of this essay.

1 G.W.F. Hegel, *Phenomenology of Spirit*, trans. A.V. Miller (Oxford: Oxford UP, 1977) 11.

2 Ibid. 11.

3 *Lectures on the History of Philosophy*, 3 vols., trans. E.S. Haldane and Frances H. Simson (Lincoln: U of Nebraska P, 1995) 3: 551.

4 In light of this maturity, it applies that as far as factual information is concerned, "what used to be the important thing is now but a trace." Thus previous times are likened by Hegel to "exercises, and even games for children." *Phenomenology of Spirit* 16.

5 Ibid. 17. Or, as Hegel also puts it, its testing of knowledge is now "not only a testing of what we know, but also a testing of the criterion of what knowing is" (ibid. 55). For a clear account of how this position critically carries on the perspective of Kant's *Critique of Pure Reason*, see Terry Pinkard, *Hegel's Phenomenology. The Sociality of Reason* (Cambridge: Cambridge UP, 1996) 191–93.

6 With regard to the history of philosophy, Hegel concomitantly claims that "Ancient philosophy is to be reverenced as necessary, and as a link in this sacred chain [spirit's development], but all the same nothing more than a link." Furthermore, he reasons that "throughout all time there has been only one Philosophy" (*Lectures on the History of Philosophy* 3: 547, 552).

7 *Aesthetics. Lectures on Fine Art*, 2 vols., trans. T.M. Knox (Oxford: Oxford UP, 1975) 1237. See also *Phenomenology of Spirit* 7.

8 *Phenomenology of Spirit* 492.

9 Ibid. 9.

10 In Hegel's lectures on the history of philosophy, the emergence of Cartesian philosophy is retrieved in the following terms: "Here, we may say, we are at home, and like the mariner after a long voyage in a tempestuous sea, we may now hail the sight of land" (*Lectures on the History of Philosophy* 3: 217).

11 Ibid. 224.

12 Ibid. 217.

13 Ibid. 218.

14 This is how Hegel defines idealism: as a direction of thought that "proceeds from what is inward; according to it everything is in thought, mind itself is all content" (ibid. 163).

15 Ibid. 166.

16 In fact, since the human being is not just spirit, but body as well, this is a problem of human self-understanding. Hegel asks how we understand the unity of soul and body when "The former belongs to thought, the latter to extension; and thus because both are substance, neither requires the Notion of the other, and hence soul and body are independent of one another and can exercise no direct influence upon one another" (ibid. 250–51).

17 According to Terry Pinkard's biography,

Hegel had been given Shakespeare's collected works at the age of eight, and while visiting Paris in 1827 he watched Shakespeare being staged at the English Theatre. See Terry Pinkard, *Hegel. A Biography* (Cambridge: Cambridge UP, 2000) 5, 551.

18 *Aesthetics* 288. See also ibid. 190.

19 Ibid. 1225.

20 Ibid. 1226.

21 The complexity of the ghost scene is elaborated in Stephen Greenblatt, *Hamlet in Purgatory* (Princeton: Princeton UP, 2001), esp. chapters 4 and 5.

22 *Aesthetics* 1228.

23 Pinkard clarifies this point by contrasting the groundedness of the Greek form of life with the groundlessness of the early modern world. *Hegel's Phenomenology* 188.

24 *Aesthetics* 1228.

25 Ibid. 1229.

26 Ibid. 1231.

27 *Phenomenology of Spirit* 17.

28 Goethe quoted in Wolfgang Stellmacher, *Herders Shakespeare-Bild. Shakespeare-Rezeption im Sturm und Drang: dynamisches Weltbild und bürgerliches Nationaldrama* (Berlin: Rütten & Loening, 1978) 110.

29 Gottsched, *Beiträge zur critischen Historie der Deutschen Sprache* (1741) in Roy Pascal, *Shakespeare in Germany 1740–1815* (New York: Octagon, 1971) 38–39.

30 Gottsched, *Beiträge* in Pascal 39.

31 See Ernst Cassirer, *The Philosophy of the Enlightenment*, trans. F.C.A. Koelln and J.P. Pettegrove (Princeton: Princeton UP, 1979) 334.

32 H.W. von Gerstenberg, *Briefe über Merkwürdigkeiten der Litteratur* (1766) in Pascal 55–56. Rehearsing the German adoption of Shakespeare, Friedrich Gundolf offers a more positive evaluation of Wieland's translation. Friedrich Gundolf, *Shakespeare und der deutsche Geist* (Berlin: Georg Bondi, 1914) 161.

33 *Briefe über Merkwürdigkeiten der Litteratur* in Pascal 56.

34 Ibid. 65–67.

35 "Shakespear (Erster Entwurf)" in *Schriften zur Ästhetik und Literatur 1767–1781, Johann Gottfried Herder Werke*, eds. Ulrich Gaier et al., vol. 2 (Frankfurt: Deutscher Klassiker, 1985–) 523.

36 "Shakespear (Erster Entwurf)" 523.

37 Ibid. 524.

38 Ibid. 525.

39 Ibid. 526.

40 Ibid. 533, 535.

41 Ibid. 545.

42 This view of Greek society and Greek tragedy, later echoed in Schiller's contrast between naive and sentimental poetry, now seems far too simplistic. For a more nuanced account of Greek tragedy and life, see Jean-Pierre Vernant and Pierre Vidal-Naquet, *Mythe et tragédie en Grèce ancienne* (Paris: François Maspero, 1972) and *Mythe et tragédie en Grèce ancienne deux* (Paris: Editions la Découverte, 1986).

43 "Shakespear (Zweiter Entwurf)" 545.

44 Ibid. 548.

45 See Herder, *Kritischen Wälder zur Ästhetik*, esp. Viertes Wäldchen (1769). *Schriften zur Ästhetik und Literatur 1767–1781*.

46 See John H. Zammito, *Kant, Herder, and the Birth of Anthropology* (Chicago: U of Chicago P, 2002) 234–37.

47 "Shakespeare" in *German Aesthetic and Literary Criticism: Winckelmann, Lessing, Hamann, Herder, Schiller, Goethe*, ed. H.B. Nisbet (Cambridge: Cambridge UP, 1985) 167.

48 Ibid. 164.

49 Ibid. 162.

50 Ibid. 172.

51 Interestingly, Kant's discussion of the misunderstanding of creative genius – as it is represented by the "charlatans" who "speak and decide like a genius even in matters that require most careful rational investigation" – entails a criticism of Herder. See Immanuel Kant, *Critique of Judgment*, trans. Werner S. Pluhar (London: Hackett, 1978) sect. 47, 310; and also John Zammito, *The Genesis of Kant's Critique of Judgment* (Chicago: U of Chicago P, 1992) 34. Kant's re-

marks seem unjustified, however, in particular when taking into account how Herder claims that mixing thinking and aesthetic practice, even within the realm of aesthetics, easily ends in "a monstrosity" in aesthetics ("ein Ungeheuer von Ästhetik"). Herder, *Kritischen Wälder zur Ästhetik, Viertes Wäldchen* 182. See also Robert E. Norton, *Herder's Aesthetics and the European Enlightenment* (Ithaca: Cornell UP, 1991) 182.

52 According to John Zammito, it applies that "For Herder, the uniqueness of an author was always a function of his historical situatedness" (*Kant, Herder, and the Birth of Anthropology* 340).

53 *This Too a Philosophy of History* in *Philosophical Writings*, ed. and trans. Michael N. Forster (Cambridge: Cambridge UP, 2002) 283.

54 *Older Critical Forestlet* in *Philosophical Writings* 258.

55 Ibid. 258.

56 Ibid. 259.

57 Ibid. 259.

58 Ibid. 258.

59 See Hans-Georg Gadamer, *Truth and Method*, trans. Joel Weinsheimer and Donald G. Marshall (New York: Continuum, 1994) 277–85.

60 Thus Gadamer, although basically Hegelian in his orientation, sets out "to restore to a place of honor what Hegel had termed 'bad infinity' [*schlechte Unendlichkeit*]," reformulated in terms of the (Platonic) idea of the "unending dialogue of the soul with itself." Hans-Georg Gadamer, "Reflections on My Philosophical Journey," trans. Richard E. Palmer, in *The Philosophy of Hans-Georg Gadamer*, ed. Lewis E. Hahn (Chicago: Open Court, 1997) 37. See also *Truth and Method* 369.

61 Indeed, throughout the early 1940s, Gadamer discusses Herder's potential for a contemporary hermeneutics, but, importantly, he does not turn to the young Herder's hermeneutics but to the later Herder's attempt to rescue the notion of *Volk* from its democratic interpretation. Herder, he claims, was the visionary of a new fundamental force in the public sphere; this is the life of the folk. He perceives the reality first in the voice of the people in songs; he recognizes the supportive and nurturing power of the mother tongue, he traces in this the imprinting force of history that fuses with the natural conditions of blood, climate, landscape and so on. Thus, through him, the word "folk [Volk]" achieves in Germany a new depth and a new power entirely remote from that political catchword, a world apart from the political slogans of "democracy." Quoted from Georgia Warnke, *Gadamer. Hermeneutics, Tradition, and Reason* (Stanford: Stanford UP, 1987) 71. See also Hans-Georg Gadamer, *Volk und Geschichte in Denken Herders* (Frankfurt am Main: Vittorio Klostermann, 1942) 22ff.

62 "Ossian and the Songs of Ancient Peoples" in *German Aesthetic and Literary Criticism* 160.

63 *This Too a Philosophy of History* 293.

64 As John Zammito puts it, "The crucial innovation in Herder's hermeneutics is recognizing the openness of the subject, not simply of the object, of interpretation" (*Kant, Herder, and the Birth of Anthropology* 339).

Kristin Gjesdal
Department of Philosophy
University of Oslo
Box 1020 Blindern
N-0315 Oslo
Norway
E-mail: kristin.gjesdal@filosofi.uio.no

Routledge
Taylor & Francis Group

ANGELAKI
journal of the theoretical humanities
volume 9 number 3 december 2004

For any teacher, student or practitioner of the architecture and the law of states, the passing of John Rawls, over a year later, is doubtless still providing an unusual moment in modern liberal democratic discourse. On one level, this is quite naturally a moment in which those who admire Rawls' powerful and intensive achievement may find themselves drawn to considering this achievement anew, as Rawls' system itself sought at every moment to renew the cause of a democratic justice. It is at this moment, then, that I wish to offer such a fresh assessment of what is arguably the most important conception developed in Rawls' corpus, his great latter-day state of nature, the hyperdemocratic construct of the "original position." More specifically, however, I want to read Rawls in a mode which has everything to do with John Rawls "himself," as this self emerges in his discourse, *as* his discourse, with all the import for the study of democracy which the passing of his material self offers in parallel.

Firstly, I want briefly to set out a short reading of the Rawlsian political subject, that agent who, from *A Theory of Justice* to *The Law of Peoples*, imaginarily dwells in the original position and guarantees the justice of the arrangements produced there. In this reading, I begin by considering further one common complaint: that this agent of Rawls' original-position exercise in *A Theory of Justice* is a subject which, though it be for purposes of egalitarianism and other sorts of fairness, is imaginatively emptied of all meaningful distinction between itself and other such subjects. It is this erasure, I want to contend, which seems to imply that "any" subject (if the idea of a plurality of subjects has not thereby lost its meaning) will carry out the original-position exercise in exactly the same way

ethan h. macadam

JOHN RAWLS AT THE ENDS OF POLITICS[1]

as Rawls' text claims, a fact which makes any enactment of the exercise after the first redundant. The original position's state of nature is thus foreclosed in favor of its very first performance, *but this performance is that of Rawls' text itself*. It is a text in/for which theory *is* practice.

Leaving aside for the moment most of the relevant definitional questions, I should note that this reading will only be a "deconstruction" of Rawls' text (to use a term as out of fashion as "state of nature") in that (a) it will illuminate a governing structural feature which, running through both the writing and reading of *A Theory of Justice*, undoes this text's own claims to present a mere blueprint for state-building,[2] and (b) it will also, in describing this structurality, make use of tools supplied by various texts

ISSN 0969-725X print/ISSN 1469-2899 online/04/030033–25 © 2004 Taylor & Francis Ltd and the Editors of *Angelaki*
DOI: 10.1080/0969725042000307619

of Jacques Derrida, from seminal writings to some of his more recent work on the explicit subject of "justice." This brings us to the second part of this presentation, in which I wish to expand this reading to show what I believe to be important intersections of Rawls' original-position thesis with the *discourse* of deconstruction, as well as with related approaches to the subject of justice which also begin from a confrontation with language. In a time in which the great democracies of global capitalism have become the world-object that we are now unsure whether we truly desired, a powerful and controversial state-building idea such as the original position can hardly be underestimated in its importance for the future of liberal democratic thinking; I want to contend also that the uniquely powerful *performative* force of the original-position argument has related and similarly important consequences for the future of our understanding of deconstructive theory in its relation to politics, and indeed for the future of "theory" itself.

I

Let us turn first, then, to the original-position exercise itself as the hypothetical imagining[3] of that most important of "pure" procedures[4] in which, according to Rawls in *A Theory of Justice*, "those who engage in social cooperation choose together, in one joint act, the principles which are to assign basic rights and duties and to determine the division of social benefits" (11). The governing device of the original position, as the site where Rawlsian civil society determines the fundamental principles of the Rawlsian state, is of course its "veil of ignorance," which obscures from participants all information regarding social, psychological and "natural" contingencies, especially as these concern any particular individual (12) – thus decisions in the original position cannot be taken so as to capitalize on those assets which are undeserved, which one has through no effort or earned merit of one's own (15). "The original position is, one might say, the appropriate initial status quo, and thus the fundamental agreements reached in it are fair" (12), and indeed what Rawls dubs

"justice as fairness" (11–17) is at the heart of this procedure which yields a conception of distributive justice[5] to which all individuals involved must agree, precisely because they have agreed beforehand on the method used to arrive at that conception (i.e., no individual has anyone but him- or herself to blame if he or she is unhappy with the outcome of the method chosen).

It is with the question of who precisely these individuals are that I begin this inquiry. Different commentators' own objections to the situation in which Rawls places the original-position's participants – even leaving aside the well-trodden practical question (not simply a question of motivation) of whether an individual could move between the original position and political realities as an integrated personality[6] – are now familiar. Ronald Dworkin has reasoned, for example, that "if we suppose that no one has any idea what talents he has, we have stipulated away too much of his personality to leave any intelligible base for speculation about his ambitions, even in a general or average way."[7] Robert Nozick characteristically takes this objection to its extreme in asking how, if all facts about individuals which stem from morally arbitrary contingencies are to be veiled in the original position, these individuals can know the most basic facts about their humanity – "rationality, [their] ability to make choices, having a lifespan of more than three days, having a memory" (Nozick 227) – let alone their "general" (noncontingent) circumstances of which Rawls asserts that they must still be aware (Rawls 142), since their very existence as human beings is entirely contingent. If the original-position exercise would therefore demand that individuals reason as though they did not know of their status as human beings, then it could clearly be discarded as impractical – to Nozick's objection at least, however, we can probably say that while there must be certain baseline traits which are contingently true of all possible persons in the original position (and therefore morally undeserved), a contingency which is true in every case is definitionally no longer a contingency, and thus does not trouble the practical problem of natural inequalities which Rawls' moral-desert argument seeks to address. And yet Nozick's reasoning of the originally positioned individual down to the nonhuman deserves our attention, since the game of identity which Nozick plays under the sign of contingency signals a nominalist dimension[8] of the original position which Rawls may not be able to control conceptually.

Principles weighed in the original position, for example, should not (says Rawls) be thought of as "appl[ying] to distributions of particular goods to particular individuals who may be identified by their proper names" (64). Perhaps this above all other aspects of the veil of ignorance should give us pause, since in one sense it cuts at the heart of the original position as an exercise which can be imagined even at the purely hypothetical level which Rawls intends:[9] that is, how can we imagine ourselves as having no proper names, since it is precisely "we ourselves" who must be imaginable as the set of "particular individuals" among whom distribution is being contemplated in the original position, and since "we" must also be satisfied that this exercise's results will be just? By attempting to efface the contingency of proper names themselves, Rawls' own stipulation sharpens the crisis of identity in the original position even more intensely than Nozick's approach to the "contingent" status of being human.

This crisis thus takes the shape of an ontic difficulty[10] in distinguishing individuals in the original position, a difficulty which signals a larger breakdown of signification in Rawls' discourse. A nominalist critique of this discourse comes to the fore, then, where Rawls himself reasons that "since the parties [in the original position] have no specific information about themselves or their situation [outside the original position], they cannot *identify* themselves" (131; emphasis added) – in this remark he seems very nearly to miss his own point (i.e., of appropriately controlled information), and to strike precisely the one we have been outlining. After all, deprived of his bank statements and tennis trophies, of all reminders of his potentially undeserved material circumstances and personal abilities, the original-position's amnesiac can still say "I, John" with some hope of a referent, but

Rawls' fuller stipulation states that "[he] cannot identify [himself] either *by name* or description" (140; emphasis added), and it is this proscription of the name which causes the true crisis of identity (and not merely of specificity) altogether. What is the amnesiac's status when he can say only "I," when his proper name is removed from play, from the original-position's verbal landscape? Not that this "I" can even be uttered by any individual person, since such a scene would reintroduce the particularity which the exclusion of proper names is meant to avoid. The "I" must function only as a floating signifier of a generic, even a *representative*, subject[11] whose sameness (with regard to all rational others) Rawls imagines will secure consensus regarding his two great principles of justice (see n. 5; we will come to the issue of such consensus shortly). This subject is one who, in representing all particularities, destroys particularity, and its accompanying "I" thus becomes the self-effacing sign of all particularity, of contingency itself, and with far broader effects than (but in the same mode as) Nozick's effacement of contingency under the sign of "humanity."

In the matter of proper names at least, Rawls acknowledges what he calls "deep philosophical difficulties" surrounding his design for the original position (131) – though doubtless we are, more than thirty years after the publication of *A Theory of Justice*, more accustomed philosophically to a conception of the proper name, or the "I," divorced from an individual consciousness.[12] But I want to hold such considerations in reserve for a few moments, and ask instead how such an individual consciousness, however generic, would practically go about "speaking" in the original position. How would this consciousness announce, pronounce or mark itself as a source of discourse which has an addressee? (And mustn't any particular "you" be as forbidden in the original position as any particular "I"?) Again, let us reserve any deconstructive critique of presence in the sign; Rawls has done as much for us and more by effectively forbidding the sign in question altogether, and thus when Rawls speaks of a "someone, as defined by the thin theory" of the good (568),[13] we can say that he has, to adapt Dworkin's phrase, stipulated any possible "someone" out of existence, that indeed we are left with only some *one*[14] (which is to say any and all *ones*), the impotent pronoun which is genderless, incapable of marking a speaker or an addressee as such, which inherently carries no threat of specificity. For a nominalist critique of the original position, then, the question is no longer "can we imagine 'ourselves' as having no proper name?" there, but rather "can we conceive of ourselves as not being marked in language there, as being inscribed nowhere in the discourse for which, and to which, we are responsible?"

Somewhere before this point, we – probably along with Nozick and others – might well discard the original position as a practically impossible and/or philosophically incoherent exercise, at least with regard to the way in which Rawls believes this exercise would work. Yet such a decision would only reflect our failure to understand how the original position actually *does* work – not as a procedural theory to be applied to particular instances requiring a just decision, but as a text which eminently contains both theory and instance. *A Theory of Justice* is virtually identical, of course, with this text which is dedicated to setting out the design of the original-position procedure, and yet this setting out in the text is also an *enactment* of that procedure, and the principles of justice which Rawls believes the procedure would yield are therefore also *actually, authentically* produced by that enactment. The substance of Rawls' claim that his theory's "particular conception of justice would be chosen" in an original-position deliberation,[15] then, has nothing to do with our evaluation of the airtightness of his arguments about what "people" who are "rational" would consent to in the original position, but rather with the fact that these are the principles which have already, as a textual event, emerged from Rawls' own unique and sole enactment/authoring of what takes place – what has already taken place, from the point of view of any particular political moment of any state – in the original position.

This enactment "counts" as authentic for two reasons: firstly, as a hypothetical, imaginative exercise designed so that "one can at any time adopt its perspective" (Rawls 139), the original position is a discursive enterprise which can be entered upon by anyone without regard to one's particular temporal moment. It would be an overliteralizing mistake, however, to suppose that, as with the traditional Hobbesian vision of free persons contracting into a state, playing out the process of the original position requires more than one person, since *discursively* all relevant persons are already called into presence.[16] Though in a powerful sense, of course, Rawls is devoted to the question of enacting social policy "[w]ithout conflating all persons into one but recognizing them as distinct and separate" (587), he has actually managed to do both at the same time, to hypostasize the natural "clash of views ... within one person" (580) as the clash of all possible views within the specialized Rawlsian individual (the individual who indulges his political judgment according to Rawls' procedure, also the individual who, I shall now show, *is Rawls*). The original position is thus one of those imaginative games for which (as Robert Frost puts it of poetry, interestingly enough) "we haven't to get a team together before we can play."[17] Its complete containment within/as the text of *A Theory of Justice* is a consequence of its own discursive mode.

Secondly (and clearly for some of these same reasons), we accept Rawls' account because Rawls "himself," which is to say the authorial presence signified by the name "John Rawls," is as much a candidate for the original position as ourselves,[18] as much as anyone who must pronounce upon questions of distributive justice. This is no less true for his being the author of *A Theory of Justice* – in fact, it is precisely the point here that his candidacy is *structurally necessary* to his mode of argument, and thus, as indicated at the start of this analysis, the passing of the material personage with whom we conflate the Rawls-subject of *A Theory of Justice* provides a momentary – or rather an eminently lasting – simulacrum of the foreclosure sustained by the intensive activity of this personage's corresponding discursive subject. When Rawls claims that "it is clear that since the differences among parties are unknown to them, and everyone is equally rational and similarly situated, each is convinced by the same arguments" – and that, "[t]herefore, we can view the choice in the original position from the standpoint of one person selected at random" (139) – we understand John Rawls himself to be this person in perpetuity, the person who in any given instance has already reasoned through the conception of justice he himself would accept in the original position, a conception which would be accepted by any rational person.[19] His description of "what would happen" in the original position is not a specimen or even a simulacrum of that event, it *is* the event. We know already that Rawls is merely *one* in this situation, specifically "one who reasons from within the original position," but the pronoun is now more important than ever, since its singularity has become the original position's governing principle: "one can at any time adopt its perspective"; "we can view the choice in the original position from the standpoint of one person." "One person selected at random," Rawls specifies, but of course Rawls' own participation in the original position *precedes all other selections*, and again this is necessarily true: Rawls has not engineered a distributive procedure and left it to determine the policy of the state, though of course this is intended to be the ultimate impact of his book – instead, he has told a story through from the formulation of a procedure to this procedure's adoption of its own results. If we accept this story, then the idea of the original position becomes not merely an imaginative exercise but an exercise *which never need be performed again*, since Rawls' own text has already performed it, played it out to its only relevant conclusion (i.e., its "first" conclusion, the conclusion of its first enactment), and therefore also given it a historical specificity which he has claimed it does not possess; we can date the original position, the Rawlsian state of nature, to Rawls' performance in *A Theory of Justice* in 1971[20] (we will return to this important point).

We now have another more powerful way of understanding how very final and *perpetual* Rawls believes decisions in the original position to be (176), although of course this perpetual authority of these decisions has really evaporated; it is now simply part of a larger necess-

ity.[21] We can also see why it does not matter to the theory of the original position that, as we have noted, its referential dimension with regard to particular individuals collapses: this theory never returns to this dimension for its execution or even for its general validity – or rather we should say that the only individual subject which matters referentially in the original position inscribes himself, as a necessary (i.e., authorial) presence, within (instantaneously with) this text which *is* the (original, only) original-position exercise, but which simultaneously accommodates the original position's proscribed names and pronouns (i.e., "John Rawls" and even "I," which pronoun Rawls occasionally uses beginning from *A Theory of Justice*'s first paragraph), and this subject is thereby able to elude this proscription and its effects. As for our question of how we might act or speak from the standpoint of a sort of ontico-grammatical nonbeing in the original position, then, this special functioning of the Rawls-subject seems to resolve this issue as well – as author of the original position, this subject is uniquely authorized to signify "our" presence there, and to do so from without, while at the same time speaking (as participant) for/as "us" from within; as in the case of proscribed identities, his text claims the advantages on both sides of the double interface which Derrida has called an "invagination."[22] Here, then, is the philosophical uniqueness of Rawls' proposal, its vision of a special deliberation between interests which, being the one and only means to the one and only conception of justice, becomes a redundant pageant from which our decisions about what is just must always begin.

As a segue to the main part of our discussion, I wish to highlight the fact that we are not interested here in a Foucauldian critique of discursive machinations on the part of Rawls "himself," understood as a discursive force inscribed in the social fabric generally (wherever it is in particular that political scientists are inscribed); after all, if Rawls undertakes the original position as he says one ought to, under the veil of ignorance – and we see that he does – it should not make a difference to any "us" that it is Rawls, and not the entire relevant group of discrete individuals (some "we," some other group, or even some other particular individual), who has determined the principles of justice. Nor would we try to portray Rawlsian theory as hypocritically anti-democratic: Rawls' is not a totalitarian stance which authentically turns its back on democratic participation, but rather one which, in attempting to perfectly embrace the ideal of such participation, ironically disassembles its grounds, the categories of multiplicity and difference.[23] Rather, we must reiterate our interest in the particular effects created by this play within a discourse on procedure, this movement whereby a total discursive authority is yielded by its author's simultaneous objectification of and subjection to process, an authority which dismantles the ostensible utility of the text in question. In the second part of this essay, then, I wish to map where this dismantling collides with related juridical "violences" explored in the texts of Jacques Derrida, Jean-François Lyotard and lastly (by extrapolation) Ludwig Wittgenstein. Only in light of a concept of violent effacement, traced through these more skeptical points of view, can we evaluate what seems, according to our analysis, to have gone "wrong" with the original position's version of the state of nature, with the intended efficacy of Rawls' great democratic architecture – an efficacy which, considering this architecture's obsession with contract within and between nations,[24] can only be an increasingly urgent priority in the world of the present moment.

II

Rawls' most sincere ideological aims, then, do not preserve his text from the charge of a particular violence. Indeed, the discursive prolepsis of Rawls' pure procedure ("we must carry out a process which will have already been carried out in the process of its exposition," one might say) may reflect in some important ways that proleptic violence which Derrida discerns as inherent in the founding of *any* political order, of "[the] law to come [which] will in return legitimate, retrospectively, [its] violence that may offend the sense of justice" – this law, says Derrida, whose "future anterior already justifies it."[25] (We

will investigate this formulation shortly.) If the Rawlsian state participates in a similarly proleptic mode of justification via the original position, then we shall find it useless, from the standpoint of practical policy, to condemn the resultant violence to the perhaps unachievable ideal of a linear (noncircular and nonproleptic) argument for justice. Instead, we can only follow out the consequences of "how justice as fairness generates its own support" (Rawls 456), though of course in a far more crucial way via the idea of the original position, rather than via Rawls' account of the original position as merely "an expository device" (21). In the second part of this essay, then, I want to investigate these consequences in their compelling connection to related standpoints – "deconstructive" and not – in certain texts by Derrida, Lyotard and Wittgenstein, as a means to realizing the significance of the original position as I have sketched it here so far: beyond Rawls' or Dworkin's distributive schemes, beyond any conventional political science of contractarianism or natural-rights theory, and into the realm of a broader concern for what is today, in a skeptical theoretical climate, perhaps more than ever desired and embattled as "justice."

The mechanism of the Rawlsian prolepsis is naturally not a perfect "match" for that discerned by Derrida, certainly not insofar as to make the former an "application" of the architecture of revolution laid out in "Force of Law"[26] – however, let us take a closer look at this prolepsis of Derrida's, quoted above from "Force of Law," and its interest for our discussion. The best example of this prolepsis, in fact, is probably to be found in another text of Derrida's entirely, a short meditation on the opening text of the USA's Declaration of Independence, in which Derrida is also preoccupied with "this future perfect, the proper tense for this coup of right."[27] "One cannot decide ...," he contends, "whether independence is stated or produced" by the Declaration's opening text (9), i.e., whether the independence being declared is only effective as of the moment of the declaration (the Declaration, the text and/as the act), or whether this independence is *already* the case (and its declaration thus *authorized in advance*, where such authorization might otherwise prove a troubling lacuna for conventional discourses of law which, as we shall see, Derrida views as interrupted by a different discourse, that of justice). Here, then, is the case under examination, from Derrida's own citation of the Declaration's opening: referring to the necessity of the American people's "assum[ing] among the powers of the earth the separate and equal station to which the laws of Nature and of Nature's God entitle them," the opening states that "all men are created equal," and that:

> We therefore the Representatives of the United States of America, in General Congress assembled, appealing to the Supreme Judge of the world for the rectitude of our intentions, do in the Name and by the authority of the good People of these Colonies solemnly *publish* and *declare*, that these united Colonies are and of right ought to be *free and independant states* ... (11)

The impending *though still future* union of the American colonies (i.e., as "free and independant states") for which the way is prepared in the first lines of this passage, then, is pronounced in its later lines by (the representatives of) that *very same union* ("the United *States* of America") whose authority we have just heard invoked, precisely *anterior to* this pronouncement. Thus a circular fallacy of this founding brand of performative is laid bare – as Richard Beardsworth puts it: "[t]he union of states is described as predating the signature of the declaration; at the same time, it is only produced *through* the signature ... The declaration of the republic straightforwardly represents the will of the people prior to the act of declaring, and yet this will is only first invented through this act."[28] Beardsworth continues that the name of God or the "Supreme Judge" at once authorizes and disguises this otherwise violent, transgressive invention (100–01), but this name also delimits the full circularity of this invention: the American people *are* "free and independent" precisely because, under the law of God, they *ought to be* so (Derrida also marks this important transition ("Declarations" 11)), i.e., entitled to a "separate and equal station." The congress of representa-

tives has a right to declare independence only because God already legitimates this independence – the name of God thus functions, in Derrida's words, as the "ultimate signature" *behind* that of the congress for which Thomas Jefferson importantly signs (we shall mention this part of Derrida's analysis again shortly), the "last instance" necessary "for this Declaration to have a meaning *and* an effect" ("Declarations" 12). This circularity, this "sort of fabulous retroactivity" of a future perfect performative ("Declarations" 10), effaces the dubious legal status of the foundation of the American colonies where divine law gives a "precedent" which makes the congress's own declaration redundant, antedated by another law (and it is the same law) which, though imminent in its declaration, remains already anterior, already past.

Much of this analysis, of course, will begin to signal a familiar pattern. Rawls' text, too, functions as both a statement and a production, or rather an exposition or description which at the same time surreptitiously produces what it describes. The resultant parallel passage of this text from description to prescription, from the Declaration's *are* to its *ought to be*, has been exposed before in Rawls' discourse (see n. 21 above), and that discourse's legitimacy in its prescriptions is ultimately derived from an absolute rule – this is a rule which Rawls claims as an empirical inevitability (the principles of justice arrived at are always the same), but which we take instead to be a discursive dictatorship of the kind I have outlined in the first part of this essay. Rawls' discourse itself functions as the sole specific instance of what it describes in general, just as the Declaration's God is the final guarantor of that text's claims. In concentrating his analysis on this latter point, too, Derrida traces the proper name of the signatory "Thomas Jefferson," a name eviscerated first by its redacted, multiply representative status, then by its deferral in favor of the name of God as the "ultimate signature" ("Declarations" 12–13) – this analysis will remind us of the original position's own emptying of proper names in favor of an impossibly generic representative subject who at once is, and is ousted by, the self-authorizing (and ultimately all-authoritative) Rawls-subject itself (which *in the instance of Rawls' text* represents this generic representative, as Derrida points out that Jefferson represented his revolutionary colleagues, themselves representatives of a people eventually representing the mandate of God, who in turn authorizes their actions, etc. (see "Declarations" 12)). At all times, the future perfect remains the tense of this subject's prescriptions ("we must carry out a process which *will have already been* carried out in the process of its exposition …").

This last point is doubtless one at which Rawls' model would require some philosophical "catching up" to Derrida's – as we have mentioned before now (n. 12), the proper name is, for Derrida, structurally empty from the start, whereas Rawls' text reinvents this emptiness by allowing the disintegration of identity in the original position to demonstrate that the proper name (or at least the "I") seems to have been creating, rather than designating, the subject all along[29] – but both circularities remain rooted in problems of that most Derridean of concerns, that of the performative speech act. Let us now, with Rawls in mind, draw out this concern in strands defined by Derrida and by other commentators as well. For the case of Rawls' theory, then, the central Derridean aporia surrounding the speech act is perhaps best expressed by Derrida's contention in "Limited Inc abc …" that "[n]o criterion that is simply *inherent* in the manifest utterance is capable of distinguishing an utterance when it is serious from the same utterance when it is not."[30] This is why – although we (with Rawls) are at first inclined to perceive the argument over the principles of justice as occurring within the context of the hypothetical original-position exercise as Rawls proposes it, i.e., where this argument "counts" (where its conclusions are final etc.) – we do not on this account seem to be able to label Rawls' own argument for those principles as merely a *demonstration*, as a simple mimetic performance or simulacrum, as itself a hypothetical version of the original position's hypothetical exercise (and thus "not serious" in Derrida's sense). And so, of course, where this latter argument ultimately turns out to be, in a potent sense, the *only* one that "counts" – i.e., the only one which is

"serious" – the serious/nonserious distinction does indeed seem undone entirely. How are we to account for the original-position discourse's attack of conventional political argument's[31] standards of the demonstrative, the mimetic, the hypothetical itself? How much and in what way is this attack related to a critique like the one offered by Derrida in "Limited Inc"? What is the status of either with regard to its own internal notions of justice, or each other's?

Before proceeding to this question, let us try to clarify its potential stakes by turning to another concern for something called "justice" as related to the speech act, a concern which, while dwelling under the umbrella of deconstructivist or even poststructuralist discourse, provides a related model of discursivity which delineates a particular set of the most extreme and concrete effects (since Rawls' argument as he presents it is in one sense, of course, quite abstract) of the sort of rupturing (occluding, excluding, disguising) of the discourse of justice indulged in by the original position, the rupture to which we are also comparing the founding violence of Derrida's revolutionary state. Specifically, then, I want to suggest initially that Rawls' own discourse about/of the original position might well be counted as an iteration of that totalizing "'last' phrase" of Lyotard's,[32] itself unarticulated though necessarily and logically ever present, that which for Lyotard may be the only hope for justice, for the signaling of the silenced "differend" at Auschwitz (see Lyotard 3–31, including the Protagoras, Gorgias and Plato Notices), of that extrajuridical wrong to the victims of the camps, a wrong created by the conjunction, or rather the nonconjunction, of discourses (Lyotard 90–101, including the Hegel Notice (91–97)). The device of the original position, after all, is what allows Rawls to offer (that democratic miracle!) a similar totalization of every possible subjectivity which might be otherwise represented *or underrepresented* – *oppressed, suppressed or silenced* – in a state-of-nature, original-contract situation. In Rawls himself, as authorial voice and subject, all discourses conjoin, all possible arguments for the optimum principles of justice are given voice in a thoroughly juridical context.

Simultaneously, however, we must consider whether Rawls' discourse thus conceived fails, on Lyotard's dialectical model,[33] to progress as far as such a "last phrase," that its chief effect may in fact be the very silencing which the "last phrase" is meant to relieve.[34] However amenable we may be to Rawls' original-position subject's representation of the relevant individuals, we must acknowledge that such representation effaces those individuals as discursive presences – this is not a juridical violence but, as I have suggested, an ontic one. Just as Lyotard's Auschwitz silences both the testimony and the very name(s) of the Jewish deportees in order to efface *them and their effacement* (Lyotard 101), where "all possible arguments" in the original position signal the sole possible argument, so this sole argument obliterates (silences) all others at a logical level, and then covers its tracks by foreclosing upon (again silencing) the original-position exercise itself, the very space of debate in which all such arguments are supposed to have subsisted, in which the sole argument itself (*and* its initial silencing of debate) has taken place. If we also consider for a moment the way in which the original position plays on a frequent mythic element in state-of-nature discourse,[35] might we not say, with Lyotard (speaking of Nazism's use of myth), that "[m]yth would then be this monster: an archaic, modern politics, a politics of the community as a politics of humanity, a politics of the real origin as a politics of the ideal future" (152)? The original position – descended from archaisms of the state-of-nature theory of Hobbes and Locke, yet modern as modern democracy, eclipsing individuals by defining them in terms of their community, an *originary* imagining *of* the "real origin" playing upon the instability of its own actuality to produce a static, "ideal future" – is it precisely such a monster, a mythic violence necessarily *opposed* to justice, indeed a violence which, Derrida reminds us, specifically shuns distributive justice ("Force" 52) counter to all Rawls' intentions? Does 1971 mark its *monstrous birth*?[36]

The potential consequences of the parallel we may or may not discern here are obviously brutal, and for this reason it is just and necessary ultimately to present Lyotard's and Derrida's theses, in this context of the original position and of the state of nature generally, in greater detail.[37] For more limited present purposes, however, I have introduced the above aporia, this double reading of a Lyotardian Rawls, as a way of leading us back, with a new sense of the stakes involved, to the similarly aporetic question of violence and deconstruction in the "Derridean" Rawls: more precisely, to the question of whether our reading of the treacherously self-effacing/self-fulfilling action of Rawls' text can be called a "deconstruction" in the specific sense in which Derrida discusses that term in its rather bald relation to the question (and of course it is also Rawls' question) of what is just:

> Justice in itself, if such a thing exists, outside or beyond law, is not deconstructible. No more than deconstruction itself, if such a thing exists. Deconstruction is justice. It is perhaps because law [*droit*] (which I will consistently try to distinguish from justice) is constructible ... [that it is also] deconstructible and, what's more, that it makes deconstruction possible, or at least the practice of a deconstruction that, fundamentally, always proceeds to questions of *droit* and to the subject of *droit*. (1) The deconstructibility of law [*droit*], of legality, legitimacy or legitimation (for example) makes deconstruction possible. (2) The undeconstructibility of justice makes deconstruction possible, indeed is inseparable from it. (3) The result: deconstruction takes place in the interval that separates the undeconstructibility of justice from the deconstructibility of *droit* (authority, legitimacy, and so on). It is possible as an experience of the impossible, there where, even if it does not exist (or does not yet exist, or never does exist), *there is* justice. Wherever one can replace, translate, determine the x of justice, one should say: deconstruction is possible, as impossible, to the extent (there) where *there is* (undeconstructible) x, thus to the extent (there) where *there is* (the undeconstructible). ("Force" 14–15)

It would be difficult, certainly, to find a better example of the later Derrida striving to signify abstractly an aporia which must come very near to denying language altogether; nevertheless, we may be lucky enough to grasp this aporia in a particular context. We know, then, not only that Derridean thought is ultimately uninterested in the material workings of Rawlsian justice qua the two principles alone,[38] but also that, by Derrida's lights in the passage above (and Rawls' intentions aside for the moment), it would not seem that even the discursive exercise of the original position itself counts as "justice" either, since we have seen how the discourse of this exercise, of pure procedure, self-de(con)structs, betraying its aim in the realm of logical and ideological argument to fulfill this aim in the realm of its own discursivity. This is to say that the original position, through the deconstruction of its own necessity, suggests itself as something other than the "undeconstructible" content of Derridean justice. On the other hand, however, it suggests itself thus only in virtue of being the object of a deconstruction *which it itself performs*[39] – what I want to suggest in turn is that *this deconstructive performance* is itself a specimen of the *un*deconstructibility which, according to Derrida, makes deconstruction possible.

It is important to note that I am making an elision here which is already present in Derrida's own text. Deconstruction is justice, and justice is undeconstructible – if we dare invoke transitivity in this context, it follows that "deconstruction" as such, that is to say an instance of deconstructive reading (opposing this, if it is possible to do so, to any notion of the *discourse* of deconstruction), is itself undeconstructible. When Derrida says, therefore, that "deconstruction takes place *in the interval* that separates the undeconstructibility of justice from the deconstructibility of *droit*,"[40] we understand this deconstructive interval to be all but indistinguishable from (undeconstructible) justice itself.[41] In the context of our original question about the relation between Rawls' text, deconstruction and justice, then, the burden lies with us to isolate the deconstructive moment (if any) of Rawls' text, there to find an undeconstructible justice coextensive with this moment. Certainly, in contradistinction to such a moment, we have seen that all the original position's political potential for such a deconstructive justice which might "excee[d] the determinable" ("Force" 28)

is compelled to yield instead what Rawls must claim as a foregone conclusion, i.e., the two principles of justice, twinned in an eminently determinable conception inscribed within the boundaries of *droit*, of static and regulative law. Alternatively, then, I wish to shift the focus of these observations onto (1) the retroactive *consequences* of this foreclosure for Rawls' ostensible discourse of procedure – where, again, the original position is understood not as a procedural blueprint for the generation of just principles but as a discursive hegemony which marks process foreclosed, which *does* mark precisely a *deconstruction of process* which denies that hegemony – and (2) on this hegemony's important affinity with the foreclosure upon deconstruction-as-justice in "Force of Law"'s account of the founding violence of the state.

Such a focus, I am arguing, yields quite a different picture of the sedimented postulates of *A Theory of Justice*. Considered thus, the movement of Rawls' text attacks the foreclosed original position at/as the very center of Rawls' authority, using the original position's discursive hegemony to give the lie to its logical/ideological hegemony. This logical/ideological dimension, as we have seen, has two parts: the writ of procedure which precedes the original position, and the legitimacy of the two principles of justice which result from it. These are twinned moments of the law which threaten the self-deconstructing justice of the original position before and behind, *precisely because they attempt to maintain its integrity*. They are iterations of the law which similarly surrounds a similarly self-effacing Declaration of Independence – the law of God prior to the text (preceding it, authorizing it), and the violent, proleptic law of that self-creating signatory, the new nation (following, to come)[42] – and which guarantees it, in the name of justice, in opposition to all justice. At Auschwitz, too, the internally divided and non-communicating law of the SS officer ("*That s/he die, I decree it*") and the Jewish deportee ("*That I die, s/he decrees it*") (Lyotard 100)[43] precedes/ authorizes a crime which attempts to tell its own story, a witness's story, before this story is silenced by this same law of death which, posterior to the crime, now destroys the witness, sacrifices justice to the law of proof ("no one can see one's own death" (Lyotard 33; see 32ff.)), and so this story becomes a differend. Lyotard's *discourse* of the differend, then, is the revelation of this story, the moment of justice outflanked by the prior law which instigates the work of the camps, and the law of death/proof which seals or preserves that work, the extermination of the name (of the) Jew ("The individual name ... and the collective name (Jew)" (Lyotard 101)). These three moments of justice (these deconstructions of the original position, of the Declaration's opening, of Auschwitz) must, like all such moments (though we shall note shortly that there can be none such as even one of these), be surrounded thus, as justice "always proceeds *to* questions of *droit*" (emphasis added), but also necessarily issues *from* such questions, since "[t]hat which threatens law already belongs to it" ("Force" 35). Deconstruction/justice is always under threat, it is structurally besieged almost before it has manifested itself. If indeed justice does occur in any case, it takes the form of this very deconstruction which is already in motion, which requires the barest reading on our part (see n. 39) in order to become a political principle, before being concealed by a prolepsis of right which then covers its own tracks – this is the nature of the original position, of the Declaration of Independence, of Auschwitz. It is the deconstructions of these three models (respectively our own, Derrida's, and Lyotard's[44] – though each reading remains immanent to *and active in* its particular text) which are marked by the vanishing interval of political discourse which presents itself in each case as the endangered or doomed moment of justice, as Derrida's "experience of the impossible."

And yet, wherever such experiences of the just are concerned, Derrida also insists *in specie* upon a feature of deconstruction in general with which we are already familiar,[45] namely that "[e]ach case is other, each decision is different and requires an absolutely unique interpretation, which no existing, coded rule can or ought to guarantee absolutely" ("Force" 23). It seems to follow from this absolute uniqueness that any comparison of the *relative* justness of these three readings (where the absolute precisely excludes

the relative) will elude us. We cannot, via some meta-jurisprudence, judge the justice of any; this is the price of post-*droit* thinking, of juridicism after legality. These three critiques of the prolepsis of right are in this sense on a par; no rule can be applied to them, *neither can any be derived from them* – indeed, from Auschwitz to liberal democracy, who would try! I want to return to this problem in some concluding remarks, but to remain for a moment longer on the subject of Rawlsian justice in itself, let us proceed to this conclusion by way of one final point of importance, namely – to attempt a return at last to Rawls' intentionally realized place in liberal democratic discourse – that this ineffable evanescence of deconstructive justice is not only borne out in the deconstruction of Rawls' text but also *reflected* in *A Theory of Justice*'s ostensible (hypothetical, theoretical) address to justice. And yet, where Derrida and Lyotard's texts are entirely at home in a register of vanishing or muted inscriptions, the intellectual tradition of contractarianism from which Rawls makes this latter intentional address remains, of course, firmly embedded in the commonsense metaphysics of presence which deconstruction rejects. It is for this reason that we may be somewhat surprised to discern in Rawls' discourse a certain semantic "dodging" of definitional ideas of justice "in itself" (though certainly not *what* is just, or what *does justice*). In fact, *A Theory of Justice* most often confines the term to an uninterrogated and imperfect binarism: circumstances are "just (or at least not unjust)" (304). If *at least some* circumstances can be neither just nor unjust, then there seem to be one or more states subsisting here *between* justice and injustice – neither would such states seem to resemble the "impossible intervals" and "silences" of the more skeptical philosophical stances we have been examining, moments which vanish between (perhaps always equally *un*just) varieties of law. Instead, Rawls' own sort of interstice is revealed in a number of incidental remarks, for example that "the sufficient condition for equal justice, the capacity for moral personality," may not be realized under "unjust and impoverished social circumstances, or fortuitous contingencies" (506): justice is balked by injustice, then, but also by other things, like contingency. Thus is seems that, in the realm of the contingent and the nonideal, in that picture of the *actual*, "real-world" Rawlsian state so often described as imperfectly just,[46] one or more intermediate conditions assure that justice and injustice do not entirely fill the field of political morality, i.e., as a positive set of conditions plus this set's negation. Indeed, we cannot be sure that "a positive set of conditions" adequately defines Rawlsian justice in even a general way. In a work which ostensibly takes justice as its sole ultimate concern, we will be surprised how often it is *not quite justice* which is at stake. After all, even the two principles of justice (or any other principles of justice a society might be based on) merely "*assume the role* of justice" according to Rawls (58; emphasis added), just as it only ever seems to be various "conceptions" of justice which he is discussing.[47]

The closest Rawls seems to come to a "working" definition of justice is his exposition of *justice as fairness*, where he nevertheless appends a telling remark concerning this apparently compound term: "The name does not mean that the concepts of justice and fairness are the same, any more than the phrase 'poetry as metaphor' means that the concepts of poetry and metaphor are the same" (12–13). It is clear that for some purposes anyway, this is not entirely so – the operator "as," as used in these constructions, naturally implies a certain similitude, but similitude almost to the point of substitution or replacement. From a certain viewpoint and/or for certain purposes – and especially where the field of definitional candidates may be otherwise empty – one term contingently ousts the other. Fairness, then, may sometimes be used to define, or stand in for, Rawlsian justice – and in Rawls' text more broadly, as we shall see momentarily, this sort of substitution proves a seemingly inevitable linguistic trope whereby the sign of similitude (*as*) is elided with the sign of everyday identity (*definition*). And yet, on the other hand, this second term, though similar enough to perform as a substitute in Rawls' discourse, is not identical to the first, or such an ousting would carry no importance, indeed would not be identifiable

as such. Is "fairness" a definition of justice, or a comparison, or a pragmatic consideration? I will return to the obviously pressing question of *definition* itself here shortly, but let us first bring these remarks about the Rawlsian career of the signifier "justice" to bear on Rawls' methodology as he himself seems to intend it.

From the beginning, then (which of course is to say, from the advent of the original position, from the "beginning" of politics), justice itself is absent – or at least offstage – and Rawls relies instead on our intuitive apprehension of this player whose role is being filled, this idea which gives way to its various substitutes. At certain points, Rawls is rather disarmingly self-conscious and explicit about this strategy:

The intuitive idea is this: the concept of something's being right is the same as, or better, may be replaced by, the concept of its being in accordance with the principles that in the original position would be acknowledged to apply to things of its kind. I do not interpret this concept of right as providing an analysis of the meaning of the term "right" as normally used in moral contexts. It is not meant as an analysis of the concept of right in the traditional sense. Rather, the broader notion of rightness as fairness is to be understood as a replacement for existing conceptions. There is no necessity to say that sameness of meaning holds between the word "right" (and its relatives) in its ordinary use and the more elaborate locutions needed to express this ideal contractarian concept of right. For our purposes here I accept the view that a sound analysis is best understood as providing a satisfactory substitute ... [W]e start with a concept the expression for which is somehow troublesome; but it serves certain ends that cannot be given up. An explication achieves these ends in other ways that are relatively free of difficulty. Thus if the theory of justice as fairness, or more generally of rightness as fairness, fits our considered judgments in reflective equilibrium,[48] and if it enables us to say all that on due examination we want to say, then it provides a way of eliminating customary phrases in favor of other expressions. So understood one may think of justice as fairness and rightness as fairness as providing a definition or explication of the concepts of justice and right. (111)

This passage is worth quoting at such length for the insight it affords us into the nature of Rawls' deferrals, not so much to "existing conceptions" of justice but more precisely to existing ways of *speaking* about justice: this play of substitution, of some expressions or "customary phrases" for others, is always a matter of *articulation*. Whether Derrida's offering of "justice equals deconstruction" can "fill in" as a viable definition which can help us to shed light on the deconstructive aspect of Rawls' text, therefore, is in some sense beside the point: Rawls' analysis depends on a readership which is *already embarked* on various other versions of the project of justice, whether or not all parts of this readership would be prepared to articulate precisely where such a project leads.[49] Rawls leans on this "intuitionist" perspective (see his chief discussion of this term in pages 34–40) when he wants to offer the possibility, as above, that there are no definitions but only descriptions or "explications"; it is this perspective, too, of course, which can lend credence (where the original position as a purely *ab ovo* device fails to do so)[50] to Rawls' claim to ground justice as fairness, or rather its "two principles," with less arbitrariness than that with which other competing conceptions (such as utilitarianism)[51] are instated in a given discourse about justice – from this perspective we can indeed make better sense of Rawls' claim that his conception constitutes an Archimedean point (520) from which to realize all other judgments. But conversely and more importantly, such intuitionism is also necessarily one of Rawls' markers for practices which we *cannot* ground via a priori conceptions or processes. In the realm of such practices, even definition, in its conventional metaphysical incarnations – for example as "an analysis of the meaning of [a] term" – escapes us.

In introducing a Wittgensteinian critique of meaning into our discussion at this late point, I am invoking a large body of work on the relationship between political theory and Wittgenstein's (not explicitly political) critique of philosophy, as well as the significant amount of commentary on the relationship between Wittgenstein and deconstruction,[52] and without being able to address either group of writings extensively. Rather, I am counting on the later Wittgenstein's determination "to bring words back from their metaphysical to their everyday use"[53] to make useful what is left of *A Theory of Justice* after (what is left of) deconstruction.[54] How might such salvage begin? Certainly Rawls might well make use of the critique of language suggested in the *Philosophical Investigations*,[55] of Wittgenstein's various demonstrations that it is possible to use words – and undoubtedly words such as "right" or "justice" – "without a *fixed* meaning" (Wittgenstein, sect. 79), and instead with *functional* meanings or "ostensive" definitions derived from existing, demonstrable uses of these words: "So one might say: the ostensive definition explains the use – the meaning – of a word when the overall role of the word in language is clear" (sect. 30). Thus, for someone with the habits of usage of which Rawls is speaking above, "the concept of something's being right" can be functionally defined as ("is the same as," "may be replaced by") "the concept of its being in accordance with the principles that in the original position would be acknowledged to apply to things of its kind."[56] However, such an application of Wittgenstein is useful for reading Rawls even before we consider the deconstruction of his text; again, my aim here is instead to investigate how the Wittgensteinian critique of language, and of philosophy more generally, might allow us to begin a reconstitution of Rawlsian theory *after* the deconstruction of its system which we have observed.

Consider then, for a moment, another of the *Philosophical Investigations*' meditations on "ostensive definition" which may provide some guidance in dealing with the seemingly thwarted aims of *A Theory of Justice*'s deconstructed text:

> The definition of the number two, "That is called 'two'" – pointing to two nuts – is perfectly exact. – But how can two be defined like that? The person one gives the definition to doesn't know what one wants to call "two"; he will suppose that "two" is the name given to *this* group of nuts!", etc. (Sect. 28)

In the next section, Wittgenstein floats a solution to the ambiguity:

> Perhaps you can say: two can be ostensively defined in *this* way: "This number is called 'two'". For the word "number" here shews what place in language, in grammar, we assign to the word. But this means that the word "number" must be explained before the ostensive definition can be understood. – The word "number" in the definition does indeed shew this place; does shew the post at which we station the word ... Whether the word "number" is necessary in the ostensive definition depends on whether without it the other person takes the definition otherwise than I wish. And that will depend on the circumstances under which it is given, and on the person I give it to. (Sect. 29)

The point of interest for us here is precisely the extent to which Wittgensteinian definition *is* "ostensive," so much a matter of showing, of *demonstration*. Certainly it flows from Rawls' text's own emphasis on "demonstration" that the passage above unpacks our problem of the mode or modes in which Rawls addresses his theory-of-justice-via-the-original-position to his reader, saying "this is or would be just" – what precisely, though? (What precisely is called "two"?) This procedure? Its results? The particular results extrapolated in this text? This text itself? The same ambiguity inheres (to use a simpler example) when I write or say "This is her problem: ...," in that it is difficult to know what will have been indicated by "this," what precisely I am about to utter – neither will it be any less ambiguous after I have uttered it. Will "this" be a description of her problem? Or will my words be the problem itself? And, if so, will the problem be these words "in general," or the words as *I* inscribe them, as their author?

That making this sort of discrimination is a reasonably simple matter for Wittgenstein (we can almost always specify that "this *number* is called 'two'"), but is far more complex for the deconstructivist outlook (remember, for example, that "Limited Inc"'s distinctions cannot be drawn from anything immanent in the phenomenon of speech ("Limited Inc" 208)), is one of the insights of Martin Stone's suggestion that

deconstruction gets us no further than metaphysics in making such judgments. Since, says Stone, *for* a deconstructivist viewpoint, "an interpretation is always required because no text is immune to *possible* doubt," i.e., no textual meaning can be absolutely fixed, this viewpoint becomes ironically tied to an "account of how meaning *is* fixed in view of 'all the possibilities'" (108; emphasis added). Stone argues for Wittgenstein that "we [should] be able to bring the word 'interpretation' back to its ordinary use, whereby interpretation is sometimes needed (i.e., in cases of real doubt and uncertainty) and sometimes not" (108). While I do not want to make out, with Stone, the everyday idea of "interpretation" as indicating clarification (see Stone 101), nor to endorse too readily the well-used dialectical type of objection to deconstruction he expresses above, I do think that such a view of Wittgenstein's project allows us to step back from the driving attraction to deconstruction which, Stone argues, is as compulsive as the attraction of metaphysics (108 and *passim*). Wittgenstein allows us to remember that *all* of these interpretations of the Rawlsian claim to justice – (1) "This procedure is just"; (2) "its results are just"; (3) "my particular results (i.e., the two principles of justice) are just"; (4) "this text itself (*A Theory of Justice*) is just"; and, of course, the current favorite, (5) "the deconstruction of this text is just" – are contingent, concrete possibilities, ineradicable from the field of our discourse (about procedure, about contract, about justice, etc.) and its "ordinary use" of these words (as Rawls himself puts it above). By radicalizing Rawls' own critique of expression in the context of our deconstructive critique, then, Wittgenstein's notion of ostensive definition might further unfix the "somehow troublesome" expression "justice" and the play of its "satisfactory substitutes." Which of the alternative interpretations above is in play at any given moment will, says Wittgenstein, "depend on the circumstances under which it is given, and on the person I give it to": to the originally positioned individual, then, perhaps *this procedure* is just. Then again – since such an individual is hypothetical only, since indeed the original position is in practice an individual "perspective" and not, even at the hypothetical level, a true procedure among individuals (see Rawls 139 for this clarification) – it is perhaps more practically the original position's *results* which are just for, say, the Rawlsian legislator (and depending on how infallible the legislator finds Rawls' own logic to be, perhaps he does indeed favor the two principles of justice themselves). Alternatively, Wittgenstein might offer "deconstructive" justice (whereby "the deconstruction of this text is just") – and again, solely on the basis of such a concept's use in political argument – to those wishing to question Rawls' discursive strategies, as I do here;[57] this offering might well take the shape of a deconstruction like the one we have been tracing, wherein Rawls' text takes the place of justice itself ("this text itself is just"), thereby paradoxically demonstrating the Derridean impossibility of such an adequation.

Indeed, Wittgenstein might be interested in deconstructive justice most of all, since it is here that the intervention of ordinary use is, from one perspective, most needed to assuage the anxiety I noted above: that we cannot, across a series of "just" deconstructions, evaluate their relative justness, or at least, pragmatically speaking (and to introduce yet another substitute definition), their relative political priority. To quickly review this point, then: as argued above, the respective deconstructions of the retroactive movements which power the discursive enterprises of the original position, the Declaration of Independence, and Auschwitz are all moments of "justice." Among these readings, however, deconstruction is deconstruction is deconstruction, impossibly incomparable and "foreign to the order of ... the rule" ("Force" 24). And yet, of course, Wittgenstein would famously be the first to note that, beyond this *theoretical* fastness of deconstructive nondifferentiation, we *do* follow rules across such series;[58] we *do* distinguish politically between the consequences of deconstructing these different events. To unravel the workings of Rawls' original position is not the same as to unravel the workings of Auschwitz; "just" both unravelings may be, but just in different ways and for different purposes, depending again, as Wittgenstein says, upon the circumstances under which the deconstruction is

performed, and on the audience of this performance. It is true, on the one hand, that Derrida has made it clear that no fixed grounds can be given for these discriminations,[59] for comparisons of deconstructions. But the Wittgensteinian reading of deconstructive justice is not, on account of this crucial region of groundlessness, forced into a relativist position, simply because, for Wittgenstein, "[g]iving grounds ... comes to an end" in every case, and "the end ... is our *acting*"[60] – Wittgenstein thus offers a means to bypass strict deconstruction's moment of discursive paralysis discerned by Stone. This alternative of the moment of simple praxis also salvages those readings of Wittgenstein which, as Alice Crary implies, run the risk of political indifference as to whether we "'cope better' by brutalizing Jews, communists, foreigners, gypsies and homosexuals," or "by talking about individuals as the possessors of certain inviolable human rights."[61] The juxtaposition is apt – deconstruction of both these positions is possible, but *we do* valuate such deconstructions differently. We do distinguish between the authorial/authoritarian hegemonies of *A Theory of Justice* and Auschwitz.

If *we do*, in spite of what we may have demonstrated or seen demonstrated in this essay, thus attach a particular value to the deconstruction of *A Theory of Justice* – if it seems to us that this deconstruction only pricks our sense that "justice" in Rawls' legalistic version also "serves certain ends that cannot be given up" – how might we hope to find value in continuing, perhaps by expanding or exploding, the project of the original position, and of the state of nature more broadly, as Rawls has bequeathed it to us? At this point, and as the barest prospectus for work toward a new reading of an astonishing corpus which for us, with the passing of its author, is now frozen – a reading which will not permit the powerful discursivity of this corpus *to freeze contractarian political discourse itself*, for this is the urgency my investigation has tried to bring to light, that the use of the original-position idea for political ends must not spell an end to politics – I wish to look briefly at one last discussion, among so many, of Wittgensteinian rule-following, this one employing the example of the observation of natives in an "unknown country" (Wittgenstein, sect. 206):

> Let us imagine that the people in that country carried on the usual human activities and in the course of them employed, apparently, an articulate language. If we watch their behavior we find it intelligible, it seems "logical". But when we try to learn their language we find it impossible to do so. For there is no regular connexion between what they say, the sounds they make, and their actions; but still these sounds are not superfluous, for if we gag one of the people, it has the same consequences as with us; without the sounds their actions fall into confusion – as I feel like putting it.

> Are we to say that these people have a language: orders, reports, and the rest?

> There is not enough regularity for us to call it "language". (Sect. 207)

Here, then, is a gap in what it seems likely that Wittgenstein would otherwise call a rule (see sect. 208). It is a practice not governed by sufficient "regularity" to qualify as a rule, and yet Wittgenstein makes it a point that a recognizable process it still occurring here (their behavior is "intelligible," "logical," etc.) – it's life, but not as we know it. What I want to draw attention to in Rawls' own great system of regularized rules, then, is a similar "gap" where the rules "let up," where indeed Rawls has neglected to give us any guide *except* his own example. This gap occurs at the point of actual debate in the original position – Rawls has famously finished out this debate for us, and, as we know, it is the very completeness of this performance, and the special architecture of the original position as its stage, which makes it so impossible to imagine deviation from Rawls' norm. But while Rawls may provide the blueprint for the original position from its first principles to its ultimate issue (and beyond), he only goes so far in telling us what the debate in between *actually looks like*. He sets constraints on what the original position's participants are like, and on what sorts of propositions can be put forward by them, but as for what actually (which is to say hypothetically) would be said by these participants, what their debate might look like, we have only

Rawls' example of a set or sequence of assertions "which, it is argued, would be agreed to" (15). And it is *only one example*, undoubled by prescription – it is, as we have said, the example of some *one* – from which not even Wittgenstein is ready to extrapolate a rule ("It is not possible that there should have been *only one occasion* on which *someone* obeyed a rule" (Wittgenstein, sect. 199; emphasis added)). What I want to suggest in closing, then, is that the very event from which I began a deconstruction of Rawls' text – i.e., Rawls' execution of his own procedure – is the same fissure from which a Wittgensteinian approach might begin to *restore* this text, a restoration in which, conversely, this same execution would now signal a gap, a lacuna. Could persons reasoning from the original position, under the proper constraints, do so in a way unimagined (though at the same time unprohibited) by Rawls' specific vision? We need not imagine that they debate by stamping their feet and shouting like Wittgenstein's chess-playing foreigners (sect. 200) – but how might the issue of the original position be imagined differently if its deliberations were carried out, say, in a theatrical mode (insofar as this is not already so)? What if speakers chose or agreed to speak ironically, in some or in all instances? Would the strange identity of originally positioned individuals breed an equally strange culture of debate, perhaps with its own religious commitments based on the precious drops of information available there? Might its debates then be written as allegorical stories? In any of these eventualities – each of which presents a tempting ingress for deconstructions of all stripes – how much would the participants be like Wittgenstein's geometer who uses a compass to trace a circle, but refuses to keep a constant distance between the stationary and moving legs (sect. 237)? I am not offering a Wittgensteinian critique here as a sort of eleventh-hour panacea for both Rawlsian and Derridean discourse – rather, I am concerned with how this critique might intersect with a larger deconstructive discourse, not of the original position but of the state of nature more broadly, beyond contractarianism, beyond utopianism as well, a discourse inspired, indeed mandated, by the Rawlsian vision of democratic justice, a subject which has already so reinvigorated deconstruction.

notes

1 I would like to acknowledge my debt to the incisive commentary and suggestions for revision provided by *Angelaki*'s anonymous reviewer – also to be thanked are Bruce Robbins and Dennis Patterson for their invaluable criticisms of earlier versions of this manuscript. Most of all, I wish to thank Derek Attridge, who has contributed his wisdom and patience to the idea presented here from its beginnings.

2 Let us say for now, then, that this reading is a deconstruction according to one of Derrida's more undemanding characterizations of this discourse as "attack[ing] the systemic ... constructionist account of what is brought together, of assembly" (*Memoires: For Paul de Man* 73; hereafter abbreviated *Memoires*).

3 While the question of the hypothetical status of the original position, and of how this status translates into real policy, is in some sense the focus of this essay (as well as Rawls' most significant revision of contractarian discourse's earlier versions of the state of nature), we will not broach it yet – for now, see Rawls' most important exposition of this matter in *A Theory of Justice* 120–21 (hereafter abbreviated TJ – all references to Rawls are made to this volume unless otherwise noted).

More generally, too, I will not be able to pause in this presentation to consider the strange and fascinating history of the state of nature's varied historicities and fictionalities as reflected by the original-position idea. As much a fleeting reality to Locke and Hobbes as it was a crucial fiction to Kant (so important to Rawls in *A Theory of Justice*; see pages 251–57 and throughout TJ) and to Rousseau (so important, of course, to Derrida's corpus as a whole), the state-of-nature idea crosses so many philosophical and literary vectors (via utopianism/dystopianism, mythology, natural-rights theory, etc.) that its reimagining by Rawls must be accounted as creating an indispensable discursive nexus for multiple branches of contemporary theory (not least for what re-

mains of deconstructive theory). Some key fragments: Locke, *The Second Treatise of Government, Two Treatises of Government*, sects. 100–01; Hobbes, *Leviathan* 186–87; Kant, "On the Common Saying: 'This May Be True in Theory, But It Does Not Apply in Practice'" 79ff.; Rousseau, "Discourse on the Origin of Inequality" 38–39.

4 Rawls' preoccupation with the workings of this type of procedure will become important further on: "pure procedural justice obtains when there is no independent criterion for the right result" of a decision concerning "distributive shares," or quantities of fundamental social goods allocated to each person in a given society, according to a method of determination to which all persons agree (86).

5 Never defined explicitly, this is justice concerning the "distributive shares" of n. 4; see also Rawls 88–89 and *passim*. Specifically, I am concerned here with the "two principles of justice" in which Rawls believes his procedure would result. Though I will not address their specific content in this essay, I cite them now so as to be able to refer to them freely from here on (two attached priority rules and a "general conception" also follow this passage in Rawls' text (302–03)):

First Principle
Each person is to have an equal right to the most extensive total system of equal basic liberties compatible with a similar liberty for all.

Second Principle
Social and economic inequalities are to be arranged so that they are both:
(a) to the greatest benefit of the least advantaged, consistent with the just savings principle, and
(b) attached to offices and positions open to all under conditions of fair equality of opportunity. (302)

6 See, for example, Robert Nozick (*Anarchy, State, and Utopia* 197) on the question of how an actual individual might be viewed as complaining against the decisions of his originally positioned self (though, as we shall see, there is also the question of how much "self," let alone how much decision, persists in the original position).

7 Ronald Dworkin, "What is Equality?: Part 2: Equality of Resources" 316.

8 I am using the perhaps somewhat obscure term "nominalist" here simply to designate that which is structured by the name, and not only by the

proper name but by the naming function of the signifier in general, that which is inaugurated precisely at the expense of *what* is named – this economy has, of course, been laid out by Derrida (see n. 12 below).

9 See n. 3 above.

10 I do not intend here a substantive engagement with Heidegger, and I have chosen to employ the term "ontic" only to specify that I am speaking of facts about persons in the original position as we (perhaps as other such persons ourselves) encounter these individuals (see Heidegger, *Being and Time* 28–35, 31 n. 3) – no ontology or metaphysics of being in such a hypothetical state, then, is suggested.

11 In *Political Liberalism*, this representative capacity (in ideological terms) becomes explicit (Rawls, *Political Liberalism* 24ff.).

12 Well before we come to our examination of Derrida's own concern with the nature of justice, then, our reading of *A Theory of Justice* moves within the structure of Derrida's seminal meditations on the fundamental alienation of this "I," this speaking "self." From "La Parole soufflée":

> Henceforth, what is called the speaking subject is no longer the person himself, or the person alone, who speaks. The speaking subject discovers his irreducible secondarity, his origin that is always already eluded; for the origin is always already eluded on the basis of an organized field of speech in which the speaking subject vainly seeks a place that is always missing. (178)

That Derrida's speaking subject has, of course, been alienated from itself long before a device like Rawls' original position – that is to say, long before, at the very advent of language – makes no difference to our argument at this point. Though it goes without saying that Rawls is no deconstructivist thinker, these tendencies of the original position begin to provide an ideological simulacrum of a field of deconstructive thinking about justice in which, I will shortly show, Rawls' presentation is more deeply implicated. (The same is true, to take another example, of any comparison that could be made between the account of the occlusion of proper names in the original pos-

ition, and Derrida's own account of the effacement of truly "proper" names in *Of Grammatology* 110ff.)

13 The "thin theory" of the good is the next-to-noncontingent moral theory which Rawls believes would be widely accepted by those seeking to structure their assumptions in the original position (see Rawls 339–407).

14 A comparison of "one" in English with the analogous German pronoun *man* (an analogy explored also by John Macquarrie and Edward Robinson (see Heidegger 149 n. 1)) is instructive, since Heidegger may come closest to Rawls' impossibly generic "one" with his hypostasization of the latter pronoun as *das Man* (see the fourth section of *Being and Time*'s Division One, 149–68).

15 Rawls 13. With regard to this dimension of Rawls' theory, the idea of a hypothetically empirical uniformity in the original position (reflecting our own autonomous discursive one), we are certainly obliged to be fair to Rawls in noting remarks like the following, on the choice of principles from among different alternatives in the original position:

> Even if there is a best alternative, it seems difficult to describe the parties' intellectual powers so that this optimum, or even the more plausible conceptions, are sure to occur to them. Some solutions to the choice problem may be clear enough on careful reflection; it is another matter to describe the parties so that their deliberations generate these alternatives. Thus although the principles of justice may be superior to those conceptions known to us, perhaps some hitherto unformulated set of principles is still better. (Rawls 122)

This suggestion, i.e., that the original position might produce different principles for others than it has for Rawls, contradictory as this suggestion is of his more typical way of speaking, is made here and at several other points in Rawls' text, and this brings to light the valuable point that Rawls is concerned to maintain the appearance of a genuine procedural process which is important, theoretically and practically, precisely because, Rawls assumes, the outcome of such a process is *not* fixed, because political possibility for any society (qua its first principles) is bound up in that process. Our notion that political possibility is instead foreclosed by the discursive nature of the original position, then, is founded on the double truth of Rawls' conviction that, given the original position as it is, "the same principles are always chosen" – where this main current in *A Theory of Justice* comes into conflict with passages like the above, it is really, so to speak, simply Rawls' word against Rawls', and we must decide where necessity lies. Neither are we critiquing Rawls here for obtuseness, let alone duplicity, concerning the logic of his own construct – rather, we are concerned with how the interaction of Rawls' text with this logic means that the original position functions in a far more powerful mode than Rawls intends.

16 By way of clarifying the full extent of the original position's hypothetical nature according to Rawls, we can note an interesting and powerful deferral in Rawls' handling of this nature: *as hypothetical*, Rawls is clear that "[n]othing resembling [the original position] need ever take place" (120), i.e., nothing resembling an actual meeting and contracting of persons. Instead, one (and only one, precisely) need merely reason about a given problem *as one would* from the standpoint of the original position (13 and *passim*). The stability of Rawlsian society, therefore, depends on the assumption that all persons (or, in the nonideal realm of political actualities (see n. 46 below), a majority (354–55)) working to render a decision about the problem will reason in the same way, to the same conclusions, in virtue of reasoning *as they would* under this constraint ("The principles must be specified so that they yield a determinate conclusion" (65)). The consensus integral to any *literal* contract situation is thus really moved one rung up the ladder into the post-contract realm of the state, and there is therefore no need to *transfer* or translate agreement from the original position to actual political states – it is already there, and it is possible that this prolepsis runs parallel to the one we are currently tracing.

17 Robert Frost, "'It Will Always Be About Equally Hard to Save Your Soul': A Letter to *The Amherst Student*" 344.

18 Rawls seems recently to have been more aware of this necessary truth in his continued assertion that the original position's conception of political justice is what would be accepted by "you and [me], here and now" (Rawls, *The Law of Peoples*, with "The Idea of Public Reason Revisited"

30) – though the "you," as we are now investigating, remains a lingering fiction of the ideology.

19 Or rather – since, all things considered, we can probably justify at this point the use of the gender-specific noun – any rational man. As for the rationality of the "man" in question, we will not be concerned here with critiquing any particular notion of rationality that Rawls may be deploying (see his own account on pages 114–17) – the point is rather that once we have accepted Rawls *himself* as rational, the issue is moot.

I should note at this point that the notion of a contractarian political theorist's impersonation of a political subject is the logical extremity of Hanna Pitkin's observation regarding an earlier social-contract theorist who, of course, remains highly important to Rawls' thinking in TJ (see, for example, 32–33 and *passim*):

> In truth, the original contract could not have read otherwise than it did, and the powers it gave and the limits it placed can be logically deduced from the laws of nature. Not only does Locke himself confidently deduce them in this way, sure that he can tell us what the terms of that original contract were, *must* have been; but he says explicitly that they could not have been otherwise …
>
> If the terms of the original contract are, as I am arguing, "self-evident" truths to Locke which could not be or have been otherwise, then the historical veracity of the contract theory becomes in a new and more profound sense irrelevant. (Pitkin, "Obligation and Consent: Part I" 996)

Pitkin goes on from here with a consent-theory argument which is no less able ultimately to escape the original contract's various historicities (we will shortly introduce yet another) than it is able to escape treating John Locke's writing *of* politics as merely writing *about* politics, about individuals' choices and obligations in real-world, everyday circumstances. It is our task here to delay this jump from theory to the real world long enough to realize (with increased clarity from Locke to Rawls) that the writing of contractarian theory actually intrudes, materially and directly, upon that world, that the state-of-nature-type construct constructs (and crosses) its own bridge to the everyday – and surely, as we have seen, Rawls seems to intend that the original position take place "every day"!

20 This is, of course, only the year of publication – we might want to be more precise by asking during how many of the preceding years, indeed at what times over the span of an entire thinking life, Rawls' performance was already begun and moving forward, and indeed unceasingly until such a comparatively recent moment.

21 It will probably not be too dramatic to say that this movement in Rawls' text breaks Lyotard's problem of how to legitimate the move from a description of justice to a prescription (see Lyotard and Thébaud, *Just Gaming* 21–24; hereafter abbreviated JG). As a process which executes itself as it proposes itself, *A Theory of Justice* (the title is really now almost taunting) is simply both simultaneously.

22 In "The Law of Genre" 236ff. – and it is certainly matters of genre that we are considering here.

23 We do not on this account, however, censure this Rawls-subject for thus "going it alone" – any authorial subject must in some sense always account itself as "on its own," and it is part and parcel of Derrida's account of such a subject as alienated "self-presence which has never been given but [is] only … always already split" (*Of Grammatology* 112) that this subject always has the resource of an illusory interiority which can, so to speak, "take counsel with itself," and we have seen the Rawls-subject do this to great effect (this interiority, of course, variously incarnated, also serves as Derrida's primary object of deconstruction in a number of texts, for example in the case of Artaud's attempted restoration of an unalienated self laid out in "La Parole soufflée"). Justice, however, would also seem to be at least partially a question of how far discourse can proceed thus isolated, how far a particular text can be singly authored before it must surrender to other authorships (and, of course, it is crucial that *A Theory of Justice* surrenders such authorship – if ever – far later than it claims to).

24 An expanded treatment of the latter is, of course, the primary subject of *The Law of Peoples*.

25 Derrida, "Force of Law: The 'Mystical Foundation of Authority'" 35; hereafter abbreviated "Force."

26 "[N]o one has ever said that deconstruction, as a technique or a method, was possible; it

thinks only on the level of the impossible and of what is still evoked as unthinkable" (Derrida, *Memoires* 135). We shall see that Derrida's rejection of a deconstructive methodology, his concern that deconstructive reading not be allowed to generate, in Derek Attridge's words, any "abstractable or applicable argument, concept, or method which could be laid out independently of [particular] readings" (Attridge, "Introduction: Derrida and the Questioning of Literature" in Derrida, *Acts of Literature* 14), remains as important as ever in the case of justice, precisely for reasons of "the irreducible singularity of each situation" ("Force" 51) (as Derrida discerns it in Walter Benjamin's "Critique of Violence," in an analysis claiming the lion's share of "Force of Law," one for which I will regrettably not have space here).

27 Derrida, "Declarations of Independence" 10; hereafter abbreviated "Declarations."

28 Richard Beardsworth, *Derrida and the Political* 99.

29 Cf. Derrida on the "good people" of the USA: "They do *not* exist as an entity, it does *not* exist, *before* this declaration, not *as such*. If it gives birth to itself, as free and independent subject, as possible signer, this can hold only in the act of the signature. The signature invents the signer" ("Declarations" 10).

30 Derrida, "Limited Inc abc …" 208; hereafter abbreviated "Limited Inc."

31 I hope it will be emergently clear that, various potential conventional/radical dividing lines aside, when I speak of "conventional political argument" in this context I am simply referring to the discourse of Rawls and many of his contemporaries (the majority of them in university political science departments), of the logical, ideological register in which many of the arguments for and against the original position – given and accepted as a hypothetical, heuristic construct that "works" or does not – have been played out since *A Theory of Justice*'s publication. It should go without saying that this is not to imply some fictitious intellectual homogeneity among scholars in the discipline of political science proper – all the less so as we move from 1971 to today, where political scientists like Aryeh Botwinick, William Connolly and others have, in different contexts, long opened this discipline to anti- or nonideological stances (from analytic philosophy,

literary theory, etc.), stances with some forms of which, indeed, thinkers such as Hanna Pitkin were already experimenting decades earlier.

32 Lyotard, *The Differend: Phrases in Dispute* 7–8, also addressed on pages 56–58 and *passim* (all subsequent references to Lyotard are made to this volume unless otherwise noted). As a variant of Derrida's own founding vision of a structural "center" which both is and is not part of the structure it produces (see Derrida, "Structure, Sign, and Play in the Discourse of the Human Sciences" 278ff., hereafter abbreviated SSP), this idea is Lyotard's brilliant calling of Derrida's bet on the autonomy of the sign: the "last phrase" is one more such "center" of discourse (and these centers are, of course, Lyotard's own earlier concern, differently framed, in *The Postmodern Condition*), but this time the discourse is that of language itself. As can be seen in the case of the differend at Auschwitz, this last phrase is also a ratifying, validating force for Lyotard, where the Derrida of *Memoires* makes such "ex-centric center[s]" (*Memoires* 73) the very "lever" of deconstruction (*Memoires* 72) – this apparent divergence is a matter for further investigation.

33 Again, see pages 154–57 for the stunted dialectic of Auschwitz.

34 Or rather that it functions not as a "last phrase" but as *the* "last instance" of the Declaration's God: prescriptive (authorizing) not descriptive (synthesizing).

35 Beyond even considerations of utopian versions of the state of nature (in Milton et al.), I believe that this is an element which is available to readings not only of Kant's and especially Rousseau's commentary but also of Locke's, thanks to his active use of biblical and classical sources – but this point will need to be developed elsewhere.

36 I invoke Derrida's remark at the birth of deconstruction, from the conclusion to "Structure, Sign, and Play," where it seems likely that he is speaking of deconstruction itself as "the as yet unnamable which is proclaiming itself and which can do so, as is necessary whenever a birth is in the offing, only under the species of the nonspecies, in the formless, mute, infant, and terrifying form of monstrosity" (SSP 293). Derrida apparently felt that philosophy was "catching a glimpse" of this birth (SSP 293) in 1966 (see

Bass' source notes on the original lecture (*Writing and Difference* 342)); here we are close to regarding *A Theory of Justice* and the state-of-nature discourse it recreated, only five years later, as a specimen of this birth, of deconstruction itself, of the newly and treacherously performative skepticism of which Derrida warns.

Warning, of course, remains intimately connected to the idea of the "monster" (derived from the Latin *monstrum* originally meaning "divine portent or warning," itself from *monere*, "to warn" (*Oxford English Dictionary* (*OED*)); for the web of variants, definitions and etymologies presented in this paragraph, see entries for the relevant words in the *OED*). And yet "monster" in English (also "monstre") is also a variant of "monstre" in another definition ("*sb.*¹" entry for monstre), i.e., as itself a variant of "monstrance" ("[d]emonstration, proof" (def. 1)), this time from *monstrare* (actually from *monstrant-em* in the *OED* – I am completing this link via the verb "monstrate" (from *monstrare* proper in the *OED*)). *Monstrare* means to "show by example" or "demonstrate" (def. 2, *Oxford Latin Dictionary*) – and this is the all-important trope of the original position as monster, as a warning of a deconstruction which it itself constitutes – but also to "*reveal*" or "*betray*" (def. 4). That which "shows," then, that which *demonstrates* as Rawls' text claims to do, must in some sense always be "monstrous," treacherous, worthy of warning, itself a warning. See the *OED* for further uses of "monstrance" ("monstre," "monster"), some of them fascinating in relation to Rawls as I am reading him: e.g., an open vessel for carrying the host (def. 2), or (as a "*monstrance of right*" in Chancery) a legal writ returning "lands or tenements" to the rightful owner from a deceased person (def. 1b).

37 And so I am bound to note that I have begun this presentation, in unpublished form, in the chapter of my doctoral dissertation from which this essay is adapted (see MacAdam, "The Republic in the Air: State of Nature Theory and the Dreaming of the State" 187–205). Such a presentation remains a crucial extension of this project.

38 "The place for justice" is not one "for calculable and distributive justice. Not for law, for the calculation of restitution, the economy of vengeance or punishment ..." (Derrida, *Specters of Marx: The State of the Debt, the Work of Mourning, and the New International* 22, hereafter abbreviated *Specters*).

39 From *Memoires*:

> As we have seen, the very condition of a deconstruction may be at work, in the work, *within* the system to be deconstructed; it may *already* be located there, already at work … One might then be inclined to reach this conclusion: deconstruction is not an operation that supervenes *afterwards*, from the outside, one fine day; it is always already at work in the work … (73)

Whether or not one would agree with Derrida that all that is therefore left for the "deconstructing" reader is perhaps "to do memory work" (73), I believe that this claim gets to the heart of Derrida's rejection of a deconstructive "methodology" (see n. 26): if any deconstructive reading on "our part" is really only a hearkening to that immanent reading, the structure of which each particular text (as the true deconstructing "agent") carries within itself, then no reader could exercise his or her own agency in applying a methodology "derived" from instances in which the reader exercises no decisive agency to begin with.

40 That is, of static law in the conventional sense – by *droit*, Derrida designates such an everyday jurisprudence, opposed to justice though derived from and aspiring to it (we will come to this shortly), a jurisprudence which we may associate with his remarks on "concepts of justice, the law and right … that have been imposed and sedimented," concepts "remaining more or less readable or presupposed" ("Force" 19) – and Rawls' law, qua *A Theory of Justice*, is nothing if not readable.

41 Why does this elision come to the fore here? Perhaps simply because its time has come. This elision's semi-covert aura, added to the strange transitivity with which Derrida defers the announcement of deconstruction's undeconstructibility (a mediation also observable in the claim that "justice in itself … is not deconstructible [, n]o more than deconstruction itself"), clearly bespeaks a philosophically consistent reluctance to grant deconstruction a privileged position which perhaps would be not unlike that once prevalently accorded to metaphysics – and yet in "Force of Law" Derrida does seem more intent than elsewhere that deconstruction *in its incarnation as justice* remain ultimately inviolate, invulnerable to its own "principle" relative to the morass of discourse it must adjudicate. (Contrast, for example, his reading of Paul de Man on allegory as the self-alienated principle which structures signification as a whole (*Memoires* 72ff.), and yet which still remains "one figure among others" (*Memoires* 78) in certain contexts.) Having witnessed over time a succession of surrogates for deconstruction's agency – various aspects of "the literary," of Freudian or Lacanian psychoanalysis, of Marxist theory, etc. – we might wonder whether the surrogate "justice" has finally brought deconstruction into an undeniable inheritance, one which *cannot risk self-effacement* (is this why deconstruction has always "done nothing but address" the question of justice ("Force" 10)?).

42 And even if this law does arrive with its declaration, the justice it promises, in Derrida's sense, remains always to come, more precisely, it remains "*à venir*" (see "Force" 27 for this term of Derrida's) – as Derrida puts it in the case of democracy in particular in *Specters*, "the idea … of democracy to come … is the opening of this gap between an infinite promise … and the … necessarily inadequate forms of what has to be measured against this promise" (65). *Droit* (the two principles of justice or any other form) always contains this promise as well as its own violence to that promise – we shall not have space here to do more than allude to the crucial work which remains to be done on such an "eschatology" (*Specters* 65) in relation to a parallel one which I believe to be discernible in Rawls (see n. 54 below).

43 See all of Lyotard for the full scenario of this mutilated dialogism.

44 Clearly I am taking a significant liberty here in accounting Lyotard's reading of the silenced "last phrase" at Auschwitz as a "deconstruction" – I should reiterate that I do so only in the local sense which I hope I have demonstrated, i.e., Lyotard's reading is such a deconstruction, and therefore "just," insofar as it reads this prolepsis of right which appears always to be present in acts of self-authorization, whether the authorization to create a people or to destroy one.

45 Cf. Derrida on the sign in "Signature Event Context" (where I consider him to be investigating the sign as the autonomous agent of deconstruction – again see n. 39): "No context can enclose it. Nor can any code …" (317).

46 For Rawls' initial statement of the idea of nonideal theory, see TJ 245ff.

47 In fairness to Rawls, we should note page 310, where "[j]ustice is happiness according to virtue"; even leaving aside the question of Rawls' use of such a moral element in the definition, this idea seems as much at sea in the rest of Rawls' argument as one would expect of a definition which arrives on its own scene so late.

48 On this concept see TJ 20–21.

49 The interaction of these varying conceptions is, of course, Rawls' chief subject in *Political Liberalism*.

50 Since, *as an ab ovo* device, the original position cannot itself admit of any grounding. Intuitionism offers such a grounding, to the original position as well as to its "product" of justice as fairness (see Rawls' remarkable account of those features of the original position "that we do in fact accept" (21) on pages 17–22; the preceding sections, of course, address our intuitions as to why a contractual viewpoint is the best approach to social justice to begin with); intuitionism achieves this by giving in to a certain circularity necessary to the justification of beginnings (beginnings which, original-position theory has the virtue of recognizing, are always artificial). This is a different *order* of circularity from that which we have seen otherwise at work in Rawls, or in the Declaration of Independence, etc. – conceptual, even metaphysical, and not discursive – but its reflection of those more skeptical investigations betrays a sophisticated perspective ripe for a new critique of political argument.

51 See, for example, TJ 180–83 for one of the strongest moments of Rawls' challenge to the utilitarian perspective.

52 On Wittgenstein and political philosophy, see Hanna Pitkin's important work, namely *Wittgenstein and Justice: On the Significance of Ludwig Wittgenstein for Social and Political Thought*, or more recently Alice Crary, "Wittgenstein's Philosophy in Relation to Political Thought"; on Wittgenstein and deconstruction, see Henry Staten's *Wittgenstein and Derrida*, and Martin Stone, "Wittgenstein on Deconstruction"; in this abbreviated discussion, I have made some use of Stone's and Crary's positions below.

53 Ludwig Wittgenstein, *Philosophical Investigations*, sect. 116. Unless otherwise noted, all references to Wittgenstein are made to this volume; paragraph numbers in the text refer to Part 1 of this volume.

54 In considering whether anything like democracy (whatever that may be like) is recoverable from Rawls' deconstructed text, we will not have the opportunity here to consider Derrida's contention that democracy as it currently exists "is a degeneracy of *droit* and of the violence of *droit*," that "there is not yet any democracy worthy of this name. Democracy remains to come: to engender or to regenerate" ("Force" 46). This remark in "Force" and its considerable elaboration in *Specters* (65–66), from which I have quoted above (n. 42), will likely present the greatest challenge to any recovery effort, except perhaps for a certain surrendering of theory which remains to be explored in Rawls' own treatment of the nonideal (see n. 46 above) – and perhaps, in these confrontations too, Wittgenstein will have a role to play.

55 And Rawls does indeed himself invoke Wittgenstein twice in TJ, in discussions of discernments about sensations (480 n. 17, 558). For the purposes of this discussion, these invocations perhaps run no deeper than Derrida's own reference to Rawls ("Force" 14), but it is instructive in either case that Rawls and Derrida seem to circle, from "opposite" sides, the ravine between skepticism and metaphysics, both conscious of the need, most urgently in matters of justice perhaps, for a crossing.

56 I am deliberately deferring here a discussion of the embattled "meaning is use" reading of Wittgenstein examined by so many commentators (including, among the texts cited above, Crary 119, 130ff., and Staten 87ff.). For present purposes, I will say only that it may be best to conceive of use as "conferring" meaning rather than as "meaning" meaning (I believe such an idea would stand opposed to that suggested by Staten (87); nevertheless, see the above discussions in Crary and Staten for a more detailed consideration of this issue of a possible reinstatement of fixed reference).

57 I will not ask here whether Wittgenstein would give his blessing to such an interrogation or count it as "nonsense" of the type he returns to throughout the *Investigations* (e.g., in sect. 40 – see also Stone 94, where his analysis appears importantly to touch upon deconstruction as a

potential Wittgensteinian nonsense, and *passim*; this issue is in one sense, of course, emblematic of the whole question of the relation between deconstruction and the later Wittgenstein, a question with which Stone's essay as a whole is largely occupied).

58 For one of the most important discussions of rule-following in *Philosophical Investigations*, and probably the most relevant here, see sect. 198ff.

59 As has, of course, in a significantly divergent argument, Lyotard – I cannot detour here into his importantly related account of why judgments in general are made "without criteria" (JG 14) – see *Just Gaming* 14–18 and *passim*.

60 Ludwig Wittgenstein, *On Certainty*, sect. 204.

61 Crary 125. Much of Crary's argument is occupied precisely with questioning "Wittgensteinian" pragmatism of Richard Rorty's stripe ("cope better" is Rorty's phrase); the example of "neo-fascism" (125) vs. human rights Crary attributes to H. Putnam, *Realism with a Human Face* (Crary 125 n. 29).

bibliography

Attridge, Derek. "Introduction: Derrida and the Questioning of Literature." *Acts of Literature*. Ed. Derek Attridge. New York: Routledge, 1992. 1–29.

Beardsworth, Richard. *Derrida and the Political*. London: Routledge, 1996.

Crary, Alice. "Wittgenstein's Philosophy in Relation to Political Thought." *The New Wittgenstein*. Ed. Alice Crary and Rupert Read. New York: Routledge, 2000.

Crary, Alice and Rupert Read (eds.). *The New Wittgenstein*. New York: Routledge, 2000.

Derrida, Jacques. *Acts of Literature*. Ed. Derek Attridge. New York: Routledge, 1992.

Derrida, Jacques. "Declarations of Independence." Trans. Tom Keenan and Tom Pepper. *New Political Science* 15 (1984): 7–15.

Derrida, Jacques. "Force of Law: The 'Mystical Foundation of Authority.'" Trans. Mary Quaintance. *Deconstruction and the Possibility of Justice*. Ed. Drucilla Cornell et al. New York: Routledge, 1992.

Derrida, Jacques. *Of Grammatology*. Corrected ed. Trans. Gayatri Chakravorty Spivak. Baltimore: Johns Hopkins UP, 1976.

Derrida, Jacques. "The Law of Genre." Trans. Avital Ronell. *Acts of Literature*. New York: Routledge, 1992.

Derrida, Jacques. "Limited Inc abc ..." Trans. Samuel Weber. *Glyph* 2 (1977): 162–254.

Derrida, Jacques. *Memoires: For Paul de Man*. Trans. Cecile Lindsay, Jonathan Culler and Eduardo Cadava. New York: Columbia UP, 1986.

Derrida, Jacques. "La Parole soufflée." *Writing and Difference*. Trans. Alan Bass. Chicago: U of Chicago P, 1978.

Derrida, Jacques. "Signature Event Context." *Margins of Philosophy*. Trans. Alan Bass. Chicago: U of Chicago P, 1982.

Derrida, Jacques. *Specters of Marx: The State of the Debt, the Work of Mourning, and the New International*. Trans. Peggy Kamuf. New York: Routledge, 1994.

Derrida, Jacques. "Structure, Sign, and Play in the Discourse of the Human Sciences." *Writing and Difference*. Trans. Alan Bass. Chicago: U of Chicago P, 1978.

Derrida, Jacques. *Writing and Difference*. Trans. Alan Bass. Chicago: U of Chicago P, 1978.

Dworkin, Ronald. "What is Equality?: Part 2: Equality of Resources." *Philosophy and Public Affairs* 10 (1981): 283–345.

Frost, Robert. "'It Will Always Be About Equally Hard to Save Your Soul': A Letter to *The Amherst Student*." *Robert Frost: Poetry and Prose*. Ed. Edward Connery Lathem and Lawrance Thompson. New York: Holt, 1972.

Heidegger, Martin. *Being and Time*. Trans. John Macquarrie and Edward Robinson. New York: HarperCollins, 1962.

Hobbes, Thomas. *Leviathan*. Ed. C.B. MacPherson. London: Penguin, 1985.

Kant, Immanuel. "On the Common Saying: 'This May Be True in Theory, But It Does Not Apply in Practice.'" *Kant: Political Writings*. Ed. Hans Reiss. Trans. H.B. Nisbet. Cambridge: Cambridge UP, 1995.

Locke, John. *The Second Treatise of Government*. *Two Treatises of Government*. Ed. Peter Laslett. Cambridge: Cambridge UP, 1991.

Lyotard, Jean-François. *The Differend: Phrases in Dispute*. Trans. George Van Den Abbeele. Minneapolis: U of Minnesota P, 1988.

Lyotard, Jean-François. *The Postmodern Condition: A Report on Knowledge*. Trans. Geoff Bennington and Brian Massumi. Minneapolis: U of Minnesota P, 1984.

Lyotard, Jean-François and Jean-Loup Thébaud. *Just Gaming*. Trans. Wlad Godzich. Minneapolis: U of Minnesota P, 1985.

MacAdam, Ethan. "The Republic in the Air: State of Nature Theory and the Dreaming of the State." Dissertation. Rutgers U–New Brunswick, 2001.

Nozick, Robert. *Anarchy, State, and Utopia*. New York: Harper–Basic, 1974.

Oxford English Dictionary. 2nd ed. Oxford: Oxford UP, 1989.

Oxford Latin Dictionary. Oxford: Oxford UP, 1982.

Pitkin, Hanna. "Obligation and Consent: Part I." *American Political Science Review* 59 (1965): 990–99.

Pitkin, Hanna. *Wittgenstein and Justice: On the Significance of Ludwig Wittgenstein for Social and Political Thought*. Berkeley: U of California P, 1972.

Rawls, John. *The Law of Peoples, with "The Idea of Public Reason Revisited."* Cambridge, MA: Harvard UP, 1999.

Rawls, John. *Political Liberalism*. New York: Columbia UP, 1993.

Rawls, John. *A Theory of Justice*. Cambridge, MA: Harvard–Belknap, 1971.

Rousseau, Jean-Jacques. "Discourse on the Origin of Inequality." *Jean-Jacques Rousseau: The Basic Political Writings*. Ed. and trans. Donald A. Cress. Indianapolis: Hackett, 1987.

Staten, Henry. *Wittgenstein and Derrida*. Lincoln: U of Nebraska P, 1984.

Stone, Martin. "Wittgenstein on Deconstruction." *The New Wittgenstein*. Ed. Alice Crary and Rupert Read. New York: Routledge, 2000.

Wittgenstein, Ludwig. *On Certainty*. Ed. G.E.M. Anscombe and G.H. von Wright. Trans. Denis Paul and G.E.M. Anscombe. New York: Torchbook–Harper, 1972.

Wittgenstein, Ludwig. *Philosophical Investigations*. Trans. G.E.M. Anscombe. Oxford: Basil Blackwell & Mott, 1958.

Ethan H. MacAdam
Department of English
University of Miami
PO Box 248146
Coral Gables, FL 33124-4632
USA
E-mail: e.macadam@miami.edu

journal of the theoretical humanities
volume 9 number 3 december 2004

introduction

"It is the irony of revolutions that they engender a power all the more absolute in its exercise, not because it is more anonymous, as people say, but because it is more reduced to the words that signify it," writes Lacan of the Freudian revolution (79). Although psychoanalysis as a Copernican revolution is a form of decentring, a centre is nonetheless surreptitiously re-installed; in becoming a science, psychoanalysis has necessarily been marked by absolutism. It is, as Lacan suggests, the sign of "an earthquake yet to come" (328), but perhaps we should be thinking in terms of an earthquake *always* yet to come. Postcolonialism, likewise, has seen its revolutionary heritage mobilized to block its revolutionary force, its current instances compared with its supposedly proper antecedents and found wanting. Structures of cause and effect, origin and prediction, have worked to police postcolonial discourses. While the hybrid, interdisciplinary nature of postcolonialism's revolutionary histories as well as concepts is accepted, there has still been an insistence on revolutionary purity.

The critique of postcolonial hybridity has often focused on Homi Bhabha's work, and his sense of interdisciplinarity is important here. In "DissemiNation," Bhabha states the following about the necessity of interdisciplinarity: "To enter into the interdisciplinarity of cultural texts means that we cannot contextualize the emergent cultural form by locating it in terms of some pre-given discursive causality or origin. We must always keep open a supplementary space for the articulation of cultural knowledges that are adjacent and adjunct but not necessarily accumulative, teleological or dialectical" (163). As in the

david huddart

THE TRANSLATABILITY OF REVOLUTIONARY IDIOMS

work of Edward Said, in the wake of whose travelling theory Bhabha is moving, this emphasis on interdisciplinarity is not only a question of adequacy to a multi-faceted object; as this passage indicates, interdisciplinarity also in principle resists transcendent critical judgements, judgements that would erase difference in an ever more inclusive total discipline. Disciplines, like cultures, may well be effects of efforts at stabilization, but they are no less real for that. Interdisciplinary postcolonialism operates on the assumption that duplicating the procedures of its objects is unlikely to prove fruitful: that, of course, is Bhabha's most general point about colonial discourse analysis. If there is necessary tension between the apparent pre-givenness of culture and the necessity of its ongoing pro-

ISSN 0969-725X print/ISSN 1469-2899 online/04/030059–15 © 2004 Taylor & Francis Ltd and the Editors of *Angelaki*
DOI: 10.1080/0969725042000307628

duction, then the critical language with which this tension is analysed and further heightened ought to mark this understanding. As Bhabha goes on to say: "Interdisciplinarity is the acknowledgement of the emergent sign of cultural difference produced in the ambivalent movement between the pedagogical and performative address. It is never simply the harmonious addition of contents or contexts that augment the positivity of a pre-given disciplinary or symbolic *presence*" (163).

According to this understanding of postcolonialism, the usual criticisms of its practices miss the point in a quite predictable manner. In referring to the usual criticisms, I mean something like the following: in talking constantly of difference, but less often of determination (economic or otherwise), postcolonial theory apparently blurs matters into indifference, making things progressively less interesting, and its analyses becoming increasingly less relevant to the realities of neo-colonialism. Regardless of the accuracy of such claims, many, situated both outside and inside the field, by themselves or others, have come to similar frustrated conclusions, and some critics strongly associated with the theoretical paradigm have determined, with the help of others, to do something about it. Robert J.C. Young, for example, is one recipient of Aijaz Ahmad's critique of postcolonial theory, but his work has increasingly taken him far away from the supposed abstractions decried by Ahmad. As the most interesting example, Young has investigated the historical routes taken by anti-colonial and postcolonial critique. He is now general editor of *Interventions: International Journal of Postcolonial Studies*, and recounts the motivation behind the journal, writing that "We seek to reinvoke the politics, political objectives and commitment through which, historically, postcolonial critique was originally generated" (1999, 29). Describing the complex of international editorial structures, Young stresses "divergences of perspective produced by different locations around the globe" (33). Despite having, of necessity, a certain centralization, *Interventions* strives towards a structural recognition and staging of the various translations that postcolonial criticism often theorizes

but perhaps more rarely practices. This essay considers the translations or piracies that anti-colonial and postcolonial theories have undergone – particularly, the very possibility of such translation and piracy, and its apparent impossibility under globalization. Interdisciplinarity is here, then, operating as a concept; when put together with revolution, it helps get at postcolonial theory's ongoing value.

translation and piracy: nationalism and revolution

First, the choice of the term "piracy" requires some comment, as it has had, and continues to have, a proliferation of meanings. Trade of various kinds (by sea or CD) is open to piracy. Anything the value of which can be traded or translated to another (intended or unintended) location is necessarily open to piracy – so clearly trade implied piracy. Copyright, also, would seem always to be a matter of intellectual copyright – and nothing is ever copywritten enough to be uncopyable. Reproducibility has "bad" reproductions built into it. Ideas, as intellectual history indicates, are often repeated – the same, but never quite the same, not quite right. A particularly pertinent example is nationalism, as examined by Benedict Anderson's widely discussed *Imagined Communities*. A central argument of *Imagined Communities* is that language is central to the imagination of the modern nation. However, he is not referring to specific natural languages but to one specific technological revolution: printed language: "Print-language is what invents nationalism, not a particular language" (134). That Anderson places such emphasis on a reproductive technology connects directly to another important argument worked into various aspects of the text, and always trying to connect nationalism more sympathetically with its perhaps more celebrated relation, revolution: that is to say, Anderson continually writes of an inherent reproducibility of nationalism, such that no one nation has a patent on even the most specific nationalist concept, aim, or action. Nationalism and revolution have been constantly pirated.

Piracy, of course, is often associated with the development of a medium or cluster of media, and that of nationalism has been no exception. In his consideration of European nationalisms between 1820 and 1920, Anderson stresses the centrality of print-capitalism, in each case with one specific print-language. These nationalisms, he suggests, worked from models: "the 'nation' proved an invention on which it was impossible to secure a patent. It became available for pirating by widely different, and sometimes unexpected hands" (67). Anderson's book, of course, makes those unexpected hands absolutely central to its arguments, with the suggestion that once this unexpected piracy had begun, if it had any simple beginning, it was always tending to hurtle out of control or predictability. He writes that "the independence movements in the Americas became, as soon as they were printed about, 'concepts', 'models', and indeed 'blueprints'" (81). There is even a rough attempt at dating this repetitious but always surprising piracy: "by the second decade of the nineteenth century, if not earlier, a 'model' of 'the' independent national state was available for pirating" (81). Wherever nationalism came from, it was going somewhere else at gathering speed through the middle of the nineteenth century onwards. The historical contexts are suggestive for Anderson because something just like this was beginning to happen with another group of ideas, those of Karl Marx, specifically those of a revolutionary Marxism. Revolutionary Marxist anti-colonial movements are testimony to just how similarly repeatable nationalism and revolution were found to be. There is an equal sense of their translatability, and at one point Anderson implies that Marxist revolution has often been an unknowing heir of nationalism. That is not, of course, to imply their equivalence, although there is more to be said here in the context of the university, which will be touched upon later. Regardless, despite the sense of the newness of nationhood and nationalism, such newness was soon displaced by interest in "precedents and models" (Anderson 194), an interest that became an obsession. If nationalism has been concerned with pasts actively reshaped, any freedom this might imply gave way to desire for control; one

cannot just reproduce and translate any way one chooses.

However, just as the originators of the groups of ideas called nationalism had no say on their further, extended, surprising uses in other contexts, those who utilized these models never quite got them "right," whatever that would mean in the variety of contexts to which they were moved. Anderson cites Tom Nairn's understanding of the *imitation* of the English state, something not ever fully realizable, and suggests that this inherent unrealizability is no less true of nationalism and revolution. Whatever elaborate schemes the Bolsheviks devised for the planning of revolutions in "backward" societies were inherently doomed. As is the way with such things, however, there is no reason to assume that the originals are therefore more effective or interesting than the failed repetitions or pirated versions. The forged is a necessary precondition, it has been argued, for the original and the genuine. Perhaps such a sentiment will seem glib when applied to nationalism and revolution, but if pushed a little further this thought helps us to understand what might be coming from postcolonial study in the university.

disavowing revolution? postcolonial theory

Anti-colonial liberation movements have usually, if not always, tended towards revolution. Postcolonial theory, as it is often understood, has apparently never had much time for revolution, favouring instead subtle, primarily discursive forms of resistance to imperialist ideology – ambivalence, mimicry, etc. These forms of resistance can be only contentiously characterized as acts of anti-colonial agency, and it has been argued that through emphasizing such forms, postcolonial theory elides historical instances of anti-colonial revolution. In an obvious example, many critics argue that Homi Bhabha's reading of Frantz Fanon[1] gets Fanon *backwards*, downplaying all talk of revolution in the name of a well-meaning but nonetheless ideologically conditioned psychiatry. Revolution talk becomes talk of the repressed – at best all talk of revolution is repressed. Of course that repressed has returned in many forms, and is given trenchant form in Aijaz Ahmad's *In Theory*. Not every postcolonial critic has been content to consign revolution to history, and criticism of postcolonial theory has often come from pragmatic perspectives; Arif Dirlik, for example, notes that "Recalling revolutions against their contemporary erasure is not to wish their return" (quoted in Duara 88). What will be argued here is that postcolonial theory translates or pirates Marxism – which does not imply that Marxism is surpassed, or superseded, or that the results of the piracy are in any way inferior. It should further be stressed that this translation or piracy was always already at work within Marxism – although that "within" might be subject to scrutiny. Tricontinental Marxism (the name recently proposed as substitute for "postcolonialism"[2]) was always engaged in a precarious attempt to translate Marxism – revolution was always something that (rather than being exported, as was famously, ironizingly, suggested) has been translated. Revolution has always been read – and reading is always in a sense a work of translation. It is perfectly true to suggest, as Crystal Bartolovich argues, that "Marx and Marxism *belong* (and have always belonged) to the whole world" (10); however, that belonging was, of course, not a pre-given but had to be worked for, and was the result of responsible, often urgent, movements of translation.

It is initially important to understand the stakes in the Marxist critique of postcolonial theory. The case against postcolonial theory is simply stated and familiar, and can be elaborated through the example of Gayatri Chakravorty Spivak, who, along with Bhabha, has been a focus for criticism of postcolonial theory in general. Spivak has a particular strategy involving the use of *catachresis*, a term that usually refers to the incorrect use of words, often through either mixed metaphor or inappropriate terminology. Given that usual or standard meaning of catachresis, when Spivak makes the following argument about postcoloniality, there is room for perhaps inevitable and serious misunderstanding:

Within the historical frame of exploration, colonization, decolonization – what is being effectively reclaimed is a series of regulative political concepts, the *supposedly* authoritative narrative of the production of which was written elsewhere, in the social formations of Western Europe. They are being reclaimed, indeed claimed, as concept-metaphors for which no historically adequate referent may be advanced from postcolonial space, yet that does not make the claims less important. A concept-metaphor without an adequate referent is a catachresis. These claims for founding catachreses also make postcoloniality a deconstructive case. (1993, 60)

In Jacques Derrida's work there is a movement of paleonymy, a re-appropriation of terminology, which often takes the form of a putting to work of previously unremarked or marginalized meaning. However, Spivak's notion of catachresis would seem to be a catachresis of catachresis, and the term concept-metaphor itself might be a source of confusion. What occurs in this catachretized catachresis is a confusion of claims to the originary status of any given rhetorical term, theory, or revolutionary model. Accordingly, when Spivak refers to "Revolutions that as yet have no model,"[3] we are again being directed to think of the postcolonial as a deconstructive case: an example, but also more than mere example – a model, exemplary, without being foundational, original or privileged. When she refers to these revolutions, Spivak is discussing Derrida's "Limited Inc a b c ...," which re-elaborates and demonstrates the argument that speech acts, even when they do succeed, are still marked by the necessary possibility of their "failure."[4] Failure in this context can be understood as what allows the translation of revolutions between contexts that necessarily vary, however minimally. Failure is the possibility, then, of another kind of success. Aijaz Ahmad, however, suggests that Spivak's gesture is a form of historical amnesia that elides the acts of revolutionary heroism constitutive of anti-colonial struggle: there are, Ahmad insists, historical referents (examples) to be found in the history of anti-colonial action ("The Politics of Literary Postcoloniality"). The word referent may help to explain the misunderstanding here, implying as it does that there have been no historical instances of the political concepts in question. Given that this essay reconsiders the reproduction of theories, it might even be argued that the Marxist critique of postcolonial theory turns on the question of *reference* and the *referent*. For example, Kalpana Seshadri-Crooks writes the following concerning Aijaz Ahmad's "literalist" critique of Spivak:

> Spivak [insists] that, insofar as socialism, nationalism, etc. function as regulative political concepts, they effectively resituate struggle within the frame of imperialism and that this is not a denial of history but a comment on the limits of historiography itself. But the literalism permits Ahmad to read ideological critique here as free-floating dehistoricizing postmodernism, thus reenacting, in the name of Marx, what Spivak problematizes: ideological regulation. (14)

Ahmad's insistence that Spivak is disallowing all reference to historical instances of postcolonialism takes her to be arguing that there have been literally no postcolonial examples of these political concepts in action. In so far as these political concepts have been regulatory in a certain sense (in that they have regulated all political talk in terms of proper, original examples, i.e., in so far as they have been owned), they have been limited in application to postcolonial contexts. So, the literal instances that Ahmad cites were not actually instances of those concepts in action – rather, they transformed those concepts in the instant of enaction in a colonial or postcolonial context. In parallel, there is the example of Spivak's essay "Can the Subaltern Speak?" In an interview, Spivak says that

> Problems arise if you take this "speak" absolutely literally as "talk." There can be and have been attempts to correct me by way of the fact that some of the women on the pyres did actually utter. Now I think that is a very good contribution, but it really doesn't touch what I was trying to talk about. (1996, 291)

Again, it happens that some critics take Spivak as arguing that subaltern women literally could not speak (however, Spivak seems to exaggerate this misunderstanding); and again, this might

come down to the choice of terms subjected to Spivak's catachresis. Speaking seems an uncertain choice for a catachretized term – at least, it requires more elaborate and explicit justification than it receives. In the movement of postcolonial translation, which minimally takes the translation into the theoretical context of postcolonial cultural studies, but also potentially involves translation between different historical and cultural contexts, there is the necessity of responsible translation, and also a certain amount of expository justification. There is much at stake in the translation of revolutionary anti-colonialism into the university classroom, and so this translation requires constant attention. Postcolonial theory has, in summary, been charged with irresponsibility in this translation movement.

tricontinental marxism

As indicated above, another focus of Aijaz Ahmad's critique is Robert Young,[5] whose *White Mythologies* is a deconstruction of one Marxist Eurocentrism. Young's more recent *Postcolonialism: An Historical Introduction*, which he characterizes as a rewriting of the earlier book, is a careful historical investigation of postcolonial theory's "roots" that performs exactly this responsible justificatory translation, insisting that revolutions as conceived by postcolonial theory have no models as such – certainly not models found in some proper original context. Young refers to a kind of "theoretical transculturation" (2001, 202), an allusion already suggesting that there is no privileged theoretical model. Young finds that the history of Marxism in its various anti-colonial contexts demonstrates that anti-Eurocentric deconstruction was already thematized within Marxism. The basic argument of Young's book is clear enough. China, 1949, assumes particular significance in his study because "For the first time, a non-white, formerly semi-colonized country achieved an independent communist government through a military campaign: national liberation and socialist revolution had been brought together" (2001, 181). However, Mao stands for what had been a source of debate within Marxism for some time – there is an untranslatability of idiomatic revolutions (which is not the same as saying that there is no connection between such revolutions, given that what is under discussion has been a form of internationalism). Young continues to argue that Mao's revolution was anti-imperial rather than anti-colonial, in the sense that China was semi-colonized, and the focus of resistance shifted between the Japanese, and landlords supported by the British and Americans: "This fact both dominated [Mao's] ideas and his rhetoric and was shared with, or transmitted to, other tricontinental revolutionaries, in comparable situations, such as Il-song Kim, Ho Chi Minh and Che Guevara" (2001, 182). Mao's rhetoric was shared with or transmitted to: in other words, translated. Furthermore, this example provided a clear demonstration of the potential reactionary quality of nationalism, and the consequent need for further revolution. Mao demonstrated the necessity of transforming Marxism for a given local context, in this case that of the agrarian peasantry:

> Mao's commitment to the cause of the peasants against the landlords was accompanied by a revision of communist politics that would transform the revolutionary potential of peasant societies throughout the three continents. It was in this sense that Mao represented for many both the example and the possibility of tricontinental revolution on its own terms. (Young 2001, 182–83)

Mao was both example and possibility: one example among others, and exemplary of the very (hitherto, seemingly impossible) chance of resistance (specifically, military resistance to the European colonial powers). Young argues that "After Lenin, anti-colonial Marxism was [...] largely the creation of the Third World: it took the preoccupations of tricontinental politics to turn it into a different instrument that could be deployed against entrenched European and American imperial power" (2001, 168). Further, "In a dialectical antithesis to Lenin, tricontinental Marxism has emphasized what one might call the untranslatability of revolutionary practices, the need for attention to local forms, and the translation of the universal into the idiom of the

local" (2001, 169). So, what Young gives in great detail is a history of Marxist self-critique, albeit critique for a time marginalized or repressed. Tricontinental Marxism, in Young's vision, was always a question of the imperfect translatability of revolutionary models and practices – revolutionary idioms.

The very split (as presented, from various perspectives) within postcolonial theory as currently formulated and formed is, it appears from Young's historical investigation, comparable to the often problematic debates within the Comintern. Indeed, for Young the resistance to or insistence upon the translatability of revolution is fully part of that very translation, both within the historical debates of anti-colonialism and in their subsequent re-appropriation in postcolonial theory. Discussing the Irish context, and its problematic insertion (or resistance to that insertion) in postcolonial theory, Young compares the figures of Connolly and Fanon. Despite Connolly's internationalist perspective, there has been resistance to his (and Ireland's) insertion into narratives of postcolonial theory. Fanon, of course, has never been less than central to debates in postcolonial theory, although, as David Macey (2001) has demonstrated most thoroughly, this centrality has involved ignoring the specificities of Fanon's engagements first with Martinique, then with Algeria. In his postcolonial theoretically translated guise, and in Young's presentation, Fanon insists upon a precarious magic of translation between anti-colonial contexts, recognizing simultaneously the inherent translatability and untranslatability of revolution:

> Although he was an active member of the FLN, Fanon's writings on Algeria have the advantage of his own lack of immediate involvement in the war. They are deliberately pitched to operate at a schematized and general level that is readily applicable elsewhere. Fanon held to the doctrine of the universal translatability of revolution developed by Lenin and Trotsky, against Castro's and Cabral's insistence on its untranslatability. Or rather, more accurately, Fanon paradoxically attempts to make the local, untranslatable principles of tricontinen-

tal Marxism translatable, universal. (Young 2001, 302)

Such a paradox suggests that Fanon's work projects and privileges a future universal revolutionary model. In other words, Fanon's notion of the translatability of revolutionary idioms works from a recognition that such translation does not work from an original text of revolution – no revolution would be privileged as providing the final exemplary model of revolution to be followed painstakingly by those seeking their own revolutionary movement. The translation plucks apparently universal principles from the range of tricontinental Marxist theories and practices, elevating them (in theory) in a given place and only for a given time. There is, then, something like an invention of a universally applicable revolutionary model. This temporary elevation would lead to translated revolution, however, as each time that model was repeated it would be not quite accurate – necessarily inflected by its recontextualization. To this extent, at least, the future universal revolutionary model would never be realized in any given present, and would always be coming from the future. So, Mao provided a model, a model that even assumed a certain privilege, but that privilege was not that of the *originary*, nor of finality, and such a non-privilege was built into the dissensus of permanent revolution. Yet, as this particular example suggests, there are no guarantees as to the outcome of this dissensus: the chance of the best is the chance of the worst,[6] which is the necessary possibility haunting the best.

revolution by analogy: singular reproductions

The complex connections found in Young's book can seem to marginalize what is usually meant by postcolonial theory, but it is obvious that these connections demonstrate that colonial and anti-colonial discourses are exemplary of certain postcolonial motifs. Taking Homi Bhabha as only the most obvious instance, his postcolonial theory is, after all, a matter of the iteration of revolution. Iteration is obviously

associated with Derrida's work, and is in Bhabha closely connected with Foucault's sense of the statement.[7] As is well known, iterability refers to the necessary repeatability of any mark, if it is to be meaningful. A mark that occurred only once would be meaningful to the extent that it could in principle occur more than once, in other times and other places. However, this repeatability is not just the simple reproduction of identical marks in those other times and places – each context makes its mark on the mark, the effect being one of non-identical repetition. Derrida is, of course, concerned not to limit this thought to language; Foucault, meanwhile, in his focus on the statement, is concerned with disciplines and institutions, many of the most important of which have been colonial. Bhabha's postcolonial theory most often operates in terms of the statement. We usually think we know what a statement means, but this is only an effect of disciplinary efforts at stabilization. The efforts are, however, always imperfect, as Bhabha remarks:

> Despite the schemata of use and application that constitute a field of stabilization for the statement, any change in the statement's conditions of use and reinvestment, any alteration in its field of experience or verification, or indeed any difference in the problems to be solved, can lead to the emergence of a new statement: the difference of the same. (22)

Such a difference coming about through repetition is what Bhabha finds in colonial statements, for example the traditions of European liberalism, but is, of course, exactly what is happening in the translation of revolution.

Following from this logic of iteration is a particular conception of critical thinking. Critical positions do not, on this logic, stand external to the situation under consideration. The fact that statements only seem to be stabilized (or that stabilization is an uncertain, hesitant product of disciplinary processes) has implications for the study of the object, in this case the revolutionary statement. Bhabha writes of critical thinking as a *process*, rather than the adoption of pre-arranged, predetermined positions; he refers to "the boundary and location of the event of theoretical critique which does not *contain* the truth" (22). The critique he has in mind, always marked by being a process rather than procedure, is just as ambivalent as the colonial discourse that is his first object of study. If we already know exactly what we think before we start reading anything, then we never quite start reading the thing itself, we merely find what we expected, and our expectations are very likely to be confirmed. Such a reading process is just as set on stabilizing itself as colonial discourse, and is just as marked by its uncertainties. To read acts of revolutionary heroism in this way is to mark them as formally the same as colonial discourse, when really they are not just a challenge to the content of that discourse but also to its form.

Bhabha's understanding of iteration relates to questions of reference and the referent, and what is argued here about reference is important for the question of Spivak's critique of regulatory political concepts, and Ahmad's consequent criticisms. The question of reproducibility – iterability – has been rehearsed at length in many contexts, and there is no reason why its implications should not be brought to bear on an interpretation of postcolonialism, especially when it seems that the various traditions covered by that term were always engaged in something like the iteration of Marxism, refusing any sense in which Marxism would remain immutable. Furthermore, postcolonial theory's suspension of acts of revolutionary heroism does not in principle deny the irreducibility of those acts' existence. Accordingly, the question of historical reference might productively be blurred into the question of any model's originary, privileged status. Postcolonial theory might seem to suspend (at its best) privileged instances of anti-colonial revolutionary heroism, in the name of a retrospective psychological or rhetorical understanding of colonialism. As it has often been accused of suspending the referent in this way, without, it would seem, much sense of distinction between referent and reference, a sense of iterability might explain what occurs in postcolonial theory's supposedly ahistorical moments. Robert Young suggestively inserts Nandy and Bhabha into some form of a tradition in the following passage:

> Just as Gandhi reinterprets the scriptures, so Nandy and Bhabha reinterpret theoretical and political texts, encouraging the individual critic to be at the center of the search for insight rather than accept received opinions or traditional dogma, and making space for transcultural exchange, translation and transformation. Both critics in their writing characteristically violate the historical integrity of the theoretical tradition from which they draw, and thereby deinstitutionalize its scope. (2001, 347)

There is in the history of anti-colonialism some minimal openness to the kinds of readings Nandy and Bhabha perform, although in Nandy's case perhaps the most obvious example of theoretical and historical translation is Freud (and so Freud would not be quite so foreign a presence in postcolonial theory as sometimes seems the case). This openness to reading applies equally to Spivak's catachretizing strategies. Anti-colonialism has been a deconstruction, which is not by any means to argue that anti-colonialism in its various forms and histories is somehow subsumed by the writings of Derrida. Ahmad, for one, has argued that Derrida's reading of Marx attempts to subsume Marxism into deconstruction – but Ahmad's complaint misleadingly assumes that deconstruction is just some theory expounded or applied by Derrida.[8]

paleonymy and metonymy

This reading of catachresis does not imply equivalence between Derrida and Spivak, for Spivak has criticized Derrida precisely on questions of revolution and what *Specters of Marx* calls the New International. To return to the vexed question of Spivak and catachresis, it seems that the subaltern is an exemplary instance of this translation question – not least because the "lessons" of "Can the Subaltern Speak?" were almost immediately subjected to generalization (something licensed by Spivak's choice of catachretized term), often without precaution, and then subjected to inevitable critique, again in general terms. The subaltern provides Spivak with an exemplary instance both of the idiomatic and of the idiomatic's necessary gathering up into totality. The idiom as what calls for translatability is what needs to be maintained, just as it is never, in being minimally readable, absolutely maintained. This question as an ethical question is also (not coincidentally) a question of reading, and of reading the new idiom – which is, then, never an absolutely new idiom. *Specters of Marx* insists upon this possibility, which is also the possibility of re-reading and re-evaluating the already established and already comfortable, particularly around the question of Marx's legacy. The general structure of the promise is a structure of precarious translation, not guaranteed and never final; this structure concerns the possibility and impossibility of system, translation, otherness, and the future: "Guaranteed translatability, given homogeneity, systematic coherence in their *absolute forms*, this is surely (certainly, *a priori* and not probably) what renders the injunction, the inheritance, and the future – in a word the other – *impossible*" (Derrida 1994, 35). Yet the question of why Derrida employs this example, so apparently specific and therefore problematic, for what he insists is a general structure, remains difficult. He indicates that his understanding of the messianic disallows any determinable messiah that would have arrived, i.e., coming from a future present; however, he appears to court confusion by his choice of name for this disallowing gesture,[9] its Benjaminian connotations notwithstanding. Frederic Jameson suggests the following in his reading of *Specters of Marx*:

> You would not evoke the messianic in a genuinely revolutionary period, a period in which changes can be sensed at work all around you; the messianic does not mean immediate hope in that sense, perhaps not even hope against hope; it is a unique variety of the species hope that scarcely bears any of the latter's normal characteristics and that flourishes only in a time of absolute hopelessness, a period like the Second Empire, or the years between the Wars, or the 1980s and 90s, when radical change seems unthinkable, its very idea dispelled by visible wealth and power, along with palpable powerlessness. It is

only in those trough years that it makes sense to speak of the messianic in the Benjaminian sense. (106)

For Jameson the specificity of *the messianic* as a name is that it marks the feeling of distance and disbarment from self-determination. Such a name might indeed sit easily alongside postcolonial studies' supposed elision or domestication of anti-colonial struggle. However, perhaps there are more sympathetic construals of its invocation. Throughout *Specters of Marx*, Derrida indicates that the category of ideology (with which Spivak is centrally concerned, for example in "Can the Subaltern Speak?") is a concept that perhaps eludes conceptuality. Derrida, after Blanchot, suggests that there is a thought of knowledge in Marx that exceeds science. A science of ideology appears to be fatally compromised, as a science, by the strange position of religion in the critique of ideology. Religion is not one ideology among others, but the exemplary ideology. There is a persistence of belief or faith in Marx that exceeds their determination as merely religion, and also exceeds their determination as mere rhetorical effects in the critique of capital. Derrida's example is the analysis of commodity fetishism at the beginning of *Capital*, with the *sensuous/non-sensuous* table, its use-value originarily haunted (1994, 150–51). Derrida does not take this originary haunting as destructive of the Marxian analysis of capital,[10] although the analysis will have undergone ruination, and become conjuration in the doubled sense on which Derrida insists (as *conjuring up* and *conjuring away*). Rather, in Derrida's analysis, this curious situation, in which the original analogy of ideology and the form of emancipatory promise both "come from" the religious, requires us to think together the universal form of the promise and the specificities of Abrahamic messianism (1994, 167–68). Derrida sets out his understanding of these issues clearly in "Marx & Sons,"[11] where he again asserts that the critique of religion does not touch *faith*, and that religion is exemplary ideology; further, Derrida acknowledges that "Marx" is "Judeo-Christian" or European, and that Marxist culture is part of *mondialatinization* – a term denying the apparent naturality claimed by and for the term *globalization*. But these facts do not simply disallow further concern with Marx. "Messianicity without messianism" is proposed as the best possibility, in a given context, for addressing the issues that Marxisms have bracketed, and that certain critiques of Marx have assumed merely relegate Marx to the place and time of his publishing (1994, 65).

So, on the one hand Derrida is acknowledging an irreducible specificity to Marx's text, its concerns, its failings, and its potential – Marx's text is just an example, with demonstrable limitations. At the same time, he finds Marx to be an exemplary location of a universal structure of experience – the promise, justice, decision, democracy. This double gesture, so familiar from Derrida's work, is, in the context of this explicit intervention in this given context, open to mis-reception. Simon Critchley, in a sympathetic reading of *Specters of Marx*, sums up what many less sympathetic commentators have wondered about the New International, asking "how is the New International to be hegemonized?" (166). Critchley's concern is focused on the issue of the party:

> how does one work outside traditional party structures without collapsing into a "divide and rule" designer politics of individualism or confining oneself to the always modest socio-economic changes of single-issue politics, or, worst of all, devoting oneself to an intra-academic politics of vacuous radicalism and reaction? (167)

Spivak extends this unease to argue that the promise "cancels the difference between democracy and Marxism"; she dismissively states that "[Derrida] would rather go for a messianism without content. By contrast, in Marx, it is the content that is spectralized" (1995, 66, 74). Stephen Morton, discussing Spivak, concurs with her diagnosis, and argues that "For Spivak, contra Derrida, this open-ended political commitment to the alterity of the other (what Derrida terms the 'messianic') is not without content; rather it is inscribed and embodied by the situated knowledge of the subaltern woman" (606). Spivak and Morton misread Derrida, par-

ticularly on the issue of content and form, but their reading is at least clear: they argue that Derrida is not only too rooted in his European specificity but simultaneously disavows that specificity in his nebulous appeals to a formless International. Spivak insists that for Derrida "all activity attaching to the South [is] ontopologocentric" (1995, 71). At the same time, Spivak argues, he privileges a language of migrancy that has been incautiously removed from its politico-economic determinants: "this privileging of the metaphorics (and axiomatics) of migrancy by well-placed migrants helps to occlude precisely the struggles of those who are forcibly displaced, or those who slowly perish in their place as a result of sustained exploitation: globality" (1995, 71).

Derrida, in Spivak's reading, has gone the way of Deleuze and Foucault (subjected to criticism in "Can the Subaltern Speak?"), benignly declaring his solidarity with subjects that his own production (necessarily) and thematization (unnecessarily) help to silence. Derrida, Spivak suggests, is just reducing complex historico-political contexts to a blandly formal logic – indeed, the same criticism as is made of postcolonial theory's treatment of anti-colonial histories. Yet perhaps we are referred back to that paradoxical gesture made by Fanon's attempt to translate untranslatable revolutionary idioms – the moment of universal translation is almost formless in the sense Derrida gives, before its recapitulation and re-appropriation into the specific forms of any given context, including the university classroom. Accordingly, the purely formal nature of Derrida's New International holds onto the possibility of translation, between class, race, gender, etc. We might continue to talk of revolution, and we might certainly continue to describe instances of revolutionary history, but this should not lead to prescriptive structures laying out the only critical paths to be followed. Insistence on propriety blocks translation.

pedagogical revolutions

Earlier, this essay discussed Benedict Anderson's connection of media and the communicability of revolutionary ideas. This closing section will gesture towards the place of universities in the cycles of revolution which, it should be clear by now, are not necessarily going to be reproducing recognizably revolutionary thought. Perhaps even the notion of cycles has been superseded; indeed, this is what Michael Hardt and Antonio Negri imply when they describe "one of the central and most urgent political paradoxes of our time: in our much celebrated age of communication, *struggles have become all but incommunicable*" (54). The impossible communication they have in mind is not quite what this essay has discussed, being a question of cause–effect, and of an immense speed of transmission that is nevertheless not instantaneous. Simultaneity has been the death of revolutionary translation, in their view. The piracies, translations, transmissions, and transformations that this essay has considered continue, and in turn may be the object of theories and descriptions in the university classroom. However, Hardt and Negri argue that in place of horizontal relations and routes, struggles under globalization instantaneously leap up and touch the global level, the level of Empire, without boundaries. Such a struggle's form of organization is as yet unimaginable, although clearly not impossible. Hardt and Negri are quite clear on this matter, however: what will come next cannot be the result of theorization. Their book explicitly views postcolonial theory, and deconstruction, as merely symptoms of the passage to Empire. All of the translation and piracy with which this essay has been concerned might even be viewed, then, as quite in keeping with Empire's management of hybrid identities.

Accordingly, if there has been an inbuilt and ongoing translation of revolutionary concepts within Marxism, this would still demand some thought of what takes place in postcolonial theory's translation of such concepts within (primarily) the university classroom, because that translation might still be what the Marxist critique of postcolonial theory puts into question. The question of postcolonial studies as a critique of globalization is closely related, for postcolonial politics implies or often elaborates theories of anti- or counter-globalization; their ambitions

are not limited to revised historical description. Hardt and Negri insist that postcolonial studies is adequate to its object, but only if that object is colonialism (156). On this view, all that this essay has to say about nationalism and revolution has historical importance but limited future applicability. For example, on the question of revolutionary struggles in the 1990s, they write that "precisely because all these struggles are incommunicable and thus blocked from traveling horizontally in the form of a cycle, they are forced instead to leap vertically and touch immediately on the global level" (5). They suggest that the blockage of horizontal translation or transmission blinds us to the importance of the vertical movement, which in its intensity and unpredictability has the potential to subvert the blankly homogeneous face of Empire at any point and any time. Even though Hardt and Negri insist that what comes next cannot be at the level of theorization, but will take place as the constituent action of the multitude, their book is itself a theory, and such theorization and translation of concepts is what this essay considers. Postcolonial theory and the postcolonial university will have its own place, even if that place starts in the circumscribed environment of the English literature department: it would be unwise, of course, to identify Australian, US or English universities as providing universal models, or to assume that postcolonial studies as practised in those universities (or their English departments only, if that is sometimes the case) stands for postcolonial studies more generally. The journal *Interventions*, mentioned at the beginning of this essay, has been one attempt to recognize and enable inclusiveness and dissensus.

Postcolonialism, then, has been rather more hybrid than Hardt and Negri, for example, will allow (their focus, Homi Bhabha, is hardly obvious given the widespread criticism he has received). Their argument about globalization and Empire invites response. Hardt and Negri's argument coincides with much of what Derrida has to say, even though they apparently dismiss his thought at various moments; more importantly for this essay, their simplified view of postcolonial theory ignores its own rethinking of its relationship with globalization. Young's *Postcolonialism* is both an historical account and a re-theorization of postcolonialism. What Young traces occurring within Marxism is a demand for translation that could be formalized as permanent dissensus, something comparable with what Bill Readings contrasts to models of consensus and transparency in *The University in Ruins*. Perhaps, rather than shutting down debate through recourse to already existent communities and identities, postcolonial criticism produces communities without, in principle, insisting on their monumentalization. Readings' analysis of the contemporary university, specifically its US and English manifestations, is organized around a critique of both "left" and "right." In the cultural studies wars, Readings argues, both sides misrecognize the situation, assuming as both do the continuation of a self-sufficient narrative of university and national identity – the professor metonymizes the university, which in turn metonymizes the nation. Readings suggests the following:

> The liberal *individual* is no longer capable of metonymically embodying the *institution*. None of us can now seriously assume ourselves to be the centered subject of a narrative of University education. Feminism is exemplary here for its introduction of a radical awareness of gender difference, as are analyses that call attention to the ways in which bodies are differentially marked by race. Both are targeted by the old guard, because they remind them that no individual professor can embody the University, since that body *would still be gendered and racially marked* rather than universal. (9–10)

As Readings traces the situation, the university has been structured around an anthropomorphic reading of Kant, in which a certain notion of communication is elevated absolutely. This communication assumes utter transparency as its *telos*. It is envisaged as commencing in a public sphere that is "anchored upon the notion of a liberal individual who participates in it" (Readings 140). This individual – the centred subject of the narrative of university education, produced as the national subject – is no longer viable, as suggested above. In its place are end-

lessly negotiating singularities, as Readings describes the situation; singularity as a term trying to capture the sense that "there is nothing you can be presumed in advance to share with someone else" (Readings 115). In such a context, the university remains a metonym of the nation, but this time with considerably different implications. Teaching becomes a mode of re-imagining affiliation after the end of the nation-state. Readings makes clear that "the University will have to become one place, *among others*, where the attempt is made to think the social bond without recourse to a unifying idea, whether of culture or of the state" (191; my emphasis). What that may be cannot be predicted. Readings' refusal to write a futurology of the university coincides with the formlessness of Derrida's New International, and also anticipates Hardt and Negri's understanding of the constitution of counter-empire. Hardt and Negri celebrate "constituent struggles, creating new public spaces and new forms of community" (56). In some form, or forms, the ruined university can be one location for these constructive activities, whatever Stanley Fish might argue.[12] Readings writes that "Exploring the question of value means recognizing that there exists no homogeneous standard of value that might unite all poles of the pedagogical scene so as to produce a single scale of evaluation" (165). His ensuing prescriptions accordingly ironize the notion of prescription: "Making audiences for this kind of pedagogy 'happen' is the task that faces those of us who find ourselves in the contemporary University – teachers and students alike" (165).

Relatedly, Spivak has often given an uneasy, or even dismissive, response to Derrida's reading of Marx, particularly *Specters of Marx*'s New International. In recent work, Spivak has been more hospitable to this notion. Her increasingly vocal disavowal of the term "postcolonial" (given most full expression in her *Critique of Postcolonial Reason*, particularly chapter 4), becomes more focused in this recent work, as postcolonial studies is remade as transnational cultural studies, bearing immediate comparison with Young's thought of tricontinentalism. We can read Spivak's response in the context of Readings' diagnoses. Spivak writes that "the idea of a collectivity without organization – that may seem hopelessly impractical at first glance as suggested in Derrida's *Specters of Marx* or *Politics of Friendship* – is actually the figure of the classroom" (2000, 33). The following discussion begins to make sense of her initial reference to "Derrida's copious teaching notes, published these days almost as is" (2000, 14). Spivak indicates her preference for the class(-room) conjured up by *Politics of Friendship* over the New International, with all that term's attendant associations. Indeed, she reads Derrida's Marx text in terms of *Politics of Friendship*, suggesting the following: "perhaps the lesson was that the presuppositions of the text of Marx should be internalized (learnt) by as large a group as possible – so that practice is changed upstream from the party line – rather than be the means of metonymically collectivizing people whose other differences will inevitably bring the 'collectivity' down" (34).

Spivak is arguing that affiliatory politics has usually dissolved because its various constituencies *to be* affiliated have always *already been* constructed or even naturalized. The suggestion remains unelaborated, Spivak instead discussing "a resistance to mere theoreticism in the classroom" (35). Perhaps that apparently different discussion is simply recognition that postcolonial theory has been constructing new audiences or communities through the university classroom. Returning to her "Revolutions that as yet have no model," there she insists that the deconstructive "lesson" will not in principle lead to just another critical school: "the range and risks of such a [deconstructive] morphology (whose examples cannot match its discourse) can go rather further than a new school of literary-philosophical criticism, or even a mere transformation of consciousness" (1996, 101–02). Even allowing for Spivak's later concerns regarding "the postcolonial," it is arguable that postcolonial theory is one name for the results of anti-colonialism's deconstructive translation into the university classroom. The stress must remain on the plurality of these results, which is to say that postcolonial theory is not only this deconstructive translation (nor is that deconstructive translation only postcolonial, of course, developed as it has been in feminism, for example).

In summary, postcolonial theory's translation of revolution can be redescribed as a recontextualization of revolution that would not, in principle, elide the many instances of heroic anti-colonial revolutionary activity. This remains only in principle, and the responsibility of this translation is never a foregone conclusion but is always to be taken on and worked through. It should be clear, however, that what results from this translation will not be predictably or traditionally revolutionary. It is not obvious, indeed, that the historical networks of displacement and recontextualization that Marxism has undergone always resulted in recognizably or traditionally revolutionary thought. Further, as Lacan understood, revolutionary thinking often brings a remarkably un-revolutionary emphasis on doctrine. Doctrines like to police the boundaries between the good translation and the bad piracy, but that boundary is a mobile construction, and the distinctions between the two will always be uncertain in advance. Any sense that postcolonial theory ought to become something more proper to revolutionary models, or be dissolved in favour of something different that is faithful to those revolutionary models, is undermined not only by what is structurally true of reference but also by the many historical instances that ignored proprieties in favour of postcolonial invention.

notes

I would like to thank *Angelaki*'s anonymous reviewers for their comments on this paper.

1 See "Interrogating Identity" in *The Location of Culture* 40–65.

2 Robert Young's *Postcolonialism: An Historical Introduction*. See also Aijaz Ahmad, "Postcolonialism: What's in a Name?" 11–32.

3 "Revolutions that as Yet Have No Model" in *The Spivak Reader* 75–106. The title comes from Derrida's "Limited Inc a b c ...," referring to what is entailed by the structure of *iterability*; see *Limited Inc* (100).

4 "Limited Inc a b c ..." is a response to John Searle, who had criticized Derrida's "Signature Event Context" for its (interest in) non-seriousness. "Signature Event Context" is in *Limited Inc*.

5 Ahmad writes that "Robert Young, who had until a decade ago devoted himself almost entirely to propagating French poststructuralism in the British Isles, with hardly a thought to spare for the erstwhile colonies, suddenly emerged as a leading theorist of what got called 'postcolonial criticism'" ("The Politics of Literary Postcoloniality" 8). Young's *Postcolonialism* insists that this separation of colonies and poststructuralism is precisely a consequence of a focus, such as Ahmad implies, on anglophone contexts.

6 Young argues that "the degree to which French poststructuralism more generally involved what amounted to a Maoist retheorization of European political and cultural theory, as well as its complex connections to Indian postcolonialism, remain as yet unexplored" (*Postcolonialism* 187). One possible exploration could be organized around the notion of dissensus.

7 Michel Foucault, *The Archaeology of Knowledge*, trans. A.M. Sheridan Smith (London: Tavistock, 1972) *passim*.

8 See John Nash's distinction between the *motif* and *movement* of deconstruction (120).

9 Geoffrey Bennington writes in terms of the *risk* around this name: "The messiah is the first casualty of this construal of the messianic, which is why the word 'messianic' can seem a risky or unduly provocative term for Derrida to use in these contexts, a perhaps extreme form of the familiar deconstructive strategy of paleonymy" (137).

10 Responding to Ahmad's claim that he aestheticizes (textualizes) Marx, Derrida writes that "It is not enough to call the idea of 'systematicity' in philosophy into question (the system is only one form of coherence or 'consistency', a form that, moreover, appears late in the history of philosophy) in order then to take refuge in the aesthetic" ("Marx & Sons" 247). Derrida's approach to Hegel (as an obvious example of system) heeds this warning.

11 *Ghostly Demarcations* 213–69.

12 In a recent article for the *Chronicle of Higher Education*, titled "Save the World on Your Own Time" (23 Jan. 2003), Fish writes that "in my view no university, and therefore no university official, should ever take a stand on any social, political, or moral issue." His assertion is that academics, *when they speak as academics*, have a duty to profess views pertaining only to academic virtue, not moral virtue; in other words, "it is immoral for academics or academic institutions to proclaim moral views." Any kind of construction (rather than description) of globality would seem to imply professing morality, and so on this view the university could only be involved in describing the problem, not producing solutions. Activism might be something one does in the morning, but come the afternoon class on globalization, one can only describe it.

bibliography

Afzal-Khan, Fawzia and Kalpana Seshadri-Crooks (eds.). *The Pre-Occupation of Postcolonial Studies*. Durham, NC: Duke UP, 2000.

Ahmad, Aijaz. "The Politics of Literary Postcoloniality." *Race and Class* 36.3 (1995): 1–20.

Ahmad, Aijaz. "Postcolonialism: What's in a Name?" *Late Imperial Culture*. Ed. Román de la Capra, E. Ann Kaplan and Michael Sprinker. London: Verso, 1995. 11–32.

Ahmad, Aijaz. *In Theory: Classes, Nations, Literatures*. London: Verso, 1992.

Anderson, Benedict. *Imagined Communities*. London: Verso, 1991.

Bartolovich, Crystal. "Introduction: Marxism, Modernity, and Postcolonial Studies." *Marxism, Modernity and Postcolonial Studies*. Ed. Neil Lazarus and Crystal Bartolovich. Cambridge: Cambridge UP, 2002. 1–20.

Bennington, Geoffrey. *Interrupting Derrida*. London: Routledge, 2000.

Bhabha, Homi K. *The Location of Culture*. London: Routledge, 1994.

Critchley, Simon. *Ethics–Politics–Subjectivity: Essays on Derrida, Levinas, and Contemporary French Thought*. London: Verso, 1999.

Derrida, Jacques. *Limited Inc a b c ...* Trans. Samuel Weber. Evanston: Northwestern UP, 1988.

Derrida, Jacques. "Marx & Sons." *Ghostly Demarcations: A Symposium on Jacques Derrida's* Specters of Marx. Ed. Michael Sprinker. London: Verso, 1999. 213–69.

Derrida, Jacques. *Specters of Marx: The State of the Debt, the Work of Mourning, and the New International.* Trans. Peggy Kamuf. London: Routledge, 1994.

Derrida, Jacques. *The Work of Mourning.* Ed. Pascale-Anne Brault and Michael Naas. Trans. P.-A. Brault, M. Naas et al. Chicago: U of Chicago P, 2001.

Derrida, Jacques. *Writing and Difference.* Trans. Alan Bass. London: Routledge, 1978.

Duara, Prasenjit. "Leftist Criticism and the Political Impasse." *Postcolonial Studies* 4.1 (2001): 81–88.

Foucault, Michel. *The Archaeology of Knowledge.* Trans. A.M. Sheridan Smith. London: Tavistock, 1972.

Hardt, Michael and Antonio Negri. *Empire.* Cambridge, MA: Harvard UP, 2000.

Jameson, Frederic. "Marx's Purloined Letter." *New Left Review* 209 (1995): 75–109.

Lacan, Jacques. *Écrits: A Selection.* Trans. Alan Sheridan. London: Routledge, 1980.

Macey, David. *Frantz Fanon: A Biography.* New York: Picador, 2001.

Moore-Gilbert, Bart. *Postcolonial Theory: Contexts, Practices, Politics.* London: Verso, 1997.

Morton, Stephen. "Postcolonialism and Spectrality: Political Deferral and Ethical Singularity in the Writing of Gayatri Chakravorty Spivak." *Interventions* 1.4 (1999): 605–20.

Nash, John. "Deconstruction and Its Audiences: A New Enlightenment for the Century to Come?" *Paragraph* 23.2 (2001): 119–34.

Readings, Bill. *The University in Ruins.* Cambridge, MA: Harvard UP, 1996.

Seshadri-Crooks, Kalpana. "At the Margins of Postcolonial Studies." *The Pre-Occupation of Postcolonial Studies.* Ed. Fawzia Afzal-Khan and Kalpana Seshadri-Crooks. Durham, NC: Duke UP, 2000.

Spivak, Gayatri Chakravorty. *A Critique of Postcolonial Reason: Toward a History of the Vanishing Present.* Cambridge, MA: Harvard UP, 1999.

Spivak, Gayatri Chakravorty. "Deconstruction and Cultural Studies." *Deconstructions: A User's Guide.* Ed. Nicholas Royle. New York: Palgrave, 2000. 14–43.

Spivak, Gayatri Chakravorty. "Ghostwriting." *Diacritics* 25.2 (1995): 65–84.

Spivak, Gayatri Chakravorty. *Outside in the Teaching Machine.* London: Routledge, 1993.

Spivak, Gayatri Chakravorty. *The Spivak Reader.* Ed. Donna Landry and Gerald Maclean. London: Routledge, 1996.

Wortham, Simon. *Rethinking the University: Leverage and Deconstruction.* Manchester: Manchester UP, 1999.

Young, Robert J.C. "Academic Activism and Knowledge Formation in Postcolonial Critique." *Postcolonial Studies* 2.1 (1999): 21–34.

Young, Robert J.C. *Postcolonialism: An Historical Introduction.* Oxford: Blackwell, 2001.

Young, Robert J.C. *White Mythologies: Writing History and the West.* London: Routledge, 1990.

David Huddart
School of Historical and Cultural Studies
Bath Spa University College
Bath BA2 9BN
UK
E-mail: d.huddart@bathspa.ac.uk

Routledge
Taylor & Francis Group

ANGELAKI
journal of the theoretical humanities
volume 9 number 3 december 2004

"Despair and a sense of loss are not static conditions but goads to our continuous labor" (*Senses* 70). This is the way Stanley Cavell describes one of the fundamental lessons of skepticism, the familiar challenge to the possibility of certainty or knowledge that emerges as a methodological tendency in modern thought with the work of Descartes. In elucidating the historical and continuing impulse to doubt in a range of examples drawn from philosophy, literature, and cinema, Cavell argues that skepticism reveals the loss of transcendental necessity – the kind of metaphysical guarantee that traditionally grounded linguistic meaning in a one-to-one correspondence between words and the objects they name, and secured the subject's relation to others on the basis of a natural order of things. For Cavell, modernity appears as an epoch where transcendental securities have irretrievably disappeared. And yet he absolutely insists on allowing the loss of such securities, the very loss that skepticism clarifies, to inform present understanding, conditioning the way we pose questions and derive answers about linguistic meaning and interpersonal relations.[1] With regard to language, Cavell draws on the later work of Wittgenstein and argues that linguistic meaning can no longer be understood as deriving from abstract principles or subject-centered paradigms, but from the context-specific nature of linguistic exchange. With regard to intersubjectivity, Cavell suggests that one's relation to another has ceased to be an issue of knowledge, at least where knowledge is equated with certainty, but must be construed as a matter of what he calls "acknowledgment": an alternative form of knowing, relating, and responding that begins with the subject's recognition of the other as separate from its own categories of understanding.[2]

tammy clewell

CAVELL AND THE ENDLESS MOURNING OF SKEPTICISM

In making the issue of lost transcendence an animating principle of his work, Cavell neither follows the trajectory that leads the skeptic to nihilism nor engages in philosophical attempts to refute skepticism. Rather, as a testament to the seriousness with which he regards the skeptical problematic, Cavell repeatedly focuses on those cases where a failure of meaning emerges when the conditions of linguistic praxis or intersubjectivity have been avoided or denied, a failure that may lead to misunderstanding, isolation, or, at its most extreme, tragic violence. The insight he gleans from the inescapable threat of skepticism, an insight derived from his rigorous, albeit unorthodox, interpretation of Wittgenstein's *Philosophical Investigations*, involves redefining the aim of philosophy. By returning to skepticism's disclosure of lost cer-

ISSN 0969-725X print/ISSN 1469-2899 online/04/030075–13 © 2004 Taylor & Francis Ltd and the Editors of *Angelaki*
DOI: 10.1080/0969725042000307637

tainty, Cavell not only discovers in skepticism a genuine effort to understand the conditions that mediate linguistic and intersubjective exchanges; he also moves on from this discovery to argue that philosophy's attempt to legitimate knowledge must be replaced by a project of therapy, a means of squarely facing and viably responding to the skeptical threat. The philosophical response to skepticism that Cavell discovers in Wittgenstein's work does not render us immune from the very real problems of using language and relating to others in a post-metaphysical age. What it does provide, however, is an antidote to meaninglessness, a therapeutic mode of living our skepticism without succumbing to its dire consequences.

Given the emphasis that Cavell places on loss, it should come as no surprise that he has recently defined his therapeutic project as a form of mourning. Critics have largely overlooked the significance of mourning in his work, an omission that is quite understandable since Cavell's remarks about the relationship between skepticism and mourning are infrequent at best, comprising little more than a handful of passages scattered throughout his writings.[3] Nevertheless, Cavell's commentary raises to consciousness the structure of loss and recovery that informs his work, promoting an unconventional and innovative model of mourning as a viable response to skepticism. In what follows, I elucidate his account of mourning by focusing on two texts: *The Senses of Walden*, where Cavell discusses the pervasive sense of cultural loss in Thoreau's book, and "Stella's Taste: Reading *Stella Dallas*," his analysis of the dynamics of mother–daughter separation in the 1937 Hollywood melodrama *Stella Dallas*. Whether the focus falls on linguistic praxis, as in *The Senses of Walden*, or on intersubjectivity, as in "Stella's Taste," Cavell articulates an approach to mourning that manages to subvert the alienation and emptiness threatened by skepticism. Mourning emerges in both texts as a process of transforming lost certainty into an enabling set of conditions that governs the possibilities for meaningful relations to language, society, self, and others.

I

Nowhere in *The Senses of Walden* does Cavell actually use the word "mourning" to describe Thoreau's response to skepticism. In fact, it is not until Cavell reflects on his own book in three later essays that he explicitly defines Thoreau's response as a work of mourning.[4] In "The Uncanniness of the Ordinary," the most extensive commentary of the three, Cavell begins by claiming that Hume responded to skepticism in the form of "distraction," that is, by leaving aside the bleak discoveries of his philosophical work and joining the company of friends (171). This type of diversion no longer cures skeptical doubt and philosophical disillusionment, for Cavell recognizes that since Hume the impulse to skepticism has pervaded all social forms of life, including our most intimate relationships. Consequently, he argues that "a more direct response [to skepticism], perhaps in a more acute stage, is that, as in *Walden*, of mourning" ("Uncanniness" 172). Rereading *The Senses of Walden* in light of Cavell's later commentary on mourning casts new significance on his repeated claim that Thoreau writes out of "a sense of loss" (*Senses* 51).[5] Cavell reads Thoreau as diagnosing a sense of loss in himself and attempting to instill in his readers an awareness of a communally shared bereavement for both lost transcendence and the unfulfilled promises of the past.

Cavell catalogs the numerous losses that Thoreau mourns in the text: the opportunities of youth, the potential for the American Revolution to forge a new political community, a relationship to the gods, the home of Walden pond itself. And yet, while he enumerates the objects of Thoreau's mourning, he also argues that "it is no set of desired things he has lost, but a connection with things, the track of desire itself" (*Senses* 51). Cavell highlights the general experience of lost connections that Thoreau takes pains to describe:

> Everything he [Thoreau] can list he is putting in his book; it is a record of losses. Not that he has failed to make some gains and have his finds; but they are gone now. He is not present to them now. Or, he is trying to put them behind him, to complete the crisis by writing his way out of it. It is a gain to grow, but

humanly it is always a loss of something, a departure. Like any grownup, he has lost childhood; like any American, he has lost a nation and with it the God of the fathers. He has lost Walden; call it Paradise; it is everything there is to lose. The object of faith hides itself from him. Not that he has given it up, and the hope for it; he is on the track. He knows where it is to be found, in the true acceptance of loss, the refusal of any substitute for recovery. (Ibid. 51–52)

Thoreau engages the problem of skepticism by describing an experience of lost connectedness to both the self and the social, as well as giving expression to a threatening and potentially paralyzing experience of nihilistic hopelessness. It is in response to these losses that Thoreau enacts a mode of recovery, a work of mourning that resolutely refuses to replace lost objects with consoling substitutes and insists, instead, on a direct reckoning with the finality of loss.

By making this argument about the aim of Thoreau's mourning, Cavell departs in innovative ways from conventional assumptions about the grieving process. In "Mourning and Melancholia," a 1917 text that continues to influence our conception of grief dynamics, Freud defined mourning as a painful and protracted process that arises when we lose either a loved one or a cherished ideal. During the work of grieving, the subject is said to detach its emotional investment in the lost object and reinvest the free libido in a new object. Mourning comes to a decisive end, according to the Freudian account, when the subject has accepted a consoling substitute for the lost object ("Mourning" 243).[6] Cavell otherwise acknowledges his debt to Freud,[7] but he rejects this notion of mourning as an economy of loss and consolation; he recognizes that installing a substitute for the object enables the mourner to act as if nothing has been lost, to console despair at the cost of a deeper confrontation with the reality of loss. Instead, Cavell finds in Thoreau's work an alternative response to lost ideals. Mourning without the hope for consolation compels Thoreau to detach emotional investments in the past, but this is a detachment that takes place without completely severing ties, without promoting the kind of absolute forget-

ting characteristic of conventional mourning. Thoreau's mourning neither seeks to recover what has been lost nor attempts to install a substitute in place of the absence. Consequently, his work emphasizes both the irrecoverable loss of the object and a sustained engagement with this loss. Thoreau embarks, then, on a work of mourning that is ongoing and endless. If a recognition of loss functions as a precondition for understanding what has disappeared irretrievably, the capacity to mourn endlessly follows, giving rise to a new understanding of future possibilities in our relation to self, language, and society.

Thoreau's representation of lost ideals and opportunities leads to a fundamental insight: our relation to society can no longer be understood in terms of connection but of separation. Mourning fosters an awareness of separateness, according to Cavell, because it teaches Thoreau and his readers "what it means that we are looking for something we have lost" (Senses 98). Mourning teaches us that we have lost a sense of immediacy or necessity governing our social forms of life; nothing preordained or essential determines the structures of our society.[8] In Cavell's account, this knowledge of social contingency cannot be grasped without an experience of self-division and laceration. We must be thrown out, so to speak, of our habitual dwelling places – our selves, traditions, beliefs, and languages – so that they appear not as transcendentally sanctioned and unalterable social forms, but ones of human creation for which we are responsible. Citing a passage from Walden, Cavell details this lacerating experience in relation to Thoreau's description of "doubleness," his discovery of the "stranger" in himself:

I only know myself as a human entity; the scene, so to speak, of thoughts and affections; and am sensible of a certain doubleness by which I can stand as remote from myself as from another. However intense my experience, I am conscious of the presence and criticism of a part of me, which, as it were, is not a part of me, but a spectator, sharing no experience, but taking note of it, and that is no more I than it is you. (Quoted in ibid. 102)

Thoreau's account of embodying various ideas and emotions at the same time as he observes himself embodying them suggests an internal or psychic space where one part of the self sets itself up against the "I" or ego. His description of an internal spectator, clearly a prefiguring of the Freudian superego, names a critical agency within the self that observes, assesses, and judges the ego. Cavell attributes the formation of Thoreau's doubleness, of a kind of alienation at the core of the self, to the way social discourses "come from outside" and produce "the sense of distance from self, or division of self" (ibid. 107). Insofar as Cavell emphasizes the social and external determinants that animate Thoreau's existence, he forfeits the notion of a unified and autonomous ego. There can be no internal voice of conscience, no opportunity for civil disobedience, without the internalization of external values and practices that partition the self. Far from a condition to be lamented or overcome, then, this internal partition must be discovered, sustained, and interpreted. Indeed, Cavell uses the term "ecstasy" to describe Thoreau's doubleness and to suggest that our own "resolve should be toward the nextness of the self to the self" (ibid. 109). The power that society has to impose its terms upon us operates to the extent that we internalize these meanings. But the very process of internalization demonstrates the failure of the social to fully constitute the subject. When Thoreau withdraws inward and evaluates what comes into the self from the outside, he is able to regard the social terms that condition the formation of the self as utterly contingent and, hence, subject to revision and change.

In his retreat from Concord to Walden, from cultural activity to solitary writing, Thoreau gives expression to the loss of ideals concerning country, liberty, the sacred, and home. But because he has turned away from the external world and withdrawn inward, compensating for these losses by imprinting them on the psyche and heightening the judgments of conscience, Cavell raises the possibility that Thoreau's civil disobedience amounts to little more than a private revolt, a personal condemnation of society that threatens to produce a paralyzing isolation in the workings of consciousness typical of skep-

ticism. "Is it the way we live," Cavell asks, "that he despises, or human life as such? Is it merely governments that he scorns, or the human need and capacity for human society altogether?" (ibid. 111). In raising these questions, Cavell acknowledges that Thoreau has substituted the internal verdicts of conscience for an active participation in the world, for social action. Since it is not immediately clear how Thoreau's work returns us to the social world, Cavell argues that his private revolt contains a discernable social text that gives expression to what remains unspeakably absent, to the longing for a set of meaningful connections to the world. In the same way that Thoreau accepts the loss of an autonomous ego when he recognizes the location of a spectator in the self, he gives his writing over to the social terms and linguistic conditions that are never fully his own. To wage a revolt against these terms does not require an act of radical independence or will, but a submission to the conditions of socio-linguistic life. If this submission calls attention to existing power structures that govern Thoreau's writing, it also establishes the conditions of possibility for thwarting the imposition of meanings from the outside.

Cavell reads Thoreau's writing as a form of social action, as an attempt to respond to the loss of past securities without succumbing to melancholic isolation or skeptical despair. Thoreau writes his way toward a meaningful relation to society by observing "the conditions of language as such," conditions that are always socially and temporally specific (ibid. 33). Cavell defines the first of three linguistic conditions that Thoreau's writing self-consciously thematizes when he suggests that "a language is totally, systematically meaningful" (ibid. 34), and adds that "[t]he occurrence of a word is the occurrence of an object whose placement always has a point, and whose point always lies before and beyond it" (ibid. 27). His emphasis on language as systematic and relational confirms what we have known at least since Saussurean linguistics, namely that linguistic meaning does not derive from any intrinsic bond between words and the things they name, but from relations of difference within a linguistic system. Saussure's work has led Derrida and other poststructuralists to postulate an endless deferral and indeterminancy of meaning. Cavell shares with poststructuralism a rejection of the assumption that linguistic meaning derives from subject-centered paradigms, whether that of the writer of a text or the speaker of an utterance; however, he departs from poststructuralism on the issue of indeterminancy. While Cavell consistently focuses on linguistic instances where meaning is far from self-evident, he argues that crises of meaning derive from specific contexts and exchanges, from ways of using language that betray the conditions of linguistic praxis. When meaning fails to be communicated, as it often does, Cavell maintains that such failures reflect the features of a particular event, rather than an indeterminancy inherent in the structure of language.[9] Thus, he offers a second condition of language represented in Thoreau's writing: "the saying of something when and as it is said is as significant as the meaning and ordering of the words said" (ibid. 34). The arbiter of meaning, as Cavell suggests here, is the specific context in which words are used. The possibility to mean what we say and communicate this meaning to others emerges, then, as a function of a concrete linguistic exchange.

Cavell's claim that linguistic meaning can be determined in relation to context-specific usage has elicited both critique and praise of his work. Taking issue with *The Senses of Walden*, Walter Benn Michaels argues that Cavell far too neatly resolves the deliberately contradictory and ambiguous formulations that Thoreau crafts. Michaels places Cavell's work on a continuum with formalism and its theory of meaning as issuing from the unity of a text: "the coherence that the formalists understood as the defining characteristic of the text becomes instead [for Cavell] the defining characteristic of the reader, and the unity which was once claimed for the object itself is now claimed for the reader's experience of it" (146).[10] Conversely, Michael Fischer, one of Cavell's most devoted interpreters, suggests that Michaels fails to appreciate the fundamentally provisional character of Cavell's account of linguistic meaning. As Fischer argues convincingly, "Cavell's

reader does not conclusively resolve crises but spends a lifetime resolving them" (400). Even when linguistic meaning can be ascertained through the procedures of ordinary language philosophy, this meaning is never fixed or absolute, but open to ongoing reinterpretation and revision.

The provisional quality of Cavell's ideas about linguistic meaning is particularly apparent with regard to the third and final condition of language laid out in *The Senses of Walden*: "that words and their orderings are meant by human beings, that they contain (or conceal) their beliefs, express (or deny) their convictions" (33). Cavell suggests that language not only describes events in the world but also reflects the value we assign to these events. In defining the capacity of words to convey conviction, a capacity as subject to reinterpretation and revision as our own convictions, Cavell criticizes the way language has been construed as a disinterested or neutral medium. He criticizes, more specifically, the way we assert objectivity and deny that our utterances contain value judgments or assume that words cannot express the precise content of our minds. The ability to return conviction to our use of language, to recognize the idea of valuing as a condition of linguistic practice, involves Cavell's notion of granting words "their full range and autonomy" (*Senses* 34).

Thoreau's "literary redemption of language" is offered as an illustration of this linguistic range and autonomy (ibid. 92). Thoreau criticizes the socio-economic order for reducing words like labor, interest, and gain to signifiers of financial profit. But he does more than simply critique; Thoreau also recovers what Cavell addresses as the "integrity" of linguistic meaning:

> Our words have for us the meaning we give to them. As our lives stand, the meaning we give them is rebuked by the meaning they have in our language – the meaning, say, that writers live on, the meaning we also, in moments, know they have but which mostly remains a mystery to us. Thoreau is doing with our ordinary assertions what Wittgenstein does with our more patently philosophical assertions – bringing them back to a context in which they are alive. (Ibid. 92)

Thoreau develops a style of writing that draws on the etymological significance of words in order to bring meaning back from a purely socio-economic context to what Cavell calls the ordinary, literal, and everyday use of language. Take, for example, Thoreau's frequent use of the word "labor" to describe the central action of building his home in the woods. At present, labor names a job done to collect a paycheck. But, as Cavell suggests, the reduction of labor to a clock-punching activity is challenged by the meaning the word has in our language. By recalling linguistic meanings lost in the present, Thoreau achieves the "ecstasies of exactness" (ibid. 44); he inflects his writing with figurative significance and restores a human value to the word "labor," a value that signifies an "edifying" activity fit for "human habitation" (ibid. 62). If our experience of labor cannot sustain such meaning, it is because, Cavell argues, we do not inhabit that activity. We have not found a home there. By recognizing that the meaning of words precedes and even exceeds any individual who employs them, *Walden* manages to transform the distinction between literal and figurative signification into a new and fuller concept of the literal, defining a way of using language in which "our words need not haunt us" (ibid. 34). As a result, Cavell argues that Thoreau's writing "is not a substitute for his life, but his way of prosecuting it" (ibid. 62), his way of engaging the terms of social life.

In his account of mourning as a therapeutic response to skepticism, Cavell establishes a relationship between lost certainty and social recovery that takes shape around a deep awareness of human mortality. His idea of bringing words home, of returning them to a context in which they transform our lives, should not be understood as an appeal to some prelapsarian meaning or plenitudinous being. Rather, the conception of home that Cavell has in mind entails returning, paradoxically, to a place we have yet to traverse. It is a place structured by an awareness of finitude. Drawing a relationship between the contingencies of linguistic and human life, between language and death, Cavell suggests that inhabiting the world requires knowing how to leave it. The homes found in language, society, and bodies, if they are found at all, are necessarily temporal and temporary. Consequently, Cavell makes much of the fact that *Walden* begins after Thoreau has already left Walden.

> The hero departs from his hut and goes into an unknown wood from whose mysteries he wins a boon that he brings back to his neighbors. The boon of Walden is *Walden*. Its writer cups it in his hand, sees his reflection in it, and holds it out to us. It is his promise, in anticipation of his going, and the nation's, and Walden's. He is bequeathing it to us in his will, the place of the book and the book of the place. He leaves us in one another's keeping. (Ibid. 119)

Thoreau is praised as a writer and philosopher who withdraws into himself and his writing as a condition for returning to society. Having abandoned his dwelling place in the woods, Thoreau returns, as if for the first time, to the place language has already happened to him. This return takes the form of mourning, for he not only discovers the loss of necessity and metaphysical guarantees in our social forms of life; he also uses this discovery as a point of departure to elucidate the conditions that mediate our relation to language and society, conditions that constrain but also mobilize new future possibilities. Thoreau's mourning enables him to "despair of despair" (ibid. 71), that is, to pass through melancholy dejection, skeptical isolation, and nihilistic meaninglessness in order to absolve them of the demonic force they have in culture, in human lives.

When Cavell retrospectively applies the term "mourning" to describe Thoreau's recovery from skepticism, he articulates an approach to grieving that is ongoing and interminable, but not pathological or melancholic. Cavell explicitly defines Thoreau's mourning as an endless work when he suggests that "encoded in the idea of a Thoreauvian pun on mourning and morning is the idea that the ecstasy in question is still part of the *work* of mourning, not a sign that mourning is all at once over" ("Stella's Taste" 221). Cavell's sense of ongoing mourning, it is worth remarking, enjoys widespread currency among numerous artists, memorial makers, and critics, who have shown how sustained attachment to loss captures our experience of bereavement much more accurately than stage theories that posit a decisive end to the grieving process.[11] This resistance to the aim of closure, all the more imperative when the loss in question is not only private and personal but also public and social, compels us to refuse consolation, perpetuate grief, and accept responsibility for living in the wake of irrecoverable loss. In the context of what Cavell sees as Thoreau's play on mourning (as a response to loss) and morning (as the dawning of new possibilities), he articulates a sustained engagement with the loss of ideals that reminds us of our longing for meaningful relationships to society. In response to the discovery that nothing natural or essential structures our social forms of life, Thoreau not only recognizes that "[t]he world must be regained every day, in repetition, regained as gone" ("Uncanniness" 172); he also engages a work of mourning to articulate "human existence as the finding of ecstasy in the knowledge of loss" (ibid. 171).

II

Mourning also emerges as a means of overcoming skepticism in "Stella's Taste," the concluding essay in Cavell's *Contesting Tears*.[12] As in his work on *Walden*, Cavell's essay defines mourning as a process of transforming the loss of necessity into an enabling set of conditions consistent with the abandonment of metaphysics. But whereas Cavell focuses his Thoreau book on the threat of skepticism in relation to language and society, he addresses *Stella Dallas*'s representation of endless mourning in terms of an experience of mother–daughter separation, not only explicating the relevance of psychoanalysis to his work but also expanding its domain to feminist concerns. Arguing that our relation to others, like our relation to the social, must begin with an affirmation of human separateness, Cavell defines mourning as a process by which we learn "to cry over separation, as for a solace preceding one's own happiness" ("Stella's Taste" 218). Moreover, he invokes the longstanding view of mourning as women's

work. But instead of perpetuating a tradition of grief expression as a feminizing and unmanly practice, Cavell counsels men as well as women to become mourners. He links "the capacity for the experience ... of mourning" to a discovery of "the feminine in one's character, whichever one's gender," showing how the experience of viewing the film makes such a discovery possible ("Freud" 386).

Ever since Freud, psychoanalysis has theorized mourning in relation to the first loss we experience, that of the mother. Theorists including Nicolas Abraham and Maria Torok have characterized mourning as a process of subject formation, a process by which the infant loses the maternal object and accepts the masculine symbol as a more than adequate compensation for the loss (5). Invariably, these models of individuation exclude the mother from playing an active role in subject formation; the child's entry into language and culture is said to be predicated on her very loss. Whether we credit the Freudian view of paternal identification as a response to horror of the mother's bodily lack or the Lacanian view of the ascendancy of the paternal Symbolic over the maternal Imaginary, the result is the same: the child acquires language and culture by repudiating the maternal object through a labor of grief that "works" by effacing the mother's difference, or what Cavell calls her separateness.

In his account of mourning as a process of subject formation, Cavell resists the myth of maternal plenitude typically spawned by theories that found culture on losing the mother and gaining the father. As a result, he defines the maternal figure as playing an active role in the child's acquisition of language and culture, as well as acknowledging her subjectivity, her identity as a mother related to yet independent from the child. Consider, for example, *Disowning Knowledge* where Cavell reads Shakespeare's *Hamlet* as sketching out "a direct psychoanalytic interpretation of skepticism" and defining "the child's sense of loss in separating from the mother's body" as a version of philosophical skepticism (13). Hamlet emerges as a paradigmatic skeptic, a male who refuses to acknowledge "that his mother is not his to dispose of" (*Disowning* 13). Cavell argues that on some level Hamlet does not fail to know he has lost his mother, that Gertrude cannot be assimilated to his own reality. But Hamlet disowns the knowledge of Gertrude's separateness. Crediting this knowledge, Cavell suggests, would entail his acceptance of symbolic castration, an acceptance that the other sets limits to the achievement of his own individuality. By denying that Gertrude exists apart from him, Hamlet indulges a fantasy of "remaining in his mother's womb," a means of possessing the mother without having to contend with her independence (ibid. 14). As Cavell suggests, Hamlet imagines reaping benefits from this fantasy, as if returning to a place prior to individuation enables him to overcome human contingency and his fear of Gertrude's "power as annihilating ... his own" (ibid. 185).

In a marked departure from the drama of maternal loss emphasized in psychoanalytic theories of mourning and individuation, Cavell also raises the issue of paternal loss. He claims that Hamlet displays a primary connection not only to Gertrude but also to his father, whose death he has failed to acknowledge and mourn. The father's ghost assigns Hamlet the task of securing paternal revenge and thereby "deprives the son of his identity, of enacting his own existence" (ibid. 188). In making this argument, Cavell moves beyond psychoanalytic accounts like Julia Kristeva's that attribute unstable or disordered forms of subjectivity to a failed reckoning with the originary loss of the mother.[13] Cavell concludes that *Hamlet* "interprets the taking of one's place in the world as a process of mourning" (ibid. 189). The achievement of subjectivity occurs, then, not by substituting the masculine symbol for the maternal object, but by negotiating both maternal and paternal loss. Dramatizing the conditions of individuation and separateness, Shakespeare's play foregrounds what Cavell calls the "double acceptance" that Hamlet has avoided: "an acceptance of one's mother as an independent sexual being whose life of desire survives the birth of a son and the death of a husband ... and an acceptance of one's father as a dependent sexual being whose incapacity to sustain desire you cannot revive" (ibid. 189).

If *Hamlet* dramatizes the tragedy that ensues as a result of the avoidance of mourning, *Stella Dallas* raises possibilities for self-discovery and transformation when loss is confronted and mourned. When the film opens, Stella (Barbara Stanwyck) marries the wealthy Stephen Dallas (John Boles), leaving her working-class life and joining her husband's refined society. But Stella fails to learn the standards of respectable dress and speech expected in Stephen's upper-class world. As an accomplished seamstress, for example, she makes her own clothes, highly ornate dresses that others see as gaudy and tasteless. Stella's failure to adopt the conventions of style and elegance exposes a rift in her marriage, and, on her urging, Stephen accepts a job in a distant city, leaving Stella to raise their daughter, Laurel (Anne Shirley), who matures into a young woman during the course of the film.

The film's turning point comes when Laurel finds herself attracted to the opportunities of love and success in her father's world, but feels she cannot leave the comforting security of her mother's. Feminist film critics, Cavell points out, have typically read the film as a troubling tale of motherly self-sacrifice, a story of a woman who compensates for her exclusion from upper-class society by securing her daughter's position in that world. This interpretation clearly merits consideration; by the film's end Stella feigns disinterest in Laurel's life and manages to secure her daughter's marriage to a wealthy young man. And yet Cavell contests the argument that Stella vacates her existence in favor of her daughter's. Rather, he sees Stella's apparent obliviousness to the public disapproval of her clothes and manners as a resolute display of difference from that world, Stella's resistance to upper-class norms which are not to her taste ("Stella's Taste" 204). Moreover, by scandalizing the respectable, Stella decidedly rejects her husband's lessons in conformity. Far from the victim she is often taken to be in feminist scholarship, Stella emerges in Cavell's account as an independent female character and a successful mother who also teaches Laurel to achieve independence. Against her daughter's protests that her "home will always be with her mother," Stella helps Laurel enter the very world she rejects, insisting her daughter must have a voice in the direction of her life (ibid. 212).

In the film's portrayal of mother–daughter separation, Cavell defines a reciprocal process of mourning and individuation that contributes to our understanding of his notion of acknowledgment – of acknowledging the other's separateness as a condition of interpersonal relations. Stella plays an active role in her daughter's education and discovers her own voice in the process. In other words, Stella not only teaches Laurel to mourn as a means of claiming a voice in her own life; the mother also learns from the daughter "to bear and express the pain of separation" (ibid. 211). Over and against the view of mourning as a one-sided contract that benefits the mourner at the expense of the mourned, which grounds the child's emerging subjectivity on the effacement of the mother's difference, Cavell sees Stella as both mourned object and mourning subject.

By shifting from the film's thematic presentation of mother–daughter separation to a discussion of its formal complexity, Cavell focuses attention on the spectator, addressing how the film directly engages the viewer in an experience of maternal mourning. In contrast to the theory of the male gaze as Hollywood cinema's organizing perspective, Cavell proposes "the infantine basis of our position as viewers" (ibid. 216). He articulates, that is, a phenomenology of spectatorship "before the establishment of human gender, that is, before the choices of identification and objectification of female and male, call them mama and papa, have settled themselves" (ibid. 209). By equating our position as viewers with infancy – with the capacity to identify with female and male characters from an infantile position of primary bisexuality – Cavell's work contests the Oedipalization of contemporary film theory characteristic of Christian Metz and Kaja Silverman. In Metz's well-known account, the film image provides the viewer with a fiction of self-presence, a means of recuperating the subject's imaginary and masterful possession of the world. So terrifying is the prospect of castration, the recognition that we exist as mortal beings subject to the contingencies of social life, that in watching films we fetishize the image, deny the

absence of reality unfolding on the screen, and recapture a lost plenitude associated with the pre-Oedipal mother. In this way, Metz argues, cinematic consumption fulfills a desire to be "a pure, all-seeing and invisible subject" (97). Although Silverman addresses the unanalyzed role of gender in Metz's account, she perpetuates his basic claims by arguing that cinema provides this fiction of self-presence only to male viewers. In denying the female gaze both on the screen and in the audience, the male spectator projects his cultural lack or discursive insufficiency onto women both on and off the screen, women who are assigned what Silverman calls a double burden of lack by being made to embody male contingency as well as their own (31).

Cavell contests the idea that "men in general … undertake to reassure themselves of their own intactness by a mechanism of substitution which allows them to disavow … the woman's horrifying lack of intactness" ("Stella's Taste" 207). In his reading, such an account might explain the particular experience of watching films for some viewers, especially some male viewers, but it cannot be upheld as a generalized theory of film reception. If men necessarily represent and perceive women in terms of a horrifying lack, then it is difficult to imagine, as Cavell wonders, why "women should converse with men at all about serious matters" (ibid. 208). Cavell objects to the idea that the dynamics of identification, fetishism, and disavowal necessarily determine female representation and film viewing. As J.D. Connor has recently suggested, "Cavell joins a long line of critics of 'the gaze,' but he does so not with recourse to an ever-more-nuanced psychoanalytic theory, but with recourse to instances" (966). Cavell does not deny that women continue to be viewed in terms of a devaluing lack, but he insists that the best way to combat such representations is in relation to an analysis of particular cases.

Cavell's analysis of the final sequence of *Stella Dallas* demonstrates the efficacy of such an approach, for it offers an alternative way of understanding the film. Unbeknownst to Laurel, Stella watches her daughter's wedding through a window on the street, an emblem of spectatorship that mirrors the viewer's own position as a seeing but unseen subject. In the film's closing shot, Stella turns from the window and directly faces the audience, her eyes slightly turned from the viewer's. In suggesting that the film fully credits the gaze of a woman and mother on the screen, Cavell writes:

> In the infantine basis of our position as viewers, Stella's gaze before the window, as the camera gives it to us, is the mother's backed by mothers; and as Stella turns to walk toward us, her gaze, transforming itself, looms toward us, as if the screen is looming, its gaze *just* turned away, always to be searched for. (For what it grants; for what it wants.) ("Stella's Taste" 216)

Cavell emphasizes that "film gazes at us" (ibid. 210), that Stella looks at the audience, draws the viewer into a direct confrontation with maternal loss, and places us in the position of infantile viewer in relation to the on-screen mother. In proposing the idea of an infantile perspective, a model of spectatorship that "assaults human perception at a more primitive level than the work of fetishizing suggests" (ibid. 209), Cavell links our emergence as viewing subjects to an awareness of human separateness, or, more precisely, to an awareness of separation from the mother. In his reading, the myth of pre-Oedipal or pre-cultural wholeness becomes an absurdity. Indeed, what Laura loses in losing Stella, what we lose in losing a mother, is quite literally nothing, the nothingness that separates us as human beings with bodies from the oblivion prior to our conception. Structured by an awareness of finitude, maternal mourning in Cavell's account teaches us that inhabiting a body requires knowing how to leave it.

Beyond exposing maternal plenitude as a nostalgic fiction of oceanic wholeness, Cavell defines mourning and the painful process of separation as an ongoing social challenge to recall mothers as desiring and speaking subjects. He concludes "Stella's Taste" with an autobiographical account of his own mother, a highly gifted pianist whose socially limited success contributed to what Cavell calls her bouts of melancholy sadness. Her way of coping was to play the piano

not for others but for herself, an experience Cavell describes as feeling abandoned by her. In fact, he criticizes his mother, recalling that he was "subjected to her moods" and worrying he would inherit her melancholia or depression (ibid. 222). However, Cavell manages to deflate the narcissism of his own position by insisting that to mourn his mother, to endlessly search for her gaze, raises "the question of what her moods are subjected to, to what scenes of inheritance" (ibid. 222). Undoubtedly, there are aspects of a mother's personal and social life that a son will never know; however, instead of focusing on maternal alterity, Cavell uses his bereavement as a means to undercut the political neutrality of mourning. He views his experience of maternal loss as an invitation to recount the story of his mother's musical talent, her wish for public recognition, and the social limitations that thwarted her aspirations.

In his recent *A Pitch of Philosophy*, Cavell acknowledges his "endless indebtedness" to a maternal gift in both the body and title of the book (9). Again addressing his mother's exceptional musical talent and her disappointment at never having achieved national recognition, Cavell remarks "My mother had something called perfect pitch" (*Pitch* 21). That he didn't inherit her pitch was one of the reasons he opted against a career in music. With *A Pitch of Philosophy*, Cavell puts into practice the endless mourning of skepticism that he champions in *Walden* and *Stella Dallas*; he confronts the irrecoverable loss of his mother and affirms a continuing engagement with this loss as an informing source of his work. To sustain attachments to loss, whether for others or ideals, is to discern a human longing for connection and meaning; to embark on the work of ceaselessly mourning these losses is to discover the conditions that govern the possibilities for interpersonal relationships and linguistic praxis. What mourning offers, then, is a way of living our skepticism about the possibility of a meaningful engagement with society and others without giving ourselves over to melancholy isolation or nihilistic chaos.

notes

I thank the anonymous *Angelaki* reader for insightful criticism of this work. My deepest gratitude goes to R.M. Berry, who has been an extraordinary source of inspiration and guidance from the beginning of my encounter with Cavell.

1 Critics have argued that Cavell's account of language and interpersonal relationships offers an alternative, indeed a viable counterargument, to the linguistic and social paralysis thought to issue from poststructuralism. Unlike poststructuralist critiques aimed at undermining conventional assumptions and power dynamics, Cavell seeks to discern what social forms of life, if any, we do share, and how the conventions or grammar governing our language games make meaningful communication and relationships possible. For accounts of Cavell's work as a viable alternative to poststructuralism, see Cantor (52); Fischer, *Stanley Cavell* (30–35); and Goodheart (8–12).

2 This is the point Bruns emphasizes in his reading of Cavell's notion of acknowledgment: "At all events acknowledgment means openness and acceptance of the other as such, that is, as other, as that which resists every effort on my part to reduce it to something containable within the legislation of my concepts" (87).

3 An important exception to this lack of critical attention to mourning is the work of Stephen Mulhall (249–62), one of Cavell's most insightful and eloquent critics. While Mulhall limits his treatment of mourning to a theme in Cavell's Thoreau study, my aim is to demonstrate how mourning functions as a response to the pervasive structure of loss and recovery that informs Cavell's project.

4 For Cavell's assessment of the therapeutic emphasis of his work as a form of mourning, see "Politics as Opposed to What?" (201); "The Uncanniness of the Ordinary" (171–72); and "Stella's Taste: Reading *Stella Dallas*" (212, 219–20).

5 Cavell's practice of self-citation, typical of his later writing, has been interpreted as a belated and failed attempt to extend his work into contemporary territory. See, for example, Esch. Rather than regard Cavell's propensity for self-citation as a sign of intellectual narcissism, I read this strategy as a form of what might be called textual mourning, his attempt to work through previous formulations in order to produce new meanings.

6 In his 1923 *The Ego and the Id* (28) Freud went on to acknowledge the inadequacy of his earlier account of mourning, citing his failure to understand the fierce resistance to consolation characteristic of bereavement. As a result, he redefined mourning as a refiguring of the subject's relation to the lost object, rather than simply a severing of ties. For an account of the development of his mourning theory, see Butler (167–98).

7 Cavell writes: "Other of my intellectual debts remain fully outstanding, that to Freud's work before all" ("Freud" 387).

8 Cavell's notion of mourning as a response to the loss of necessity or metaphysical securities invites comparison to Peter Homans (262–63, 338), who interprets Freud's mourning theory as a process of creating new personal and social opportunities in the wake of lost religious transcendence, arguing that psychoanalysis itself derived from Freud's ability to mourn the loss of cultural meaning in the aftermath of secularization.

9 For Cavell's critique of the notion of indeterminancy in the work of Paul de Man, see "Politics" (181–202). When Cavell turns his attention to Derrida, he remarks an affinity between his own interest in lost necessity and Derrida's account of the loss of metaphysics. While both may share a concern with the loss of transcendence, Cavell argues that Derridean philosophy "institutes an (a false) absence for which it falsely offers compensations" and concludes that in "Derrida's heritage we 'cannot' truly escape from the tradition of philosophy; in mine we cannot truly escape to philosophy" ("Uncanniness" 173, 174). For alternative accounts of Derrida's work as a melancholic refusal to let go of lost metaphysical certainties, see Rose (11–12); and Abrams (75–78).

10 Other critics have drawn on insights derived from poststructuralism to critique Cavell's work; see Bearn (65); Spivak (353–54); and Ziarek (130–36). My account differs from these by emphasizing the provisional character of Cavell's concept of linguistic meaning and by demonstrat-

ing how the ongoing work of mourning facilities the ceaseless creation of new significations.

11 For an excellent introduction to the concept of sustained mourning, see Woodward (93–110).

12 Cavell reads the film as part of a genre he terms "the melodrama of the unknown woman," a genre that supplements his work on "the comedy of remarriage." For a discussion of the relationship of the two genres, see Cavell, *Contesting Tears* (3–6).

13 Kristeva ventures the highly criticized claim that "matricide is our vital necessity," suggesting that the stable forms of selfhood depend on killing off – or more precisely, separating from – the mother and accepting the linguistic resources in the symbolic order to neutralize the guilt that follows the murderous deed (27).

bibliography

Abraham, Nicolas and Maria Torok. "Introjection – Incorporation: Mourning or Melancholia." *Psychoanalysis in France*. Ed. and trans. Serge Lebovici and Daniel Widlöcher. New York: International UP, 1980. 3–16.

Abrams, Marsha Lynne. "Coping with Loss in the Human Sciences: A Reading at the Intersection of Psychoanalysis and Hermeneutics." *Diacritics* 23.1 (1993): 67–82.

Bearn, Gordon. "Sounding Serious: Cavell and Derrida." *Representations* 63 (1998): 65–92.

Bruns, Gerald. "Dialogue and the Truth of Skepticism." *Religion and Literature* 22.2 (1990): 85–92.

Butler, Judith. *The Psychic Life of Power: Theories in Subjection*. Stanford: Stanford UP, 1997.

Cantor, Jay. "On Stanley Cavell." *Raritan* 1 (1981): 48–67.

Cavell, Stanley. "Freud and Philosophy: A Fragment." *Critical Inquiry* 13 (winter 1987): 386–93.

Cavell, Stanley. "Hamlet's Burden of Proof." *Disowning Knowledge in Six Plays of Shakespeare*. Cambridge: Cambridge UP, 1987. 179–91.

Cavell, Stanley. *A Pitch of Philosophy: Autobiographical Exercises*. Cambridge, MA: Harvard UP, 1994.

Cavell, Stanley. "Politics as Opposed to What?"

The Politics of Interpretation. Ed. W.J.T. Mitchell. Chicago: U of Chicago P, 1982. 181–202.

Cavell, Stanley. *Pursuits of Happiness: The Hollywood Comedy of Remarriage*. Cambridge, MA: Harvard UP, 1976.

Cavell, Stanley. *The Senses of Walden: An Expanded Edition*. Chicago: U of Chicago P, 1992.

Cavell, Stanley. "Stella's Taste: Reading *Stella Dallas*." *Contesting Tears: The Hollywood Melodrama of the Unknown Woman*. Chicago: U of Chicago P, 1996. 197–222.

Cavell, Stanley. "The Uncanniness of the Ordinary." *In Quest of the Ordinary: Lines of Skepticism and Romanticism*. Chicago: U of Chicago P, 1988. 153–78.

Connor, J.D. "Disappearing, Inc.: Hollywood Melodrama and the Perils of Criticism." *MLN* 112.2 (1997): 958–70.

Esch, Deborah. "No Time Like the Present." *Surfaces* 3.19 (1993): 16 (26 June 2004). Available < http://www.pum.umontreal.ca/revues/surfaces/vol3/esch.html > .

Fischer, Michael. "Speech and Writing in *The Senses of Walden*." *Sounding* 68 (fall 1985): 388–403.

Fischer, Michael. *Stanley Cavell and Literary Skepticism*. Chicago: U of Chicago P, 1989.

Freud, Sigmund. *The Ego and the Id*. Vol. 19 of *The Standard Edition of the Complete Psychological Works of Sigmund Freud*. Ed. and trans. James Strachey. London: Hogarth, 1953–74. 3–66.

Freud, Sigmund. "Mourning and Melancholia." Vol. 14 of *The Standard Edition of the Complete Psychological Works of Sigmund Freud*. Ed. and trans. James Strachey. London: Hogarth, 1953–74. 239–59.

Goodheart, Eugene. *The Skeptic Disposition in Contemporary Criticism*. Princeton: Princeton UP, 1984.

Homans, Peter. *The Ability to Mourn: Disillusionment and the Social Origins of Psychoanalysis*. Chicago: U of Chicago P, 1989.

Kristeva, Julia. *Black Sun: Depression and Melancholia*. Trans. Leon S. Roudiez. New York: Columbia UP, 1989.

Metz, Christian. *The Imaginary Signifier: Psycho-analysis and the Cinema*. Trans. Celia Britton, Anwyl Williams, Ben Brewster and Alfred Guzzetti. Bloomington: Indiana UP, 1982.

Michaels, Walter Benn. "*Walden*'s False Bottoms." *Glyph* 1 (1977): 132–49.

Mitchell, W.J.T. (ed.). *The Politics of Interpretation*. Chicago: U of Chicago P, 1982.

Mulhall, Stephen. *Stanley Cavell: Philosophy's Recounting of the Ordinary*. New York: Oxford UP, 1994.

Rose, Gillian. *Mourning Becomes the Law: Philosophy and Representation*. Cambridge: Cambridge UP, 1996.

Silverman, Kaja. *The Acoustic Mirror: The Female Voice in Psychoanalysis and Cinema*. Bloomington: Indiana UP, 1988.

Spivak, Gayatri Chakravorty. "The Politics of Interpretations." *The Politics of Interpretation*. Ed. W.J.T. Mitchell. Chicago: U of Chicago P, 1982. 347–66.

Woodward, Kathleen. "Freud and Barthes: Theorizing Mourning, Sustaining Grief." *Discourse* 13.1 (1990–91): 93–110.

Ziarek, Ewa Plonowska. *The Rhetoric of Failure: Deconstruction of Skepticism, Reinvention of Modernism*. Albany: State U of New York P, 1996.

Tammy Clewell
Department of English
Kent State University
PO Box 5190
Kent, OH 44242
USA
E-mail: tclewell@kent.edu

journal of the theoretical humanities
volume 9 number 3 december 2004

We start with the assumption that, confronted with a work such as the *Recherche*, the reader is in much the same position as the narrator who has lost his beloved.

How does Proust describe the narrator's relation to Albertine, especially after her sudden disappearance and her unexpected death? From the beginning he is separated from her. Just as her disappearance has an impact on him which, initially at least, eludes both his intelligence and his imagination, her appearance amounts to a revelation which remains unintelligible. Everything meaningful about Albertine is revealed the moment the narrator encounters her for the first time, but the meaning takes flight before he can grasp it. There is something specific about the end of the relationship only in so far as the impossibility of bringing her back in the flesh highlights the separation inherent in the relationship itself.

Albertine's presence seems to be an effect of her absence. It is doubtful whether her death does make a difference. What would be a presence that is not the effect of an absence? In the *Recherche*, such a presence assumes the form of a stupefying habit or calls for a relation bereft of responsiveness, of "the power to awaken the dead," as the narrator puts it.[1] At this point, a reader could be tempted to say that, for Albertine to come back in the flesh, she must be dead in the first place. She must be a character in a novel. It is not surprising that the narrator keeps stressing the importance of the beloved's image. Albertine never presents herself to him as one single being, for he remains separated from her by virtue of the delay with which his intelligence relates to her appearance and to her disappearance. The name Albertine stands for a collection of photographs taken successively

alexander garcía düttmann

SEPARATED FROM PROUST

from angles that never form a whole. Each of Albertine's many aspects is a sort of image, a memory contingently and at the same time inextricably intertwined with other memories. Only the unattainable and perhaps illusionary view of the whole, only the idea of Albertine, would abolish the imagery in favour of a presence no longer in need of a relation.

Will the narrator be capable of forgetting Albertine and freeing himself from the images of a fragmented and therefore haunting memory? He can undergo a transformation because his own self is not exempt from the fragmentation that also binds him to the other.

Time and again the narrator emphasizes the negativity of a relationship mediated by images and sometimes reduced to the mere repetition of

ISSN 0969-725X print/ISSN 1469-2899 online/04/030089–02 © 2004 Taylor & Francis Ltd and the Editors of *Angelaki*
DOI: 10.1080/0969725042000307646

a name. This is why the *Recherche* raises the question of scepticism. Can I ever know an other who is but a name forever repeated? Inasmuch as a relationship has a history, this history consists in the production of a reassuring stereotype which allows *me* to recognize the other immediately. The other is a surface on which I project my desires and fears regardless of who he is. Should an image of the other ever turn into something real, should an idea I conceive in connection with the other ever enter the realm of reality, should my wishes come true and a possibility I discern become actual, I would feel disappointed. An image is always more and less than life itself, and its indifference and even hostility towards reality renders it irresistibly attractive. When the other dies I will have killed him, for I constantly wish for the suffering his absence provokes. My torment helps me to make a discovery which is not valuable in itself but which serves my appropriation of the other. Is this not the predictable picture a sceptic would draw, claiming that its predictability has no bearing on its truth?

Indeed. The assumption that guides the sceptic here is that, in a relationship, I aim at reaching the other and that my attempt to do so must fail. The sceptic sees the other as an entity which exists independently of the relationship itself and which therefore keeps withdrawing from my understanding or calling for an infinite understanding I cannot provide. Does it make sense to conceive of the other in these terms? All the doubts I may have about the other I would not have if I did not already relate to him. The other does not precede the relationship even though he may surprise me or make the relationship change. The self and the other are abstractions and cannot be considered in isolation. But a relationship comes into existence and is maintained only if, rather than endlessly wondering who the other may be and what I may be doing to him, I keep responding, not simply in an arbitrary fashion or by way of imposing my will upon him, but in a creative manner to which the concept of understanding cannot be applied unreservedly. The power of the work of art, the power to awaken the dead,[2] is precisely the power at work in such a response. The dead

awoken by the artist are neither the living whom death has spared so far nor creatures who have not existed before. There may well be a response to the *Recherche*, but there is no other Albertine behind the Albertine the narrator introduces. In a response, be it a work of art or a reply in a conversation, the difference between the self and the other is erased. However, there is no response outside the relationship. Thus each response allows and perhaps requires the other to take a stance – to respond in turn, to suspend all responding or to break off the relationship. I am as dead as the other is before a response is given, and yet one of us gives a response which awakens us both to life while a threshold is crossed beyond which it proves futile to distinguish between me and the other, between the one who responds and the one addressed.

When a third party takes over, when the academic starts talking about the *Recherche*, rules are set down and roles are identified at the expense of genuine responsiveness.

notes

1 Marcel Proust, *A la recherche du temps perdu*, vol. IV (Paris: Bibliothèque de la Pléiade, 1988) 158.

2 Luchino Visconti's *Death in Venice* is an impressive film once the viewer realizes that it is almost a silent movie, with the flashback sequences functioning not as the enunciation of a conflict between doctrines that the plot itself illustrates but as a contrasting and ironic reminiscence of words and their triviality. As a silent movie this film points to itself, as it were to the awakening of the dead.

Alexander García Düttmann
43 Blenheim Terrace
London NW8 0EJ
UK
E-mail: aduttmann@aol.com

journal of the theoretical humanities
volume 9 number 3 december 2004

"Give me a body then": this is the formula of philosophical reversal. The body is no longer the obstacle that separates thought from itself, that which it has to overcome to reach thinking. It is on the contrary that which it plunges into or must plunge into, in order to reach the unthought, that is life. Not that the body thinks, but obstinate and stubborn, it forces us to think, and forces us to think what is concealed from thought, life.

Gilles Deleuze, Cinema 2, *188*

elizabeth walden

LANGUAGE, SPECTACLE AND BODY IN ANTHONY DRAZEN'S *HURLYBURLY*

The dearth of action and the relatively underdeveloped narrative structure of *Hurlyburly* (dir. Anthony Drazen, 1998) allow us to observe more readily the subtle action that takes place in and among the film's words, images and bodies. In the quotation from Gilles Deleuze that serves as this paper's epigraph, our situation is described as one that requires thought to "plunge into" the body. Body is no longer, as it was for Descartes, "the obstacle that separates thought from itself," but that without which thought remains separated from "life." The drama that unfolds within *Hurlyburly*, particularly through the character of Eddie (Sean Penn), serves as an allegory of this situation and forces us to confront the need to think the embodied conditions of thought that are often invisible to it.[1] This is not just fortuitous; cinema helps enact this "philosophical reversal." It brings before us the audiovisual, sound and image, and "plunges" us below the surface/image of the body: through mimetic connection to its characters, through the phenomenological context of its spectators, and, indeed, through the materiality of the film itself.[2] In short, cinema brings closer to thought what is unthought in our ordinary experience. Still, as Deleuze says, cinema cannot give us a body; it can, however, give us the "genesis of an unknown body" (201). It can provoke us to consider the forgotten body and thereby bring us closer to "what is concealed from thought, life." In *Hurlyburly* it is "the genesis of an unknown body," a force that demands that Eddie think differently, that saves his life.

It isn't possible to address the body in *Hurlyburly* directly; we must approach the "unthought" as it reveals itself within the context of the audiovisual. Rather, it is language that clamors for attention in the foreground of *Hurlyburly*. David Rabe, who wrote the screenplay for the film, is second only to David Mamet in creating works that rain down words without

ISSN 0969-725X print/ISSN 1469-2899 online/04/030091–10 © 2004 Taylor & Francis Ltd and the Editors of *Angelaki*
DOI: 10.1080/0969725042000307655

cessation. The result is less like dialogue, communicative exchanges among speakers, than, indeed, a "hurlyburly" that ventriloquizes the characters and assaults the audience with a rapid-fire verbal barrage. Rabe, in his stage directions, writes:

> in the characters' speeches, phrases such as "whatchamacallit," "thingamajic," "blah-blah-blah," and "repateta" abound. These are phrases used by the characters to keep themselves talking and should be said unhesitatingly ... In general, the play should proceed without pauses between speeches or words. (167)

The velocity of the words, the will to expunge silence, overtakes meaning itself as it overtakes its characters. *Hurlyburly*'s language is never their language, but an almost seamless force beneath which we witness the inexpressible – isolation, rage, confusion, pain – and its inevitable consequences – violence, misogyny, anesthetization, and suicide. This "hurlyburly" presents a spectacle from which it is difficult to turn away.[3] As we examine it and the themes introduced thereby in the characters' dialogue (meaninglessness, the inaccessibility of feeling, the absurdity of life, etc.), we move beyond the film's language to its intertwining with image and then to the body whose material participation in the filmic experience is always something other than merely visible.

Hurlyburly has a loosely structured narrative organized around a series of vignettes primarily involving Eddie (Sean Penn) and his male friends and taking place in the chic minimalist condominium shared by Eddie and Mickey (Kevin Spacey). It has an ensemble cast composed of Penn, Spacey, Robin Wright Penn (Darlene), Chazz Palminteri (Phil), Garry Shandling (Artie), Anna Paquin (Donna) and Meg Ryan (Bonnie). The film begins in the Hollywood Hills, "a little while ago,"[4] develops its characters and context and then jumps ahead one year for its final scenes. Except for Donna, a teenage waif who comes to Eddie and Mickey as a gift from Artie, all the characters are involved in the entertainment industry. Eddie and Mickey are casting agents, clearly near the top of

this rigidly hierarchical world; Artie is a successful but insecure producer; Phil, Eddie's pal, is a failed actor, with a criminal past and a tendency toward violence; Darlene, Eddie's love interest, who has also slept with Mickey, is a costume designer and Bonnie is a stripper at the margins of the Hollywood game. Most of the film revolves around the guys partying, their endless verbal sparring, narcissistic monologues, and their complaints about women. Mickey is "having a break" from his family and intends to return to his wife. Phil abuses his wife; they divorce, but eventually have a baby, despite Phil's reservations; finally his wife kicks him out for good. Eddie and Darlene have a relationship that doesn't seem to satisfy either of them, since they are each "their own greatest distraction" and Darlene seems to have a continuing interest in Mickey. The pivotal off-screen event is Phil's suicide, who drives off a cliff on Mulhulland Drive. This event hastens Eddie's breakdown and brings the film to its final scene.

Arguably, *Hurlyburly* thematizes the relation between the sexes and the duality of thinking and feeling that is typically mapped onto gender. Such a theme is in accord with much of what Rabe says himself about the piece, whose working title was "Guy's Play." Rabe was motivated to explore the confusion that men were feeling between traditional expectations that they control their feelings and think, and new expectations that they feel and express feelings. He says:

> It was a confusing melee of contradictory exhortations, a great many of which, both past and present, came from women. On the one hand these men had the admonitions and codes of their childhoods, while on the other there were their companions and contemporaries, who, awakened by the Women's Liberation Movement, were now pointing angrily to claim obvious rights for which they had, to all appearances, in the past lacked all desire. (362)

The film shows men in the midst of crisis, men who are angry, violent, cut off from their feelings to varying degrees, men who abuse women in a variety of ways, hurl insults at each other, and are absorbed by their particular narcissistic preoccupations. These are men who come quite close to voicing Rabe's motivating insight – that the Women's Liberation Movement, and the particular women in their lives, had "flung them out from the haven of their sexual and marital context" (361). Such a reading captures the perspective of the characters, and perhaps of Rabe, but seems inadequate for understanding the situation that the film presents to us. The outmoded notion of "the war between the sexes" explains little of the source of the conflicts shown in the film, in which men *and* women, while clearly having different levels of access to the mechanisms of power, are equally cut off from their feelings, equally self-destructive and equally unmoored from themselves and others. It is, indeed, precisely this theme of the duality of thinking and feeling that is the source of the grab bag of clichés that limits these characters and shapes their shiny, but barren, world.

Consider one of the movie's most wretched scenes. During yet another night of drinking and drugging, the "guys" reminisce about the time that they greeted a visiting celebrity actor at the airport with a limousine and a complimentary blowjob from Bonnie. They laugh at the thought of the celebrity's surprise and Bonnie's utter helplessness before the celebrity image become flesh. The unseemly memory of the fact that Bonnie's young daughter was present during this episode and deeply traumatized ("the kid was catatonic") is something Eddie and Mickey argue over as Mickey attempts to deny or mitigate the despicable nature of their actions ("I was personally blotto"). We see emotion flash across their faces, but it has no currency in their exchange, and the fact that they are once again setting Bonnie up for degradation is a connection they seem to miss altogether. As for Bonnie, she too has feelings, as she informs us, but as with the other characters her feelings remain a discrete part of her "inner emotional subjective experiences" with no effect on her actions, as the sacrifice of her daughter's well-being indicates. Women have a particular function in the imaginations of these men as tokens of a lost or hoped for bliss, but the real flesh-and-blood women in the film are suffering the same malaise as their male counterparts.

Though the characters are preoccupied with the conflict between feeling and thinking and, in the case of Eddie, with "getting in touch" with their feelings, this does not bring them, or us, very far in understanding their predicament. The problem with the men in the movie is not that they don't have feelings – all of Rabe's "guys" have feelings – but that these feelings are privatized, inaccessible and without effect. The characters do not examine or interrogate their feelings, considering them discrete immediate facts of experience, and hence are not able to use them as factors in their reasoning or as guides to actions. As the likes of Martha Nussbaum and Antonio Demasio have argued recently, feeling and thinking are inextricably linked and sound behavioral choices require attention to emotion.[5] The preoccupation of the characters with emotion is a marker of their refusal to think. The guys laugh it off any time anything that might provoke reflection arises, snort another line, have another drink. It seems plausible that these feelings that they have, but which remain private and inaccessible, are impulses to think simultaneously emerging and being squelched.

While the dichotomy between thinking and feeling is a cliché that traps the characters in their state of confusion and fuels their misogyny, the problems it presents are critical for understanding their situation. Feelings are required for moral action; they are a powerful ground of our sense of connection to others and to the world beyond us. When they are privatized, as they are for these characters, they fail to inform their actions. The characters have no sense, as Eddie says, of how things "pertain to them." The characters are isolated with feelings that seem little more than nagging sensations that they could do without. In light of this, Eddie's intuition that he needs to "get in touch with his feelings" is a powerful tug in the right direction. Despite (or because of) the fact that Eddie is the character most evidently in crisis, he is the closest to Deleuze's "philosophical reversal." Teresa Brennan says in *Exhausting Modernity*:

> affects are especially important as a category in which some of the original indissolubility of

thought and substance are retained; they keep the tie to matter, as emotions are indubitably corporeal, at the same time as they reflect ideational responses; we can regard them as the slower motion residue of the original connection between thought and substance. (67)

Feelings, hence, are one avenue for "plunging into" the body. They are the corporeal corollary of thinking. To the extent that the characters refuse to give currency to their feelings, to the extent that they regard their feelings as private commodities, they never begin to think. The characters may think that they are thinking, rather than feeling, but what the film makes clear is that above all they are just talking and their talk is nothing but a "hurlyburly." And it is Eddie who suffers this circumstance most acutely.

At one point in *Hurlyburly* Eddie reflects upon his linguistic predicament, saying "I know what I'm saying. I don't know what I mean, but I know what I'm saying." This is, of course, the opposite of what we expect: regardless of theories of language which suggest otherwise, the subjective experience of speaking to another lends itself to the feeling that meaning is prior to or concurrent with its expression. But Eddie *is* saying what he means here. He and other of the characters in *Hurlyburly* know what they and their interlocutors are saying: their words are calculated and often exhibit a nuance and subtle attention to shadings of signification. But language fails these characters as a source of expression and as communication. It is at once a vast system of signification and utterly meaningless.

While theories of language since Saussure and Wittgenstein have decentered the subject with regard to language itself, all such theories nonetheless acknowledge that for language to function the speaking subject must appropriate it for his or her own purposes; but the language of *Hurlyburly* barely even allows the appearance of communication and the characters struggle continuously with its inadequacy. While the language of *Hurlyburly* appears to its characters to be a "hurlyburly," it has not become mere noise, commotion or empty signifiers. Rather, if we entertain Giorgio Agamben's suggestion, we

could say that language in *Hurlyburly* has attained the condition of spectacle. For Agamben, in *The Coming Community*, the legacy of Guy Debord and the French Situationists, the theorists of the "Society of the Spectacle," is the recognition that the spectacle is language itself. Agamben presses Debord's analysis to its furthest degree.

For Debord, in societies such as ours all of life "presents itself as an immense accumulation of *spectacles*. All that once was directly lived has become mere representations" (12). Our society produces a separation of people from their own lives, from their own experience and from each other, in compensation for which the spectacle provides an ersatz commonality within the realm of representation. For Debord the spectacle was mediated by mass-media images, that carnival of representation that distracts us from the poverty of everyday life. There is much in *Hurlyburly* that suggests a society of the spectacle, beginning with the film's setting, Hollywood, and the significance it gives celebrity and image ("I'm a real person, not some goddamn TV image," Eddie tells us). The mass media are an omnipresent part of Eddie's life and a marker of his confusion. When the film begins, Eddie is verbally raging at his TV. We see its images crosscut with his nightmare come true, his best friend and his love interest in bed. The TV is prominently placed, in the American fashion, in the living room where it remains on during much of the film. Later, when Eddie is spiraling to collapse, and holding forth to Bonnie, he rails about how TV news brings him terrible pain, but he is unable to discern what is true or how the horror that he views pertains to him.[6] Eddie's final collapse is indicated visually by acceleration through his many cable TV channels, a phantasmagoria of the disturbing preoccupations of late modern life. In all of this, Eddie displays the dislocating effects of the society of the spectacle.

Agamben's claim is that the society that finds a commonality within the spectacle is a society that has experienced "the expropriation of human sociality itself":

capitalism (or any other name one wants to give the process that today dominates world history) [is] directed not only toward the expropriation of productive activity, but also and principally toward the alienation of language itself, of the very linguistic communicative nature of humans, of that *logos* which one of Heraclitus' fragments identified as the Common. The extreme form of this expropriation of the Common is the spectacle, that is, the politics we live in. (80)

There is a commonality, a system that binds us together, but no community, not even the false community of Debord's spectacle. Language is stripped of its lived features. It still provides the means of interaction, but does so for the sake of a system that is no longer identifiably human. If "we are constituted in language in a continuous becoming that we bring forth with others,"[7] the situation that Agamben describes would be not only the death of community but also of the functional self. Eddie shows us both the requirement of linguistic social interaction to produce a world for the self as well as the crisis its breakdown produces: he tries to talk to Mickey about his feelings for the woman they share in order to develop the shared terrain of their friendship. Mickey doesn't want to talk, but Eddie defends their conversation on the grounds that it "is just [he] trying to maintain a viable relationship with reality" instead of getting lost in some "solitary paranoid fantasy system of my totally unfounded and idiosyncratic invention."

The extent to which language has ceased to belong to its speakers in *Hurlyburly* is evident in the way that semantic arguments substitute for communicative exchanges. The characters' exchanges often display careful attention to each other's words, not in order to understand but rather to develop a strategic response. The effect is an endless battering of each other that hardens their separation. Consider the following exchange, which occurs after Mickey has mocked Eddie's reaction to Phil's death:

Eddie: "Keep your sarcasm to yourself."

Mickey: "What sarcasm? ... I've indulged in nothing even remotely sarcastic here, and I want that understood. If I've been flip, it's to put some humor into what could be totally and utterly morbid."

Eddie: "'Flip' is 'sarcastic.'"

Mickey: "'Sarcastic' is 'heavy.' It's mean. Funny sure, but mean. I do both, but this was flip."

The exchange amounts to semantic hair-splitting, but what is really at stake is the ability to control the moment and, more fundamentally, but out of the grasp of their language, their respective relationship to Phil, their understanding of the meaning of his death and their own friendship.

Language here calls for decoding and interpretation as a system independent of its speakers. While this work of decoding demands intelligence and sophistication, it presupposes a self wholly isolated from the other and goes along with a paranoid reading of the motives of other speakers. These characters do not so much communicate as desperately seek linguistic clues as to each other's meanings. This is the end of meaning, however, as it ceases to provide what Eddie calls "a viable relationship to reality"; it is unable to bring forth a world, as the connection of language to context, to life, to purpose, is severed.

In one scene, Eddie becomes angry with his girlfriend, Darlene, and breaks up with her (and abandons her on the side of the road) when she has no preference as to whether they eat at a French or a Chinese restaurant. Eddie decodes their exchange, concluding that she is incapable of loving him exclusively. He may be right, but his interpretation and ensuing anger bypass their relation as interactive selves by focusing on the traces of such in a frozen system of language.

Phil, who is portrayed as inarticulate and violent, also views language as a code, but a code he cannot decode, a fact not unrelated to his failed acting career. Eddie sets up Bonnie on a date with Phil. As they are driving around, Bonnie suggests they go to her place. Phil says that he is hungry and so Bonnie suggests that they go to Jack-in-the-box. Phil asks if that is code for something and, becoming increasingly paranoid about Bonnie's quite banal suggestions, ends up yelling that he doesn't understand the code and ejecting her from the moving car.

Perhaps the most extraordinary example of language's existence merely as code comes when Phil has killed himself and left behind a cryptic note for Eddie: "the guy who dies in an accident understands the nature of destiny." Rather than seeking a context for understanding the note in their relationship or in his knowledge of Phil, Eddie begins frantically to search the words for a secret meaning, to crack the code. He begins to count letters, to look the words up in a dictionary, to consider whether it is an anagram. The madness of his search for a code is a measure of his love for Phil, a fact that utterly eludes him.

The idea of the spectacle is linked to what Laura Marks, following Deleuze and Guattari, calls "optical visuality" (162). Optical visuality is vision as we habitually conceive of it: it "sees things from enough distance to perceive them as distinct forms in deep space" and "depends upon a separation between the viewing subject and the object" (162). Agamben's claim that language has become spectacle, like Debord's society of the spectacle, depends upon the perceptual commonplace of optical visuality for its plausibility, elaborating it as a metaphor delineating a realm of representation cut loose from its origins in life.

Drazen is able to underscore the spectacle of Rabe's language by using techniques that reinforce our perceptual habit. The camera focuses obsessively on our characters and we are called to study them with a clinical detachment. The camera never lingers on objects or on sensory experience, eschewing Marks' "haptic visuality" (xi), visuality that mimetically evokes a tactile relation to the image, or any evocation of the embodied sensorium. While we have the visual clues of sexual intimacy, we see little of its caresses and all evidence indicates that the contact is perfunctory. (This is true not only in the case of "meaningless" sex but also in the case of Eddie and his girlfriend. After a lengthy separation, now reunited, we see the couple in bed. Eddie takes a phone call and jumps up to respond, already apparently forgetting what he was doing, and waddles off to the bathroom, pants still around his ankles.) Moreover, the quick

tempo of the editing is such that our eyes never settle upon anything that elicits a non-visual sensory relationship to the image.

Drazen captures a number of perfect static images that crystallize the relationship among the characters. In a particularly effective one, Eddie is lying underneath the glass-topped coffee table that serves so well for laying out lines of coke. Artie is peering through the table and the coke at Eddie, growing frustrated at Eddie's inability to appreciate that Artie is angry with him. As Artie moves away, we see Mickey peering down at the two of them from the second floor railing. Later, Mickey further clarifies where Phil fits into this visual economy by saying that the reason Eddie likes Phil is that no matter how low Eddie sinks, Phil will be lower. Eddie could be "crawling along the sidewalk," he says, and "Phil is going to be on his belly in the gutter looking up in wide-eyed admiration."

While Drazen confirms our habits of perception to underscore the spectacle, an attention to the sensory situation of the cinema subverts its claim on us. While optical visuality produces the effect of a view from nowhere, we know there is no such view, that sensory experience cannot ultimately be separated from embodiment, and hence that the sight of objects in space and the separation of subject and object in cinema is an incomplete account of vision per se. To the degree that our view of the spectacle depends upon an elaboration of optical visuality, it too is incomplete. It is in an attempt to capture the complexity of our sensory relationship to cinema that Vivian Sochack, in *The Address of the Eye*, calls film a "viewing view/viewed view" (22). It has, she says, a "double embodiment": it depends upon the viewing subject, embodied and enworlded, for whom it is "a viewed view" (23). But it presents to that spectator a view that is already embodied, in the sense that it presents an embodied and enworlded vision, "a viewing view."

With this reflection in mind, we can revisit the image discussed above that so well crystallized the relation among our characters. This image was able to accomplish such by drawing us, embodied and enworlded and yet unconsciously so, into relation with these men whose separation we are able to see only upon the ground of their evident and constant embodied and enworlded interrelation. The achievement of film, in Sobchack's words, is that it:

thus transposes what would otherwise be the invisible, individual, and intrasubjective privacy of direct experience as it is embodied into the visible, public, and intersubjective sociality of a language of direct embodied experience – a language that not only refers to direct experience but also uses direct experience as its mode of reference. (11)

We see the characters' separation, but we see that separation upon the ground of their interrelation. So, Drazen presents us with the spectacle, but also with the cinematic experience that implicitly subverts it.

What is true of visuality and visual representation – that it always comes with and depends upon body and world – is true of all representation. In the quotation above, Sobchack is right to point out cinema's unique ability to apprehend what often goes unthought in ordinary experience, but even the "intrasubjective privacy of direct experience" depends upon the world that we bring forth together as linguistic and socially interactive beings. The idea of "direct experience" involves again the forgetting of our embodied and enworlded condition. The spectacle is not, nor can it be, pure representation, the literal "expropriation of human sociality." Regardless of its seeming transcendence of all things human, there is always a mimetic trace in representation: even though cinema is ostensibly an audiovisual medium, it allows us, as Marks shows, to participate with all our senses. We "watch" movies with our whole bodies. What the spectacle is, then, if not literally the "expropriation of human sociality," is the furthest degree of forgetting of the body and its material interconnection with other bodies and the world we bring forth together.

There is nothing about the intersubjective experience of phenomenology, or the mimetic trace of representation, however, that precludes the social atomism that we see in the film. Intersubjectivity and mimesis are not "human sociality" per se. Nor does the fact of the ma-

terial condition of representation necessarily change the violence of its appearance of separation and its effects on us. But such do suggest the persistence of the basis for connection, give credence to the characters' recurring flashes of emotion despite attempts to deny them and explain their need for anesthetization to continue to forget. But why does this matter? What is changed by our attempt to "plunge into the body" with thought? It may seem that nothing is changed. What Agamben refers to as "the politics we live in" is not transformed by this "philosophical reversal." Such is work that remains, now more than ever, to be done. But attempts to think the body do constitute significant change. If our world is one that is "brought forth together" and thinking the body shows how that is so, this certainly seems to expose as false the inevitability of a system that depends upon the invisibility of the material conditions of its production. For Eddie, it makes the difference between life and death, between the impossibility of living in a world which doesn't "pertain to him" and his recognition that, although he "has a lot to learn," it is possible with others to make some sense of it.

Agamben, it needs to be said, is himself not without hope, but his view leads him to a hope that goes beyond the unthought to the unthinkable. "In the spectacle," he says, "our own linguistic nature comes back to us inverted. This is why ... the spectacle retains something like a positive possibility that can be used against it" (80). Language that cannot reveal anything because it has lost its communicativity, eventually "reveals the nothingness of all things" and, hence, threatens the very system that depends upon it (Agamben 82). What comes next, according to Agamben, we cannot say. He heralds the rising of a new community, a community of "whatever singularity," beyond identity and identification (ibid. 1). This gesture celebrates, thereby, the end of thinking in a way that is evocative and chastening to intellectual pretension (always a temptation), but offers us nothing to go on. Thinking, as indeed Agamben's example shows us, is what we do. Ironically, it is perhaps film that shows us this better than philosophy, which is always in danger of becoming its own "hurlyburly." In *Hurlyburly*'s final scene, Eddie faces "the nothingness of everything." He is ready to cease thinking and feeling altogether and submit to death, but unlike Phil, who we may imagine discovered his body at the moment of its dissolution, Eddie, in that moment between life and death, rediscovers his own materiality and the materiality of the world, which buoy him back into life.

After Phil's funeral, in a drugged stupor and suicidal, Eddie plunges into the swimming pool. This nihilistic collapse, however, proves to be a tactile immersion that floods the screen with an evocation of the sensorium that Drazen has not permitted hitherto in the film. What seems like the end of Eddie, then, is really an opportunity to slip beneath the surface of the spectacle. ("When the hurlyburly's done. When the battle's lost and won."[8]) We see Eddie's face in extreme close-up under the water, eyes open, still mouthing a cigarette, bubbles of air leave his lungs as his body is buoyed by the water. The anticipated crash is more of an embrace as Eddie discovers slowly that there is more to bodily death (and to life) than the collapse of meaning. Then we hear something, not quite yet a voice, begin to coalesce into words. Donna has returned to the house and is hailing Eddie from above the water.

In many ways, Donna is the antithesis of the powerful guys in the story. When we meet her she has been homeless and is now in the grips of men who couldn't care less about her well-being; nevertheless, her greatest concern is to use the pool. After she swims she goes from man to man like a wet puppy looking for tactile comfort. Donna is a cautionary figure; she appears to be a creature of the body, not subject to the order of the spectacle, but she is another of its victims. Her worldview seems to be a challenge to the spectacle, but is a distorted effect of it. If the men are all ego, narcissism and control, Donna is egoless, with no clear boundaries or sense of autonomy. When Eddie talks to her about his inability to understand the meaning of things and how they pertain to him, Donna replies with a radically reductive materialism telling him that things do not pertain to him, that the universe is indifferent to him, that a flow interrelates all

things without distinction. Her sense of the flow of life is a counterbalance to Eddie's atomic self-absorption, but for Donna nothing really matters, everything is undifferentiated, a view that is the simple inversion of Eddie's view that all representations are equally indifferent to him. Donna is cautionary, then, in the sense that her engagement with body, with materiality, is as simple undifferentiated presence. She forgets the subject altogether – what Maurice Merleau-Ponty called a "fold" in being[9] – and doesn't appreciate the degree to which we together, through our linguistic social interaction, bring forth the world. As a result she has become merely an object for herself and others. Nevertheless, Donna has a sense of what is important and is able to lead Eddie away from the brink, because, as she shows him, "it's great when people know what each other are talking about."

So, when Eddie surfaces upon hearing the sound of Donna's voice, what follows is a simple, ordinary conversation: that is, an exchange the likes of which we haven't seen in the film. Donna asks him about his day and Eddie says he was at Phil's funeral. "So that's why you are such a wreck, Eddie," she says. Eddie looks a little confused, as if the connection between his physical and emotional state and Phil's death had not occurred to him, but Donna persists. She asks about Phil's funeral. At first Eddie merely describes what one would have seen at the funeral. But when Donna asks (repeatedly) if it was sad, his tone changes. He seems to experience the funeral in relating it to Donna. We saw the funeral: Eddie, like the other guys, was standing alone, away from the crowd, stoic, affectless in dark glasses. But he tells Donna:

> The Priest could say anything, a lot of nice things; sad things; nothin' … this guy was singing with a beautiful voice and you couldn't pick out the words even. You just heard this high, beautiful, sad sound, this human sound and we would all start to cry along with him.

Instead of the hurlyburly of language from which human sociality has been expropriated, Eddie, faced with the material fact of Phil's death, hears in the singing a "human sound" and he is moved. His attention is diverted from meaning to its embodied source. This moment is significant not because the sound, by focusing Eddie's attention upon sensory experience and affect rather than representation, is closer to an unalienated human presence or body per se, but because Eddie requires this circuitous route from the unthought back to thought, to language, to life. It is not merely the human sound that saves Eddie, nor is it simply the water's embrace of his forgotten body, but the simple conversation with Donna as well, the recovery of linguistic social interaction capable of bringing forth a world which is not solitary, paranoid, dead. For those of us who watch *Hurlyburly*, Eddie's journey provokes a "philosophical reversal," the intertwining of word and image forcing us to remember our fragile, shared embodiment at a time in history which makes TV entertainment of global disaster.

notes

This paper has benefited from the comments of *Angelaki*'s anonymous reviewers.

1 I am not claiming that this paper represents Deleuze's view of cinema or of body. And indeed to the degree that Deleuzians explicitly reject phenomenology, I am working against the tradition tied to his work (cf. Olkowski). Rather, I take inspiration from Deleuze's insistence that cinema inform philosophy and from the quotation serving as this paper's epigraph, which evokes the spirit of recent interest in thinking the body including, but not restricted to, Deleuze's own.

2 This paper owes a great deal to the work of Laura Marks whose loving attention to the materiality of film and the filmic experience I consider exemplary. This last body, the materiality of the film, is something I consider significant to the issues raised in this paper, but cannot pursue here (cf. Marks).

3 Apparently for many, however, it requires turning away. When I have mentioned working on this film, many people have expressed disgust

with it and a surprising number said that they left the theater before the film's end.

4 This quotation, and all further quotations without page references, come from the film's dialogue, much of which was improvised by the actors.

5 The claim that feelings inform reason has been part of a certain strand of feminist criticism for decades, and now seems to be a commonplace in various discourses: in ethics (Nussbaum's *Upheavals of Thought* insists upon the cognitive content of emotions and the necessity of processing emotion for ethical and political thought), in cognitive science (Demasio makes a convincing case that emotion is necessary for rational behavior), and even popular culture (cf. Daniel Goleman's *Emotional Intelligence* and its various spin-offs).

6 *Hurlyburly* seems like a timely film, not only because of the extreme form of the Spectacle it presents but also because the news that disturbs Eddie is of Gulf War I, weapons of mass destruction, and the sowing of domestic fear through perverse preoccupation with horrible crimes and bizarre cults.

7 I take this quotation from Humberto Maturana and Francisco Varela (234–35); they have a keen sense of language within its evolutionary and biological context, which ties it closely to embodiment.

8 Rabe talks about how he discovered the validation for the play's title when he found this line in Shakespeare's *Macbeth* (Rabe 371).

9 Maurice Merleau-Ponty, *Phenomenology of Perception* 215.

bibliography

Agamben, Giorgio. *The Coming Community*. Trans. Michael Hardt. Minneapolis: U of Minnesota P, 1993.

Brennan, Teresa. *Exhausting Modernity*. New York: Routledge, 2000.

Debord, Guy. *Society of the Spectacle*. Trans. Donald Nicholson-Smith. Cambridge, MA: MIT P, 1995.

Deleuze, Gilles. *Cinema 2: The Time-Image*. Trans.

Hugh Tomlinson and Robert Galeta. Minneapolis: U of Minnesota P, 1989.

Demasio, Antonio. *Descartes' Error: Emotion, Reason, and the Human Brain*. New York: Avon, 1994.

Goleman, Daniel. *Emotional Intelligence*. New York: Bantam, 1997.

Hurlyburly. Dir. Anthony Drazan. With Sean Penn, Kevin Spacey, Robin Wright Penn, Chaz Palminteri, Carry Shandling, Anna Paquin and Meg Ryan. Fine Line Features, 1998.

Marks, Laura. *The Skin of the Film: Intercultural Cinema, Embodiment, and the Senses*. Durham, NC: Duke UP, 2000.

Maturana, Humberto and Francisco Varela. *The Tree of Knowledge: The Biological Roots of Human Understanding*. Trans. Robert Paolucci. Boston: Shambhala, 1998.

Merleau-Ponty, Maurice. *Phenomenology of Perception*. Trans. Colin Smith. New York: Routledge, 1962.

Nussbaum, Martha. *Upheavals of Thought*. Cambridge: Cambridge UP, 2001.

Olkowski, Dorothea. *Gilles Deleuze and the Ruin of Representation*. Berkeley: U of California P, 1999.

Rabe, David. *Hurlyburly and Those the River Keeps*. New York: Grove, 1995.

Sobchack, Vivian. *The Address of the Eye: A Phenomenology of Film Experience*. Princeton: Princeton UP, 1992.

Elizabeth Walden
Department of English and Cultural Studies
Bryant College
1150 Douglas Pike
Smithfield, RI 02917-1284
USA
E-mail: ewalden@bryant.edu

Routledge
Taylor & Francis Group

ANGELAKI
journal of the theoretical humanities
volume 9 number 3 december 2004

Carroll's uniqueness is to have allowed nothing to pass through sense, but to have played out everything in nonsense, since the diversity of nonsenses is enough to give an account of the entire universe, its terrors as well as its glories: the depth, the surface, and the volume or rolled surface.

Gilles Deleuze, "Lewis Carroll," Essays Critical and Clinical

alan lopez

DELEUZE WITH CARROLL
schizophrenia and simulacrum and the philosophy of lewis carroll's nonsense[1]

With the notable exception of Gilles Deleuze's famous prolegomenon on Lewis Carroll's *Alice* books, *Logique du sens* (1969), in which Deleuze explores the intersections between sense and nonsense around the axes of theory and philosophy, there has been relatively scant attention paid to the philosophical questions raised in Carroll's *Alice* books, especially around the subject of nonsense.[2] Indeed, there are arguably only two other works that could be said to offer a sustained philosophical treatment of *Alice* and nonsense, namely Peter Heath's *The Philosopher's Alice* and Jean-Jacques Lecercle's *The Philosophy of Nonsense*. At the same time, it is perhaps because of the pivotal space nonsense *has* occupied within conventional and theoretical readings of *Alice* that it has found itself interrogated within literary studies as representative of that common ground in which literature and theory meet. Structuring this exemplarity is what Jean-Jacques Lecercle's book refers to as "anachrony," an obvious play on the word "anachronism." Here, "anachrony" refers to the uncanny way in which nineteenth-century Victorian nonsense could be said to anticipate (and thus have within itself) the still-inchoate seeds of philosophy and postmodernism. This is indeed the project of Lecercle's book. As Lecercle writes: "the declared object of this book [*Philosophy of Nonsense*] is the intuitions of Victorian nonsense writers – how literary practice anticipates theory" (166; hereafter PN). Yet, for Lecercle, philosophy is likewise indebted to literature for *its* construction of the object of nonsense. Lecercle is perhaps nowhere more clear on this dual indebtedness between nonsense and philosophy than in his description of nonsense *as* that (dialectical) site of intersection between literature and philosophy. As Lecercle notes, following up on the above proposition, "I have also attempted to use Victorian literary texts to read philosophical texts, so that the interpretation of philosophical texts in and

ISSN 0969-725X print/ISSN 1469-2899 online/04/030101–20 © 2004 Taylor & Francis Ltd and the Editors of *Angelaki*
DOI: 10.1080/0969725042000307664

through nonsense is given anachronically, in advance – an interpretation of unwritten texts" (PN 223). Of interest to me here is the latter half of Lecercle's proposition, namely "the interpretation of unwritten texts," the determinations of which are perhaps found around Gabrielle Schwab's claim that Carroll anticipates and perhaps marks "the beginning of those far-reaching challenges to our cultural notions of mimesis and representation which culminate in what we have come to call the simulacrum of postmodernism" ("Nonsense and Metacommunications" 177). (While we might debate whether Carroll's works alone announce what we have come to identify as our postmodern condition – an assertion that, while common within traditional readings of Carroll, can perhaps also be addressed around Lawrence Sterne's *Tristam Shandy*, or Robert Browning's "Child Roland" – I would nonetheless like to underline Schwab's proposition as the guiding principle structuring Lecercle's (and other commentators') ostensibly theoretical interventions around the question of an anticipated or missed encounter between Carroll and postmodernism.) What Lecercle's and Schwab's interventions arguably bring into sight is that earlier question posed by Peter Heath exactly twenty years prior, specifically the question of locating in the *Alice* books an "indigenous philosophy attributable to Carroll himself" (*The Philosopher's Alice* 8). Though inevitably answering the question in the negative, Heath nevertheless underscores (if not exaggerates) Lecercle's anachrony when he wryly claims, in a rehearsal of Humpty Dumpty's earlier aphorism,[3] that the *Alice* books "can explain all the philosophies that ever were invented, and a good many that hadn't been invented when it was written" (8).

What I might underline as symptomatic about the above readings is the way in which they foreground the anticipatory character of nonsense but nonetheless foreclose a space of inquiry into that search for a critical subject within the *Alice* books. We might read this omission as a symptom of an ironic reluctance to question the character of the "indigenous philosophy attributed to Carroll." Or, in more emphatic

terms, as reluctance to identify a critical discourse within the texts, perhaps out of fear *of performing* a vulgar anachronism. Over such readings, I would like to suggest that a more productive examination of the question of a critical subject in *Alice* would occur in the context of the complex negotiations between the madness of nonsense and the epistemic and ontological doubt grounded in the simulacrum. By taking up the *Alice* books in the context of the discourse of postmodernism and its correlative counterpart in the simulacrum, I hope to put at stake the *philosophical* determinations of what Schwab identifies as those "affinities between nonsense and schizophrenia" (168). It is in the context of this convergence between nonsense and schizophrenia that, I want to suggest, is foregrounded the above-mentioned neglected and, heretofore, minor philosophical orientation to *Alice* and nonsense. By way of an investigation of the latter half of this above proposition, I might underline Lecercle's claim in *Philosophy of Nonsense* that postmodernism and nonsense are the (retroactive) inheritors of a certain tradition in philosophy, namely the "philosophy of mind" and therein that area "concerned with [the spatio-temporal determinations] of personal identity" – an empiricist tradition most notably delineated around the writings of John Locke and David Hume (PN 162).[4] At stake in this reformulation, then, is an attempt to read the *Alice* books philosophically but, more importantly, an attempt to recover (or uncover) a *specific* tradition of philosophical inquiry performed in the *Alice* books. As I will elaborate below, at issue is the opening of that space where the anticipatory and philosophical character of Carroll's nonsense converge – a convergence that I will argue may be read under the sign of Descartes's famous proposition over the "proof" of the *cogito* and the "I-think," namely that search for truths "clear and distinct" (*Meditations* 9).

The following reading thus proceeds as an attempt to foreground a certain, though marginal, tradition of reading the *Alice* books, a reading predicated upon the assumption that there is, as Lecercle words it, an "implicit philosophy in nonsense … a philosophy in act or *in nuce*" (PN 4). I suggest this reading for three independent reasons, which I might summarize here. First, and following Lecercle, if we begin with the assumption that nonsense *is* unconsciously philosophical, we may perhaps understand why traditional and even ostensibly theoretical readings of *Alice* have missed, and indeed sought, that philosophical character of nonsense within its more *conventional* or *traditional* modes of expression, for instance analytic philosophy, philology, and linguistics.[5] Second, we may understand the failure of traditional approaches to discern those philosophical contours conditioning wonderland's nonsensical games. That is to say, we may understand the failure of such approaches to discern the philosophical problems posed by the *Alice* books, problems which arguably achieve their greatest articulation in the form of a rehearsal of the Cartesian mind–body problem and the question therein of an immediate coincidence between mind and body. Finally, we may discern a critical subject within *Alice*, one whose positivity qua schizo could be said to be produced through the confluence of the above-mentioned axes of madness, doubt, and simulacrum.[6] To address this question, I will juxtapose Lecercle's reading of *Alice* with Gilles Deleuze's reading of *Alice* in *Logic of Sense* and *Essays Critical and Clinical*, taking up this juxtaposition between Deleuze and Lecercle as exemplary of a divergence in tendencies between literature and philosophy over the status of nonsense, particularly as this division is figured within Carroll's *Alice* books. In *Logic of Sense* and *Essays Critical and Clinical*, though elsewhere as well,[7] Deleuze cites Antonin Artaud and Lewis Carroll as exemplary of these two opposed treatments of nonsense. By taking up the question of nonsense between these two tendencies in the context of *Alice*, however, and particularly around the writings of Deleuze, I hope to disclose a certain *affinity* between Carroll's and Artaud's treatments of nonsense – a reading perhaps provocative in its opposition to Deleuze's own reading of Artaud and Carroll in the "13th Series of the Schizophrenic and the Little Girl" chapter in

Logic of Sense, where, Deleuze tells us: "Carroll and Artaud do not encounter each other" and, in fact, may be "oppose[d] point for point" (93, 91; hereafter LS). Taking as my point of departure this potential site of disagreement with Deleuze over the status of nonsense between Carroll and Artaud, therefore – a division perhaps also rendered as the division of nonsense between linguistics and philosophy – I will address the *Alice* books as the site of a *convergence* between these two seemingly opposed tendencies toward nonsense, principally linguistics and philosophy, a convergence consequently understood as twofold in the context of the *Alice* books. On the one hand, it is a convergence around surface and depth and, on the other, around thought and affect, the latter categories being the two formally opposed determinations of nonsense qua surface and depth.

II

Before I turn to an examination of the status of a critical subject within the *Alice* books, however, I must first explicate the above proposition that there exists within literary studies (or philosophical interventions, for that matter) a certain hesitancy to identify a critical discourse within *Alice*. More precisely, I would like to address the condition of this reluctance, in particular, *why* a critical subject has yet to be discerned within *Alice* and nonsense. Given the above discussion, we might speculate that structuring this question of "why" is a certain misrecognition of nonsense, one that always puts at stake the character of nonsense: its ostensible lightness, its intangible, impalpable, ethereal form. Put differently, reluctance to locate a critical subject within *Alice* may be understood as symptomatic of the very lightness of nonsense, its non-theoretical and ostensibly benign character (where "benign" refers to the linguistic and philological games and constructions often enacted under the aegis of "nonsense"). Understandably, and perhaps arguably, it is this lightness which could be said to *cover over* those philosophical lines along which a critical subject may be discerned. This misrecognition is highlighted within a return to Lecercle's reading of Carroll. Lecercle, as I have suggested above, argues for a close propinquity between *Alice* and philosophy (or philosophy and nonsense). Or, in different terms, Lecercle discerns no clear point of termination between linguistics and philosophy. As Lecercle writes, the "attitude of philosophers towards nonsense does not differ from that of linguists ... philosophers, both analytic and continental, seem to find reading nonsense texts rewarding" (PN 162). For Lecercle, then, there is a sharing of tendencies or interests between linguists and philosophers over the status of nonsense, such that nonsense texts "raise questions that fascinate [analytic and continental] philosophers" (PN 162). That Lecercle does suggest such a close, almost liminal, relationship between nonsense and philosophy should not surprise us, for it is that liminality which, Lecercle suggests, conditions the importation of the *Alice* books within a philosophical context. As Lecercle puts it, reflecting on that liminality, the *Alice* books "are plastic enough to be inserted in the philosophical tradition ... intuitive enough to enable us to raise questions about the present state of the art – even perhaps to go over to the other side" (163). The "other side," here, is Lecercle's taciturn reference to Continental philosophy. Accordingly, we might underline this passage as exemplary of Lecercle's anachronic reading of *Alice*, namely a reading which posits the *Alice* books as if in anticipation of that postmodern dissolution of the subject and object relation, a certain eschatological point at which the *Alice* texts and philosophy coincide with each other.

If we then take Lecercle at his *word*, that is, if we take at face value his suggestion that nonsense anticipates questions for both analytic and Continental philosophy, where what is anticipated is the possibility that philosophy may "have something to learn from a consideration of the workings of nonsense texts" (PN 162), I believe we would expect to discern within Lecercle's intervention an attempt to bring into relief what have heretofore been understood as the marginal dimensions of *Alice* and nonsense (i.e.,

the dimensions of theory and Continental philosophy). I would suggest, however, that it is exactly the opposite which we find at work in Lecercle's reading. Though I grant Lecercle's illuminating reading of the affinity between nonsense and philosophy, I would critique Lecercle for his failure to carry out his announced proposition: an identification of both the analytic *and* Continental questions raised by nonsense. We might also read this division as existing along the lines of linguistics and philology on the one hand and postmodernism or philosophy on the other, with the suggestion that it is the latter half of the equation that is neglected by Lecercle. I would argue, in other words, that Lecercle ironically marginalizes the very dimensions he was to highlight: the philosophical dimensions of nonsense, those in keeping with the Continental tradition. This marginalization, I want to suggest, is done unconsciously, carried out in light of Lecercle's failure to discern any substantive difference between linguistics and philosophy (particularly around the subject of *Alice* and nonsense), and no substantive distinction between the "questions" raised by linguistics and the "questions" raised by philosophy. Absent from Lecercle's reading, that is, is any imperative to bring into relief the questions of one dimension of nonsense over another (for example the questions of philosophy over those of linguistics), since, indeed, for Lecercle, there is no substantive difference between the two. Both belong to the genre of nonsense. If this reading is correct, we might read Lecercle's philosophical treatment of *Alice* as indeed symptomatic of several other, non-theoretical (or traditional) readings, at least in character, if not in scope and breadth. Both kinds of readings, in other words, could be said to extinguish the marginal or peripheral in favor of the traditional, such that what remains unexplored within such readings are those radical dimensions of nonsense, dimensions which have been jettisoned in favor of examination of the more surface-level counterparts of nonsense, specifically, linguistic and philological language games, paradoxes and portmanteau words. Here, again, Lecercle could be said to dramatize one of my earlier three points in response to the lightness of nonsense: on the one hand he identifies the philosophical within the linguistic; on the other hand he conflates the two fields, destroying any possibility of finding within Carroll that which Carroll ostensibly anticipates: unique philosophical problems putatively grounded in that Continental tradition of the dissolution of a heretofore given accord between mind and body, reason and affect.

Because I could be accused here of offering a reductive reading of Lecercle's text, I might acknowledge Lecercle's identification (if not outright examination) of those marginal structures of nonsense, here understood as madness, doubt, and simulacrum, philosophical and theoretical structures which (historically) have been subordinate to the more conventional and thereby linguistic dimensions of Victorian nonsense. "The most striking feature of Victorian nonsense," Lecercle tells us, "is the quality of its intuitions, this mixture of diachrony (the genre reflects, refracts and arranges the elements of a historical conjecture) and anachrony: it anticipates, and it *criticizes in advance, the developments of philosophy and linguistics*" (PN 224; emphasis mine). If developed within a Lacanian analysis, nonsense here performs the discourse of the critical hysteric. Deeply suspicious of all critical theory, nonsense seeks to reveal it as pure simulacrum, merely a "grand narrative" (Lyotard's term)[8] posturing as so many discourses and counter-discourses. I suggest a comparison between Lacan and nonsense because of the metonymic relation Lecercle himself could be said to have to the discourse of the hysteric. The discourse of the hysteric, curiously enough, occupies an integral place within critical theory, with striking appearances within (for example) race theory, queer theory, and gender theory. I emphasize the word *critical* (as in critical hysteric) to highlight a certain ethical imperative within the hysteric's otherwise suspicious and doubting discourse, specifically, an imperative to locate difference where previously there were only vulgarly consolidated categories of identity (here we can refer to arbitrary markers like race, gender, sexuality), categories which totalize and stand in for what is invariably heterogeneous: the fractured and fragmented subject. This formulation led Lacan to famously announce that

"Woman does not exist,"[9] insofar as "Woman" (i.e., All Women) as a marker of identity reduces to the level of the imaginary what precisely is not merely imaginary: *women.* I would argue that we find a similar undertaking (and suspicion) within Lecercle's reading of Carroll, in which Lecercle attempts to *reveal or uncover* the philosophical character of the different discourses through which nonsense has historically been enunciated (linguistic, social, philological, logical). That is, we might read Lecercle's anachronic reading as an epistemological and genealogical excavation, where what is at stake is the revelation of that quintessential discourse around which (for Lecercle) nonsense is both grounded as well as brought into discourse qua nonsense, specifically the discourse of philosophy. However, it is only within the last section of Lecercle's work, a section entitled "The Polyphony of Nonsense," that Lecercle could be said to allude to a properly philosophical subject within *Alice*, one articulated around the discourse of "madness," one of four discourses Lecercle identities as structuring nonsense, in addition to "fiction, logic, and the natural sciences" (196). Though these last three discourses do not individually constitute a proper concept of nonsense, insofar as they rather constitute what we might call its traditional and historical modes of expression, we might nevertheless underline them as those rational and literary structures against which Lecercle will define and, finally, circumscribe that fourth and final discourse of nonsense (i.e., "madness").

If I have devoted some time to a discussion of the discourses of nonsense, it is thus only to highlight their underlying philosophical sincerity. The three aforementioned discourses are necessary, in other words, insofar as they collectively define that genealogical backdrop of hyper-logic and reason *against which* Lecercle will posit the discourse of madness, one which will henceforth be incarnated in the discourse and subjectivity of what Lecercle identifies as the "nonsense subject." Like Alice, the nonsense subject is identified through its sense of alienation and estrangement from wonderland's vulgarized and parodic reason and rationality. Its perspective organized around a certain external-ity and otherness, the nonsense subject merely looks *into or at* Carroll's maddening worlds, "isolated and pointed at, subjected to the wondering gaze of an audience of readers who laugh and gape at [her] eccentricities, as if [she] were a freak in a fair ... or who prod and interpret" (PN 206). While I agree with Lecercle's reading of the nonsense subject, I would nevertheless like to examine further those questions of self-doubt and ontological uncertainty inaugurated around nonsense, questions that *acknowledge yet go beyond a reading* of *Alice as mere spectacle, a mere object of difference*. In more emphatic terms, I would like to put at stake Alice's own skepticism and self-doubt as regards the phenomenality of her being. That is to say, I would like to address the ways in which such doubt could be said to reveal those axes around which a radical erasure of the self occurs: namely, madness, doubt, and simulacrum.[10]

III

It is in fact through such an examination that I believe we may discern within Lecercle's reading a certain division of kind between Carroll's "nonsense" and Antonin Artaud's "madness," a division constitutive of Carroll's and Artaud's respective treatments of nonsense. Here I cite Artaud as that paradigmatic (and idiosyncratic) figure for whom language was of the most personal and painful experiences, something felt and experienced rather than thematized or metaphorized. Though I will return to address the relationship between Carroll and Artaud, here I merely wish to highlight a certain philosophical elision of Lecercle's, an elision located in the division of that object of nonsense in Carroll between literature and philosophy. As indicated above, the madness Lecercle discerns in Carroll is one organized around rhetoric and visuality, whose logical paralogisms and absurd rhetorical flourishes may be read as a response to Carroll's Victorian England's well-ordered and rational structures of reason and rationality. That is, even as nonsense twists and bends out of shape those semiological structures, insofar as it works within those structures it nonetheless re-

tains – rather than suspends – that basic semiology between signifier and referent – even if, as Linda Shires observers, "it breaks signifiers from signifieds" ("Fantasy, Nonsense, Parody, and the Status of the Real" 281).[11] It is perhaps worth underlining Carroll's retention of this basic semiology, since it is around an understanding of this semiology as merely *rearranged* that Lecercle can conclude that at the base of Carroll's nonsense is a difference in *type* rather than *kind* with idiomatic rhetorical conventions: namely, an understanding of those structures as rather *shuffled* and *gone awry*. In Lecercle's hands, and in contradistinction with Schwab's and Clark's distinctions between sense and nonsense, Carroll's nonsense both is and is *not* a perverted mirror-like image of those principles of idiomatic speech, insofar as it is more properly a transvaluation thereof. Because both nonsense and idiomatic speech necessarily obey the same basic rhetorical and semiological principles, Carroll's nonsense, Lecercle wants to suggest, does not so much constitute an irreducible other to sense as it rather discloses the arbitrariness (figured through metonymic ambiguity, synecdoche) constitutive of language itself. In sum, for Lecercle, Carroll's nonsense, to the degree it retains a basic semiology of signifiers and referents, similarly retains a kind of sense, even if a duplicitous one.

Recalling that above-mentioned division between Carroll's and Artaud's sense of nonsense, therefore, it is perhaps around this last point that we find the punctuation of their divergence. For if the above reading is correct, the madness Lecercle discerns in Carroll's nonsense is not the schizophrenic madness of pain and affect, sensation and depth. It is not the madness that resists literary and semiological codifications, a madness of radical self-abnegation and hatred. I would even argue that within Lecercle's reading is a certain *reluctance* to approach the schizo qua schizo, a reluctance to approach madness qua madness. That is, we might accuse Lecercle of committing what Gabrielle Schwab cautions as a "*critical evasion,*" an evasion around which both Lecercle and ourselves are "spared the pains of actually encountering the ... pathologies of schizophrenia *on their own terms*" ("Nonsense and Metacommunications" 178; emphasis mine). If we grant, in other words (once again to use Schwab's language), Lecercle's aim to "recuperate these forms of [literary nonsense] within a tradition from which they have broken away" (178), philosophy in particular, we might nevertheless fault the recuperation insofar as what is recuperated is less the philosophical disclosure of the aforementioned "pathologies of schizophrenia" than their concealment within a *"postmodern simulacrum* of schizophrenia" – a reinscription around which we are "saved ... the tortures of a schizophrenic experience" (178). This is not to suggest, however, that Lecercle's "critical evasion" is the move to discern the philosophical contours of Carroll's nonsense; on the contrary, it is the particular *way in which* the move is carried out: Lecercle's intervention does not so much disclose the philosophical determinations of those schizophrenic contours as it rather reinscribes them within a still-overarching linguistic framing of the question. Lecercle's error, then, is doubly pernicious; it is in a sense a rehearsal of Deleuze's criticism of Carroll's nonsense as a mere "reading of the surfaces": a reading around which the schizophrenia of nonsense is given over in favor of its more surface-level and linguistic counterparts. Deleuze is perhaps most clear on this point in *Logic of Sense*, where we find that "the mistake made by the logicians, when they speak of nonsense, is that they offer laboriously constructed, emaciated examples fitting the needs of their demonstration, as if they had never heard a little girl sing [Kafka's little girls, for instance], a great poet recite, or a schizophrenic speak [Artaud]" (LS 83). As Deleuze continues,[12] at stake here is a "clinical problem ... a problem of [not] sliding from one organization to another ... a problem of the formation of a progressive and creative disorganization" (LS 83). At stake in this "critical evasion," in other words, is nothing less than what Deleuze identifies as a *"problem of criticism,"* where what is problematic is that failure to *distinguish* "the differential levels at which nonsense changes shape, the portmanteau words undergo a change of nature, and the entire language changes dimensions" (LS 83; emphasis mine). As Deleuze puts it, we must:

be attentive to the very different functions and abysses of nonsense, and to the heterogeneity of portmanteau words, which do not authorize the grouping together of those who invent or even those who use them. A little girl may sing *"Pimpanicaille,"* an artist may write "frumious"; and a schizophrenic may utter "perspendicace." But we have no reason to believe that the problem is the same in all of these cases and the results roughly analogous ... With all the force of admiration and veneration, *we must be attentive to the sliding which reveals a profound difference underlying these crude similarities.* (LS 83; emphasis mine)

These criticisms might appear strident were it not for the fact that, in his own words, Lecercle circumscribes the schizophrenia of nonsense within the linguistic trappings of a literary metanarrative, one in which the depth of nonsense is safely delimited and contained. As Lecercle observes, "the text of nonsense is a verbal asylum, in which madmen speak, but within the limits and constraints of the text, which phrases both the discourse of madness and the discourse on madness" (PN 208). To the extent that for Lecercle nonsense is principally rhetorical and linguistic, it is also narratological, in mimetic relation to discourses which oppose it and attempt to subvert it (i.e., the above-mentioned discourses of rationality, logic, scholasticism, etc.). Here we might also observe Schwab's definition of nonsense as a "collision of systems of meaning – a collision that invites a new relationship between the involved systems or even causes them to collapse" (159). At stake in both definitions, consequently, is a sense of nonsense organized less around a "lack of order" than a "collision between different systems of order within a larger system" (159). In sum, then, we might say that "the critical evasion" performed by conventional or traditional readings of nonsense is nothing less than a certain *willfulness* to treat nonsense as (or only as) a literary genre, as something *not* in "fearful symmetry" (Frye[13]) with literature. The price paid for such a formulation, however, a formulation which mediates the schizophrenic through the literary, is that, as Schwab words it, "life and death lose their cutting edge" (178). And what is this "cutting edge"? In Deleuze's hands it is the schizophrenic experience of nonsense, the loss of self, what I will argue is the disclosure of a schizophrenic subjectivity in the *Alice* books, one mapped principally around the figure of Alice.

IV

The question posed to us by Carroll, I wish to suggest, one picked up by James Kincaid, Peter Heath, Linda Shires, Gabrielle Schwab, and of course Gilles Deleuze, is thus the question of how Alice answers the ineluctable void lurking and hiding behind Carroll's surfaces. The status of this void within the context of Carroll's wonderland and looking-glass worlds can most readily be discerned by summarizing the principle dimensions of the "schizo" within Deleuze's commentary in *Logic of Sense*. It is in fact around this question of the status of nonsense within *Alice* that Carroll and Artaud encounter each other. Specifically, it is around an interpretation of the schizo as the instantiation of the *breakdown* of those divisions between sense and signification that Deleuze will conclude that the void lurking at the bottom of wonderland is nothing less than the confrontation with the *real* of nonsense: the phenomenological and affective encounter with transcendent immanence. According to Deleuze, the void of nonsense is the world of depths, the world of the schizo. In contradistinction with Carroll's surfaces, for instance, the realm of schizophrenia eschews the surface-level world's metaphorical enjambments, rhetorical sophistry, metaphors and similes. These differences between the two worlds turn on wonderland's and looking-glass world's sense of language, which, from the schizo's perspective, remains structurally constrained around a capricious play between sign and signified, word and thing. The two worlds, in other words, oppose each other around the schizo's "use" of language, an opposition turning on the dissolution of that "frontier between things and propositions" within the realm of schizophrenia (LS 87). This frontier evacuated, in other words,

"[e]verything is body and corporeal. Everything is a mixture of bodies" (LS 87). Consequently, if devices like metaphor and synecdoche are meaningless for the schizo it is because the schizo refuses that frontier (or space) between the signifier and the signified – the condition of possibility for such catachresis. Put simply, then, the main difference between the two realms of depth and surface is the equivocal status of language unevenly divided between them. While reading Deleuze's *Logic of Sense* around this last point I happened upon the passage in which Deleuze takes up Artaud's epistle to Lewis Carroll, an epistle written while Artaud was at the asylum at Rodez (*c*.1945). We might recall this passage here to remark more rigorously this division of nonsense between the phenomenal and linguistic determinations of language, a difference that comes to a head within Artaud's reading of Carroll's poem "Jabberwocky" (one organized around the enjambment of several portmanteau words). Deleuze writes:

> As we read the first stanzas of "Jabberwocky," such as Artaud renders it, we have the immediate impression that the two opening verses still correspond to Carroll's criteria [of nonsense] and conform to the rules of translation generally held by Carroll's other French translators, Parisot and Brunius. But beginning with the last word of the second line, from the third line onward, a sliding is produced, and even a creative, central collapse, causing us to be in *another world and in an entirely different language*. With horror, we recognize it easily: it is the language of schizophrenia. Even the portmanteau words seem to function differently, being caught up in syncopes and being overloaded with gutturals. (LS 84; emphasis mine)

Unlike Carroll, Artaud's sense of nonsense belongs to the realm of affect and somaticism, its "enunciations" understood as brute physical gestures that pulverize all traces of the sign and its referents – a nonsense, that is, which pulverizes that difference that makes a difference between the signifier and the signified. Artaud's nonsense is thus not sense *sans* sense, nonsense absent of sense; and it is not, insofar as such predicative determinations would merely reinstall those semiological indices of nonsense *already in place, maintaining that frontier between affect and language*. Rather, as Artaud bemoans, the relation between nonsense and schizophrenia is spatio-temporal, exclusive of *all* linguistic formulations: nonsense, if we are to maintain fidelity to Artaud, must more properly be understood as that which is *underneath or behind* the syntactic. Accordingly, for Artaud, the criterion around which is determined one's *proper* relation to nonsense is the "depth" relative to one's approach to that language. Artaud is, of course, somewhat more explicit around this last point. As Artaud thus continues, in the above-mentioned epistle:

> *I do not like poems or languages of the surface* which smell of happy leisure and intellectual success ... One may invent one's language, and make pure language speak with an extra-grammatical or a-grammatical meaning, but this *meaning must have value in itself, that is, it must issue from torment* ... When one *digs* through the shit of being and its language, [Jabberwocky] necessarily smells badly, [it] ... is a poem whose author took steps to keep himself from the uterine being of suffering into which every great poet has *plunged*, and having been born from it, smells badly. (LS 84; emphasis mine)

Perhaps most remarkable within Artaud's extended conceit is its proleptic announcement of what Deleuze several decades later in *Critique et Clinique* (1993) would baptize as the condition of "becoming minoritarian." As outlined by Deleuze in *Essays Critical and Clinical*, becoming minoritarian refers to a forceful decomposition of language, the "creation of [new] syntax [toward] the invention of a new language within language" (*Essays Critical and Clinical* 5; hereafter CC). According to Deleuze, decomposition refers to that moment or series of moments "when another language is created within language ... a language [that] in its entirety tends toward an 'a-syntactic,' 'a-grammatical' limit, or that communicates with its own outside" (CC iv). Here we might also recall those lines in Deleuze's *Kafka*, in which Deleuze likens the process of decomposition to "language ... torn

from sense, conquering sense, bringing about an accentive neutralization of sense, no longer find[ing] its value in anything but an accenting of the word, an inflection" (*Kafka* 21; emphasis mine). If read this way, Carroll's approach to nonsense is bereft of "value" insofar as Carroll refuses to excavate at the level of the affective, refuses to move toward a new language, which remains enfolded within the pleasant veneer of metaphor. Indeed, what Carroll would seem to neutralize and deny access to is exactly and precisely that language of nonsense. Though Carroll expresses an interest in "creating a language within language," such "passages of fecality," as Artaud puts it, are undermined inasmuch as it is the "fecality" of a figure who "*curls the obscene within himself* like ringlets of hair around a curling iron" (CC iv; emphasis mine).

Given this admittedly brief discussion of the differences between Carroll's and Artaud's treatments of nonsense, we might be tempted to conclude that at stake in Artaud's criticism of Carroll is the latter's refusal to *go far enough* (literally, to *dig* deep enough) in his treatment of language. Artaud's criticism runs in just the opposite direction, however: for Artaud, Carroll's "critical evasion" (like Lecercle's) materializes as a *willful* (*en*)*folding and concealing* of the schizophrenia of nonsense. In curling the obscene within himself, Artaud wants to say, Carroll parses out the schizophrenia of nonsense through its metaphorical surface-level counterparts. It is around this doubled act of *enfolding* and *unfolding* that the schizophrenia of nonsense is reduced to its merely linguistic and metaphorical determinations. What Carroll maintains, in Artaud's view, is that incorporeal border between sonorous words and physical bodies, a border which maintains, on the one hand, the phenomenal determinations of words and, on the other, the logical attributes of bodies – a border around which, as we saw, "sonorous language is sheltered from any [mingling] with the physical body" (LS 91). At the same time, Artaud's criticism is similarly undercut insofar as he fails to recognize the world of depth (i.e., the world of schizophrenia) as anything other than a purely affective space. To the extent that Artaud grounds nonsense in affect, he also and necessarily excludes the possibility of difference therein. For Artaud the schizophrenia of nonsense materializes only ever *outside* the particular psychical and linguistic vicissitudes of the subject. Yet if, as Artaud suggests, Carroll conceals the obscenity within himself, conceals the "fecality" and "depth" of nonsense, *why* is Alice (and wonderland and looking-glass world) still threatened with the loss of self? The answer, as Deleuze elegantly puts it, is because "*Even unfolded and laid out flat, the monsters still haunt us*" (CC 22; emphasis mine). The schizophrenia of depth, that is, still "rumble[s] under the surface, and [always] threaten[s] to break through it (CC 22). At stake in both Artaud's and Carroll's "errors" is the belief that, if left unfolded or unearthed, nonsense is divorced of its schizophrenia. The significance of this mistake cannot be overstated. For if Artaud is in fact correct, if nonsense "has teeth" (LS 84), it matters little, finally, if Carroll retains that frontier between sense and signification. It matters little, for nonsense, even if "emitted [only] at the surface," is still "carved into the depth of bodies" (LS 84). Indeed, as we saw above, in this realm of schizophrenia, in which the aforementioned border between word and thing has been "reabsorbed into [schizophrenia's] gaping breath," the only duality left is "*between the actions and passions of the body*" (LS 91; emphasis mine). We might highlight this last point, insofar as it is around this dissolution that Deleuze can conclude that, though only monsters on the surface, the Snark and the Jabberwock, in their "terror" and "cruelty," are nonetheless *still* "monsters" (LS 93). Though they are not of the depths, in other words, "they have claws just the same and can snap up one laterally, or even make us fall into the abyss which *we believed we have dispelled*" (LS 93; emphasis mine).

V

What we are after in Deleuze's discussion of *Alice* is thus this characterization of the world of depth as structured around a certain spectrality

or haunting. For it seems to me that what the above discussion puts at stake exactly is that thing which could be said to "haunt" wonderland: a nervousness that there is actually *something* rather than nothing lurking beneath wonderland, beneath its affable realm of surfaces and appearances. What Deleuze identifies as "haunting" may in fact be understood under the principle of radical contingency: as a question over the *possibility* of the appearance of the world of depths onto and into the world of surfaces. From the perspective of the inhabitants on the "surface" (i.e., wonderland's inhabitants), the world of depths *can only ever exist as a possibility*. It threatens – but does not penetrate – wonderland. What is between the two realms, what establishes (but does not guarantee) difference between them, is nothing but the *possibility* of the presence of the other, of that which threatens – but does not arrive. There is nothing between the two realms (surface and depth) save for the impossible possibility of the arrival of the Other, an Other as the "expression of [that] possible world" (LS 310). As Deleuze puts it, we must:

> understand that the Other is not one structure among others of perception ... *It is the structure which conditions the entire field* and its functioning, by rendering possible the constitution and application of the preceding categories. It is not the ego but the Other as structure which renders perception possible. In defining the Other ... as the expression of a possible world, we make of it ... the *a priori* principle of the organization of every perceptual field in accordance with the categories; we make of it the structure which allows this functioning as the "categorization" of the field. (LS 308; emphasis in original)

If read through these lights, in other words, the *Alice* books disclose an irreducible interdependence between surface and depth, an irreducibility around which nonsense is figured as nothing less – and nothing more – than the "expressible of the expressed of the proposition, and the attribute of the state of affairs" (LS 22). What we might remark here, however, and insofar as the event is not (or is not reducible to) "an attribute of the state of affairs," is that nonsense "does not *merge* with the proposition which expressed it ... [rather] it is the *boundary* between propositions and things" (LS 22; emphasis mine). Though the realms of surface and depth could be said to touch each other, insofar as they mutually constitute those two determinations of nonsense, they remain in opposition to each other, an opposition understood under the principle of metonymy:

> Surface nonsense is like the "Radiance" of pure events, entities that never finish happening or withdrawing. Pure events without mixture shine above the mixed bodies, above their embroiled actions and passions. They let an incorporeal rise to the surface like a mist over the earth, a pure "expressed" from the depth: not the sword, but the flash of the sword, a flash without a sword like the smile without a cat. (LS 84)

It is thus not that surface has less nonsense than depth; it is simply not the same nonsense. Accordingly, and by this principle, we ought not to conceive the relations between sense and nonsense in correspondence with *categories true and false*. On the contrary,

> when we assume that nonsense says its own sense, we wish to indicate ... that sense and nonsense have a specific relation which cannot copy that of the true and false, that is, *which cannot be conceived simply on the basis of a relation of exclusion*. The condition cannot have with its negative the same kind of relation that the conditioned has with its negative. (LS 68; emphasis mine)

All of which is to say, finally, and in accordance with the above observation of the two realms as cathected together, the relations between sense and nonsense are grounded in a "*type of intrinsic relation, a mode of co-presence*" (LS 68). It is in this sense, consequently, that we might understand the relationship between madness and nonsense as exemplary of the relationship between philosophy and nonsense: one establishes the conditions of possibility for the other – at least to the degree that both fields of knowledge implicitly or explicitly raise questions concerning the limits of knowledge, especially as such limits could be said to address the *(in)finitude of the subject*. Though Kincaid's "Alice's Invasion of Wonderland" raises this question of finitude, it is nevertheless an issue whose treatment is reserved until the end of his essay, in a provocative section on Alice's unresolved dream. I would like to take up, then, a reexamination of that question of finitude, a question that Kincaid identifies in terms of "an impossible choice ... [whose] final point is not so much aggressive as deeply and profoundly sad" (99).

Over readings by Beverly Lyon Clark and James Kincaid I would thus like to suggest that the *Alice* books inaugurate an epistemological and ontological break with reality, a break which ultimately forces Alice to encounter what Heath identifies as that Kantian terror of transcendentality: the experience of "a mind driven almost to the verge of unhingement" (*Philosopher's Alice* 6). While Heath grants, in his own words, that "Carroll is no Kant," particularly in the former's treatment of the relation between reason and consciousness, he nonetheless locates within Carroll the ideational determinations of Kant's project: a concern with "Critical Philosophy itself, with the bounds of sense and the limitations of reason" (6). The ostensible precursor to Kant's mature philosophical writings, the *Critique of Pure Reason* in particular, Descartes's *Meditations* may similarly be said to be inscribed within the *Alice* books. Though the *Meditations* initially betray skepticism around the certainty of consciousness, Descartes ultimately attenuates this skepticism by concluding that there is something "certain": namely the *cogito*. Yet, as I suggest below, the epistemological (and, finally, ontological) certainty granted to the *cogito* by Descartes is exactly what the *Alice* books ultimately undermine. Carroll and Descartes encounter each other in several places in the *Alice* books, with perhaps the most provocative encounter in the coda, if not also the scene around the slumbering Red King. In both, though, we find the same question: the certainty of the *cogito*, most notably around Carroll's final question: "which dreamed it?" (*Alice* 238). While the answer might seem clear to the readers, if not quite Alice, we nonetheless might highlight Carroll's non-response to underline the sincerity of Alice's unresolved questions over this not so *clear and distinct truth*. Alice's concluding admonitions to Kitty are exemplary here: "Now let's consider who it was that dreamed it all. This is a serious question, my dear ... it *must* have been either me or the Red King. He was part of my dream, of course, but then I was part of his dream, too! *Was* it the Red King, Kitty?" (*Alice* 240; emphasis in original).

The two principles of Carroll's around which the coeval problems of finitude and epistemic doubt are posed are the principles of repetition and causality, both of which (in the books) take the form of narratological overdetermination. Though visibly apparent in the above example, the *subject* of that question (i.e., loss of the predicative "I" and the proceeding infinite regress toward its procurement) is first introduced in Alice's encounter with Humpty Dumpty in looking-glass world. What most interests me here is the story's dissolution of those boundaries between what Deleuze calls literature and life, a dissolution figured through Alice's curious role as both the story's narrator and (heretofore hidden) cause of its crashing crescendo – a dissolution the implications of which Humpty Dumpty blissfully and also *necessarily* disavows or otherwise feigns ignorance before. I recall, for instance, and following Alice's recognition of Humpty Dumpty from his progressive development from an egg ("and when she came close to it, she saw clearly that it was Humpty Dumpty himself"), the ensuing debate between the two over Humpty Dumpty's precipitous position on that wall:

> "Don't you think you'd be safer down on the ground ... That wall is so *very* narrow." "Of course I don't think so! Why, if ever *I* did fall off – which there's no chance of – but if I did ... If I *did* fall," he went on, "*the King has promised me ... The king has promised me – with his very own mouth* – to – to ..." "To send all his horses and all his men," Alice interrupted, rather unwisely. "Now I declare that's too bad," Humpty Dumpty cried. "You've been listening at doors – and behind trees – and down chimneys – or you couldn't have known it!" "I haven't, indeed!" Alice said very gently. "It's in a book." (*Alice* 183)

His heretofore given identity as "real" brought into question as perhaps nothing more than a rehearsed nursery rhyme, Humpty Dumpty's above lines to Alice double as both the conditions of his existence qua Humpty Dumpty but also – and insofar as they do – concomitantly mark the negation of his identity *as anything more than that narrative of fiction*: against his protests, Humpty Dumpty *will* fall, and (as the nursery rhyme goes), "all the king's horses and all the king's men will not be able to put Humpty together again." By way of implication, what we might observe around this admixture is the curious way in which Alice consequently finds herself interpellated as both reader *and* signer of that Humpty Dumpty "book" – almost as if to suggest, in some strange way, that Lewis Carroll actually *precedes* the famous nursery rhyme. One can imagine, for instance, an infinite number of encounters between the two, in which Alice tries, but fails, to prevent Humpty Dumpty's fall, each failure a remark on the overdetermination of Carroll's worlds and their characters. Each failure, that is, is a remark on the constitutive impossibility of ever (re)telling (i.e., revising) the fable, of ever *completing* their conversation, insofar as its incompletion is exactly and precisely the nursery rhyme's status qua complete (i.e., Humpty Dumpty's crashing to the ground). We find, then, perhaps, a structural convergence between these two "characters": though both equivocate between positions active and passive, listener and storyteller, neither is fully free from the authorship of wonderland and looking-glass worlds – not even, as we will see, in the coda, in which these questions of personal finitude and freedom reappear.

VI

I would like to address this notion of the decentered subject partly through the analysis provided by Linda Shires, in her essay "Fantasy, Nonsense, Parody, and the Status of the Real." Though not privy to Lecercle's discussion of nonsense, which would appear about eight years later, Shires provides a useful framework through which to examine the relationship between Carroll and nonsense, in particular the ways in which such a decentering of the subject may reveal that subject yet to be located within the *Alice* books. Of particular interest to Shires are the ways in which nonsense and fantasy "question the basis of a known reality, unsettle fixed positions for the reader and for characters of speakers, put our mastery and control into question" (272). As Shires writes: "what is at stake – whether in the unreal of fantasy, the more real of parody, or the non-real of nonsense – is ourselves" (268). Each inaugurates a specular trauma in which one's self or "I" disappears and can no longer be guaranteed. Shires treats nonsense in dialectical terms. Like a "trip to the fun house," nonsense "offers" and presents us with a "similar kind of risk, pleasure, loss, and reassurance" (268). I would like to extend Shires' reading here, in particular Shires' position that nonsense "aim[s] toward a breakdown of linguistic coherence, of a reassuring sense of identity, of known meaning" (272).

We need only refer to Alice's encounter with Tweedledum and Tweedledee to highlight this point, one which Tweedledum manages to encapsulate within a single sentence. Here we might quickly summarize the main points of their exchange over the meaning of the slumbering Red King's sleep:

He's dreaming now, said Tweedledee: and what do you think he's dreaming about? –

Nobody can guess that –

Why, about *you*! ... And if he left off dreaming about you, where do you suppose you'd be?

Where I am now, of course, said Alice –

Not you! You'd be nowhere. Why, you're only the sort of thing in his dream! (*Alice* 164–65)

Regarding the possibility that Alice may simply be a manifestation of the Red King's dream (a possibility that I would argue is never put to rest), Tweedledum says to Alice "If that there King was to wake ... you'd go out – bang! – just like a candle!" (*Alice* 165), to which Alice responds "I shouldn't! Besides, if *I'm* only a sort of thing in his dream, what are *you*, I should like

to know?" (*Alice* 165). What we might discern within Alice's response to Tweedledum is an inverted though categorical response to the diffident one earlier offered to the laconic Caterpillar: "I can't explain myself, I'm afraid, sir ... because I'm not myself, you see" (*Alice* 41). Nonetheless, to this question both Tweedledum and Tweedledee respond with "Ditto." They, too, we are to believe, are merely the imaginings of the Red King's dream. As their exchange continues, though, we arrive at a disturbing parallel between the slumbering Red King and Descartes's Evil Genius, a parallel posed in the form of a question over the determinations of the distinction between dream and reality – a parallel Kincaid will allude to in his essay. Following Alice's curious admonition to Tweedledum and Tweedledee to quiet down for fear of rousing the king from his slumber, we find Tweedledum's own admonition to Alice, admonitions most provocative in their denouement: "Well, it's no use *your* talking to him ... when you're only one of the things in his dream. You know very well you're not real" (*Alice* 165; emphasis in original). In response, we find Alice's famous lament, "I *am* real! (*Alice* 165). Alice's justification of this claim is empirical at its base: "If I wasn't real ... I shouldn't be able to cry" (*Alice* 165). Alice's claim turns on a perceived distinction (which the brothers disavow) between our sensible and rational apprehension of the world, a distinction turning on the former's *immediate* and the latter's *mediate* relation to the world. If Alice appeals to physical categories of experience (e.g., I can cry) as exemplary of her "realness," it is because (for Alice) such are "concrete" examples of her bodily extension in the world. To the extent, in other words, that her tears are registered as experience (similar to pinching oneself), the tears are an example of an external sensation (e.g., I feel). They are, in short, "proof" of her existence outside the space of mere "thought." Too clever, though, are the brothers-as-philosophers Tweedledum and Tweedledee. Aware of Alice's logical error (not that Alice should be ashamed, of course), namely the remaining – and begged – question of the status of the "I" to which that experience ostensibly refers, Tweedledee responds to Alice's proof with the glib comment: "You won't make yourself a bit realler by crying ... *there's nothing to cry about*," to which Tweedledum intercedes with the "formal rebuke": "I hope you don't suppose those are *real* tears" (*Alice* 165; emphasis in original).

Around this last point we might turn to Descartes's similar hypothesis in the opening book of his *Meditations*, the former a rehearsal of sorts of Alice's (if not Tweedledum's and Tweedledee's!) question over the certainty of her subjecthood. Beginning with the supposition that some "evil genius ... has employed his whole energies in *deceiving* me," Descartes concomitantly surrenders himself to the possibility that:

> the heavens, the earth, colours, figures, sound, and all other *external things* are nought but the illusions and dreams [of this genius] ... I [thus] shall consider myself as having no hands, no eyes, no flesh, no blood, nor any senses, yet falsely believing myself to possess these things; I shall remain obstinately attached to this idea, and if by this means it is not possible [to find the truth], I may at least suspend my judgment, and ... avoid giving credence to any false thing imposed by this arche deceiver. (*Meditations* 62; emphasis mine)

It is perhaps worth noting here that, insofar as Descartes doubts all that has heretofore arrived through experience, he nonetheless – and precisely – does *not doubt* the mind within which the intuitions of these objects are located. For, according to Descartes, the mind is given. The mind is the unconditioned condition of possibility for the thought experiment. Accordingly, what Descartes doubts are all objects *external* to him, namely "body, figure, extension, movement and place," all of which are supposed as mere "fictions of [that] mind" (*Meditations* 63). For Descartes, the *cogito* is nothing less than the "guarantor" of our subjectivity as sentient subjects. Descartes offers such proof in Book II of the *Meditations*, when he writes, following the above rehearsed experiment:

> was I then not likewise persuaded that I did not exist? Not at all; of a surety I myself did exist

since I persuaded myself of something ... So that after having reflected well and carefully examined all things, we must come to the definite conclusion that this proposition: I am, I exist, *is necessarily true each time that I pronounce it, or mentally conceive it.* (*Meditations* 64; emphasis mine)

That is, to the extent Descartes thinks, or, more correctly, insofar as he doubts this possibility, he finds he necessarily *cannot not exist*, for in "wishing to think all things false, it was absolutely essential that the 'I' who thought this should be somewhat" (*Meditations* 21). However, since for Descartes the *cogito* is only ever phantasmatic, his thought experiment inevitably ignores anything that we might experience qua experience, for the qualification of these experiences qua experiences obliges proof in the form of a physical body – which, as we saw above, Descartes has already put into question. For Descartes, in other words, certainty of the *cogito* can be posited only at the level of a *division* between the mind and body, a division in the certainty that what doubts is *only* the *cogito*. Thus, in a rehearsal of the sentiments above:

> I am, I exist, this is certain. But how often? Just when I think; for it might possibly be the case if I ceased entirely to think, that I should likewise cease altogether to exist ... to speak more accurately I am not more than a thing which thinks, that is to say a mind or a soul. I am, however, a real thing, and really exist; but what thing? I have answered: *a thing that thinks* ... What is a thing which thinks? It is a thing which doubts, understands, affirms, denies, wills, refuses, which also imagines and *feels*. (*Meditations* 65, 66; emphasis mine)

Though Descartes might assume an absence of the body, assume even an absence of the world, insofar as he does, he necessarily posits an "I" to whom such doubt would be ascribed:

> And although possibly ... I possess a body with which I am very intimately conjoined, yet because, on the one side, I have a clear and distinct idea of myself inasmuch as I am only a thinking and unextended thing, and as, on the other, I possess a distinct idea of body, inasmuch as it is only an extended and unthinking thing, it is *certain* that this I (that is

to say, my soul by which I am what I am), is entirely and absolutely distinct from my body, and can exist without out. (*Meditations* 100; emphasis mine)

At the same time, present within Descartes's *Meditations* is the negation of the certitude of that "I." Insofar as for Descartes consciousness materializes only in the act of saying "I think," or "I doubt," consciousness can be posited only in terms of a self-reflexive prepositional grammar: in non-coincidence with a material body, the *cogito* affirms nothing more than its own linguistic structurations. The *cogito*, that is, is constituted only and precisely around the enunciation of that "I" that speaks, an "I" which nevertheless surreptitiously reintroduces – rather than suspends – an *interdependency* between itself and the body. If this reading is correct, the upshot is that the self can be posited only outside language, a consequence of its being determined outside all spatio-temporal considerations. Insofar as it is, though, that is, to the extent the "I" is posited beyond experience, it is necessarily beyond and outside all sensible apprehensions of it: *the self cannot be reduced to, nor is it in coincidence with, the phenomenal subject who says "I think, therefore I am."* If read this way, the *Alice* books could be said to literalize that epistemological and ontological terror that Kant and Descartes could *only* philosophize about. Within theological terms, Alice is not before the Caterpillar, nor is she really before the Red King. In theological terms, she is before Descartes's "evil genius," that is to say, before God.

What we might underline here is what Kincaid similarly discerns – if only implicitly – as a relationship between nonsense and the *cogito*, a relationship founded on Kincaid's sense of nonsense as simultaneously subversive as well as affirmative. Relying on Elizabeth Sewell's reading of nonsense, Kincaid finds that "nonsense, in its pure form, is not frightening but deeply reassuring, since it actually only appears to be disorderly and actually establishes so many structures and limits that it functions to keep disorder in check" ("Alice's Invasion of Wonderland" 93). Accordingly, let us now place the above discussion within the context of Kincaid's examination of nonsense in Carroll, so as to address what Kincaid identifies as this "reassuring" void at the heart of wonderland. Like Shires, Kincaid observes a certain dialectical contiguity between death and nonsense. Unlike Shires, though, Kincaid's treatment of death is only narratological in character, by which I mean that Kincaid only glosses the more ontological dimensions of nonsense, which are conceived as exemplary of Carroll's "nonsense." Though Kincaid addresses the question posed by Carroll in *Alice's* denouement, the one over which is divided Alice's existence or extinction, he nevertheless repeats the same move by Carroll, preferring not to answer to the two possibilities: "Which do you think it was?" (*Alice* 240). Instead, Kincaid retreats into what Derrida identifies as a "willful naïveté," which evokes that Hegelian "beautiful soul" that "seeks to protect itself from an encounter with Error" (Lambert, "The Subject of Literature between Derrida and Deleuze" 183). Rather than confront the two possibilities offered by Carroll (existence or extinction), which would force him (Kincaid) to address head on the implications of Alice's being or not being imaginary, Kincaid defers to Carroll, just as Carroll defers to the reader. As Kincaid writes, commenting on the chiasmus conditioned by the question, "[w]e are back where we started, and the closing question … significantly returns to the issue of whether or not Alice is only part of the Red King's dream" (99). Kincaid foregrounds the question itself as meaningful; his mournful response turns on the presence of the question, the fact that it is even posed by Carroll. Insofar as Kincaid's emphasis falls on the status of Carroll's question, subsequently elided are those ontological and epistemological implications raised by the books. Over Kincaid's reading, I would suggest that at stake in Alice's peregrinations is in fact the *subversion* of the syntactic and grammatical structure of the Cartesian "I," the disclosure of self as only and exactly self-reflexive.

VII

This discussion returns us to the aporias of self-constitution that we discussed initially, namely the constitutive impossibility of securing the "I" and its concomitant evacuation by that specular trauma inaugurated around nonsense. My intent here, though, I want to be clear, is not to rehearse the critical dialogues surrounding this disappearance within Carroll. Such enterprises have productively been performed by individuals elsewhere, notably, by Linda Shires, Gabriele Schwab, Jean-Jacques Lecercle, and Gilles Deleuze. I would argue, however, that in these interventions (with the possible exception of Deleuze's) a certain kind of misreading has been performed, often at the price of obscuring Carroll's quite significant and even scandalous ideas on subjectivity and consciousness. Such interventions have indeed dramatized Deleuze's greatest criticism of Carroll: a hesitancy to probe beneath the surface level of language, beneath its rudimentary syntagmatic transparency. The critical genealogy informing Alice's relation to nonsense has in fact been a genealogy complicit in the reduction of what is invariably terrifying and frightening to what is essentially innocuous and even superficial, merely a dream of Alice's: confrontation with her own finitude. Though I am in sympathy with Lecercle's claim that Carroll's *Alice* books may not explicitly address the erasure of consciousness or the vanishing *cogito*, I take heed of Deleuze's claim that there is an implicit epistemological and ontological terror lying beneath wonderland's surfaces, one which threatens to destroy (reveal as artifice) Alice's Cartesian subjectivity. Over Beverly Lyon Clark's reading,[14] for instance, we see this threat of erasure only partly through Alice's problems with growth. Such problems are rather undertaken through wonderland's perversion of that which is most cherished by Alice: the specular relationship between herself and the Other. For Alice, the Other is herself, insofar as "I" no longer equals "I," especially as dramatized through Alice's encounter with the Caterpillar, Tweedledum and Tweedledee. At stake in these exchanges are the continual slippages between the signifier and the signified over that "I,"

slippages around which is revealed Alice's position as merely another signifier within Carroll's fantastic worlds – a signifier predicated on the mistaken assumption of an absolute signified that will guarantee the positivity of one's being *as* unique and singular, that is, predicated upon the (im)possibility of a difference without difference.

Yet, even around this last point, perhaps especially around this point, we must be careful not to *reduce* Alice's confrontation with the schizophrenia of nonsense to a series of topological exchanges carried out *only* at the level of the linguistic or syntactic. For this reduction would merely reproduce the aforementioned "critical evasions," namely the subordination of the linguistic to the affective (or the failure to distinguish between the two). The burden of my argument has been to show how the simulacrum of wonderland *opens into and is in fact implicated within the production of those conditions around which is called into question the givenness of Alice's subjectivity.* I have claimed that Alice's "adventures" disclose a fundamental displacement of self, a displacement around which is dramatized (contra Descartes) the non-coincidence between the *cogito* and the body. What I have argued is at stake in Carroll's *Alice* books is exactly and simply this: the erasure of the rational and bourgeois Cartesian subject, a subject predicated on the condition that it can self-reflexively know itself, that it can know itself vis-à-vis its ostensibly known and empirically fixed position as a subject outside of language ("I am I"). If anything, the Cartesian subject's hyper-logic and rationality, its adherence to a purely linguistic grammatical conception of consciousness (i.e., the prepositional status of consciousness, figured in Descartes's "I think, therefore I am") conditions its very erasure within wonderland. Following this last point, let us return to our earlier discussion over the ontological significance of the above-mentioned void at the heart of *Alice*. Recall that this void is crucial insofar as it is the fundamental bedrock around which is constitutively barred (at least within Alice's mind) the possibility of a coincidence between her intuited and enunciatory "I." This problem makes a curious appearance in Alice's encounter with the Caterpillar and the Pigeon, where divided between both is that philosophical question, "Who are you?":

> "Who are you?" said the Caterpillar ... "I – I hardly know, Sir, just at present – at least I know who I *was* when I got up this morning, but I think I must have been changed several times since then." "What do you mean by that? ... Explain yourself! I can't explain *myself*, I'm afraid ... because I'm not myself, you see." "I don't see," said the Caterpillar ... "Who are *you*?" [and later] "But I'm *not* a serpent, I tell you! ... I'm a – I'm a –" "Well! *What* are you? ... I can see that you're trying to invent something!" "I – I'm a little girl" said Alice rather doubtfully. "A likely story indeed!" said the Pigeon ... (*Alice* 41, 48; emphasis in original)

To the extent that the Caterpillar "sees" Alice, he sees her as empty and hollow, a sentiment doubled around the Pigeon's understanding of Alice as less an *individual* and *particular* person than a general *kind* of *thing*. While the Caterpillar's exchange with Alice is dialogic, for instance, the Caterpillar never conceives Alice as more than a repetition of that iterative – though empty – "I." To the Caterpillar and, indeed, Alice as well, her identity is nothing less – and nothing more – than the syntactic predicate of that grammatical "I," *an "I" that even here refers not to "Alice" but to that category of identity in which that "I" is inscribed, namely the category "little girl."* Accordingly, part and parcel of Alice's reconciliation of this aporia (or rather the failure thereof) is the divestiture of the givenness and immediacy with which Alice had heretofore invested being, a divestiture revealed around the above-implied non-coincidence between who Alice "was" in the morning and who she is now. Per the evacuation of a semblance of self and "I," Alice/"Alice" consequently becomes merely a placeholder for her experiences, a repository of sorts within which that experience, only ever a succession of images and impressions, is continually (re)inscribed. Divested of that certainty, in other words, Alice's repeated moves toward self-apprehension disclose nothing less than the infinite regress correlative with the above-mentioned Kantian terror of

the Real, namely the possibility that she may not exist at all. Here, then, we might recall those lines in the opening pages of the English translation of Deleuze's *Empiricism and Subjectivity*, in which, in answer to the question "What are we?," Deleuze responds with "we are habits, nothing but habits, the habit of saying 'I'" (x). "Perhaps," as Deleuze continues, "there is no more striking answer to the problem of the self" (x). To slightly modify Shires' argument, "uncanny" does indeed refer to Alice's recognition of herself as "multiple" or "spatially" represented. However, it *also* refers to Alice's apprehension of herself as not unique, not special, not singular, not possessed – by herself. Deleuze puts this all very clearly:

> once substantives and adjectives begin to dissolve, when the names of pause and rest are carried away by the verbs of pure becoming and slide into the language of events, *all identity disappears from the self, the world, and God*. This is the test of *savoir* and recitation which strips Alice of her identity. In it words may go awry, being obliquely swept away by verbs. It is as if events enjoyed an irreality which is communicated through language to the *savoir* and to persons. (LS 3; emphasis mine)

The anxiety enacted upon Alice is the radical confrontation with her finitude, a confrontation similarly dramatized around Alice's acrimonious encounter with Humpty Dumpty:

> Don't stand chattering to yourself like that, Humpty Dumpty said ... but tell me your name and your business –
>
> My name is Alice, but –
>
> It's a stupid name enough! Humpty Dumpty interrupted impatiently. What does it mean?
>
> Must a name mean something?
>
> Of course it must ... my name means the shape I am – and a good handsome shape it is, too.
>
> With a name like yours, you might be any shape, almost. (*Alice* 182)

What Humpty Dumpty's avowedly cantankerous "insight" highlights is that "truth" that Alice has heretofore (and even here) fought to dismiss as irrational, absurd or just plain mad: that non-coincidence between the intuited and experienced "I," where what is at stake is the former's ostensibly fixed and given sense of self and the latter's unstable and polymorphously perverse sense of one. Much to Alice's consternation, and insofar as the dichotomous gap between the intuited "I" and the experienced "I" is constitutive, Alice cannot ignore or dismiss but, rather, must confront, the totality of this non-coincidence, a non-coincidence in congruence with a figure like Humpty Dumpty, who wanted merely to be "real."

VIII

While it may seem natural to conclude from our discussion thus far what Derrida identifies in "La Parole soufflée" as a kind of "unpower,"[15] especially in the context of our attempts to determine just what discourse can fully accommodate the nonsense within Carroll, what is perhaps now clear is that Carroll's nonsense does indeed betray the articulation of a philosophical subject, one which I have claimed may be located over and above the Cartesian subject and, finally, a subject materialized *as* the radical *potentiality* suturing Alice's three worlds: namely, wonderland and looking-glass worlds, but also, and perhaps more importantly, Alice's waking "real world." In our attempt to appreciate the first two realms "on their own terms," however, I do not mean to suggest that it is only philosophy that can appreciate Carroll's nonsense. On its own it is as helpless as literature in the attempt to render sensible Carroll's nonsense. As an alternative, I have claimed that such may be appreciated through the intersection of both, an intersection figured here around the writings of Deleuze and, in particular, the Deleuzian schizo, a figure who, at best, literalizes the trauma only dramatized by Carroll and experienced by Alice, and, at worst, rejects Carroll for himself not "feeling" the depth of nonsense.

If Artaud's assessment of Carroll's *Alice* books is correct, we might, Deleuze tells us,

attribute the books' treatment of nonsense and schizophrenia to the playful imaginings of a "pervert ... who holds onto the establishment of a surface language" (LS 84). Perhaps, though, and as I have claimed, an argument may yet be made by which Carroll's nonsense may properly be recuperated and rescued from that (invariably) Artaudian charge of a critical evasion, the failure to "feel the real problem of a language in depth – namely the schizophrenic problem of suffering, of death, and of life" (LS 84). By way of conclusion, therefore, I might recall one of Deleuze's earliest writings on the question of sense and signification, namely *Difference and Repetition*. Situated within the context of our earlier discussion over the "haunting monsters" in the world of depths, whose haunting alterity is nothing less than their suspended potentiality, we find that in order to "grasp" the schizophrenia of nonsense "we [must] insist upon special conditions of *experience* – however artificial – namely ... that the expressed has (for us) no existence apart from that which expresses it: the Other *as the expression of a possible world*" (*Difference and Repetition* 261; emphasis mine). The Other, that is, insofar as it grounds the possibility of a(nother) world, must necessarily be understood as nothing less – and, consequently, nothing more – than qua the "inscription [of] the *possibility* of a frightening world when I am not yet afraid, or, on the contrary, the possibility of a reassuring world when I am really frightened by the world ..." (LS 310). Accordingly, if, as Deleuze suggests, Carroll's "*Alice in Wonderland* was originally to have been entitled *Alice's Adventures Underground*" (CC 21), we might speculate that Carroll made the change in recognition of the fact that the two realms of nonsense are fundamentally cathected together, continually enveloping into but also *away* from each other – caught in a Liebnitzian incompossibility around which the question of the schizophrenic status of "suffering, death, and life" can only ever be posed as an unanswerable cryptic cipher whose conditions of openness are also the conditions of its infinite enfolding.

notes

1 I would like to thank Linda Shires, Pelagia Goulimari, and an anonymous *Angelaki* reviewer for their very helpful and careful comments on an earlier draft of this essay. My thanks also to Gregg Lambert and David Johnson, both for their encouragement of my work and for the many hours of invigorating discussion on the writings of Deleuze and Descartes.

2 I mean only to highlight a division in Carroll scholarship over the subject of nonsense, an object traditionally taken up less under the protocols of what we might call Continental philosophy and postmodernism, than that of linguistics and mathematics and certain analytical strains of philosophy. On the latter, see Martin Gardner's *Annotated Alice* and subsequently revised in two separate editions, *More Annotated Alice* and *The Annotated Alice*.

3 I'm referring to Alice's exchange with Humpty Dumpty, where, in response to Alice's question over whether Dumpty can explicate the poem Jabberwocky, Humpty Dumpty replies "I can explain all the poems that were ever invented – and a good many that haven't been invented just yet" (187).

4 See, for instance, Locke's *An Essay Concerning Human Understanding* (1690) and Hume's *An Enquiry Concerning Human Understanding* (1748), as well as Bishop Berkeley's *A Treatise Concerning the Principles of Human Knowledge* (1710).

5 Here I am thinking of works by Jean-Jacques Lecercle, Peter Heath, and James R. Kincaid in particular.

6 The following discussion over the division of nonsense between Antonin Artaud and Lewis Carroll is indebted to Gregg Lambert's discussion over Gilles Deleuze and Jacques Derrida and the question of literature divided (shared) between them (see "The Subject of Literature between Derrida and Deleuze").

7 Deleuze's references to Carroll and Artaud occur in a number of his works, but perhaps the most well known occur in his works with collaborator Félix Guattari, namely *Anti-Oedipus* and *A Thousand Plateaus*.

8 See Jean-François Lyotard's critique of the normativity of metadiscourses in *The Differend*, in particular Lyotard's characterization of the "crisis of legitimacy" as an epistemic rupture in modern society over the basic question of consensus and of whether any discourse (or discourses) may legitimately (be said to) organize and adjudicate various truth-claims or claims-to-truth (3–32, 128–30, 123–50).

9 Cf. Jacques Lacan, "God and the Jouissance of the Woman."

10 I thus disagree with interpretations which have occluded discussion of the philosophical dimensions of this confluence, especially as this appears around the question of Alice's dream, in favor of a less radical approach – such that what is reinstalled, rather than subverted, are those rhetorical protocols ostensibly subverted by nonsense.

11 For instance, Alice's discussion with the Mad Hatter over the subject of time. Whereas the Hatter's is a personified "Time" Alice's is a conventional definition of "time." As Cohan and Shires suggest, "Alice and the Hatter each use the word 'time' to refer to something different because the words they use keep pointing to other signifiers of time within two mutually exclusive syntagms, each producing a different meaning for time" (16).

12 See Deleuze's *Essays Critical and Clinical* over the question of the (im)proper division of literature between the two discourses, a division most striking within what Deleuze calls psychoanalysis's "botching" of the clinical discourse (LS 92) – a problem itself taken up much earlier by Deleuze around the figures of de Sade and Masoch in his *Coldness and Cruelty*, originally published in 1967.

13 Cf. Northrop Frye, *Fearful Symmetry* 3–29. The phrase is borrowed from Frye's characterization of romantic poet William Blake's "The Tiger." The expression refers to the juxtaposition between fear and awe incarnated in the observer in the face of his reciprocal gaze with the contained animal. The phrase's use of "symmetry" underscores the potential of the encounter: the sense of an irreducible other that, while contained, and even while fearful, nonetheless (or precisely therefore) remains a source of wonder and captivation.

14 Cf. Beverly Lyon Clark, *Reflections of Fantasy*.

15 In Jacques Derrida, *Writing and Difference* 176.

bibliography

Carroll, Lewis. *Alice's Adventures in Wonderland and Through the Looking-Glass.* Ed. Hugh Haughton. London and New York: Penguin, 1998.

Clark, Beverly Lyon. *Reflections of Fantasy: The Mirror Worlds of Carroll, Nabokov, and Pynchon.* New York: Lang, 1986.

Cohan, Steven and Linda Shires. *Telling Stories: A Theoretical Analysis of Narrative Fiction.* New York: Routledge, 1988.

Deleuze, Gilles. *Coldness and Cruelty.* Trans. Jean McNeil. New York: Zone, 1989.

Deleuze, Gilles. *Difference and Repetition.* Trans. Paul Patton. London: Athlone, 1994.

Deleuze, Gilles. *Empiricism and Subjectivity.* Trans. Constantin Boundas. New York: Columbia UP, 1991.

Deleuze, Gilles. *Essays Critical and Clinical.* Trans. Daniel W. Smith and Michael A. Greco. Minneapolis: U of Minnesota P, 1997.

Deleuze, Gilles. *Kafka: Toward a Minor Literature.* Trans. Dana Polan. Minneapolis: U of Minnesota P, 1986.

Deleuze, Gilles. *The Logic of Sense.* Ed. Constantin Boundas. Trans. Mark Lester and Charles Stivale. New York: Columbia UP, 1990.

Deleuze, Gilles and Félix Guattari. *Anti-Oedipus: Capitalism and Schizophrenia.* Trans. Robert Hurley, Mark Seem and Helen R. Lane. Minneapolis: U of Minnesota P, 1983.

Deleuze, Gilles and Félix Guattari. *A Thousand Plateaus.* Trans. Brian Massumi. Minneapolis: U of Minnesota P, 1987.

Derrida, Jacques. *Writing and Difference.* Trans. Alan Bass. Chicago: U of Chicago P, 1978.

Descartes, René. *Discourse on the Method and Meditations on First Philosophy.* Ed. David Weissman. Trans. Elizabeth S. Haldane and G.R.T. Ross. New Haven: Yale UP, 1996.

Frye, Northrop. *Fearful Symmetry: A Study of William Blake.* Boston: Beacon, 1947.

Gardner, Martin. *Annotated Alice: Alice's Adventures in Wonderland and Through the Looking Glass.* New York: Potter, 1960.

Gardner, Martin. *The Annotated Alice: Alice's Adventures in Wonderland and Through the Looking Glass. The Definitive Edition.* New York: Norton, 2000.

Gardner, Martin. *More Annotated Alice: Alice's Adventures in Wonderland and Through the Looking Glass and What She Found There.* New York: Random, 1990.

Heath, Peter. *The Philosopher's Alice: Alice's Adventures in Wonderland and Through the Looking-Glass.* New York: St. Martin's, 1974.

Kincaid, James R. "Alice's Invasion of Wonderland." *PMLA* 88 (1973): 92–99.

Lacan, Jacques. "God and the Jouissance of the Woman." *Feminine Sexuality: Jacques Lacan and the école freudienne.* Ed. Juliet Mitchell and Jacqueline Rose. Trans. Jacqueline Rose. London: Macmillan, 1982. 137–48.

Lambert, Gregg. "The Subject of Literature between Derrida and Deleuze: Law or Life?" *Angelaki: Journal of the Theoretical Humanities* 5.2 (2000): 177–90.

Lecercle, Jean-Jacques. *The Philosophy of Nonsense: The Intuitions of Victorian Nonsense Literature.* New York: Routledge, 1994.

Lyotard, Jean-François. *The Differend: Phrases in Dispute.* Trans. Georges Van Den Abbeele. Minneapolis: U of Minnesota P, 1991.

Schwab, Gabrielle. "Nonsense and Metacommunications: Reflections on Lewis Carroll." *The Play of the Self.* Ed. Ronald Bogue and Mihai I. Spariosu. Albany: State U of New York P, 1994.

Shires, Linda M. "Fantasy, Nonsense, Parody, and the Status of the Real: The Example of Carroll." *Victorian Poetry* 26.3 (1988): 267–83.

Alan Lopez
Department of English
306 Samuel Clemens Hall
SUNY Buffalo
Buffalo, NY 14260
USA
E-mail: alopez@buffalo.edu

journal of the theoretical humanities
volume 9 number 3 december 2004

Language would exceed the limits of what is thought, by suggesting, letting be understood without ever making understandable [*en laissant sous-entendre, sans jamais faire entendre*] an implication of meaning distinct from that which comes to signs from the simultaneity of systems or the logical definition of concepts. This possibility [*vertu*] is laid bare in the *poetic said* [...] It is shown in the *prophetic said*.

    Emmanuel Levinas, *AE 262/OB 170*

Thinking otherwise than he thinks, he thinks in such a way that the Other might come to thought, as approach and response.

    Maurice Blanchot, *ED 41/WD 36*

Thus there are not two discourses: there is discourse – and then there would be dis-course, were it not that of it we "know" practically nothing. We "know" that it escapes systems, order, possibility, including the possibility of language, and that writing, perhaps – writing, where totality has let itself be exceeded – puts it in play.

    Maurice Blanchot, *ED 141/WD 134*

gabriel riera

"THE POSSIBILITY OF THE *POETIC SAID*"
between allusion and commentary (ingratitude, or blanchot in levinas ii)

In his effort to elucidate a more originary difference than Heidegger's, as well as an *ethicity* of thinking able to respond to the trace of transcendence of the other's face, Levinas's philosophy redefines language radically and does so in uneasy proximity to poetic writing.[1] Most critics agree that Levinas's philosophy is inhospitable to aesthetic phenomena and ambiguous toward poetic language. His severe condemnation of the work of art in "Reality and Its Shadow," whose conceptual system is still present in *Totality and Infinity*, leaves little doubt of this fact.[2] This does not mean that Levinas did not acknowledge "poetic" language's ability to suggest significations that exceed the order of discourse; indeed, he even endows it with a (quasi-)ethical force. The acknowledgment goes without saying, however, or is merely implied (*sous-entendu*), since in *Otherwise than Being* it will appear only by way of an *allusion* to Maurice Blanchot's *The Madness of the Day*. As I will show in this paper, this indirect reference marks the site of a complex intertextual grafting: what the poetic *said* simply *suggests*, that "language would exceed the limits of what is thought" (AE 262/OB 170), becomes operative in Levinas's own text. It enables it to welcome the *otherwise than being* and to put into place a writing whose double temporality (diachrony) lets the other "come to thought, as approach *and*

ISSN 0969-725X print/ISSN 1469-2899 online/04/030121–15 © 2004 Taylor & Francis Ltd and the Editors of *Angelaki*
DOI: 10.1080/0969725042000307673

response" (EI 78/IC 67). That something more is at stake in this allusion becomes clear when read through the magnifying glass of the essay that Levinas devotes one year later to *The Madness of the Day*, where the proximity of *the poetic* and *the prophetic* said weave an intrigue of *the otherwise than being*.[3] My purpose here is to read the allusion through the essay "Exercises on *The Madness of the Day*" because it is here that something crucial occurs concerning the destiny of the "possibility [*vertu*] of poetic language" (AE 262/OB 170). It also allows us to re-evaluate, retroactively, what takes place by means of the allusion in *Otherwise than Being*. But before analyzing the essay I will situate the allusion within the frame of Levinas's overall reflections on art and poetic language in view of isolating continuities and displacements in Levinas's philosophy.

The apparently constitutive incompatibility between the aesthetic sphere and a philosophy that seeks to welcome not only another saying but also a saying *of* the other – a signifyingness (*significance*) of the human being that retains the trace of transcendence – should still remind us that Levinas must necessarily confront what Blanchot calls the "question of writing" (EI 12–21/IC 6–18): a way of conceiving "literary" or "poetic" language "beyond" aesthetics and in an oblique relation with the philosophical *logos*. By approaching writing in this way, Levinas not only reconsiders his early position regarding the work of art but also radically revises his conception of language in order to shape a textual matrix in which to welcome the other. Levinas's rapport with Blanchot's thinking is symptomatic of his complex attitude toward writing and poetic language and thus a privileged site to explore how Levinas engages "the question of writing."

I

Poetic language appears as a reservoir of experiences, themes and examples in Levinas's early works. By *Existence and Existents*, however, the activation of poetic language's latent potentialities gives way to one of his most important

concepts: the "there is" (*il y a*). Levinas appeals to the imagination in order to isolate being's underside, the terrible dimension of pure being, impersonal and anonymous (DEE 57/EE 93): what remains after the world's negation (including the negation of this negation). Levinas secures the *il y a*'s deduction by means of the imagination, and in a footnote gives credit to Maurice Blanchot's *Thomas the Obscure* for making this dimension explicit. From then on, the *"possibility [vertu] of poetic language"* (AE 262/OB 170) in particular and the destiny of the aesthetic phenomenon in general are sealed. They are the privileged means for exposing us to being in general, although they break neither with the *il y a*'s hold nor remove us from its suffocating neutrality. Levinas thus locates aesthetic phenomena at the antipodes of his philosophy.

Levinas does not elaborate on the "possibility [*vertu*] of the poetic said" (AE 262/OB 170) until well into his second major book, *Otherwise than Being*, and he does so in a decisive context. It is an even more audacious operation here than the earlier elucidation of the "there is" (*il y a*) since it now concerns the reduction of the said (*le dit*) and the securing of an ethical saying (writing) that retains the trace of the other in the language of the Same. In the language of philosophy, Levinas appeals to a different law from that of discourse, a law "before the law."[4] However, he does not summon up the imagination here. Neither does he introduce any philosophical or biblical reference. Indeed, Levinas's way of dealing with "the possibility of literary language" (AE 262/OB 170) goes almost unnoticed: it is simply an *allusion*. As in the case of the "there is" (*il y a*), his friend Maurice Blanchot is again summoned to testify on poetic language's behalf, but this time his writing gets entangled with the *emphatic* writing of the *otherwise than being*.

Marked by a general condemnation of art, the distance between *Existence and Existents* and *Otherwise than Being* also separates Levinas's two uses of Blanchot. The pitfalls of the aesthetic phenomenon that Levinas circumscribes early on in *Existence and Existents* cohere into a system of concepts that go against the grain of all the tenets of modern aesthetics in "Reality and Its Shadow." A *shadow* of the "there is" (*il y a*), the *plasticity* of the work of art turns into the gelid stone of the *statue* or *idol* of fate, whose *rhythm* has a hold upon the subject and transports him into the *meanwhile*. The subject has no hope of breaking away from the deadly fascination of pure being because it is hostage to the interval of time deprived of the other's face. Against phenomenology's idealization of the image (a window to the *noema*), Levinas claims that art's proper dimension is obscurity or non-truth and that the production of images entails a form of magic or participation. And contra Sartre, Levinas argues that the artist is a possessed individual whose irresponsibility, disengagement and evasion are dangerously contagious. Levinas disqualifies the image by putting it under the heading of *idol*, a concept that brings together the opacity of aesthetic materiality and the fixed temporality of the work of art: "a stoppage of time, or rather its delay behind itself" (RO 791/CPP 8).[5]

Totality and Infinity exacerbates the precarious nature of the work of art by privileging the *face-à-face* and speech without mediation over the artwork's façade (beautiful form). This book appeals to a sober and demanding word; the other summons the self in a severe *prose* that exorcises plasticity's rhythm and rhetoric's simulacra. But prose does not seem to have the last word on the *virtue* of the poetic said since Levinas does not determine the precise place of the "there is" (*il y a*) until *Otherwise than Being*. It is also in this work that Levinas's conception of language undergoes a profound re-articulation where the structure of the Socratic word breaks its dependency on a metaphysics of presence.[6]

Throughout Levinas's work, his discussion and his use of the "possibility [*vertu*] of the poetic said" (AE 262/OB 170) oscillate between two sometimes-overlapping versions. On the one hand, *possibility* appears as being's verbality (rumor of the "there is," rhythm, statue, idol, all the elements that can be subsumed under the concept of the said (*le dit*)) and, on the other, *possibility* denotes the "otherwise than being" or saying (*le dire*) endowed with a (quasi-)ethical dimension. So we are faced with an ontological

possibility and a metaphysical one, in the sense of an ethical anteriority that Levinas isolates in *Totality and Infinity*. This oscillation is never fully settled and compels Levinas to re-assess the aesthetic phenomenon time and again. It also explains why Levinas does not fully address the "possibility [*vertu*] of the poetic said" (AE 262/OB 170) in all its complexity until *Otherwise than Being*, where he not only indicates this (quasi-)ethical dimension but also unfolds it in his own textuality.[7] This double operation occurs precisely within the frame of the capital reduction of the said (*le dit*), where the *allusion* to Blanchot's *The Madness of the Day* allows Levinas to re-articulate poetic language vis-à-vis the ethical saying that *Otherwise than Being* not only elucidates but also produces as call *and* response. This response is out of sync because it is a word in two-times (*dia-chrony*), a mad word that no longer simply obeys the law of discourse (in *The Infinite Conversation* Blanchot calls it an "always already written speech" (EI 80/IC 67)).

In *Otherwise than Being* the destiny of poetic language seems to unfold on the hither side or beyond the region that in *Existence and Existents* Levinas called "existence without world" (DEE 55–57/EE 93–95). It is also no longer simply cast as a *shadow*, as in "Reality and Its Shadow," but envisioned as a "given word" (AE 233/OB 149). Now it is a voice that comes from "the other shore" (AE 280/OB 183); a mad voice that, as in Blanchot's story (*récit*), refuses to tell stories and yet manages to bear witness to an *intrigue* of the other in a "quasi-hagiographic style" (DQVI 65/GWCM 59). However, while in *Existence and Existents* Levinas acknowledges Blanchot's "description of the *there is*" by explicitly referring to *Thomas the Obscure* (DEE 103, n. 1/EE 98), in *Otherwise than Being* he does not mention *The Madness of the Day*.[8]

It is crucial to consider the reasons for Levinas's discretion. Inasmuch as the allusion functions under a double register, the *virtue* of poetic language falls on the side of the said (*le dit*) and thematization (order of discourse). However, a textual grafting takes place in *Otherwise than Being*: the matrix of a double law that unfolds in *The Madness of the Day* becomes the model of the ethical reduction of the said and the possibility of a word whose spacing subtracts itself from the law of discourse (totality, the Same). In the poetic *said*, Levinas localizes a double temporality that could potentially exceed discourse's power of assimilation. It is this dimension of poetic language that Levinas explicitly recognizes and values under the heading of "possibility [*vertu*]." Levinas describes the refutation of skepticism, the oppressive dimension of the order of discourse and its rejection of anything that could escape its grasp in terms of *The Madness of the Day*. He alludes to this text at a strategic moment: before the performative inscription of the ethical saying, an operation *of writing* that marks the ethical interruption of essence (AE 262–63/OB 169), and before the last chapter titled "Outside" ["Au Dehors"], in which Levinas elucidates the form of openness that pertains to substitution, an ethical form of openness different from Heidegger's "letting be" (AE 274–75/OB 178–79).

Because the first use of these literary figures responds to a classical philosophical treatment of tropes, Levinas does not hesitate to qualify it as a *said*: it belongs to ontology and offers a satisfactory description of totality's topology. The second use, however, does not belong to this configuration. We could call it a poetic *saying* that, while going unacknowledged, silently provides Levinas with a formal structure to describe and inscribe the ethical saying as what exceeds ontology and totality. The poetic *said* allows Levinas to describe how discourse accomplishes the mending of the saying's "latent diachrony," what we may call the first version of interruption: "coherence thus dissimulates a transcendence, a movement from the one to the other, a *latent diachrony*, uncertainty and a fine risk" (AE 263–64/OB 170). Levinas conveys the violence of coherence and its dissimulation of the *intrigue* in terms of a literary scene that presents the "association of philosophy with the State and with medicine" (AE 264/OB 170). Repression and mediation appear here under the guise of the ophthalmologist and the psychiatrist, the two discursive positions that interrogate "the interlocutor that does not yield to logic" (AE 262/OB 168) and, therefore, that resists the complete

assimilation of the saying to the said, as well as the violent suppression of the saying. However, Levinas still circumscribes the *possibility* of poetic writing as a *said*, without mentioning or elucidating the interruptive force of Blanchot's story (*récit*) as the *saying* that subtracts itself from the order of discourse.[9] This literary scene (that, strictly speaking, is neither "literary" nor "aesthetic") allows Levinas to ask whether another way of dealing with interruption is possible. Is there a *second version of interruption* that does not depend on the violence of coherence (the forceful extraction of a testimony by interrogation, which is precisely how Blanchot figures the coercive nature of the order of discourse and the law of narration)?

The poetic *saying* provides Levinas with a formal structure to describe this other version of interruption and to inscribe the ethical saying, since what he proposes is the possibility of understanding interruption as different from interruptions in discourse. Levinas focuses on what discourse represses or on what a conventional version of interruption discards, but nonetheless preserves on the underside of its fabric. The dissimulating effect that the first version of interruption accomplishes comes to the forefront as a continuous thread, but the inscription of a no less forceful interruption sparks Levinas's interest (the series of knots). In order to relate these two series, Levinas first exposes the discursive work of interruption (its thread) and shows that it is a "broken thread" unable to fully reduce the knots of interruption. He then interrupts the interruption of discourse and demonstrates that the continuous thread and the knots of interruption no longer relate to each other in terms of simultaneity or correlation.[10]

Levinas's *allusion* to the "possibility [*vertu*]" of poetic language goes hand in hand with the deployment of a series of *textual* tropes (thread, knots, tissue, weaving) through which the ethical reduction of the said takes place, since in the poetic *said* language *suggests* "an impossible simultaneousness of meaning" (AE 262/OB 169). Levinas attempts to write precisely this simultaneity of meaning that philosophical discourse betrays.

Levinas invokes the *possibility* of poetic writing as *said, at the very moment* when he speaks of language as "skepticism" and energizes his ethical reduction of discourse through a textual graphics that bears striking similarities to *The Madness of the Day*. It is as if the language of *Otherwise than Being*, which shows a different understanding of its own operations from that of *Totality and Infinity*, were making peace with poetic writing. One can claim that a *substitution* of "poetic" and "philosophical" writing has taken place, yet doubts still remain, given Levinas's discrete acknowledgment of the "possibility [*vertu*]" of poetic language to *un-say* the said. The only way to dispel these doubts is by supplementing Levinas's allusion with a reading of his 1975 essay "Exercises on *The Madness of the Day*." However, to do so entails shifting away from discretion and into the concept of *ingratitude*, a concept in which Levinas ciphers an ethics of reading.

Levinas's essay provides an enlarged version of what was earlier just a discrete allusion. Does Levinas wish to make up for the allusion's ingratitude and to acknowledge the pivotal role that Blanchot's writing plays in *Otherwise than Being*? This is a tempting explanation given that only one year separates the allusion and the essay, except that *ingratitude* is precisely the concept that organizes the latter. As we will see, the fate of the "possibility [*vertu*] of poetic language" (AE 262/OB 170) hangs on this final confrontation with Blanchot and will also allow us to evaluate retroactively what took place in *Otherwise than Being*.

II

Does Blanchot think there is no longer any book? No reading, no writing, no expression.

Emmanuel Levinas, SMB 70/PN 167

We must give up trying to know those to whom we are linked by something essential; by this I mean we must greet them in *the relation with the unknown* in which they greet us as well, in our distance [*éloignement*]. Friendship, this relation without dependence, without episode, [...] [is] *the movement of understanding* in which, speaking to us, they reserve, even on the most

familiar terms, an *infinite distance*, the *fundamental separation* on the basis of which *what separates becomes relation*.

Maurice Blanchot, A 24/F 29

Maurice Blanchot's writing occupies a privileged place in Levinas's reflection on art in general and poetic language in particular. Because it spans over twenty years the relation between their texts is fraught with shifts, reformulations and ambiguities. Levinas first situates Blanchot within a Hegelo-Kojèvian philosophical context (the end of philosophy, the end of art, the closure of the system) and then gradually places him within a space that is neither philosophical nor aesthetic. Although he approaches Blanchot's writing in terms of ethics as "first philosophy," Levinas's re-articulations of the "there is" and language are determining factors in his reading of Blanchot, as the three essays he publishes between 1956 and 1975 (later collected in *Sur Maurice Blanchot*) make clear.[11]

Levinas reads Blanchot as the signpost of a "way out of Heidegger" (SMB 25/PN 139), a path that his own thinking sets as a goal in the early *On Escape* [*De l'évasion*]. The effects of this approach are still visible today in intellectual histories, as well as in more analytical works.[12] Although this account finds its justification in Blanchot's own critique of Heidegger, it hides as much as it reveals. Within the context of this critical account the *neuter* and its relation to writing marks a point of total divergence between Levinas and Blanchot. While for the former the *neuter* names the impersonality of pure being (*il y a*) and the violent realm of ontology (including Heidegger's fundamental ontology) from which the other becomes the only way out and the only true process of *de-neutralization*, for the latter it indicates a space of subtraction from being that thinking must preserve in its radical alterity (without recourse to any form of presence or de-neutralization). To be unable to endure the emptiness of the neuter entails a failure for thinking: the inability to respond to the injunction to keep watch on the other and the temptation to cover up its emptiness with the remains of the Same.[13]

In his seminal "The Poet's Vision" Levinas attempts to specify the peculiarity of Blanchot's writing, whose "reflection on art and literature has the highest ambitions [...] [T]he book [*The Space of Literature*] is, in fact, situated beyond all critique and all exegesis. And yet it does not tend toward philosophy" (SMB 9/PN 127). Levinas situates Blanchot's reflexive writing in proximity to philosophy, although the former does not fully coincide with the traditional hierarchical emplacement of philosophy, especially given that Blanchot's writing subtracts itself from power and possibility. Does this mean that his writing is irreducible to philosophical discourse? Before answering this question, it is necessary to make the two basic predicates of Levinas's reading explicit and to focus on its overall teleology.

After situating the peculiarity of Blanchot's writing, Levinas claims that

> Blanchot determines writing as a quasi-mad structure in the general economy of being, by which being is no longer an economy, as it no longer possesses, when approached through writing, any *abode* – no longer has any *interiority* [*aucune habitation, ne comporte aucune intériorité*]. (SMB 17/PN 133; my emphasis)

This is an ambiguous assessment of writing. On the one hand, writing exceeds the restricted economy of being and is conceived as something radically *strange*. On the other, it does not entail an inwardness and a dwelling, the two crucial concepts that for Levinas constitute the possibility of the face-to-face with the other.[14] We must recall that this essay was published in 1956, at the time Levinas was writing *Totality and Infinity*; consequently, the principles guiding his reading are those he outlined in "Reality and Its Shadow" and in some of the essays that make up the basic argument of *Totality and Infinity*:[15]

> It is literary space, that is, absolute exteriority: the exteriority of absolute exile [...] Modern art speaks of nothing but the adventure of art itself [...] No doubt the critical and philosophical work, relating that adventure, is far below art, which is the voyage into the end of the night itself, and not merely the travel narrative. And yet Blanchot's research *brings to the*

philosopher a "category" and a new "way of knowing" that I would like to clarify, independently of the philosophy of art proper. (SMB 18/PN 133; my emphasis)

At first, Levinas recognizes that *writing* exceeds the frames of "the general economy of being" as well as philosophical discourse, since no discourse operating under the law of the Same would be able to approach its specificity or absolute exteriority. There is therefore agreement between Levinas and Blanchot on "the question of writing." Yet in spite of all the precautions that Levinas takes, such as his use of quotation marks to signal the impropriety of certain philosophical concepts within this context, he ultimately recuperates what exceeds or resists philosophical conceptuality. He does so by a double movement whose necessity is systematic.

The first turn of this appropriating movement is marked by a lexical slippage: Levinas begins by referring to writing (*écriture*) and concludes in the realm of *art*. As soon as he conflates writing *and* art, he activates the legitimacy of a philosophical approach to art (even if Levinas's clarification functions "independently of the philosophy of art proper" (SMB 18/PN 133)).[16] The second turn in this movement consists of a reduction and final appropriation of what by Levinas's own definition seems to resist appropriation. The appropriated excess is put to work against philosophy itself (Heidegger), but this confrontation takes place *within* philosophy's economy, as could not be otherwise: Blanchot's search is thus profitable for the philosopher. If in "Reality and Its Shadow" the work of art had no claim whatsoever on knowledge because it "[let] go of the prey for the shadow" (RO 794/CPP 12), Blanchot's writing now provides the philosopher with a *"new way of knowing"* (SMB 18/PN 133):

> Does Blanchot not attribute to art the function of uprooting the Heideggerian universe? Does not the poet, before the "eternal streaming of the outside," hear the voices that call away from the Heideggerian world? (SMB 25/PN 139)

In Levinas's schema Blanchot is a writer who

evolves from an early Hegelian phenomenological position in the 1940s to a late Heideggerian in the 1950s and finally leaves Heidegger behind. Blanchot thus marks a way out of the thinking of Being. Although Levinas draws the outline of his own trajectory through Blanchot, it is still not clear whether this escape leads to an ethical thought understood as "first philosophy" (SMB 22/PN 137).

Levinas attenuates the complexity of Blanchot's relation to Heidegger, which cannot be interpreted simply as carrying out a transformation of the thinking of Being (Heidegger) into *ethics*[17] – not only because it would be possible to isolate an *ethicity* in Heidegger but also because Blanchot disavows the pertinence of the term *ethics* to refer to the "wholly other relation" (*rapport tout autre*) (EI 101–03/IC 84–86).[18] In fact, Blanchot separates his elaboration of the question of the other from Levinas's and this move will not only activate Heidegger's *Ent-fernung* (proximity in distance) as a way of undermining any notion of immediate presence but will also explore the question of the ontological difference that takes him to a radical exploration of language.[19] While for Levinas the *face-à-face* with the other human being is irreducible, for Blanchot it is not the final term of the "wholly other relation" since what is decisive for him is what circulates in and through the *face-à-face*. The other (*autrui*) is not the final term but rather the knot of an intrigue through which the *neuter*, the (an-archic) unnamable origin of language, passes. The ethical (infra-) structure that Levinas isolates in the *face-à-face* is part of a larger one that encompasses the Outside (*le Dehors*), an element as old or older than Levinas's diachrony.

Levinas shifts from descriptive language to a more judgmental one when he specifies Blanchot's understanding of writing:

> To write is to return to essential language, which consists in moving things aside in words, and echoing being [...] To be is to speak, but in the absence of any interlocutor. An impersonal speech without "you," without address, without vocative, and yet distinct from the "coherent discourse" which manifests a Universal Reason belonging to the order of the Day. (SMB 15/PN 130–31)

Although Levinas recognizes that writing does not belong fully to totality, he juxtaposes writing and speech by characterizing the former as speech that occurs in the interlocutor's absence; he thus asserts the non-ethical nature of writing. Levinas reinforces this view when he adds that the two basic modalities of ethical speech – interpellation and the vocative – do not belong to writing. In other words, Levinas evaluates Blanchot's writing from the perspective of the conceptuality elaborated in *Totality and Infinity*, where the opposition of speech to writing is in solidarity with a metaphysics of presence.[20]

Levinas returns to Blanchot ten years later in "The Servant and His Master" (1966), which includes a reading *L'Attente l'oubli* and marks a major shift in conceptuality.[21] Levinas's understanding of language and poetic writing in *Otherwise than Being* is crucial to his re-assessment.[22] Blanchot's text challenges Hegelian dialectics, says Levinas:

> *L'Attente l'oubli* denies the philosophical language of interpretation, which "speaks incessantly," the dignity of being and ultimate language. To seek – beyond the poetic discourse that expresses, dispersedly, the impossible escape from discourse – the *logos* that gathers, is to block the opening through which the circularity of coherent discourse announces (but also denounces, and in so doing transcends) itself. Could one not venture further, and think what speech wants to say? *And perhaps we are wrong in using the designation art and poetry for that exceptional event, that sovereign forgetting that liberates language with respect to the structures in which the said maintains itself.* Perhaps Hegel was right as far as art is concerned. What counts – *whether it be called poetry or what you will* – is that a meaning be able to proffer itself beyond the closed discourse of Hegel; that a meaning that forgets the presuppositions of that discourse becomes *fable.* (SMB 33/PN 143; my emphasis)

Levinas locates Blanchot's text "beyond Hegel" (even if the syntax of Blanchot's writing –

ni ... ni – voids the step (*pas*) to a beyond by means of a discrete negation) and, more importantly, outside of the space of "art." In spite of Levinas's lack of specificity regarding the status of that space, this statement marks a distance from "The Poet's Vision," where he conflated the space of art with that of writing (*écriture*), a difference that Blanchot distinguishes systematically since at least *The Infinite Conversation*.

What is traditionally called art or poetry becomes an "exceptional event" in which saying (*le dire*) exceeds the prepositional dimension of language (*le dit*) and no longer amounts to a "return to essential language, which consists in moving things aside in words and echoing being" (SMB 33/PN 143). Considered an ethical event, poetic writing shares some structural features with ethical *saying* because it "signals to us, without the sign's bearing a meaning by giving up meaning" (SMB 39/PN 147).[23] In a footnote that still shows a certain reticence toward poetic language, Levinas clarifies what he understands by "poetry":

> I have already said above, that the word poetry, to me, means the rupture of the immanence to which language is condemned, imprisoning itself. I do not think that *this rupture is a purely esthetic event*. But the word poetry does not, after all, designate a species, the genus of which would be art. Inseparable from the verb, it overflows with *prophetic meaning*. (SMB 79, n. 3/PN 185, n. 4; my emphasis)

Poetic writing interrupts totality from its nonaesthetic emplacement because "poetry" no longer names an artistic genre, but rather something endowed with "prophetic significations." We must remember that in *Otherwise than Being* the term *prophetic* defines the "reverting in which the perception of an order coincides with the signification of this order given to him that obeys it" (AE 232/OB 149; translation modified). *Prophetic* is an ethical term because, strictly speaking, it refers to the other in the Same or to ethical signification. It is precisely this ethical dimension that, according to Levinas, Blanchot's writing liberates by disrupting the power of assimilation proper to the totality and by opening language from within to

its most "external intimacy" (*extimité*).[24] Blanchot's poetic saying "preserves this movement that is located between seeing and saying [...] a language going from one singularity to the other without having anything in common, a language without words that *beckons before signifying anything*" (SMB 41/PN 148; my emphasis).

This decisive change in the conception of language and the "possibility [*vertu*] of poetic writing" informs Levinas's 1975 essay and is crucial for determining its relation to the allusion in *Otherwise than Being*. By referring to Blanchot's text as a "no longer recent text" (SMB 51/PN 156) Levinas indicates that he is not writing a chronicle, review or note and that his reading of the *Madness of the Day* is extemporaneous.[25] However, one should not overlook the fact that in 1974 Blanchot published a series of fragments titled "Discours sur la patience," devoted to two key concepts in *Otherwise than Being*, passivity and responsibility.[26]

"Discours sur la patience" and "Exercises on *The Madness of the Day*" may be read as a diptych, as some critics have done, in which Levinas reciprocates Blanchot's gesture, but only if their "infinite conversation" is figured as an exchange rather than a *friendship*, which supposes asymmetry and lack of reciprocity. Levinas's notion of work (*œuvre*), however, also stresses non-reciprocity and asymmetry: "[it] demands a radical generosity from the Same who, in the work, goes toward the Other. The work demands the Other's *ingratitude*. Gratitude, on the other hand, would mean the movement's return to its point of origin" (EEHH 191; translation mine). Not unlike Blanchot, Levinas questions the circular economy of the Same by opposing the story of Ulysses' return to the safety of Ithaca to the dispersal and exile condensed in the figure of Abraham.[27] What remains to be seen is whether Levinas preserves the *ingratitude* that the work demands or if a more complex gesture takes place.

Ingratitude is a movement that interrupts the return to a point of origin; it alters and therefore accomplishes a series of reversals that allows a substitution of "discourse" for "exercises." There are good reasons for this movement since Blanchot's fragments not only bear little resemblance to "continuous speech" but also propose a reflection on patience and passivity that puts the order of discourse in disarray. Levinas's essay, meanwhile, where a "translation" of a poetic text into prose (ethical language) takes place, seems to operate under the order of discourse. It would be a mistake, though, to overlook the fact that Levinas's essay also functions under the exigency of a double law and performs a series of displacements on Blanchot's text.

What relationship can we establish between the allusion and the essay? Can one simply read the latter as a more explicit development of what was only elliptical in the former? If *ingratitude* is indeed the principle of the work (*œuvre*) does it "do justice" to Blanchot's text? The allusion to *The Madness of the Day* in *Otherwise than Being* enables Levinas to condense several threads of his argument (diachrony, substitution, saying and skepticism) and arrives at a strategic point (the reduction of the said by saying). Since only one year separates *Otherwise than Being* from the "Exercises," one could reasonably expect that the basic premises of the book would also apply to the essay. In fact, the so-called quasi-hagiographical style that dominates *Otherwise than Being* energizes the deployment of some of the essay's crucial figures. Its rhythm marks the pace of a double set of operations: the interpretation of Blanchot's text, and a re-writing (in filigree) of "Reality and Its Shadow," in which a reassessment of the ethical "possibility [*vertu*] of poetic language" (AE 262/ OB 170) is at stake. For this reason the essay is made up of two different sets of premises that juxtapose each other: those of *Otherwise than Being* and those of "Reality and Its Shadow" that the "linguistic turn" of the former should have superseded. I will separate these two different sets of premises to see the kind of figure they compose in response to *The Madness of the Day* and then determine whether there are differences or displacements between Levinas's allusion to this text in *Otherwise than Being* and what he explicitly affirms in the "Exercises."

Levinas opens his essay with a section titled "From Poetry to Prose," where he defines expression as "inspired meaning" (*sens inspiré*) (SMB 55/PN 156),[28] according to the principles

of *Otherwise than Being*. At the same time, he performs a reduction, a "translation" of the text's musicality (poetry) into prose reminiscent of "Reality and Its Shadow." This "translation" removes the text from the jurisdiction of "artistic criticism" into that of "philosophical criticism" (SMB 57/PN 157). The movement "from poetry to prose" allows the "Exercises" to operate as discourse, even if in *Otherwise than Being* Levinas suggests the possibility of other significations and of the interruption of discourse through *The Madness of the Day*. This movement introduces a distance between "philosophical criticism" and an "artistic criticism" that does not "interrogate [the] figures [of Blanchot's text] indiscreetly, as if a code were applicable to them by which their poetry could be translated into prose. All back away from such presumption, such profanation or treason" (SMB 57/PN 157). As in "Reality and Its Shadow," Levinas contraposes a "philosophical criticism" against those interpretations that preserve the text in its own "musicality." However, if in "Reality and Its Shadow" Levinas could not manage to develop the logic of a philosophical criticism of the work of art, here he does introduce "the perspective of the other" (RO 796/ CPP 13). Levinas's philosophical (ethical) reading of *The Madness of the Day* translates the "musicality" of Blanchot's text into "prose": into a philosophical statement according to which the story (*récit*) is "a *fable* about the closure of being" (SMB 57/PN 158). He also condenses the reading's *telos* in the syntagm "relation to the other – a last way out" (*rapport avec autrui – dernière issue*) (SMB 68/PN 165) that organizes the last part of the essay.

What is at stake in Levinas's commentary is the very possibility of reading the opening of being's closure as the approach of the other. It is for this reason that he appeals to the notion of intelligibility, to the space of the Book:

> The reading proposed here of a short and no longer recent text of Blanchot's touches upon a few points of its texture as if they had been singled out solely for their *symbolic power*. A hesitant pedantry? Lèse-poetry? Indeed so, but it is also one of the possible lives of that work, even if you reject the idea behind my *decipher-*

ing: the idea that *the irreducible* (inspired) *exoticism* of poetry refers back to [*en appelle au*] a saying *properly so-called* [*dire proprement dit*], a saying that thematizes, even if it may be obliged to unsay [*dédire*] itself in order to avoid disfiguring the secret it exposes. (SMB 56/PN 156–57; my emphasis)

Levinas anchors his interpretation in the "symbolic power" of certain textual elements. This term seems out of place within the context of a writer who had systematically questioned all the values of plenitude associated with the symbol. Although Levinas's "symbolic" ought to be understood in a broad sense, it is not clear whether the figures or sequences he analyzes are endowed with the same "symbolic power." Levinas first isolates an "optical focus" (*foyer optique*), the madness of the day, which unfolds in a temporal figure he calls "hell" and associates with the name of Auschwitz (SMB 58/PN 158). Second, he takes into account the lacerating and transparent opening of truth and, finally, the appearance of a baby carriage.[29] Do these textual elements belong to the same level of the story or of narration? Levinas refuses the presuppositions of a criticism that does not "touch" the materiality of the text, but deprives himself of the resources of a narratology that would allow him to delimit levels and form series, even if it is true that one cannot take them very far when it comes to Blanchot. Although the first two textual elements that Levinas focuses on are metonymic sequences that deploy a topology of essence and truth, the last one (the baby carriage) is a much more discrete element and it is in the latter that he grounds his reading. Levinas's exercises confine themselves to a semantics (expression, space of Intelligibility and the Book are the dominant coordinates) underwritten by an archi-pragmatics: the ethical a priori Saying that inhabits every historical language, according to the principles of *Otherwise than Being*.

The idea that an "irreducible exoticism" (SMB 56/PN 156–57) characterizes *The Madness of the Day* is a confirmation that some of the underlying principles of "Reality and Its Shadow" still shape the essay. We are familiar with the expression "irreducible exoticism" that, as in 1948, must be brought back to the straightforwardness of prose. What *remains* of this "*irreducible* exoticism" once translated into "prose"? To the familiar expression "irreducible exoticism" Levinas adds a new term: the adjective "inspired" that in *Otherwise than Being* emigrated from the realm of aesthetics to that of ethics. It is for this reason that Levinas claims that this "irreducible (inspired) exoticism" refers back to a saying properly so-called ("en appelle au dire proprement dit") (SMB 56/PN 156–57)? Does this mean that the said is equivalent to a saying *as such* (that the nominal verb *dire* is the subject of a nominal verbal phrase modified by an adverbial clause), or is it rather a said (*dit*) that, properly speaking, can only achieve its maximum level of "symbolic power"? Is the "irreducible (inspired) exoticism" a saying of "being otherwise" or of "the otherwise than being" (AE 13–14/OB 3–4)? This is an important distinction given that Levinas reads Blanchot's story (*récit*) as an *inspired* "fable about the *closure of being*" (SMB 58/PN 158), where the term *inspired* indicates that a breaching of totality or the Same has taken place.

Levinas's procedure is double: on the one hand, he channels poetry into prose, while on the other, in the very text on the closure of being he localizes the possibility of an opening, of an "otherwise than being." However, this possibility is quickly transferred from the text to an act of reading that seeks to find some "breathing room":

> […] the irresistible temptation of commentary attests to the fact that for this reader this text on *closure* is inspired – that in it the *other* of the Image and the Letter rend the *same* of the Said, according to a modality of awakening [*réveil*] and sobering up [*dégrisement*] and that this writing is Book. (SMB 58/PN 158)

Inspiration tears the texture of the Same at the very heart of the fable that tells what the closure of being signifies. For Levinas this implies that Blanchot's "writing is Book" (SMB 58/PN 158) and it is here that the *ingratitude* of the commentary reveals itself. The interruption of the *said* is not a textual trope because no figure of writing can convey it, but rather an ethical trope that Levinas expresses by the figures of "awakening" (*réveil*) and "sobering up" (*dégrisement*). This gesture may be justified given that the Same of the work (*œuvre*) goes in the direction of the other without a return to the point of origin or any hope for restitution. In addition, Levinas transfers these ethical tropes to the space of the Book, and it is in this space that the reader manages to find some "breathing room." Even if one agrees that restitution does not command ingratitude, how far can one go in establishing a "difference" separating the writer from the reader? Levinas goes so far as to restore Blanchot's writing to the order of the Book, an order that Blanchot himself rejects from *The Infinite Conversation* on.[30] Is this just ingratitude or does it summon Blanchot to a space alien to his writing?

Levinas's commentary on *The Madness of the Day* is in line with the allusion he made to this text in *Otherwise than Being*. He deploys the text's *said* in terms of a philosophical proposition, the fable of the closure of Being, but he also inflects this proposition with an ethical torsion: the figure of an inspired exoticism that, in the end, belongs to the space of the Book. This commentary confirms that the "possibility [*vertu*] of poetic writing" (AE 262/OB 170) that *The Madness of the Day* elicits has been decisive for Levinas's writing of the "otherwise than being" at the same time that it affirms the discrete character of his acknowledgment (the allusion). However, the altering principle called ingratitude runs the risk of being compromised by the presence of elements of a previous axiomatic that, although stated in terms similar to those in *Otherwise than Being*, are less fluid and dichotomous. In the final analysis, if philosophy is the "wisdom of love," poetry's virtue "that beckons without taking its place within the eternity of the signified idea is circumvented by the ancillary word that follows its traces and does not cease talking" (SMB 41/PN 149), a deceiver's virtue that loves the madness "he keeps watch over" (SMB 42/PN 149).

abbreviations

A	*L'Amitié.*
AE	*Autrement qu'être; ou, Au-delà de l'essence.*
CPP	*Collected Philosophical Papers.*
DEE	*De l'existence à l'existant.*
DQVI	*De Dieu qui vient à l'idée.*
ED	*L'Écriture du désastre.*
EE	*Existence and Existents.*
EEHH	*En découvrant l'existence avec Husserl et Heidegger.*
EI	*L'Entretien infini.*
F	*Friendship.*
GWCM	*Of God Who Comes to Mind.*
IC	*Infinite Conversation.*
OB	*Otherwise than Being: or, Beyond Essence.*
PN	*Proper Names.*
RO	"La Réalité et son ombre."
SMB	*Sur Maurice Blanchot.*
WD	*The Writing of the Disaster.*

notes

1 For a comprehensive study of literature in Levinas, see Jill Robbins, *Altered Reading. Levinas and Literature.*

2 For a reading of "Reality and Its Shadow," see Françoise Armengaud, "Éthique et esthétique. De l'ombre à l'oblitération" 605–19; Robert Eagleston, "Cold Splendor: Levinas's Suspicion of Art" in *Ethical Criticism: Reading after Levinas* 13–38; Jill Robbins, "Aesthetic Totality and Ethical Infinity" in *Altered Reading: Levinas and Literature* 75–90; and Thomas C. Wall, "The Allegory of Being" 13–30.

3 I have analyzed the functioning of this allusion in "Literary Language in *Otherwise than Being* (Allusion, or Blanchot in Levinas I)," *Diacritics* (forthcoming).

4 See Jacques Derrida, "Before the Law" in *Acts of Literature* 181–220; and *Parages* 60–64.

5 In a forthcoming essay, "Art's Inhumanity," I explore how "Reality and Its Shadow" juxtaposes a critique of Heidegger's ontological use of the work of art to a more general critique of the materiality of the work of art. Levinas's argument

revolves around a debatable interpretation of the biblical prohibition of representation.

6 It is necessary to stress that in *Otherwise than Being* the reversal of ontological difference is followed by its re-inscription and displacement. This is a precondition for writing the "otherwise than being," as Levinas states explicitly in the Preface to the second edition of *De l'existence à l'existant* (1977) and in part as a response to Jean-Luc Marion's objections in *L'Idole et la distance*. Levinas's treatment of Heidegger's ontological difference is a contentious issue, as evidenced in Derrida's "Violence and Metaphysics." For an assessment of this problematic, see Silvano Petrossino, "D'un livre à l'autre. *Totalité et infini* et *l'Autrement qu'être*"; and Silvano Petrosino and Jacques Roland, *La Verité nomade: Introduction à Emmanuel Lévinas*.

7 For an analysis of the peculiar structure of *Otherwise than Being* see Paul Ricouer, *Autrement. Lecture d'Autrement qu'être; ou Au-delà de l'essence d'Emmanuel Lévinas.*

8 Simon Critchley has systematically studied the different conceptions of the *il y a* in Levinas and Blanchot in his *Very Little … Almost Nothing! Death, Philosophy and Finitude.*

9 For a reading more attuned to the dimension of a saying that exceeds the grasp of the said, see Jacques Derrida, "La Loi du genre" in *Parages.*

10 I base my reading of this crucial section of *Otherwise than Being* on Derrida's "En ce moment même dans cette ouvrage me voici" in *Psychè. Les Inventions de l'autre* and on Simon Critchley, *The Ethics of Deconstruction. Derrida and Levinas.* A consideration of the allusion to *The Madness of the Day* does not form part of these studies.

11 Emmanuel Levinas, *Sur Maurice Blanchot.*

12 Joseph Libertson, *Proximity: Levinas, Blanchot, Bataille and Communication.*

13 See Maurice Blanchot, "Knowledge of the Unknown" in *The Infinite Conversation.* The thinking/writing of the neuter can take place only by presupposing that the working of totality has already been accomplished (Hegel) and that the neuter does not constitute a form of opening (Heidegger). In the first part of *The Infinite Conversation* the neuter becomes the question of the "other than being" or "the most profound question" (EI 1–39/IC 5–47). This turning point opens

a new period in Blanchot in which writing, understood as the question of the neuter, is also conceived as the question of the other in the ethical sense of the term. This period closes with *The Step (Not) Beyond* (1973) and *The Writing of the Disaster* (1980).

14 See Emmanuel Levinas, "Interiority and Economy" in *Totality and Infinity* 109–21.

15 "Is Ontology Fundamental?"; "Freedom and Command" (1953); "The Ego and the Totality" (1954); and "Philosophy and the Idea of Infinity" (1957).

16 This distinction was never overlooked by Blanchot, as the following formulation makes clear: "Writing, without placing itself above art, supposes that one not prefer art, but efface art as writing effaces itself" (ED 89/WD 53).

17 Taking into account the different ways that Heidegger and Levinas understand this term. While for the former ethics refers to an ontic or regional domain grounded in metaphysics (*Letter on Humanism*), for the latter ethics refers to a breaching of ontology.

18 Much like Heidegger, Blanchot is apprehensive regarding the term "ethics," but does not elude the force of the ethical injunction, as *The Writing of the Disaster* and *The Step (Not) Beyond* clearly show.

19 See Maurice Blanchot, *The Space of Literature* and his *Au moment voulu.*

20 See Jacques Derrida, "Violence and Metaphysics" in *Writing and Difference.*

21 "Le Servant et son maître" originally appeared in *Critique* 229 (1966).

22 These concepts are the trace, the distinction between the said and saying, as well as the ethical reduction of the said to the saying.

23 The French text reads: "fait signe sans que le signe soit porteur de une signification en se déssaisant de la signification" (SMB 39).

24 Blanchot has insistently questioned the modern doxa on writing's self-referentiality. That writing becomes a question as "the question *of* writing" (objective and subjective genitives) means that the borders separating inside and outside open themselves up in a complex manner. The inner core of language (the other, the

referent) becomes the strange par excellence. A good way of characterizing Blanchot's project would be by employing a Lacanian expression: "the extimate [*extimité*] writing." Lacan used the term *extimité* in his seminars. Jacques-Alain Miller gave currency to this term in his unpublished *Seminar 1, 2, 3*.

25 Maurice Blanchot, *La Folie du jour*. The text was originally published as "Un récit" in the journal *Empedocles* in 1948.

26 Maurice Blanchot, "Discours sur la patience" 19–44. These fragments later became part of *The Writing of the Disaster*.

27 "The work […] is a movement from the Same toward the Other that never returns to the Same. To the myth of Ulysses returning to Ithaca, we would like to oppose Abraham's story leaving his homeland for good for a land yet unknown" (EEHH 191; translation mine). For Blanchot's reading of Odysseus as a conceptual persona of the man of power, see "Le Chant des sirènes" in *Le Livre à venir* (Paris: Gallimard, 1959). Odysseus' figure has to be opposed to Orpheus', the poet whose infidelity is both toward the realm of action and power, as well as to that of the artwork.

28 The reader should note that the expression "sens inspiré" is deleted from the English translation, although it appears in the second paragraph within a less decisive context.

29

> Outdoors, I had a brief vision: a few steps away from me, just at the corner of the street I was about to leave, a woman with a baby carriage had stopped, I could not see her very well, she was maneuvering the carriage to get it through the outer door. At that moment a man whom I had not seen approaching went in through that door. He had already stepped across the sill when he moved backward and came out again. While he stood next to the door, the baby carriage, passing in front of him, lifted slightly to cross the sill, and the young woman, after raising her head to look at him, also disappeared inside. (See "The Madness of the Day" in *The Station Hill Blanchot Reader* 189–200)

30 See Maurice Blanchot, "The Absence of the Book" in *The Infinite Conversation*. For a compel-ling reading of this demanding text, see Leslie Hill, *Maurice Blanchot. Extreme Contemporary*.

bibliography

Armengaud, Françoise. "Éthique et esthétique. De l'ombre à l'oblitération." *Cahier de l'herne. Emmanuel Lévinas*. Ed. Catherine Chalier and Miguel de Abensour. Paris: Editions de l'Herne, 1991.

Blanchot, Maurice. *L'Amitié*. Paris: Gallimard, 1971.

Blanchot, Maurice. "Discours sur la patience." *Nouveau Commerce* 30–31 (1975): 19–44.

Blanchot, Maurice. *L'Écriture du désastre*. Paris: Gallimard, 1980.

Blanchot, Maurice. *L'Entretien infini*. Paris: Gallimard, 1969.

Blanchot, Maurice. *L'Espace littéraire*. Paris: Gallimard, 1955.

Blanchot, Maurice. *La Folie du jour*. Paris: Fata Morgana, 1973.

Blanchot, Maurice. *Friendship*. Trans. Elizabeth Rottemberg. Stanford: Stanford UP, 1997.

Blanchot, Maurice. *The Infinite Conversation*. Trans. Susan Hanson. Minneapolis: U of Minnesota P, 1993.

Blanchot, Maurice. "The Madness of the Day." *The Station Hill Blanchot Reader*. Ed. George Quasha. Station Hill, NY: Barrytown, 1998. 189–200.

Blanchot, Maurice. *Au moment voulu*. Paris: Gallimard, 1951.

Blanchot, Maurice. *Le Pas au-delà*. Paris: Gallimard, 1971.

Blanchot, Maurice. *The Space of Literature*. Trans. Ann Smock. Lincoln: U of Nebraska P, 1992.

Blanchot, Maurice. *The Step (Not) Beyond*. Trans. Lycette Nelson. Albany: State U of New York P, 1992.

Blanchot, Maurice. *The Writing of the Disaster*. Trans. Ann Smock. Lincoln: U of Nebraska P, 1986.

Bruns, Gerarld L. *Maurice Blanchot: The Refusal of Philosophy*. Baltimore: Johns Hopkins UP, 1997.

Challier, Catherine and Miguel Abensour (eds.). *Emmanuel Lévinas*. Paris: L'Herne, 1991.

Critchley, Simon. *The Ethics of Deconstruction. Derrida and Levinas*. Oxford: Blackwell, 1992.

Critchley, Simon. *Very Little ... Almost Nothing. Death, Philosophy and Literature*. London: Routledge, 1997.

De Vries, Hent. "Levinas." *A Companion to Continental Philosophy*. Ed. Simon Critchley and William R. Schroeder. Oxford: Blackwell, 1998.

Derrida, Jacques. *Adieu to Emmanuel Levinas*. Trans. Pascale-Anne Brault and Michael Naas. Stanford: Stanford UP, 1995.

Derrida, Jacques. "Before the Law." Trans. Avital Ronell and Christine Roulston. *Acts of Literature*. Ed. Derek Attridge. London: Routledge, 1991. 181–220.

Derrida, Jacques. *Parages*. Paris: Galilée, 1986.

Derrida, Jacques. *Politics of Friendship*. Trans. George Collins. London: Verso, 1997.

Derrida, Jacques. *Psychè. Les Inventions de l'autre*. Paris: Galilée, 1988.

Derrida, Jacques. *Writing and Difference*. Trans. Alan Bass. Chicago: U of Chicago P, 1978.

Docherty, Thomas. *Alterities: Criticism, Theory, and Representation*. Oxford: Clarendon, 1996.

Eaglestone, Robert. *Ethical Criticism: Reading after Levinas*. Edinburgh: Edinburgh UP, 1997.

Féron, Etienne. *De l'idée de transcendance à la question du langage: L'itinéraire philosophique d'Emmanuel Lévinas*. Grenoble: Millon, 1982.

Gibson, Andrew. *Postmodernity, Ethics and the Novel: From Leavis to Levinas*. London: Routledge, 1999.

Heidegger, Martin. *Basic Writings*. Ed. David F. Krell. New York: Harper, 1977.

Heidegger, Martin. *Gesamtausgabe*. Frankfurt: Vittorio Klosterman, 1977.

Heidegger, Martin. *An Introduction to Metaphysics*. Trans. Ralph Manhein. New Haven: Yale UP, 1959.

Heidegger, Martin. *On the Way to Language*. Trans. Peter Hertz. New York: Harper, 1971.

Heidegger, Martin. *Pathmarks*. Ed. William McNeill. Cambridge: Cambridge UP, 1998.

Heidegger, Martin. *Poetry, Language, Thought*. Trans. Alfred Hofstadter. New York: Harper, 1971.

Heidegger, Martin. *Sein und Zeit*. 15th ed. Tübingen: Max Niemeyer, 1984.

Heidegger, Martin. *Unterwegs sur Sprache*. Pfullingen: Günter Neske, 1959.

Heidegger, Martin. *Vorträge und Aufsätze*. Pfullingen: Günter Neske, 1954.

Heidegger, Martin. *Was heißt Denken?* Tübingen: Max Niemeyer, 1984.

Heidegger, Martin. *What is Thinking?* Trans. J. Glenn Gary. New York: Harper, 1968.

Hill, Leslie. *Maurice Blanchot. Extreme Contemporary*. London: Routledge, 1997.

Lescourret, Marie-Anne. *Emmanuel Lévinas*. Paris: Flammarion, 1994.

Levinas, Emmanuel. *Autrement qu'être; ou, Au-delà de l'essence*. Paris: Kluwer, 1978.

Levinas, Emmanuel. *Collected Philosophical Papers*. Trans. Alphonso Lingis. Pittsburgh: Duquesne UP, 1998.

Levinas, Emmanuel. *De Dieu qui vient à l'idée*. Paris: Vrin, 1982.

Levinas, Emmanuel. *En découvrant l'existence avec Husserl et Heidegger*. Paris: Vrin, 1967.

Levinas, Emmanuel. *Existence and Existents*. Trans. Alphonso Lingis. The Hague: Nijhoff, 1978.

Levinas, Emmanuel. *Of God Who Comes to Mind*. Trans. Bettina Bergo. Stanford: Stanford UP, 1998.

Levinas, Emmanuel. *Otherwise than Being: or, Beyond Essence*. Trans. Alphonso Lingis. Pittsburgh: Duquesne UP, 1998.

Levinas, Emmanuel. *Proper Names*. Trans. Michael Smith. Stanford: Stanford UP, 1996.

Levinas, Emmanuel. "La Réalité et son ombre." *Les Temps modernes* 38 (1948): 781–89.

Levinas, Emmanuel. *Sur Maurice Blanchot*. Paris: Fata Morgana, 1975.

Libertson, Joseph. *Proximity: Levinas, Blanchot,*

Bataille and Communication. The Hague: Nijhoff, 1982.

Llewelyn, John. Emmanuel Levinas. The Genealogy of Ethics. London: Routledge, 1995.

Llewelyn, John. The Hypocritical Imagination. Between Kant and Levinas. London: Routledge, 2000.

Nancy, Jean-Luc. "L'"Ethique originaire' de Heidegger." La Pensée dérobée. Paris: Galilée, 2001. 85–113.

Peperzak, Adrian. To the Other: An Introduction to the Philosophy of Emmanuel Levinas. West Lafayette, IN: Perdue UP, 1993.

Petrossino, Silvano. "D'un livre à l'autre. Totalité et infini et l'Autrement qu'être." Emmanuel Lévinas. Le Cahier de la nuit surveillée 3. Paris: Verdier, 1984.

Petrosino, Silvano and Jacques Rolland. La Vérité nomade: Introduction à Emmanuel Lévinas. Paris: La Découverte, 1984.

Ricouer, Paul. Autrement. Lecture d'Autrement qu'être; ou, Au-delà de l'essence d'Emmanuel Lévinas. Paris: PUF, 1997.

Riera, Gabriel. "Abyssal Grounds: Heidegger and Lacan on Truth." Qui parle? 9.2 (1997): 51–76.

Riera, Gabriel. "For an Ethics of Mystery: Philosophy and the Poem." Alain Badiou. Philosophy under Conditions. Ed. Gabriel Riera. Albany: State U of New York P, forthcoming 2004.

Riera, Gabriel. Intrigues of the Other: Ethics and Literary Writing in Levinas and Blanchot. Unpublished.

Riera, Gabriel. "Poetic Language in Otherwise than Being (Allusion, or Blanchot in Levinas I)." Diacritics (forthcoming 2004).

Robbins, Jill. Altered Reading. Levinas and Literature. Chicago: U of Chicago P, 1999.

Wall, Thomas C. "The Allegory of Being." Radical Passivity: Levinas, Blanchot and Agamben. Albany: State U of New York P, 1999.

Wyschogrod, Edith. Emmanuel Levinas: The Problem of Ethical Metaphysics. The Hague: Nijhoff, 1974.

Wyschogrod, Edith. Saints and Postmoderns. Chicago: U of Chicago P, 1990.

Gabriel Riera
Department of Comparative Literature
103 East Pyne
Princeton University
Princeton, NJ 08544
USA
E-mail: Riera@princeton.edu

Routledge
Taylor & Francis Group

ANGELAKI
journal of the theoretical humanities
volume 9 number 3 december 2004

I

And God said, Let us make man in our image, after our likeness ...

Genesis 1.26

In the beginning there was the word, but there was also the image and the concept of likeness, and in the course of the present essay I revisit the story of Man's creation for the purpose of exposing an ancient, but never more topical, relation between Man and the concept of the image. I should say at the outset that my analysis of this relation and the tradition (art history) which has this relation at its crux proceeds from a willful but *precedented* misreading: namely, the a-historical conflation of image and picture, such that the story of *Man's* origins can be made to function as the origin of my own story about an essential and evolving link between people and pictures.[1] Indeed, although I am aware that the image featured in Genesis 1.26 is said to have little to do with what we, today, call "pictures," the present essay nevertheless persists in their conflation, for it is my contention that *this* (mis)reading has been the misreading of Western culture *writ large*, the consequences of which are the subject of this essay.

isabelle loring wallace

FROM THE GARDEN OF EDEN AND BACK AGAIN
pictures, people and the problem of the perfect copy

II

As is well known, Genesis begins with a series of repetitive verses which relay the creation of heaven and earth and all their contents, and in each instance, excepting Man, these creative feats are accomplished by utterance alone in the form of the famous "Let there be ..." Achieving and in this way narrating the creation from nothing of heaven and earth, land and sea, sun and moon, fish and fowl, cattle and that which creeps, Genesis turns in its twenty-sixth verse to *Man's* creation. Of Man and Man alone God will say that he is made *after* – *after* not only in the sense of being made after the other creations but *after* in the far more crucial sense of being modeled, of being, in other words, not a creation or a presentation but rather a re-presentation, something made, as God is said to have said, in the image of another.

Born of this iterative logic, Judeo-Christian Man is aligned from the outset with the notion of

ISSN 0969-725X print/ISSN 1469-2899 online/04/030137–19 © 2004 Taylor & Francis Ltd and the Editors of *Angelaki*
DOI: 10.1080/0969725042000307682

Fig. 1. Michelangelo (1475–1564). *The Creation of Adam*. Sistine Chapel, Vatican Palace, Vatican State. Photo credit: Alinari/Art Resource, NY.

representation. But just what kind of representation are we talking about here? And, more pointedly, what exactly is it that Man re-presents? Certainly, the reliance of the text on the notion of the image (*tselem, eikon, imago*) complicates matters, as does my own inclusion of the verse's belated, but equally well-known, illustration (see Fig. 1).[2] Indeed, as aides to this discussion of the link between representation and subjectivity we now have *two* texts – one written, one painted – which establish the primacy of Man's relation to God in ways that cannot be extracted from the notion of the image, however defined.

A tremendously complicated and important issue, the precise meaning of the word *image* in the context of the creation myth has occupied many scholars both in and beyond the field of theology. Asserting that image *does not* mean

picture, and that *likeness* (*demuth, homoioos,* or *similitude*[3]) is, in this context, a clarifying synonym for (immaterial) similitude, biblical scholars working to preserve the iconoclastic impulse of the Judeo-Christian tradition have gone to great lengths to undo the confusion of the modern anglophone, who assumes, however wrongly, that the image in question is visual.[4] About this confusion – a confusion which is both the subject and springboard for this paper about people and pictures – I have three things to say, two of which will require further elaboration: (1) the confusion of images and pictures is ancient history; *tselem, eikon,* and *imago* – the words used in the original Hebrew, Greek and Latin Bibles – have always meant both similitude and picture;[5] (2) the more recent confusion of image and picture exceeds philology; it derives from genuine, historical developments in the fields of theology and aesthetics, which together have altered both the meaning of the original verse *and* our conception of images;[6] (3) the confusion of image and picture is today an ineluctable part of the story Westerners tell themselves about their origins; it is their inheritance and perhaps their destiny.

As regards the first point, I defer to the work of specialists in the field, noting only for the record here that there are many documented instances of *tselem*, *eikon* and *imago* meaning *picture* or *visual object* – as in, for example, Plato's use of *eikon* to refer to an image in a mirror, Cicero's use of *imago* to refer to statuary, and several Old Testament passages in which *tselem* refers to outward, visible form: Numbers 33.52, Samuel I 6.5, Kings II 16.10, etc. As regards the second more involved point, I defer in large part to the influential work of W.J.T. Mitchell whose seminal study on images asks and answers virtually all of the relevant questions: how, when and why did images become identified with pictures, and spiritual likeness become synonymous with visual similitude?[7]

It goes without saying that the conflation of image and picture does not have a precise point of origin, but for Mitchell, Milton's seventeenth-century treatment of Adam and Eve as *imago dei* in *Paradise Lost* stands as a concrete example of the modern – i.e., the avowed and deliberate – conflation of image and picture:

Two of far nobler shape erect and tall,
Godlike erect, with native Honour clad
In naked Majesty seemed Lords of all
And worthie seemed, for in their looks divine
The image of thir glorious Maker shon,
Truth, Wisdome, Sanctitude severe and pure,
Severe, but in true filial freedom plac't.

(*Paradise Lost* 4.288–94[8])

Calling attention to Milton's use of the word "looks" in the preceding verse, Mitchell deduces that Milton's reading of Genesis is purposefully confused: on the one hand, Man *looks* like God in that he can be called God's *picture* and, on the other hand, Man looks like God in that he and God share attributes which allow them *to see* the world in similar, but, of course, not identical ways. A reading of Genesis that acknowledges its irreducibly double meaning, Milton is thus among the first to openly concede the role played by the visual image in Man's creation. The question remaining, then, is this: what factors contributed to this shift in our understanding of the image, such that it was at last possible to concede the role played by *imaging*, indeed by *pictures*, in the book of Genesis? Or, put otherwise, how can we explain ambiguity's embrace in the verse of Milton, given centuries of clarifying disavowal in the form of iconoclastic biblical commentary?

By way of explanation, I return our attention to Michelangelo's fresco – both because Michelangelo cannot help but describe the likeness of Man and God in terms of *visual* similitude, and because it is, as W.J.T. Mitchell has suggested, the Renaissance, and more precisely the Renaissance invention of perspective, which leaves as its legacy the conflation of which we (and Milton) now speak. First systematized by Alberti in 1435, perspective played a major role in the revolution we call the Renaissance, and we are well accustomed to rehearsing its importance for a visual tradition that would become increasingly more (and then less) concerned with reproducing the look of the real.[9] Less well established is the impact this development would have on our conception of images *as such*, and it is *this* issue that Mitchell takes up in his study.

Put simply, perspective's great accomplishment was that it allowed pictures to accurately reproduce the look of the real. Much has been written about the errors implicit in this line of thought, yet what is of interest to Mitchell and me are the *received* truths of perspective, for it is they that produced a fundamental shift in our conception of the image. Prior to the invention of perspective, images were many; there were mental images, visual images, verbal images, etc. After the invention of perspective there were still many kinds of images, but one kind of image reigned supreme and was indeed the paradigm under which all other images were seen to operate. This kind of image is, of course, the *visual* image and it was in large part perspective which granted it this supremacy. And why not? With the invention of perspective, pictures could now claim to be coincident with reality in ways that seemed to conclusively subvert long-standing rhetoric about the *difference* between image and essence. Having made appearance and reality more or less the same, the invention of perspective implied a fundamental philosophical shift, one that would eventually lay waste to the theologically important distinction between looking like a God and seeing like he sees.[10]

More than a crucial passage in the history of art, the invention of perspective can thus be credited with effecting a profound shift in our perception of images and their relation to both reality and Man. Understood to be linked to the truth of *what is*, visual images were now believed to be inextricable from other kinds of similitude which may or may not have been visible previously. As such, Man's resemblance of God, post-perspective, is *necessarily* a matter of the visual; after the Renaissance, *being* like God means *appearing* like him, as is perhaps evidenced by the careful mirroring of Adam and God in Michelangelo's fresco. Returning to Genesis 1.26 with this in mind, we might say that the invention of perspective – an invention which was both catalyst and symptom of a larger cultural shift – retrospectively altered (revealed?) the meaning of the story of Man's creation, and with *that* the meaning and identity of Man. Indeed, when read from the perspective inaugurated in the Renaissance, Genesis 1.26 can be seen to speak of God's appearance and essence *simultaneously* – a fact which brings us to the other question posed at the outset: what exactly is it that Man re-presents at the moment of his making?

Like the related question of the image, the question of what Adam re-presents is answered in historically determined ways. Consider: if *image* is interpreted in immaterial terms, then it is some aspect of God's character that Adam re-presents. If *image* is interpreted in light of the developments we've been tracking here, then Adam re-presents God's *appearance*, which is

itself necessarily a reflection, or re-presentation, of the divine's essential characteristics. As such, the point isn't simply that with the Renaissance images give way to pictures, it is also that, as image, or indeed *as picture*, Adam can now be said to picture *another picture*, and thus represents for his more modern audience not only the primacy of Man's relation to God but also the primacy of Man's relation to the visual image. And it is with *this* contention that we arrive at a more direct description of my essay's subject and the final of my three comments concerning this more recent conflation of image and picture.

If Genesis 1.26 is typically invoked for the purpose of establishing the singularity of Man's relation to the divine, by now it is clear that I have invoked this verse for the alternative purpose of establishing the importance of a less theorized, but no less foundational, link: namely, the link the verse implies between Man and the historically constituted concept of the image. Asserting that the meaning of *image* in this context has always been multiple, and that Man's conception of his creation has always been inflected by the often repressed role of the visual, I have nevertheless followed Mitchell in asserting that the meaning of the verse has evolved *toward* this once unpopular reading, and will claim in what remains that this evolution has had dramatic consequences for our conception of pictures, people and the relation between them.

Arguing that Genesis 1.26 *does* speak to us of the visual and that it may have spoken to the West of the visual all along, I assume in what follows (here is my third point concerning the conflation of image and picture) that whatever the historical truth (or textual multi-valency), the story of Western Man's origins, as read today, *is* the story of the visual and the role it has played in Man's formation and fate. Taking seriously an idea I see everywhere reflected in the present – the idea that Man is made in the image *of an image* – I propose in the remainder of this essay that a historically conditioned (mis)reading of Genesis 1.26 can clarify the terms of an essential and evolving relation between people and pictures, to which my own text now adds a third, never more relevant, concept – that of the perfect copy.

III

By way of a second beginning and by way of introducing the idea of the perfect copy – an idea that has played a significant role in the history of art and which will lead us, however perversely, to the *literal* intersection of people and pictures – consider one of art history's foundational myths: the story of the rivalry between Apollodorus, who is said to have begun art, Zeuxis, who is said to have perfected art, and Parrhasius, who can be said in the end to remind us that perfection in art is impossible.[11]

According to Pliny, the rivalry between Apollodorus and Zeuxis was resolved in favor of the latter, for, as the story goes, Apollodorus was unable to compete with the level of realism achieved by Zeuxis – the emblem and proof of which was a bird's attempt to pluck a grape from Zeuxis' painted, two-dimensional vine. Thus, though Pliny will say of Apollodorus in book 35 of *Natural Histories* that his paintings made obsolete his predecessors, he will also say in that same book that his *greatest* accomplishment was that "he opened the gate" for Zeuxis, his grape-painting rival and successor (307).

Already a compelling story, there is yet another chapter in Pliny's account of this artistic triumvirate, one that concerns the competition between Zeuxis and *his* successor, Parrhasius. As with the tale of Zeuxis and Apollodorus, the tale of Zeuxis and Parrhasius will turn on the issue of realism – a fact which testifies to the privileged status afforded to realism in the West, both then and now.[12] Indeed, however obvious, it seems important to note that Pliny's narrative retains currency today because, though artistic media and subject matter have changed, the idea of the perfect copy continues to dominate both within and, as we shall see, beyond the boundaries of fine art.[13]

Having said that, it is important to note of "the perfect copy" that its attainment, both then and now, is by definition impossible, as representation is necessarily a re-presentation of – which is to say a necessarily different and thus imperfect version of – the thing to which it refers. Seen in this light, it is not so much that art continues to fail in its attempt to achieve the perfect copy, though this is of course true; it is more that the perfect copy is *by design* an impossible and paradoxical goal – a fact acknowledged long ago by Pliny in his account of Zeuxis' rivalry with Parrhasius:

> Parrhasius entered into competition with Zeuxis, who produced a picture of grapes so successfully represented that the birds flew up to the stage buildings; whereupon Parrhasius himself produced such a realistic picture of a curtain that Zeuxis, proud of the verdict of the birds, requested that the curtain should now be drawn and the picture displayed; and when he realized his mistake, with a modesty that did him honour, he yielded up the prize, saying that whereas he had deceived the birds, Parrhasius has deceived him, an artist.[14]

Always out of reach, mastery of the perfect copy is shown by Pliny to be short lived and illusionary. Indeed, the moral of the story is that painting can *always* be more realistic. Thus, though Zeuxis' *trompe l'oeil* painting of grapes earned him a reputation as the man who perfected art under the paradigm of realism, this accolade is quickly rescinded, for in the aftermath of his encounter with Parrhasius the insufficiency of his likeness, and by extension the insufficiency of *all likenesses*, is revealed to be an essential part of art history's narration within the paradigm of realism. Indeed, if the story of Zeuxis' success and failure is a testament to the *centrality* of the perfect copy within aesthetic discourse, it is at the same time a testament to its absence, and to the benefits this absence engenders.

One such benefit concerns the discipline of art history, for, as we have seen, it is perfection's unattainability that lends to art history's narration a certain innate drama and *dynamism*. After all, it isn't just that the paradigm of realism gives us a theatrical and/or decisive way of staging aesthetic rivalries; it's that it "opens the gates," as Pliny might say, for an endless number of similarly dramatic episodes. Indeed, looking back at a trajectory that seems always to look forward, tales like the one we've just considered seem to multiply and cohere, resolving as they do into a cumulative succession of increasingly heroic attempts to achieve the unachievable. We call this progression "art history," and do so in the knowledge that art's romance with the "perfect copy" makes for consistently good *art historical* copy, the drama of which is measured by the heroism of successive failures along the asymptote.[15]

Though failure will be my focus in the pages that remain, I should note that certain episodes in the history of art have been credited with producing the elusive perfect copy.[16] I'm thinking here of the invention of the photograph in the 1820s and the still more promising invention of the readymade by Marcel Duchamp in the 1910s. So as not to get waylaid by either of these crucial and complex moments in modern art history – moments to which I attend elsewhere – I'll simply concede that both the invention of the photograph and the iconoclastic gesture of the readymade *did* bring art dangerously close to the perfect copy, which is *also* to say dangerously close to art's extinction.[17] Indeed, though many things link the photograph and the readymade, what I want to stress here is that the flirtation of each with perfection as defined within the paradigm of realism resulted not in jubilation at the realization of representation's long-standing goal (*At last! At last! The perfect copy is here!*), but rather in theatrical expressions of despair, the precise form of which would be a series of hyperbolic claims about the death of painting and the death of art more broadly.[18] As these audiences came quickly to realize, the copy is perfected *only* at representation's expense, which is of course why the story of art's quest for perfection is the asymptotic tale that it is.

Dramatic moments within this tale, the invention of the photograph and readymade did more than challenge the investment of art in traditional notions of authorship; in addition, their extreme pursuit of representation's obsolescence made uncomfortably visible what one might call the underpinning nihilism of art as conceived in the West. Exposing the threat that the perfect copy always carries and the danger implicit in its pursuit, the photograph and readymade brought to the surface the strange logic of the Western tradition, and in that way forced an acknowledgement of representation's desire to replace representation with its referent. Seen through the lens of the photograph and readymade, art in the West emerges as a tradition compelled by the possibility of its own demise, and is thus best characterized by a distinct and near-consistent self-loathing. In light of this suicidal profile, I suggest that the terms of this discussion be rearranged; the real question is not how representation negotiates the problem of the unattainable, perfect copy, but rather how the perfect copy negotiates what I will call hereafter "the problem of representation."[19]

IV

What is the problem of representation? A return to the texts with which we began may provide us with something of the answer. In conjunction with a second fresco from the Sistine (see Fig. 2), here is a second passage from the book of Genesis:

> Now the serpent was more subtil than any beast of the field which the Lord God had made. And he said unto the woman, Yea, hath God said, Ye shall not eat of every tree of the Garden?
>
> And the woman said unto the serpent, We may eat of the fruit of the trees of the garden:
>
> But of the fruit of the tree which is in the midst of the garden, God hath said, Ye shall not eat it, neither shall ye touch it, lest ye shall die.
>
> And the serpent said unto the woman, Ye shall not surely die:
>
> For God doth know that on the day ye eat thereof, then your eyes shall be opened, and ye shall be as Gods, knowing of good and of evil.
>
> And when the woman saw that the tree was good for food, and that it was pleasant to the eyes, and a tree to be desired to make one wise, she took the fruit thereof, and did eat, and gave also unto her husband with her; and he did eat.
>
> And the eyes of them both were opened, and they knew, that they were naked ... (Genesis 3.1–7)

Two questions emerge from this passage, the answers to which will return us to the link

Fig. 2. Michelangelo (1475–1564). *The Temptation and Expulsion from Paradise*. Detail of Sistine ceiling. Sistine Chapel, Vatican Palace, Vatican State. Photo credit: Alinari/Art Resource, NY.

between people and pictures, while at the same time clarifying the so-called problem of representation: (1) what is the nature of the knowledge gained by Adam and Eve in the Garden and (2) what exactly are the consequences of that knowledge's attainment? After all, Adam and Eve do not, in fact, die on the day that they partake of the tree. Rather, having been expelled from the Garden, Adam and Eve go on to bear Cain, Abel and others, dying of natural causes several years later. Thus although they *do* acquire in this moment the certainty of a deferred death, they are for that momentous day nevertheless unharmed.

Interestingly, what *does* happen in the immediate aftermath of the fruit's consumption – and this by way of answering the first of our two questions – is Adam and Eve's knowledge of their mutual nakedness. Again, paradoxes would seem to abound. Adam and Eve have, of course,

always been naked, yet in the wake of the forbidden fruit they are suddenly ashamed, as is evidenced by their subsequent adoption of fig leaves. The conventional way of understanding this gesture is to imagine that Adam and Eve are, having eaten from the Tree of Knowledge, newly *aware*, and thus newly ashamed of their nudity. Such a reading seems right but also simplistic, in that it does not examine enough the nature of the knowledge gained in that instant. Certainly on *one* level what they now know is indeed their nakedness, yet knowledge of nakedness presumes a far deeper knowledge of which "shame" is only a symptom. The knowledge of which I speak is the knowledge of one's self *as seen*, or, to put that in slightly more pointed terms, it is the knowledge of oneself as a visual object in the mind of another subject who gazes upon you.

So, although Adam and Eve do not die a

literal death in the aftermath of the forbidden fruit, they nevertheless *do endure* a kind of death in this moment. That death is the death of authentic and unmediated subjectivity (unself-consciousness, if you will), and it occurs in the moment that Adam and Eve are each riven by a deeper knowledge – specifically, knowledge of themselves as representation, as the visual images that readers of Genesis already knew them to be. That the experience of being seen is thus comparable to, and thus takes the place of, an implied, immediate death is a fact that establishes a compelling link between representation and mortality, while at the same time adding a fatal layer to the relationship Genesis had already established between people and pictures.

A final thought on the link between death and the image, before looping back to our discussion of the perfect copy's intervention in the problem of representation. In the immediate context of Genesis, representation's link to death has to do with seeing oneself as seen – i.e., with understanding that one is always from another perspective only the mortified image of the Other. Yet it is possible to forge a more abstract relation between representation and death, the essence of which can be summed up *à la* Blanchot in the following way.[20] Arguing that the strangeness of the cadaver is also the strangeness of the image, Blanchot suggests that the connection between representation and death turns on the violent severance, in each, of form from an original context. Consider: in the instant a woman is photographed her appearance is replicated and thus proves separable from its original context, however broadly or narrowly the idea of context is defined. A similar dynamic takes hold at the moment of death, for although form and content still seem united in the figure of the corpse they are in fact asunder, as the *original* context and meaning are, in the most profound sense, no longer present. Thus in both corpse and image, meaning and materiality are wrenched apart, and as such, we might say, it is the logic of death that makes the image possible, if also in the end unbearable.

It is interesting to consider Michelangelo's fresco with this in mind. As if in accordance with the shared logic of representation and death

– the discovery of which *is*, in some sense, the subject of the Fall – Michelangelo's composition turns on the problem of severance as articulated by the divisive *Tree of Knowledge* at the composition's center, and on the separation of oneself from oneself, as articulated in the doubling, indeed the re-presenting, of both Adam and Eve. Though surely not Michelangelo's intent, his work nevertheless manages to articulate in exactly the right context in impossibly knowing ways a fundamental and uncomfortable connection between death and representation, each of which Adam and Eve come to know in the very moment the fresco is given to describe. Indeed, having eaten from the Tree of Knowledge, it is this that they come to understand: between representation and death there is the deepest and most unnerving connection, the existence of which *is* representation's so-called problem.

Enter here the paradigm of realism and its mascot, the perfect copy. After all, what better solution to the problem of representation than its elimination, and what better agent of elimination than an entity capable of suturing the divide that representation inevitably is. Rendering unintelligible the difference between representation and referent, the perfect copy's realization would substitute unified plenitude for the moribund fragment that is the image, and would in this way dissolve representation's reliance on the logic of severance. Of course, here it must be recalled that this sought-after solution to the problem of representation is one that comes at representation's own expense, and as such we might conclude that the Western tradition and its quest for "the perfect copy" are at one and the same time a symptom of, and the inadequate solution for, the problem of representation and its unseemly relation to death.

V

At this point it is clear that the problem of representation has to do with mortality. Aligned with Man's literal death in the future and with the more abstract and immediate mortification that comes from seeing oneself seen, representation emerges in the West as a problem in need

Fig. 3. Albrecht Dürer (1471–1528). *Melancholia I*. Engraving (1514). 23.8 × 18.9 cm. Victoria and Albert Museum, London, UK. Photo credit: Victoria and Albert Museum, London/Art Resource, NY.

of solving – a fact which may help to explain the West's two-thousand-year-old pursuit of the perfect copy, as well as the West's more recent demonization of art that elects *not* to take as its goal this self-defeating *but nevertheless imposs-ible* end.[21] Indeed, here it must be said that the sheer *duration* of this self-destructive romance only returns us to the fact of the perfect copy's unattainability – an unattainability that I claim is the core of representation's equally long-standing battle with melancholia, as testified to by Dürer in the North at the very same moment that Michelangelo is unwittingly testifying to the related fact of representation's link to both Man and death in the South (see Fig. 3). A key part of the story I am telling about people and pictures, the relation between art and melancholia has many facets and has generated a good

deal of scholarship, but to my knowledge the following has not yet been said in precisely this way: Man and the image after which he is made are each potentially melancholic entities, defined, as in keeping with the illness they keep at bay, by a loss that cannot be mourned.[22]

Let's put the image on the couch first.[23] Characterized by Freud in 1917 as the inability to productively mourn an intolerable loss, melancholia is easily associated with representation, given the constitutive loss of the referent, without which representation ceases to be.[24] Defined by the loss of a referent it compulsively strives to duplicate in the form of an unachievable perfect copy, representation can neither repair this loss – as we've seen, that happens only at representation's expense – nor mourn it. Indeed, it isn't merely that the loss has always already happened, it's also that the loss in question is one that cannot be articulated in accordance with the demands of the "talking cure." After all, how would representation articulate, which is to say mourn, the trauma of the referent's loss without inflicting upon itself again via symbolization the trauma from which it hopes to escape?

Condemned to live with a loss it can neither amend nor accept, representation seems to have found an alternative means of coping with the loss that defines it, and in this regard the psychoanalytic theories of Nicholas Abraham and Maria Torok may be of some help. Building on Freud's ground-breaking work in this area, Abraham and Torok maintain that a bereaved subject has two options for processing loss: introjection and incorporation.[25] On their account, introjection is like mourning in that it is a "normative" procedure in which the loss in question is conscious, and successfully negotiated through a process of reclamation in which the bereaved recovers that which had been displaced onto the object recently lost. Needless to say, this procedure is not an option for representation, for were it to reclaim for itself the plenitude of the referent it would engender its own annihilation in the process. What to do, then, with a loss that cannot be mourned? How to rise above mourning's impossibility such that the inertness pictured by Dürer can be transformed into the productive lineage we call art history?

On Abraham and Torok's account, there *is* a means of negotiating losses which defy expression. As they argue in *The Shell and the Kernel*, the subject who cannot mourn often engages in an unconscious process called incorporation, in which he or she swallows whole and unprocessed both the lost object and the trauma associated with its loss.[26] Erecting an internal tomb in which to house both the lost object and the trauma of having lost it, the subject unwittingly encrypts what it cannot bear to loose and continues to identify with the object preserved therein.[27] The status quo thus maintained, the traumatized subject avoids melancholia and proceeds as before, asymptotically approaching but never in fact achieving complete identification with the object whose loss cannot, and effec-

tively need not, be acknowledged.[28]

At this point the relationship of incorporation to representation is perhaps clear, but a final detail should drive the point home. According to Abraham and Torok, incorporation typically occurs given a very particular type of relationship between the bereaved and the lost object. In psychoanalytic terms, that relationship can be described as the relationship of the subject to the necessarily unattainable ego-ideal – a relationship not at all unlike the one *we've* been tracking between representation and *its* unattainable ideal: the perfect copy and/or referent.[29] Seen in this light, the subject diagnosed by Abraham and Torok is *very much* like the entity we call representation. Fated by a loss it can neither assimilate nor mourn, representation nevertheless manages to transcend melancholia, perhaps through the erection of a crypt which contains both the idea of the referent and the trauma associated with this constitutive loss. Looking at a posthumous work like Marcel Duchamp's *Etant donnés* – a work whose installation at the Philadelphia Museum is exactly contemporaneous with the publication of Abraham and Torok's theory[30] – I'm tempted to say that it shares with Michelangelo's *Temptation and Expulsion* a kind of impossible knowing, assuming on behalf of all representation the characteristic structure of the crypt (see Fig. 4). Indeed, as we look at this crypt's façade, we need not peer inside to know something of its contents; unknown and unknowable, it is the referent and the trauma of its loss that resides therein, assuming for the shell that is representation the role of the traumatic and inassimilable kernel.

At the same time, if we *were* to peer inside, we would only see further evidence to support the (utterly theatrical) idea that death allowed Duchamp to know and picture the very essence of representation, the truth of which he seems to affirm through the inclusion of an illuminated gas lamp, visible, as it were, on the door's *other side* (see Fig. 5). Speaking to us from the grave, Duchamp presents a headless female (?) body, access to which for us is eternally foreclosed given the presence of multiple barriers which together can be seen to symbolize the constitu-

Fig. 4. Marcel Duchamp. *Etant donnés: 1. La Chute d'eau, 2. Le Gaz d'éclairage (Given: 1. The Waterfall, 2. The Illuminating Gas)* (1946–66). Exterior view. © 2004 Artists Rights Society (ARS), New York/ADAGP, Paris/Succession Marcel Duchamp. Philadelphia Museum of Art: Gift of the Cassandra Foundation, 1969.

tive inaccessibility of the purely material referent or thing-in-itself. Divided in its structure and morbid in its content, Duchamp's work thus speaks to *and is* representation's double bind in attempting to access and re-present that which remains unknowable outside the context of certain ineluctable *givens*: tradition, language, time, space, etc.[31] Adding another layer to our discussion of the referent's loss, the *Given* manages to concisely picture the problems of picturing, all the while recalling that these problems ultimately intersect with the idea of the crypt, symbolic as it is of both death and the will to preserve.

As I move to a consideration of Man's constitutive loss, a confession must be made concerning this paper's original conceit. I began this essay with a re-reading of Genesis, and in the spirit of

literalism I argued that Man is made in the image of an image, and that there is, therefore, a primary and mutually reflexive bond between people and pictures in the West. The truth of the matter is that images are made in the image *of Man*, and are that which provides him with an externalized picture of himself through which he can observe his own constitution, evolution, and logic. Indeed, if we live with a category of objects we call pictures, it is because we are ourselves *seen*, and feel ourselves divided by that seen-ness, the burden of which we displace onto a category of objects which exist for precisely the purpose of their witnessing. Mirroring Man's status as visual object, the image is thus both after us and of us, reflexive of us and somehow formative of us, a category of objects which compulsively restages for our consideration not only our seen-ness but also, because of

Fig. 5. Marcel Duchamp. *Etant donnés: 1. La Chute d'eau, 2. Le Gaz d'éclairage* (*Given: 1. The Waterfall, 2. The Illuminating Gas*) (1946–66). Interior view. © 2004 Artists Rights Society (ARS), New York/ADAGP, Paris/Succession Marcel Duchamp. Philadelphia Museum of Art: Gift of the Cassandra Foundation, 1969.

that, the distilled essence of the experience that was the Fall, at the precise moment Man became both seen and mortal.

At the same time, we might say that the image reflects Man's predicament *in the aftermath* of the Fall, reflecting back to its traumatized creators his own bereft structure, characterized as it is by a comparably constitutive loss. Indeed, if we can say that the image incorporates whole the memory of the referent and its absence, and does so for the purpose of continuing to identify with this unattainable ego-ideal, then we can also

say that it does this because on some level it is serving to reflect Man's incorporation of *his own* constitutive loss as narrated by Man in the myth of the Expulsion: the loss of unmediated subjectivity as it occurred in the Garden at the moment Man comes to know he is the mortified picture Genesis consigns him to be.[32] Further, we might also say that if representation is riven by a loss that is constitutive, and if it is therefore obsessed with the distracting but ultimately ineffectual fetish the West has called the perfect copy, it is because representation is the playing

Fig. 6. Jake and Dinos Chapman. *Tragic Anatomies* (1996). Fiberglass, resin, paint, smoke devices. Dimensions variable. © The artists. Courtesy Jay Jopling/White Cube (London).

field on which Man unwittingly rehearses the trauma of his own loss, and, as we shall see, his own ineffectual pursuit of the perfect copy, however nihilistic and moribund its achievement might (also) be.

VI

In essence, this essay has concerned the relation between people and pictures, and tangentially the relation between pictures and the concept of the image. Maintaining that images and pictures *have never been* fully extricable concepts, I proposed at the outset that time has made them still less so, and suggested that the Renaissance's more purposeful confusion of image and picture allowed for a re-reading of Genesis which secured via the logic of likeness a fateful relation between people on the one hand, and on the

other the (divine) picture after which they were made. In conclusion, I propose an end to this trajectory, and at the same time a highly problematic return to the beginning – a double movement I claim is now possible given a culture defined by genetic engineering, cosmetic surgery and, above all, the soon-to-be-realized phenomenon of the human clone.[33]

Read as the logical terminus of a story about the link between people and pictures, these scientific developments also immediately conjure our story's third term – the perfect copy – and are in many ways our story's end, for they manifest in no uncertain terms not a simple *relation* between perfect copies, people, and pictures, but rather the possibility of their complete and literal *conflation*. Simultaneously, these developments also return us to the beginning, and do so in ways that round out the more abstract

Fig. 7. Jake and Dinos Chapman. Detail of *Tragic Anatomies* (1996). Fiberglass, resin, paint, smoke devices. Dimensions variable. © The artists. Courtesy Jay Jopling/White Cube (London).

analogy we've been tracking between the bereftness of people and pictures, for which the perfect copy continues to be a most imperfect solution.

As we have seen, the perfect copy promises to solve the so-called "problem of representation" by eliminating the difference between image and referent; so, too, genetic engineering, cosmetic surgery and the clone, each of which promises, with varying degrees of viability and success, to solve the problem of being after the Fall by eliminating any trace of difference, and with that the possibility of death. Thus, however one may feel about cloning and face-lifts, it is fair to say that Man's attempt to realize his own version of "the perfect copy" makes manifest the utter complexity of the relation between people and pictures, while also recalling the problem to which the perfect copy is always addressed. That problem is, of course, mortality, and through genetic engineering and the clone that problem may be solved in ways that return us to the beginning – by which I mean not only the Garden of Eden, but also a much more primordial past in which immortality and sameness were "humanity's" defining characteristics. Indeed, by replacing procreation and difference with the clinical and surgical reproduction of the same, cloning and the rest threaten to return us to the innocence and immortality of the Garden, itself a compelling myth for our shared *biological history* as single-celled, asexual organisms that lived eternally, given their own exact duplication.

The perfect copy's elusiveness has been a recurring theme of this paper, and whether or not the technologies under discussion here can in fact produce the perfect copy, and whether or not they will thus return us to the Garden of Eden, remains to be seen. But looking at the perversely Edenic work of the Chapman brothers, it's plain to see that many remain dubious – both about the possibility of the perfect copy's realization and about the desirability of that phenomenon (see Fig. 6).[34] Of course, at the end of this essay it goes without saying that artists have particular insight into the nature of the perfect copy, insight that might temper their enthusiasm for the solution it promises to deliver. Indeed, as we've said, the artist knows all too well the consequence of the perfect copy's realization; eliminating difference, and thus representation, the perfect copy makes everything, and thus nothing, an image, and in this regard we might say that the work of the Chapman brothers visualizes not the essence of representation *à la* Michelangelo and Duchamp, but rather the essence of representation's elimination as it would occur at the hands of the perfect copy. Comparing Michelangelo's representation of the Expulsion with the Chapman brothers' ironic representation of Man's return, and looking specifically at the *Tragic Anatomy* of the Chapman's identical, eternal youths, we see that while knowledge of representation doubles, divides and mortifies, *representation's elimination*, or conversely representation's transcendence at the

hands of the perfect copy, doubles *without division* and without the mortification that that division has always entailed (see Fig. 7). Born together in the mind of Man at the moment of the Fall, death and representation would thus die together, and with them Man as he has been defined in the West for centuries.

I have maintained throughout this paper that pursuit of the perfect copy is an exercise in nihilism, and that its achievement would mark the end of representation and the difference on which it depends. What I didn't say, and what Pliny could not have anticipated, is that an attempt to realize the perfect copy would also result in the end of both image and Man as defined by their essential characteristics. Absolving the image of its difference from the referent, and Man of his mortality and the need of sexual difference, not to mention the burden of his constitutive difference from himself, the perfect copy may well return us to a Garden of Eden, but in the process Man will undoubtedly find himself and his pictures fundamentally changed, given an unprecedented conflation of the terms this paper has sought to track and distinguish: perfect copies, pictures, and people.

notes

A version of this paper was delivered at the "Inventions of Death" conference at the University of Warwick in June 2001, and again at Bryn Mawr College in spring 2003. Thanks are due to these audiences, my students, and the following individuals in particular: Steven Z. Levine, David Cast, Lisa Saltzman and Linda Wallace.

1 My introductory remarks draw heavily on the work of W.J.T. Mitchell whose seminal analysis of the idea of the image did much to inspire and inform the present remarks. See his *Iconology: Image, Text, Ideology* (Chicago: U of Chicago P, 1986) 5–52. For an account of the creation which is attentive to the role played by gender and difference, see Mieke Bal, "Sexuality, Sin, and Sorrow: The Emergence of a Female Character (A Reading of Genesis 1–3)" in *The Female Body in Western Culture*, ed. Susan Suleiman (Cambridge, MA: Harvard UP, 1986) 317–38.

2 For an analysis of the Creation in relation to another work of art, see Penny Howell Jolly, *Made in God's Image? Adam and Eve in the Genesis Mosaics at San Marco, Venice* (Berkeley: U of California P, 1997).

3 Mitchell, *Iconology* 31.

4 Here is a standard example:

> A further hint of a lower theological position has been seen by some in the repeated phrase *in our image, in his image, in the image of God*, which is thought to point to a time when men believed that God had a material frame like that which man possesses. Yet is it more probable that the expression *in the image of God* has no physical implications, but is meant to suggest that man differs from all the rest of creation in the possession of self-conscious personality, in which he alone of all creatures resembles God. (*Abingdon Bible Commentary*, ed. Frederick Carl Eiselen (New York: Abingdon, 1929) 221)

For commentary which entertains the opposite view, arguing that the incorporeality of God was too abstract a thought for Israelites of the fifth century, see *The Interpreter's Bible*, ed. George Buttrick (New York: Abingdon, 1952) 482–85. Lending credence to the idea that the Bible references God's material form are several Old Testament references to his hands, feet and mouth: Psalms 119.73, 33.6; Isaiah 60.13; Zechariah 14.4.

5 Seen from this perspective, the modern confusion of image and picture is only a retrospective illumination of an uncertainty that has always been present and in large part repressed.

6 My own remarks will concentrate on developments in the field of aesthetics which necessarily intersect with the complex history of iconoclasm.

7 Mitchell, *Iconology* 31–40.

8 John Milton, *Paradise Lost* (Menston: Scholar, 1968).

9 The most sustained and rigorous work on perspective has been that by E.H. Gombrich and Hubert Damisch. See, *Art and Illusion: A Study in the Psychology of Pictorial Representation* (Princeton: Princeton UP, 1960) 242–87 and *The Origin of Perspective*, trans. John Goodman (Cambridge, MA: MIT P, 1995), respectively.

10 Here I do not mean to suggest that debates about the meaning of *image* in Genesis ceased, nor do I mean to suggest that there was anything like an acknowledgement of the fact that the meaning of the verse had changed. Rather, I mean to imply that the invention of perspective contributed to, but did not on its own *cause*, a general trend toward the material which had obvious consequences for everything, but in particular the West's conception of Man's relation to the divine.

11 Pliny offers the definitive account of this rivalry. See *Natural Histories*, vol. IX, trans. H. Rackham (Cambridge, MA: Harvard UP, 1961) 307–15. For an account of this legend's implications for the conception of tradition in the West, see Norman Bryson, *Tradition and Desire: From David to Delacroix* (Cambridge: Cambridge UP, 1984) 1–31.

12 I am aware that "realism" is a tremendously complicated term, which has inspired a great deal of specialized literature. Here, I use the term in a very general way to refer to the common notion that art ought to "look like" its subject. That some movements – Mannerism and the Rococo, for example – will be excluded by a definition of art that privileges visual similitude is interesting in and of itself. What does it mean that we tell the story of the history of art in a way that marginalizes art that refuses to participate in its own self-effacement? Might it be that the West only tolerates art that is intolerant of itself? On realism and the marginalization of Rococo art, see Norman Bryson, *Word and Image: French Painting of the Ancien Régime* (Cambridge: Cambridge UP, 1987).

Also, here is as good a point as any to assert that the idea of the perfect copy looms large even in, and perhaps especially in, those moments when realism seems to have been abandoned for an alternative schema. Abstract Expressionism, for example, seems to have had little to do with the concerns of realism in so far as it abandons entirely the language of reference. Yet one of the most popular and enduring ways of thinking about Abstract Expressionist paintings is to see them as the unmediated reflections of the men who made them. Realism by another name, Abstract Expressionism thus shares with any realist painting the desire "to be true" to its subject, to truly re-present it, and in that sense, it might be possible to say that virtually all Western art is produced within a realist paradigm, and is therefore plagued by the notion of perfect and unattainable copy. In this regard, it might also be interesting to consider the relationship between the tradition of icon painting and the story of St Luke painting the Virgin, as it is this presumed event which transforms all icons into realistic likenesses.

13 Today, the drive toward the perfect copy is most clearly expressed outside the terrain of traditional fine art and applies mostly to Man's duplication of himself. Here, I'm thinking of developments in the field of virtual reality (in theory this technology allows you to be an *even more real* version of yourself, given the mutability of one's appearance in this arena), and other developments I discuss in closing: genetic engineering, cosmetic surgery, and, of course, cloning. Together, these technologies may undo the West's faith in the truth of the image, as established by the invention of perspective.

14 Of course, the story does not end with Parrhasius. As Pliny will say of Apelles, he "surpassed all the other artists put together and all who were to come after" (319). Significantly, Pliny's account of Apelles also manages to maintain the logic of the perfect copy's unattainability, noting of Apelles that he was inferior to several contemporaries in some very particular respects: to Melanthius in terms of grouping, to Asclepiodorus in terms of measurement, etc. Pliny, *Natural Histories* IX: 319–33.

15 Norman Bryson's account of tradition in the West will choose to stress the belatedness of the artist in light of the past's accumulation. I see no reason to disagree with this account, and in fact second his emphasis on failure. See Norman Bryson, *Tradition and Desire*, throughout.

16 And there are certainly mythological examples of the perfect copy's realization, among them the story of Pygmalion and Galatea. Here, as elsewhere, the realization of the perfect copy means the loss of representation, for at the end of the story Pygmalion, happily, has a woman *instead* of a statue, the thing *instead* of the thing's representation.

17 On the death of painting and the implications of the readymade for art, see my own "From the Death of Painting to the Death in Painting: Or, What Jasper Johns Found in Marcel Duchamp's *Tu m'/Tomb*," *Angelaki* 7.1 (2002): 133–55. See also Yve-Alain Bois, *Painting as Model* (Cambridge, MA: MIT P, 1990) 229–44.

18 Most famously, Paul Delaroche's remark concerning the invention of photography: "From today painting is dead!" (though there is no hard evidence that the French painter ever made such a statement).

19 Interestingly, loathing also plays a role in the myth of Pygmalion, as it is his loathing of women that propels his art, and in turn his quest for the perfect copy.

20 See Maurice Blanchot, "Literature and the Right to Death" and "Two Versions of the Imaginary" in *The Gaze of Orpheus and Other Literary Essays* (Barrytown: Station Hill, 1981) 21–62, 79–89. More recent efforts to address the relation between art and death are: Gregg Horowitz and Tom Huhn, "The Wake of Art: Criticism, Philosophy and the Ends of Taste" in *The Wake of Art: Criticism, Philosophy and the Ends of Taste* by Arthur Danto, eds. Greg Horowitz and Tom Huhn (Amsterdam: OPA, 1998) 1–56; and Peter Schwenger, "Corpsing the Image," *Critical Inquiry* 26 (spring 2000): 395–413.

21 See n. 10.

22 Actually, I will argue that Man and image triumph over melancholy through the erection of an intra-psychic crypt. Also, in terms of art's relation to melancholia, I should note that what goes for art also goes for art history, as the historian is always searching for a lost object, context, etc. that cannot be found. On this point, see Michael Ann Holly, "Mourning and Method," *Art Bulletin* 84.4 (2002): 660–69.

23 If psychoanalyzing art history seems to confuse traditional distinctions between people (the usual objects of psychoanalysis) and pictures, it is an intentional and welcomed side-effect of arguing that the two are each other's mirror reflection.

24 Sigmund Freud, "Mourning and Melancholia" (1917), vol. 14 of the *Standard Edition*, ed. and trans. James Strachey 239–58. In light of the diagnosis I am making, it seems important to note a couple of additional things: (1) mourning and melancholia are distinguishable from one another at the level of symptom in only one way: the loss of self-esteem, which is experienced only in the case of melancholia; (2) melancholics experience this loss of self-esteem because their identification with the lost object is of a narcissistic variety in that the lost object somehow resembles the bereaved. For me, each of these points tracks well with the idea of representation

as: (1) suicidally convinced of its unworthiness and (2) narcissistically attached to the referent via the idea of resemblance.

25 See Nicholas Abraham and Maria Torok, *The Shell and the Kernel*, trans. Nicholas Rand, vol. I (Chicago: U of Chicago P, 1994) 99–156. Introjection and incorporation are terms inherited from other psychoanalysts including Ferenczi, Freud, and Klein.

26 Here it is important to note the following stipulation concerning incorporation: "*The abrupt loss of a narcissistically indispensable object of love has occurred, yet the loss is of a type that prohibits its being communicated. If this were not so, incorporation would have no reason for being.* Cases of reluctant mourning are well known. Yet they do not inevitably lead to incorporation" (Abraham and Torok, *The Shell and the Kernel* 129).

27 Abraham and Torok refer to this process as "preservative repression" by which they mean to imply the dramatic consequences the subject would have to face were he or she to introject the incorporated loss. The idea is that the incorporated loss is one whose introjection would fundamentally reorganize the bereaved, something which is, of course, true of representation *vis-à-vis* the loss of the referent.

28 On Freud's account, normal psychology requires that there be an appreciable difference between the ego and its ideal. Omnipotent mania is the unhappy result of their conflation – hence the asymptotic nature of this identification.

29 Though I do not wish to push this too far, there are two more preconditions of the crypt which have obvious resonance for this paper: (1) the existence of a love totally free of ambivalence, such that only a "real and traumatic cause" could put an end to it; and (2) a previous experience tainted with "shame … death, disgrace, or removal" (136). Needless to say, stipulations *more* evocative of the Fall would be difficult to come by, though it should be noted that it is the ego-ideal's shame that is in question here and not, strictly speaking, the shame of the subject him/herself. In the context of our discussion, the original mirroring of Man and God renders difficult the distinction between Man and ego-ideal, as does the related distinction between Man pre- and post-Fall (Abraham and Torok, *The Shell and the Kernel* 131–38).

30 According to the translator and editor Nicholas Rand, Abraham and Torok's theories of incorporation were, with one exception, all published between 1967 and 1975. Duchamp worked on *Etant donnés* in secret between 1946 and 1966; in accordance with Duchamp's wishes, it was installed at the Philadelphia Museum of Art in 1969. For a sustained analysis of the work, see Dalia Judovitz, "Rendezvous with Marcel Duchamp: *Given*," *Dada/Surrealism* 16 (1987): 184–202.

31 Of course, it is possible to read Duchamp's work in a myriad of ways, none of which are negated by my own reading here. Also, though I cannot pursue this here, I find Duchamp's readymades intriguing in light of the following passage concerning the crypt's dissolution:

> It should be remarked that as long as the crypt holds there is no melancholia. It erupts when the walls are shaken, often as a result of some secondary love-object who had buttressed them. Faced with the danger of seeing the crypt crumble, the whole of the ego becomes one with the crypt, showing the concealed object of love in its own guise … Consequently, the ego begins the public display of an interminable process of mourning. (136)

Might it be that having shaken the walls of the crypt the readymade inaugurated a new chapter in modern art history – high modernism – in which self-reflexivity ensured complete and total identification of the image with its referent? Certainly the notion of interminable mourning can be applied to modernism, given its asymptotic approach toward what Greenberg might call the absolute essence of each medium; further, in so far as Abraham and Torok also note that this process all culminates – if it is, in fact, to culminate – in the fantasy of the love-object's suicide – an outcome not at all unlike the fate of the referent (i.e., reality) which is said to have disappeared in postmodern culture (see Abraham and Torok, *The Shell and the Kernel* 136–38).

32 In this regard, it is interesting to note that Abraham and Torok repeatedly use the word *idyll* to describe the contents of the crypt.

33 My thoughts on the clone are influenced by the work of Jean Baudrillard, especially *The Vital Illusion*, ed. Julia Witwer (New York: Columbia UP, 1999). For an overview of cloning and the

debate it has generated, see Nicholar Agar, *Perfect Copy: Unraveling the Cloning Debate* (Cambridge: Icon, 2002). Despite its suggestive title – a title I came across while well immersed in the present text – *The Perfect Copy* does not engage the intersection of aesthetic and scientific or psychoanalytic discourse. For an analysis of cloning's implications for the idea of sex and gender, see my own "Sex, Sameness and Desire: Thoughts on Versace and the Clone" in *WAR: Women, Advertising and Representation: Extending beyond Familiar Paradigms*, eds. Sue Abel, Anita Nowak and Karen Ross (New Jersey: Hampton, forthcoming 2004).

34 There is a great deal that one could say about the Chapman brothers' work, especially as it concerns the implications of recent technologies for the issues of sex and gender. Here, the sameness wrought by these phenomena ends up making heterosexual sex (and perhaps all sex) impossible – both because we've been returned to the age of innocence in the Garden and because our attempts to get there via genetic engineering and cloning have resulted in dysfunctional amalgams like the ones that populate their work. Also, I should note that the relevance of this work to the Judeo-Christian tradition is acknowledged by the Chapman brothers in various ways; most obviously the corresponding exhibition catalogue, which took the form of a Bible (gold edges, thin pages, etc.) and was entitled *Unholy Libel*. See *Unholy Libel* (London: Gagosian, 1997). For other artists working along these lines, see the exhibition catalogue *Paradise Now: Picturing the Genetic Revolution*, ed. Ian Berry (New York: D.A.P., 2000); and *Gene(sis): Contemporary Art Explores Human Genomics*, available < http://www.gene-sis.net/splash.html >.

Isabelle Loring Wallace
Lamar Dodd School of Art
University of Georgia
Visual Arts Building
Athens, GA 30602-4102
USA
E-mail: iwallace@uga.edu

journal of the theoretical humanities
volume 9 number 3 december 2004

I introduction: heidegger's turn away from figuration

Heidegger's writings are an object of study for many readers interested in poetry, poetic language, poetic thinking, and even metaphor, despite the fact that Heidegger explicitly resists the ascendancy of metaphor and figurative language. In his 1955–56 lecture course on Leibniz's principle of reason, for instance, Heidegger famously declares that metaphor exists only within metaphysics and that the separation of sensible and nonsensible realms upon which metaphor depends is untenable.[1] Likewise in Heidegger's 1942 lectures on Hölderlin's poem "The Ister" Heidegger opposes an approach to Hölderlin's poem in terms of symbols or symbolic images (*Sinnbilder*), because symbols are said to presume a framework wherein a distinction – again the metaphysical distinction – is made between a sensuous and a nonsensuous realm. Heidegger claims that the river named in the poem is not an image or metaphor for journeying, nor is it a figure for human life.[2] Nonetheless he also makes such assertions as "[t]he poet is the river. And the river is the poet."[3] As Heidegger stresses, these statements are not to be understood metaphorically, insofar as he considers metaphor one species of symbolic image; but then we are left with the question of how such statements can be understood at all.

In the following pages I would like to suggest that Heidegger's rejections of metaphor on the grounds that it is metaphysical belong to an evocation of a dimension of language that might be described in terms of performance, effecting, enactment and even performativity. It is my argument that Heidegger's discrediting of meta-

karen s. feldman

HEIDEGGER AND THE HYPOSTASIS OF THE PERFORMATIVE

phor is itself a step in the evocation of this dimension, i.e., that Heidegger's explicit rejection of metaphor and symbolic representation constitutes a step in his texts in the evocation of, or access to, the order of enactment and performance. But how might we understand *texts* as doing, enacting or performing? Is there a way to describe this dimension of textual performance in accurate and straightforward terms, if, indeed, performance can be attributed to texts at all? In order to answer these questions I turn to criticisms by J. Hillis Miller of Heidegger's treatment of figurativeness that, in view of Miller's accustomed concern in his work for performativity, demonstrate an anomalous blind spot on Miller's part. This is not Miller's *personal* blind spot, but an indication of a particular difficulty

ISSN 0969-725X print/ISSN 1469-2899 online/04/030157–11 © 2004 Taylor & Francis Ltd and the Editors of *Angelaki*
DOI: 10.1080/0969725042000307691

with respect to *seeing* the performative dimension of texts; indeed, given that Miller is otherwise notoriously sensitive to questions of textual performativity, Miller's reading of Heidegger illustrates particularly acutely the difficulty of describing, or even of evoking, this performative dimension directly. That is, Miller's criticisms inadvertently show that the dimension of performativity or textual event at stake for Heidegger is inherently evanescent; it turns out to be represented only and at best by means of hypostases that are inadequate to capturing the event-like and dynamic character that Heidegger attempts to evoke.

II de man, miller and passages to the performative

Heidegger's discussions of poetic naming and poetizing involve a shift from a figurative reading of the poem to a reading attuned to what Paul de Man in another context refers to as "textual event," or to what Jean Greisch refers to as a way "in which one might think the stylistic gesture together with the event or 'thing itself' of which this thought speaks."[4] What is, however, a textual *event?* How is it related to the performative? Despite Miller's criticisms – to which I will turn in a moment – of Heidegger's rejection of figurativeness in favor of what I am characterizing as a turn toward performativity, Miller has throughout the corpus of his work demonstrated himself to be a supreme thinker of the event-like character and performativity of texts, in a way that is closely related to de Man's work on rhetorical reading.[5] Hence I will first clarify the notion of performativity and its relationship to the rejection of figurativeness by way of a brief examination of its characterizations in the texts of de Man and Miller.

In his readings in the history of literature and philosophy, de Man mentions performativity by name infrequently, but his analyses are concerned throughout with the tensions between what a text *explicitly* says and what it also *implicitly* says and, moreover, what a text *does*. Thus, for instance, three of de Man's chapters on Rousseau in *Allegories of Reading* concern

types of speech acts – i.e., promises in *The Social Contract*, excuses in *Confessions* and a profession of faith in *Émile*. In each case, de Man's readings focus on the "disruptive intertwining of trope and persuasion or – which is not quite the same thing – of cognitive and performative language."[6] In de Man's posthumous essay "Kant and Schiller" de Man explains, albeit rather cryptically, the radical disjunction between the tropological and performative modes and the passage from the former to the latter:

> [T]he linguistic model for the process I am describing, and which is irreversible, is the model of the *passage* from trope, which is a cognitive model, to the performative, for example. Not the performative in itself ... but the transition, the passage from a conception of language as a system, perhaps a closed system, of tropes ... to *another* conception of language in which language is no longer cognitive but in which language is performative.[7]

For de Man, tropology is a form of cognition, a linguistic process of understanding and knowing. The epistemological function of tropes, however, is not sufficient to account for all of language; there is also a performative aspect. But we do not seem to ever fully reach a performative conception of language; it appears that we only ever undergo the passage *from* the cognitive, tropological model of language *to* the performative model, without actually attaining the latter: "[T]he passage from trope to performative ... occurs always, and can only occur, by ways of an epistemological critique of trope."[8]

In a statement of his own interest in the particular figure of personification, Miller elucidates de Man's references above to the distinction between cognitive and performative language: "personifications, like prosopopeias in general, seem a form of knowledge but are in fact potent speech acts. They have to do with doing rather than knowing."[9] In these references to knowing vs. doing – which may be understood to translate, albeit within certain limits, the cognitive and performative language to which de Man refers – we can see the common terrain on which Miller and de Man operate.

Miller writes, in explanation of the title of his book *Speech Acts in Literature*:

> "Speech acts in literature" can mean speech acts that are uttered within literary works, for example promises, lies, excuses, declarations ... and the like said or written by the characters or by the narrator in a novel. It can also mean a possible performative dimension of a literary work taken as a whole. Writing a novel may be a way of doing things with words.[10]

Thus Miller inquires into whether texts themselves may be understood as performatives that call into existence the world to which they seemingly merely refer.[11] Nonetheless, I will show below, Miller's otherwise scrupulous sensitivity to the potential performative dimension of texts appears to falter in his reading of Heidegger's "Building Dwelling Thinking." Although Miller seems to be a thinker of the "doing" performed by figures and of textual events, with regard to Heidegger he is strangely inhospitable to considerations of performativity.

This is, of course, just one of many deployments of the term "performative" that have come to prominence in contemporary disciplines including philosophy of language, literary criticism, gender studies, queer theory, theater studies, communications, and anthropology. J.L. Austin initially defined performatives as utterances in which "the issuing of the utterance is the performing of an action,"[12] and offered such examples as christening, betting, and promising. In the course of lectures 4–6 of *How to Do Things with Words*, however, the performative/constative distinction is shown to be problematic, and later in the lectures Austin introduces the locutionary/illocutionary/perlocutionary schema to account for the various ways in which utterances can have effects and produce results. Philosophers of language who draw on Austin, including John Searle, have focused largely on the concepts of illocution and perlocution in order to talk about the relationship between language and the results it can effect. In other disciplines, however, and in Continental philosophical thought, the performative, in all its ambiguity – indeed, perhaps owing precisely to the opportunities this multivalent concept offers for thinking speech and act together – has become the center of a range of discussions concerning sexual, political, social and personal identity. Some of the significance of Austin's notion of the performative for these multidisciplinary discussions derives from Jacques Derrida's essays "Signature Event Context" and, in response to Searle's criticisms, "Limited Inc a b c ..." In his readings of Austin, Derrida derives the concept of a generalized iterability at the heart of the Austinian performative.[13] This plain repeatability of any utterance – i.e., the lability of the material signifier that allows it to be deployed in contexts parodic, staged, inappropriate, and unexpected, in addition to the normatively defined contexts for particular performatives – is the condition of both successful and failed performatives. This iterability therefore also constitutes the possibility of subversion, irony, comedy and infinite other exploitations of performatives, including, as is the present topic, the doings that texts might be said to accomplish.

III performativity and the call of conscience in *being and time*

Where in Heidegger's analyses is the turn away from a figurative (or, in de Manian/Millerian terms, tropological) dimension linked to a turn toward something of the order of enactment, performance and even performative? In *Being and Time*, I suggest, the call of conscience is peculiarly situated at this nexus. That is, Heidegger's analysis of the call of conscience, in which he explicitly rejects a figurative understanding of the call, turns out to be linked to what could be seen as a performative mode of the very text *Being and Time* as a whole. Heidegger's analysis of conscience implicitly instructs us as to the task performed by *Being and Time* – i.e., *Being and Time* turns out to *be* the instantiation of the call of conscience that is described within it. While *Being and Time* may indeed also be seen to instruct us by way of descriptions of being-in-the-world, phenomenology, ontology and so forth, the call of conscience, in contrast to these other elements, is not only described *by* the text but could also be said to *be* that which the text performs for *us*, its readers. In other words, as itself an incarnation of the call of conscience, the text *performs* an appeal to our own Dasein and thus surpasses the *description* of conscience that it offers.

This characterization and singling out of the call of conscience in *Being and Time* requires further explanation. First some review: Heidegger introduces the call of conscience in Division II of *Being and Time*, as an "existential" re-interpretation of what in Division I was discussed as care, where "existential" refers to an ontological mode of consideration, namely having to do with Dasein's possibilities, as opposed to an ontic mode of consideration that focuses on entities and the everyday.[14] The call of conscience is said to summon Dasein to its own self,[15] where this self is not understood as any thing or essence, but as possibility, as "its ownmost possibility of existence."[16] Heidegger's characterization of conscience bears little resemblance to traditional philosophical and theological descriptions of conscience – for instance in Augustine, as the seat of God within us or the witness that testifies against us; or in Kant, as a moral conviction of our duty. Heidegger's characterization of conscience as a *call* would seem to depend on figuring it as voice, as involving hearing, saying, and so forth, and thus would be in accord with familiar depictions of conscience as an inner voice or the call of duty. And yet Heidegger insists that the call of conscience is not to be understood figuratively, that it is not an image (*Bild*) in the same way that the court of conscience is an image in Kant.[17] So what is the call, if not a figure? It does not seem possible for it to be a literal call, because Heidegger claims that it says nothing, speaks in the mode of silence, and has nothing to tell. What kind of call could be described in these terms? Heidegger evacuates the call of conscience of the qualities that might allow it to be understood literally as a call and yet he rejects a figurative understanding of the call. My contention is that the rejection of figuration verges on enactment or performance in two respects. First, where the call is said not to be a figure, but cannot be

understood literally either, the absence of a viable alternative in cognitive terms effects or produces an incomprehension as to what conscience might be. In its very unfathomability the predicament of how to understand the call of conscience lands us readers in the perplexity that Heidegger exhorts us to retrieve in the opening prologue to *Being and Time*.[18]

This first point explains how in the analysis of the call of conscience the rejection of figuration effects our perplexity. The call of conscience is, however, peculiarly and significantly related to considerations of textual performativity in the following way: in addition to landing us in perplexity the call of conscience can also be read as encapsulating and in effect allegorizing the function of the entire text of *Being and Time*. For the turn to conscience in *Being and Time* is governed by a demand in the text for an attestation, in answer to the question whether an attestation can be found of Dasein's authentic potentiality to be itself.[19] Hence the call of conscience serves initially within the text of *Being and Time* as an attestation of that potentiality of Dasein. But if the call of conscience is an attestation, the text's very reference to that call serves as an attestation *of* that attestation. *Being and Time*, then, in doubling the attestation contained in itself, can be seen as performing that which the analysis of the call of conscience describes. This doubling of attestation by the text itself, i.e., the call's *allegorization* of the function of the text, is what renders the description of the call of conscience unique among the elements Heidegger examines in *Being and Time*.

Indeed, the attestation that is described as the call of conscience breaks off Dasein's listening to the they-self and provokes another kind of hearing.[20] But this is also the very task of *Being and Time* with regard to each of us, as a Dasein who reads. This is the task of *Being and Time*, which in its enigmatic and difficult language forces another kind of hearing, a hearing not dominated by ontic and everyday expectations and things. In other words, *Being and Time* as a whole can be read as a performance of conscience, writ large, such that what Heidegger writes about conscience's call can in fact also be said of the text *Being and Time*, i.e., "it reaches him who wants to be brought back" (271). This includes reaching Daseins like us, Daseins who read. The inquiry that is *Being and Time* calls the *reading* Dasein to its ownmost ability-to-be, and thus it would seem that *Being and Time* could be said to be its reader's conscience. The text enacts the function that is described in Heidegger's analysis of the call. In this regard, the text is a performance, an enactment, of that which it describes as the call of conscience. There are certainly other ways and moments in which *Being and Time* can also be described as being concerned with enactment and performance, and even as enacting or performing. But the call of conscience in *Being and Time* demonstrates that Heidegger's rejection of a figurative approach to conscience coincides with a uniquely recursive site of performance and enactment; *Being and Time* itself performs a work of conscience with respect to the Dasein who reads it.

IV from figuration to naming: heidegger on hölderlin

Throughout Heidegger's 1942 lecture course on Hölderlin's "The Ister," in contrast, the connection between the rejection of figure and the shift to a mode of enactment and performance is more explicit, as Heidegger develops a series of enigmatic claims regarding what he calls poetizing and naming. In section 3 of that lecture course Heidegger discusses what he considers to be the metaphysical interpretation of art, wherein such things as rivers and waters assume the role of symbols. According to the metaphysical, symbolic interpretation, the sensuous images of the things mentioned in a poem are presumed to evoke or refer to a nonsensuous or spiritual meaning. Heidegger declares that Hölderlin's hymnal poetry is not, however, to be understood in terms of symbols at all and that specifically the rivers in that poetry are not symbols or symbolic images.

Heidegger goes on to make some statements that, in accordance with his rejection of a symbolic approach to the river of Hölderlin's poem,

are not to be understood figuratively and yet are seemingly impossible to take literally – for example the river is said to be the locality of human abode, to vanish, to be full of intimation, and to be the locality of journeying. As with the call of conscience, the most obvious rhetorical effect here is to run the reader up against the difficulty of understanding these statements and thereby to land the reader in perplexity. Heidegger writes:

> The river is the locality of journeying. Yet the river is also the journeying of locality. Such statements make it sound as though empty words were being strung together and exchanged ... This illusion of a mere playing with words cannot be overcome immediately. We must even concede that such statements cannot be understood directly at all in the way that we understand the assertion that today is Tuesday ... Yet why do we then pronounce such statements? ... simply so that we may know that the river is an "enigma [*Rätsel*]."[21]

The "is" which equates "today" and "Tuesday" is not the same "is" that appears in the statement that the river is the locality of journeying. The latter statement is not merely an assertion *about* the river; rather, the statement evokes a reflection on our own knowledge of the river, a reflection that puts our knowledge into question and evokes the enigmatic character of the river in contradistinction to our everyday understandings of "river" and of what it is to say that the river "is" this or that. But in evoking the enigma, the "is" therefore opens the *possibility* of a different thinking not only of river and of journey but also of the "is" and of being, where "is" is not simply constative and not metaphorical, but in a specific fashion "names" the river and, in Heidegger's words, unveils the river's activity and brings it to its essence.

Indeed, the very function of Hölderlin's poem, according to Heidegger, is not symbolizing or representing, but is instead just such evocative naming. This naming is neither a referring nor a mentioning; rather, Heidegger terms this naming a poetic telling. This naming is, in Heidegger's words, an elevation and poetization of what is named into its essence.[22] Naming, as Heidegger understands it, is what I am calling a form of enactment, transitivity, performativity, or founding. Heidegger's turn to what he calls naming is thus an explicit moment where the rejection of a tropological modality is tied to a claim to an enacting one. Still, what naming does, or what this enacting is, is not explained in any transparent fashion. This is precisely my point: what naming is, in its founding and performative dimension, is not said more clearly or directly by Heidegger because it *cannot* be said directly. The saying of what naming *is* ends up as a *figure* for that performativity; indeed, it risks appearing to be a literalization of that figure. The same holds true for any classificatory definition of "poetizing," "poetic telling," and the essence of poetry. What the performing, enacting naming to which Heidegger refers does is, on one hand, sayable only in figurative terms; and yet the figurative term gets taken literally precisely because there is no proper term for what this performing-enacting-naming does. The definition of this performing, enacting, poetic element is thus necessarily tropological.

For these reasons what naming is cannot be said *directly* by Heidegger's analyses of poetry. Naming is, rather, *exemplified* by the hymn, which is the name of both a Greek celebratory song and of Hölderlin's river poetry. Heidegger writes:

> The ὕμνος is not the "means" to some event, it does not provide the "framework" for the celebration. Rather, the celebrating and festiveness lie in the telling itself.[23]

The hymn accomplishes itself and that for the sake of which it exists in one gesture. The "what" that is told in the hymn and the "how" of its telling are one. Hence in the hymn the noun and verb are one; for the word of the hymn celebrates and is the celebration, *tells* and *is* in one gesture, without any pointing toward something else, without recourse to any outside, and without separating the being of the celebrating from the being of what is celebrated.

V miller against heidegger

Can human thinking be faithful to the simultaneity of nonmetaphysical telling and the celebration of the hymn? Can thinking operate on a register of poetizing and performativity? Heidegger's reading of Hölderlin's hymn clearly attempts to evoke a possibility of thinking otherwise than in terms of literal and figurative, otherwise than in terms of metaphysics. This attempt is, however, entirely open to resistance, to such a reply as "No, there is no other way to read the poem than in terms of figures. Poems do not name rivers into being, rivers cannot literally be localities or journeying, and so these *must* be figures." Here, a reading by Miller of Heidegger's 1952 essay "Building Dwelling Thinking" seems to offer convincing criticism of Heidegger's evocations of an other, nonfigurative, nonliteral and hence nonmetaphysical thinking.[24]

The example of the "Ister" course indicates that Heidegger attempts an other thinking than one determined by a literal/figurative opposition. According to Miller's reading of the essay "Building Dwelling Thinking," however, Heidegger's rejection of figurativeness leads him to fall into a confusion of words with things and of figurative with literal meanings. This sort of confusion is what Miller, with Paul de Man, also refers to as a confusion of linguistic with phenomenal reality, and it is the defining characteristic of what Miller and de Man call "ideology."[25] Specifically, Miller suggests that Heidegger confuses the "is" of figurative equivalence with the "is" of simple identity. In fact much of what Miller characterizes as the "vaulting," "slipping" and ideological confusion of linguistic and phenomenal reality takes place by means of the "is" as Heidegger makes use of it – for example, where in "Building Dwelling Thinking" building is said to *be* dwelling and dwelling is said to *be* thinking. Miller numbers these among Heidegger's "many small performative positings" that Miller characterizes as "vaultings" and "stark juxtapositions that vault across fissures and crevasses in Heidegger's thinking."[26] Heidegger is said to literalize tropes in order to make equivalences without acknowledging his positings as positings, and he is said to treat them as assertions of fact. In sum, "Heidegger's trick is to affirm that analogies or figurative displacements are identities. He must forget, and lead us to forget, that they are figurative substitutions."[27] Hence Miller accuses Heidegger of writing as though language were only grammar and logic, and not also rhetoric; he says that for Heidegger authentic language is purely literal, and that Heidegger does not allow for the unauthorized performative power of language. According to Miller, Heidegger covers over and denies the rhetorical strategizing of his own essay by reading figurative statements literally.[28] In effect, Miller retrieves the figurative/literal distinction in order to criticize Heidegger for being unable to bear the uncontrollability of figurative language and its proneness to unauthorized, ungoverned slippages and performative effects. Where for Heidegger metaphor depends on an untenable metaphysical distinction between the sensuous and nonsensuous – a distinction from which he attempts to turn away – for Miller the figurative/literal or linguistic/phenomenal distinction is essential and insuperable.

Miller's criticisms focus on "Building Dwelling Thinking" but are also applicable to Heidegger's claims for poetic naming in the "Ister" lectures, precisely because of Heidegger's assertions in those lectures of the founding, essential character of the poetic word. Miller's claims rest on a decision or preconception that Heidegger is in fact writing an *argument*, and Miller takes as his task to show us Heidegger's rhetorical moves and strategies, along with what Miller characterizes as Heidegger's disavowal of those moves and strategies. Ironically enough, Miller – an outstanding practitioner of rhetorical reading – ends up telling Heidegger how to be logical and philosophical, how to respect and obey the rules of argumentation. What is also ironic, from the point of view of those sympathetic to Heidegger, is that Heidegger would appear to be in the converse position of offering Miller a lesson in literary reading, in being open to poetry, as opposed to logical argument.

Now Miller would seem to be supremely qualified to judge Heidegger's readerly and rhetorical sensitivity, as Miller is himself a rhetorical reader of great care and thoughtfulness. For this very reason it is remarkable that these criticisms of Heidegger come from *Miller*, whose model of reading and the tropological/performative connection is so close to that of Paul de Man, and whose readerly concerns are *precisely* at the nexus of tropes and performatives. Indeed, the relationship between the rejection of figure and the turn to enactment in Heidegger seems to have distinct affinities with what de Man in *Aesthetic Ideology* refers to in terms of a passage from a tropological or cognitive model to a performative one.[29] What is more, Heidegger could in many instances be seen as an exquisite rhetorical reader, precisely because of his apparent awareness of the performative, event-like elements of the text that exceed the epistemological dimension. It seems, for instance, a consummately rhetorical reading when Heidegger discloses the second intonation of Leibniz's principle of reason – not the first intonation that goes "*Nothing* is *without* a reason" and thus tells us about things, about beings, and how they all have reasons – but the second intonation that goes "Nothing *is* without *reason*" and thereby reveals the ground-like character of reason with regard to beings, and the ground-like character of being as well.[30] Heidegger's scrupulously simple double reading in his lecture course *The Principle of Reason* discloses the proliferation of meanings from the single grammatical construction "Nihil est sine ratione." With his reading of the Angelus Silesius verse "The rose is without why, it blooms because it blooms," Heidegger elucidates the differences between "whys" and reasons, "becauses" and grounds, in a fashion that is entirely compatible with what de Man characterizes as rhetorical reading and its distinctive attention to meanings produced or performed above and beyond the grammatical and cognitive levels of a sentence (*The Principle of Reason* 35–43).

Miller's criticism of Heidegger is peculiarly caught in a literal/figurative opposition that, while it attends to the rhetorical strategies of Heidegger's text, nonetheless takes no notice of the dimension of performativity, enactment, or execution that is at stake. In his reading of Heidegger, Miller unaccountably reduces rhetoric to "strategy" and seems to miss what he so painstakingly describes elsewhere regarding how "what happens in readings happens."[31] Indeed, Miller writes of de Man, "his own work becomes a performative utterance working to lead the reader to the edge of unintelligibility," a statement that seems perfectly applicable to Heidegger and even to the very same Heidegger whom Miller describes in "Slipping Vaulting Crossing."[32] It appears that while Miller sees Heidegger as trapped by his rejection of figurativeness, Miller does not see that this very rejection might be precisely a way to "lead the reader to the edge of unintelligibility."

So, for example, with regard to Miller's claim that in "Building Dwelling Thinking" Heidegger confuses the "is" of identity with the "is" of figurative equivalence, it could instead be said that Heidegger in his "Ister" lectures does not *confuse* the "is" of identity and the "is" of figurative equivalence, but rather he *thematizes* this confusion instead of falling into it. In the "Ister" lectures the "is" is in quotation marks when Heidegger writes, "The river 'is' the locality and the journeying."[33] The "is" is in italics when Heidegger writes "The journeying that the river *is* prevails."[34] The punctuation and italicization of the word "is" indicates precisely the caution and special attention with which the word is employed in those contexts, i.e., these marks of emphasis reflect a sensitivity to the very possibility of confusion.

Indeed, Miller wrongly restricts the notion of figuration in such a way that it is conceived as referring only to tropes of substitution. Thus in contending that Heidegger rejects *tropes*, Miller's reading of Heidegger suppresses what P. Christopher Smith refers to in his book *The Hermeneutics of Original Argument: Demonstration, Dialectic, Rhetoric* as the diachronic tropes, i.e., the tropes of delivery and diction, which concern the sequence and juxtaposition of like and different terms.[35] What is more, Miller overlooks the significance of *dispositio* and hence overlooks the disjunction between rhetoric and logic in Heidegger's statements. The statement "The poet is the river" can be read as not a logical statement but instead as an evocation of pathos and affect, as an attempt to render the listener or reader receptive, namely to another thinking besides that of constative, descriptive thought.

VI the hypostasis of the performative

My point here is not, however, to rebut Miller's essay. Instead I would suggest that Miller's resistance to Heidegger's rejection of figurativeness is telling, telling of a performative dimension that cannot be approached directly or in proper substantive terms. Miller's argument concerning "Building Dwelling Thinking" allegorizes the difficulty of *seeing* the other thinking that Heidegger thematizes, of *seeing* performativity, enactment, poetizing, and of *seeing* the step away from figurativeness in terms of anything but a step into literalness. In this regard, my interest in Miller's criticisms of Heidegger is ultimately directed toward what they offer to an understanding of performativity and to a necessary hypostatization and indirectness that are required when discussing it. This consideration exceeds, of course, the proximate concerns of Heideggerians, Millerians, and de Manians, and is relevant to any inquiry into the legacies of the concept of performativity. For Miller's blind spot regarding the shift Heidegger offers from figurative to performative demonstrates that the step away from figurativeness *cannot* be accomplished in anything but figurative terms, for there are only tropes and hypostases for what enacting or performative saying does; it is impossible to argue about it or to even mention it without recourse to some sort of trope and some sort of hypostasis. The performative dimension is, in being talked about at all, necessarily figured and hypostatized, because it is, if it exists at all, thoroughly evanescent, an operation rather than a thing or actuality. The figure for that dimension and for that step takes on the appearance of literalness insofar as there is no proper literalness with which to contrast the tropes by means of which it is characterized. Thus the step away from figuration may look like a step into literalness, but in fact if there is a performative dimension toward which one *can* step, it has no proper language with which to be described and thus appears as at best a literalized trope for that performativity or for that enacting. In this regard, then, Heidegger's enactment in his text of the rejection of figuration, without a compensatory offer of a concrete alternative, is where he *shows* something about performativity that Miller is, at least in his reading of Heidegger, unable to *say*, namely that it is at best evoked hypostatically and figuratively.

Miller's reading presents one outcome of the decision that reading Heidegger in terms of performativity and enactment raises. The outcome of this decision cannot be said to rely solely on the argumentative value of Heidegger's texts, but rather on a preconception regarding whether in fact the split between literal and figurative can be said to be overcome or at least rethought or undergone otherwise in terms of the inaugural, naming, event-like character of language. Is there inaugural, performative, enacting saying, i.e., is there textual event – or isn't there? Is there a performative dimension apart from the literal/figurative opposition – or is there nothing beyond that opposition?

This decision, as I've already indicated above, is not at all only a matter for Heidegger studies and literary critics. The nexus of figuration and enactment at stake here, or in other words of "textual event," is not something that can be divorced from questions of the body and the efficacy of language upon the body, on political formations and the constitution of nationhood, or on the construction of racial identity. Indeed, the question of repercussions of the spillover between tropological rhetoric and philosophy in these areas is already present in Heidegger, in the very questioning as to whether saying is restricted to representing, asserting and describing or as to whether saying can breach its own apparent distance from that which is spoken about. Heidegger's inquiries in the "Ister" lectures as to whether the poetic river is other than the actual one are precisely an entanglement in the question of the performativity or enactment of language with regard to the thing that is *apparently* only referred to, but in actuality becomes what it is in a textual event. The very proliferation of discussions of the social construction of sex or of the founding force of law suggests that we are already in a theoretical space where figurative/literal is not the only or even primary tension at stake; at play is rather the tension between the dualism figurative/literal

and a further dimension of enactment, a dimension that nonetheless can be described only in tropes.

The small "performative positings," such as those for which Miller condemns Heidegger's "Building Dwelling Thinking" on the grounds that Heidegger does not take responsibility for his own rhetorical strategies, may also be read as self-conscious experiments with the relationship between linguistic invention and discovery, between saying something *about* something and a saying that does not simply refer but somehow discloses or even constructs something – although construction is here again a trope for performativity, a trope, easily literalized, for what this saying does.[36] These experimental positings cannot prove definitively that the poetic telling is performative or that there is such a thing as a textual event; they can only evoke for us these possibilities. But this uncertainty is intrinsic to any representation of enacting, founding, or performativity. If we or Miller do not see this performativity – whether in Heidegger or elsewhere – except in terms of a literalized trope, this does not prove that it does not exist. It may go unseen because it is not there to be found, but on the other hand it may be, in its own way, found only as hypostasis and figure.

notes

I am grateful to an anonymous *Angelaki* reviewer for constructive suggestions.

1 Martin Heidegger, *The Principle of Reason*, trans. Reginald Lilly (Bloomington: Indiana UP, 1991) 48.

2 Martin Heidegger, *Hölderlin's Hymn "The Ister,"* trans. William McNeill and Julia Davis (Bloomington: Indiana UP, 1996) 42–43. For a more thorough discussion of Heidegger's reading of this poem, see my essay "The Naming of the Hymn: Heidegger and Hölderlin" in *Between Philosophy and Poetry: Writing, Rhythm, History*, eds. Massimo Verdicchio and Robert Burch (New York: Continuum, 2002) 117–24. For important discussions of Heidegger and metaphor, see Ronald Bruzina,

"Heidegger on the Metaphor and Philosophy" in *Heidegger and Modern Philosophy: Critical Essays*, ed. Michael Murray (New Haven: Yale UP, 1978); Samuel Ijsseling, *Rhetorik und Philosophie: Eine historisch-systematische Einführung* (Stuttgart: Fromann-Holzboog, 1988) 177–80; David Halliburton, *Poetic Thinking: An Approach to Heidegger* (Chicago: U of Chicago P, 1981) 156–58; Joseph J. Kockelmans, "Heidegger on Metaphor and Metaphysics," *Tijdschrift voor Filosofie* 47 (1985): 415–50; and Ernesto Grassi, *Kunst und Mythos* (Frankfurt: Suhrkamp, 1990) 115–28.

3 Heidegger, *Hölderlin's Hymn "The Ister"* 165.

4 Paul de Man, *Allegories of Reading: Figural Language in Rousseau, Nietzsche, Rilke and Proust* (New Haven: Yale UP, 1979) 279; Jean Greisch, "Les Mots et les roses: La Métaphore chez Martin Heidegger," *Revue des Sciences Philosophiques et Théologiques* 57 (1973): 433–55 (436). Neither de Man, Greisch nor Miller takes Heidegger as exemplary for an understanding of textual events, but here I claim that Heidegger's rejection of metaphor is an indirect way to thematize the event-like character of the text.

5 See, for example, Miller's essay "The Disputed Ground: Deconstruction and Literary Studies" in *Deconstruction is/in America*, ed. Anselm Haverkamp (New York: New York UP, 1995); and Miller's volume *Tropes, Parables, Performatives: Essays on Twentieth-Century Literature* (New York: Harvester Wheatsheaf, 1990).

6 De Man, *Allegories of Reading* ix.

7 Paul de Man, *Aesthetic Ideology* (Minneapolis: U of Minnesota P, 1996) 132.

8 Ibid. 133.

9 J. Hillis Miller, *Topographies* (Stanford: Stanford UP, 1995) 8.

10 J. Hillis Miller, *Speech Acts in Literature* (Stanford: Stanford UP, 2001) 1.

11 Miller, *Topographies* 5: "… [T]he text and its reading, it may be, are performative speech acts bringing the terrain into existence."

12 J.L. Austin, *How to Do Things with Words* (Cambridge, MA: Harvard UP, 1962) 6.

13 Jacques Derrida, "Signature Event Context" in *Limited Inc*, trans. Samuel Weber and Jeffrey Mehlman (Evanston: Northwestern UP, 1988)

17: "For, ultimately, isn't it true that what Austin excludes as anomaly, exception, 'non-serious,' *citation* (on stage, in a poem, or a soliloquy) is the determined modification of a general citationality – or rather, a general iterability – without which there would not even be a 'successful' performative?" Eve Kosofsky Sedgwick offers extremely helpful explanations of the genealogy of performativity in *Touching Feeling: Affect, Pedagogy, Performativity* (Durham, NC: Duke UP, 2003) 3–8; and in her introduction (co-authored by Andrew Parker), "Introduction: Performativity and Performance" in *Performativity and Performance* (New York: Routledge, 1995) 1–18. Also noteworthy is the role that Stanley Cavell has played in the reception of performativity and the Austin/Derrida discussion. See Stanley Cavell, *A Pitch of Philosophy: Autobiographical Exercises* (Cambridge, MA: Harvard UP, 1994) 55–127.

14 For the difference between existentiell and existential understanding, see Martin Heidegger, *Being and Time*, trans. Joan Stambaugh (Albany: State U of New York P, 1996) 12–13. Page numbers for *Being and Time* are referenced according to the original German pagination that is noted in the margins of the English translation.

15 Heidegger, *Being and Time* 273.

16 Ibid. 265.

17 Ibid. 287.

18 Ibid. 1.

19 Ibid. 267.

20 Ibid. 270–71.

21 Heidegger, *Hölderlin's Hymn "The Ister"* 33–34.

22 Ibid. 21. See also my "The Naming of the Hymn: Heidegger and Hölderlin." For an exhaustive treatment of naming in Heidegger's thought, see Dieter Thomä, *Die Zeit des Selbst und die Zeit danach: Zur Kritik der Textgeschichte Martin Heideggers, 1910–1976* (Frankfurt am Main: Suhrkamp, 1990) 659–84.

23 Heidegger, *Hölderlin's Hymn "The Ister"* 13.

24 J. Hillis Miller, "Slipping Vaulting Crossing: Heidegger" in *Topographies* 216–54.

25 Paul de Man, *The Resistance to Theory* (Minneapolis: U of Minnesota P, 1986) 11; Miller, "Slipping Vaulting Crossing" 223, 230–31.

26 Miller, "Slipping Vaulting Crossing" 235.

27 Ibid. 238.

28 Ibid. 236.

29 De Man, *Aesthetic Ideology* 133.

30 Heidegger, *The Principle of Reason* 33–49.

31 Miller, "Paul de Man as Allergen" in *Material Events: Paul de Man and the Afterlife of Theory*, eds. Barbara Cohen, Tom Cohen, J. Hillis Miller and Andrzej Warminski (Minneapolis: U of Minnesota P, 2001) 183–204 (198).

32 Miller, "De Man as Allergen" 197.

33 Heidegger, *Hölderlin's Hymn "The Ister"* 142.

34 Ibid. 30. In *Being and Time*, particularly in the introductory sections, the word "being" is placed in quotation marks and italics in order to call attention, it would seem, to the catachrestic use that is being made of it. In Heidegger's writings on poetry and language where the "is" is not italicized, framed in scare quotes, or otherwise marked, it would seem that the catachrestic character of the usage of the term "is" has become thematized to such a degree that quotation marks and italics may themselves be left off – precisely because the usage of "is" and of the word "being" are presumably everywhere what is in question.

35 P. Christopher Smith, *The Hermeneutics of Original Argument: Demonstration, Dialectic, Rhetoric* (Evanston: Northwestern UP, 1998). This excellent book makes no reference to Miller or to the sorts of claims that are being proposed here, but rather discusses Heidegger's work in terms of what could be called a retrieval of original argument, based mainly on Aristotle's *Rhetoric*. Using Smith's analysis, one could argue that the statement "the river is the poet" is not a literalization of a trope and not a confusion of the "is" of identity with the "is" of figurative equivalence, but rather a play on a trope – not a trope of substitution such as metaphor, but a diachronic trope wherein the very unfolding of the sentence is a figure, a temporal connection of elements that performatively associates the terms that are thereby connected. This operation is already rhetorical; it is not sheerly grammatical and certainly not sheerly logical.

36 These considerations of the literalization of the trope for performativity and specifically of the trope of construction are indebted to Judith Butler's "How Can I Deny that These Hands and This Body Are Mine?" in *Material Events: Paul de Man and the Afterlife of Theory* 253–73.

Karen S. Feldman
Department of Rhetoric
University of California
Berkeley, CA 94720-2670
USA
E-mail: kfeld@socrates.berkeley.edu

journal of the theoretical humanities
volume 9 number 3 december 2004

Gilles Deleuze is no phenomenologist. At least that is what he leads us to believe in his strident efforts to distinguish his radical empiricism from phenomenology. In *Cinema 1: The Movement-Image*, he puts his position clearly, stating that:

> What phenomenology sets up as a norm is "natural perception" and its conditions. Now, these conditions are existential co-ordinates which define an "anchoring" of the perceiving subject in the world, a being in the world, an opening to the world which will be expressed in the famous "all consciousness is consciousness of something …" [Whereas] [t]he cinema can, with impunity, bring us close to things or take us away from them and revolve around them, it suppresses both the anchoring of the subject and the horizon of the world. Hence it substitutes an implicit knowledge and a second intentionality for the conditions of natural perception. (57)

Deleuze's critique of phenomenology's anchored subject and his revision, for cinema, of Henri Bergson's model of perception as "a flowing-matter in which no point of anchorage nor centre of reference would be assignable" (*Cinema 1* 57), opens up the possibility of theorizing spectatorship as a form of immersion in an image.

This may seem to be a paradoxical claim. After all, Deleuze is quick to cast aside the category of the spectator in *Cinema 2: The Time-Image*, as the term, in its usage in psychoanalysis-influenced film theory, introduces categories of subjective identification and position that are antithetical to Deleuze's emphasis on the flow of images. In Deleuze's cinema of direct time-images, the spectator disappears, becoming a seer absorbed into and by the image, immersed in the film's unfolding from one image to the

maria walsh

THE IMMERSIVE SPECTATOR
a phenomenological hybrid

next. "This is a cinema of the seer and no longer of the agent."[1] However, not taking a psychoanalytic/structuralist approach to film need not automatically exclude the notion of the spectator. I shall argue in this article that while Deleuzian concepts are crucial to conceiving of a relation to the image in terms of immersion rather than alienation (much cultural theory adopting the latter position), the concept of the spectator is still useful. Without a concept of the spectator, it is difficult to consider how the body is imbricated in the state of being immersed in the image. In order to consider immersion and embodiment as co-existent, I shall perform a juggling act between Deleuze and Maurice Merleau-Ponty's phenomenology. Again, this may seem to be a paradoxical position, as it is Mer-

ISSN 0969-725X print/ISSN 1469-2899 online/04/030169–17 © 2004 Taylor & Francis Ltd and the Editors of *Angelaki*
DOI: 10.1080/0969725042000307709

leau-Ponty's *Phenomenology of Perception* that Deleuze is critiquing in the above citation. However, turning to the Merleau-Ponty of *The Visible and the Invisible*, one finds a theory of embodiment that is strangely commensurate with aspects of the subjectless subjectivity that Deleuze explores in his two cinema books. A hybridization of these two thinkers is not only in line with Deleuze's own philosophical procedure of assemblage but also allows for the insertion of embodiment into the infinite unfolding of images that Deleuze describes. It simultaneously prevents Merleau-Ponty's notion of embodiment from being reduced to traditional notions where embodiment is considered as the sensuous, mute, ground of being.[2]

The background to my desire to theorize a form of spectatorship where the spectator is immersed in the image yet is aware of his or her bodily coordinates stems from distinctions between cinematic and digital media that are currently in vogue. In contemporary media discourse, immersion is largely referred to in relation to digital technology where "principles of envelopment and temporal simultaneity" are contrasted with the "distance and sequential unfolding" of the cinematic apparatus.[3] However, these distinctions stem from literal categorizations of medium specificity and do not take into account the fact that a spectator (or user) may be engaging with the image in a mode that is not reducible to the mechanics of the medium. A cinematic spectator's engagement with the screen is not bounded by his or her location in front of it and immersion in the diegesis need not be thought of as illusory, as it has been conceived in much film theory. A digital user's engagement with the computer screen need not mean the disappearance of the body in favour of a free-floating, dislocated engagement in the deep space of an immersive environment. Instead, a case can be made for crossovers between these media-based categorizations. Immersion in the image can be theorized, I shall argue, as a mode of spectatorial engagement whereby the simultaneity of envelopment and the sequential nature of montage are not mutually exclusive. The notion of immersive spectatorship can be applicable to specific instances of moving-image

work rather than immersion being the sole feature of a medium per se. There is no doubt that digital technology reconfigures how we think about spatial density and temporal flow but there is no reason to suppose that engagement with cinematic images cannot follow the principles of immersion that have been identified with the digital.[4] Deleuze's writing on cinema suggests the possibility for conceiving of immersion as a more generalized form of image engagement, bypassing the reduction to medium specificity. In what follows, I shall attempt to combine the usually distinct categories of immersion and spectatorship to theorize a state where a viewer is enveloped by a moving-image scenario, yet, at the same time, is aware of shifting bodily coordinates in relation to the image flow. I am not claiming that all images have the same effects but that instances of contemporary cinema, experimental film, gallery film installation, and digital media that emphasize the senses in a way that seems to dissolve bodily boundaries can engender the state I am calling immersive spectatorship.

In beginning to theorize this state, Deleuze is an inspirational guide. As I have already said, in Deleuze's taxonomy of images the spectator becomes a seer absorbed into and by the image, immersed in the film's unfolding from one image to the next. His concern is not with the narrative trajectory of a character's passage from one state of being to another but in the way a character's hallucinatory visions allow the director to move from one kind of image sequence to another. This proffers a different kind of narrative trajectory for the viewer where images follow one another according to their own logic rather than following the dictates of (linguistic) narrative. In this, Deleuze takes issue with dominant psychoanalytic/structuralist approaches to film, claiming that, in replacing the image by an utterance, those approaches give the image "a false appearance, and its most authentically visible characteristic, movement, is taken away from it" (*Cinema 2* 27). On the face of it, Deleuze's dynamic suggests a smooth, non-conflictual image-space rather than the tension of conflictual identification that abounds in psychoanalytic accounts of spectatorship. While this trajectory is liberating in terms of releasing the image from the dictates of language, it is my contention that in Deleuze's embrace of image narration something vital is lost, i.e., the spectator's embodiment. Merleau-Ponty also employs the term "seer," in his case to refer to an embodied and yet immersed subject in the world. For Merleau-Ponty there is always a "strange adhesion of the seer and the visible," rather than the dispersal of the seer into the acentred state of things, which is why I will go on to appropriate aspects of Merleau-Ponty's philosophy for a theory of immersive spectatorship.[5] Also, in a twist to my argument, Deleuze, read in tandem with film theory's appropriation of phenomenology in the 1970s, will be shown to recuperate phenomenology's "transcendental subject" which he claims is antithetical to his project and which is certainly antithetical to mine.[6]

from duration to dust: immersion as disembodiment in deleuze

Initially at least, Deleuze's dissolution of the spectator into the seer offers possibilities for theorizing immersive spectatorship. Deleuze articulates the dissolution of the seer in the screened image by way of the infinite spiralling motion of temporality itself. In the shift from the pre-war cinema of the movement-image to the post-war cinema of the time-image (Deleuze's loose historical categorization), "perceptions, actions and affects underwent such an upheaval [...] because a new element [time] burst onto the scene [...] to prevent perception being extended into action in order to put it in contact with thought" (*Cinema 2* 1). In this process, action is transformed into hallucination, an expanded duration in which a character, as seer, becomes immobilized. The sensori-motor schemata are suspended and a "pure optical *situation*" takes over (ibid. 2). In relation to the shots of empty interiors and deserted exteriors in Yasujiro Ozu's films, Deleuze claims that these instances of "pure optical situations" become instances of "pure contemplation" (ibid. 16). However, more pertinent to my purposes in theorizing immer-

sive spectatorship as a state that involves an awareness of change rather than hypnotic dissolution is Deleuze's discussion of the dynamic exchange in Ozu's films between empty interiors and still lifes (for example, the vase in *Late Spring*). For Deleuze, "[i]f empty spaces, interiors or exteriors, constitute purely optical (and sound) situations, still lifes are the reverse, the correlate" (ibid. 17). Still lifes show the changing states of a duration, which would otherwise be invisible, "pure" perhaps, and thereby without the capacity to register the human passage of time. While "time does not itself change," it needs to be embodied in human terms to punctuate and change the direction of its eternal nature (ibid. 17). Otherwise, the immersive, hypnotic encounter with the image would dissolve into the flux of the "inhuman narration" of a non-organic lifeworld, Deleuze's ultimate trajectory (ibid. 102).

As we shall see shortly, the emphasis on a pure perception that moves beyond human embodiment is the direction that Deleuze's discussion of Michael Snow's films takes and is perhaps why Deleuze is referred to by theorists who celebrate the supposed escape from the body in virtual space.[7] While Deleuze does insist on the body as a marker of temporal change in chapter 8 of *Cinema 2: The Time-Image*, he generally abandons the emphasis on everyday banality in neo-realism and in Ozu in favour of references to the production of images as a kind of perceptual cosmological dust. For example, in discussing the importance in contemporary cinema of the image of absence, the black screen or the white screen, Deleuze states that in the films of Philippe Garrel:

the series of anterior images has no end, while the series of subsequent images likewise has no beginning, the two series converging towards the white or black screen as their common limit. Moreover in this way, the screen becomes the medium for variations: the black screen and the under-exposed image, the intense blackness which lets us guess at dark volumes in the process of being constituted, or the black marked by a fixed or moving luminous point, and all the combinations of black and fire; the white screen and the over-exposed image, the milky image or the snowy image whose dancing seeds are to take shape ... (Ibid. 200)

Deleuze, in expanding the field of the film scenario to the expanse of a temporality without limit, moves towards the end of the spectrum whereby the spectator becomes vaporized in a pure perceptual unfolding. Initially locating time in the body, Deleuze goes on to divorce the two, or rather, to locate the body in the empty form of time. Appropriating Henri Bergson, Deleuze writes:

Bergsonism has often been reduced to the following idea: duration is subjective, and constitutes our internal life. And it is true that Bergson had to express himself in this way, at least at the outset. But, increasingly, he came to say something quite different: the only subjectivity is time, non-chronological time grasped in its foundation, and it is we who are internal to time, not the other way round. (Ibid. 82–83)

While Deleuze does say that "[t]ime is [...] the interiority in which we are, in which we move, live and change," his processual occlusion of space from this picture makes it difficult to see where, and in relation to what, movement and change could occur, other than being the infinite unfolding of pure virtuality (ibid. 82). To be subject to this virtual unfolding paralyses the body. When Deleuze, in relation to Louis Malle's *Lift to the Scaffold*, says that "bodily states themselves link up with movements of the world," he is referring to the murderer's movements in the film which are blocked by the halting of the lift and which, in turn, extend into a kind of cosmic dream-like state (ibid. 60). But what of the spectator's bodily states? By inference, they perhaps mirror those of the character become seer. However, while Bergson does insist that the body is a special kind of image within the field of images, what interests me is how this imagistic body differentiates itself in relation to other images rather than melting into the vertiginous mass of an infinitely unfolding cosmic vision.[8] For Deleuze:

the before and after are no longer themselves a matter of external empirical succession, but of the intrinsic quality of that which becomes in time. Becoming can in fact be defined as that which transforms an empirical sequence into a series: a burst of series. A series is a sequence of images, which tend in themselves in the direction of a limit, which orients and inspires the first sequence (the before), and gives way to another sequence organized as series which tends in turn towards another limit (the after). The before and the after are then no longer successive determinations of the course of time, but the two sides of the power, or the passage of the power to a higher power. The direct time-image here does not appear in an order of coexistences or simultaneities, but in a becoming as potentialization, as series of powers. (Ibid. 275)

For Deleuze, the before and after, the passage of time through the body, becomes liberated from any particular body. However, I would insist that, rather than dissolving the body into the heady vaporosity of the movements of time itself, the problematic of thinking the body still remains here, albeit a different kind of body.

from luminous dust to material affect: the return of mute phenomena

Attempting to marry thinking the body and Deleuzian theory, Barbara Kennedy unabashedly embraces Deleuze's language of flows and intensities to discuss the affective nature of immersive film experience. For Kennedy, a Deleuzian approach situates the spectator's body beyond phenomenology's emphasis on the "lived body," instead proffering "the complex understanding of 'body' as processes of congealment, imbrication, consilience, assemblage, aesthetics and the molecular."[9] Kennedy's thesis is relevant to my argument. Desiring to "counter the negativity of cine-psychoanalysis," she too is attempting to articulate an immersive spectatorial scenario, but her consumption of Deleuze causes her to celebrate "subjectless subjectivity" on the one hand, and to emphasize the visceral nature of affect on the other ("Towards an Aesthetics" 2, 45). This reassertion of binary thinking re-substantializes the "visceral" body as the ground of anonymous being, a position which Deleuze is actually at pains to avoid, as it falls back into the trap of positing a mute materiality beneath or beyond symbolic meaning.[10] As she puts it: "mind/body/brain meld with the image in an assemblage of filmic sensation where affect affords the ultimate 'material emotion' which is beyond any subjective vision" (ibid. 53). Kennedy's tendency to reduce the viewing space to an undifferentiated mass of matter, whereby "brain/body/image are coagulated into a malleable set of images, into a materiality of emotion" (ibid. 144), can perhaps be seen in her attribution of the same descriptive terms to different films. Discussing the landscapes in *Orlando*, *The English Patient*, and *The Sheltering Sky* she says: "Something grand, intangible and molecular is emitted across the gestural movements of the screenic event. The emptiness and solitude of the landscape enable a connection of intensities which are about process, continuums, becoming, and, ironically, are far removed from transcendent notions of inorganic origins, death, and fixity."[11] This position would tend, in Deleuze's terms, to actually deny difference, resulting instead in "undifferenciated being, without difference."[12]

Undoubtedly, there is much in Deleuze's trajectory in the cinema books that lends itself towards this vision of undifferentiated mass, and Kennedy is not the only reader to proffer it. While Kennedy emphasizes an undifferentiated visceral ground of affect, John Johnston embraces the infinity of Deleuzian gaseous perception as a way of describing the decoded field of electronic imformational impulses of global telecommunications. Johnston appropriates the chapter on the brain in *Cinema 2: The Time-Image* where "Deleuze identifies the 'irrational' cut of modern cinema with a specific type of synaptic, neuronal transmission."[13] In that chapter, Deleuze claims that:

[e]verything can be used as a screen, the body of a protagonist or even the bodies of the spectators; everything can replace film stock, in a virtual film which now only goes on in the head, behind the pupils, with sound sources taken as required from the auditorium. A disturbed brain-death or a new brain which would be at once the screen, the film stock and the camera, each time membrane of the outside and the inside. (*Cinema 2* 215)

This move in Deleuze exemplifies the merging of screen and disembodied consciousness that features in much theorizing of digital media. It is this sentiment of the screen as a boundless mental landscape, "a new brain" that I am taking issue with. The emphasis in digital media on immersion need not rule out embodiment and in effect redraws our attention to the fact that, in the early days of film theory, cinema itself was seen as an immersive environment capable of carrying the spectator away.[14] The issue here in theorizing immersive spectatorship via Deleuze is whether the absorption of the seer in the image can also be considered in terms of embodiment, in terms of location rather than purely mental contemplation.

Before moving on to a consideration of Merleau-Ponty's phenomenology, which, contrary to Kennedy's alliance of "subjectless subjectivity" with the viscerality of material affect, allows for a process of differentiation between the particularity of subjective vision and the anonymity of a-subjective vision, I now want to look at another attempt in film theory to marry a Deleuzian approach to the image and embodiment. The purpose of this is to show why traditional readings of embodiment are to be avoided and to extract other elements from Deleuze that I will hybridize with Merleau-Ponty for my theorization of the paradox of immersive spectatorship.

deleuzian derangement of the senses vs. the sensuous phenomenological body

Laura Marks' *The Skin of the Film: Intercultural Cinema, Embodiment, and the Senses*, which refers to both Deleuze and Merleau-Ponty, gives credence to Kennedy's otherwise debatable claim that "the phenomenological body" is somewhat regressive.[15] Marks reads Deleuze's assertion that cinema "can give us 'the genesis of an unknown body, which we have in the back of our heads, like the unthought in thought'" as a commonsense assertion that "cinema may indeed be capable of bringing us to our senses"

(147–48). However, the senses as Deleuze conceives them are certainly not the senses we assume as being rooted in the body and are far removed from the traditional phenomenological framework that Marks uses.

> Given the nature of memory, the audiovisual image necessarily evokes other sense memories, perhaps even memories that belong to that "unknown body." For example, when I am watching a scene shot in a garden in Shani Mootoo's *Her Sweetness Lingers* (1994), close-ups of magnolia flowers remind me of how they feel and how they smell, and the buzzing of insects reminds me of the heat of summer. For me the tape calls up associations with gardens I have known in my ancestral Alabama, associations that are probably somewhat different from the artist's and other viewers' associations with them. (Marks 148)

I cite this lengthy quotation as an example of the personal, autobiographical level of association that pervades Marks' analysis of the tactility of immersive spectatorship.

While I am sceptical of Deleuze's emphasis on "pure contemplation," I would not want to reassert a return to the particular in terms of the corporeal self-possession of the spectator. For Deleuze, the unknown body is removed from autobiographical knowledge and ownership, which is why it can offer liberation and transformation rather than habitual repetition. Marks does not examine the constitution of the body that she claims is a container of sensuous knowledge. Also, in emphasizing how postcolonial cinema and experimental film use senses beyond the visual, such as smell and touch, to engage and recover bodily memories, she unwittingly reasserts the very hierarchy that she wants to readdress between mind and body, dominant and marginal. She claims that films that "blur" and "muffle" the experience of the visual point "to the possibility of less ocularcentric ways of seeing" (Marks 135–36). While there is a case to be made for this opposition between the ocular and the haptic in Deleuze's own work, his endowment of touch with haptic vision is not to assert a specific bodily sensation of tactility but to overrule such distinctions between eye and hand. This is exemplified in his book on the painter Francis Bacon, *Francis Bacon: Logique de la sensation.*

> To characterize the connection between eye and hand, it is certainly not enough to say that the eye is infinitely richer, and passes through dynamic tensions, logical reversals, organic exchanges and vicariances ... We will speak of the *haptic* each time there is no longer strict subordination in one direction or the other ... but when sight discovers in itself a function of touching that belongs to it and to it alone and which is independent of its optical function.[16]

The fact that the sensations engendered by film stem from or lean on the visual realm does not necessarily mean that the visual operates as an isolated facet in the space of viewing. Nor does it mean that soft-focus or blurry imagery is necessarily tactile, bodily and in opposition to the supposed distancing of harsh contour. Taking a Deleuzian approach, the visual becoming haptic does not necessarily mean that one is propelled out of the optical. What this means is that the visual is broken down as a component sense. In fact, the capacity of the component senses is broken down by the impact of the image of sensation and what is unleashed is a kind of sensory chaos. No one sense is available for any recognized channel. Rather than the return of a familiar memory or the rupture of a buried one, for Deleuze the image of sensation generates the return of something new.

In *Proust and Signs*, Deleuze refers to the famous scene from Proust's *Remembrance of Things Past*, where the taste of a madeleine cake sends a shudder through Marcel and he begins to "hear the echo of great spaces traversed. Undoubtedly what is thus palpitating in the depths of my being must be the image, the visual memory which, being linked to that taste, is trying to follow it into my conscious mind."[17] For Deleuze, the visual memory that occurs here is not the return of the Combray that Proust knew as a child. What returns in the image is Combray "not as it was experienced in contiguity with the past sensation, but in a splendor [...] that never has an equivalent in reality."[18] In other words, the process of translation, or mediation, which could also be called time itself, has transformed the image into a scene both familiar and estranged. Rather than the senses being interrelated as in traditional phenomenology, Deleuzian derangement of the senses causes each one to attain its own singularity, a singularity that is not owned by a particular body but casts that body adrift on a clamorous ocean in which "each drop and each voice has reached the state of excess – in other words, the difference which displaces and disguises them and, in turning upon its mobile cusp, causes them to return" (*Difference and Repetition* 304). Deleuze's notion of the derangement of the senses is crucial to avoid the reassertion of the selfsame body, a body re-found or a body returned to its owner in the immersive spectatorial space. To be fair to Marks, and also to Kennedy, on occasion Deleuze seems to come close to asserting a kind of phenomenology. As Gaylyn Studlar points out, while Deleuze is critical of phenomenology's insistence on the anchored subject, he is "interested in the power of the image in *phenomenologically positive terms*, in the cinema's ability to provoke wonder, awe, and astonishment."[19] While Kennedy attempted to combine a "subjectless subjectivity" with viscerality, the problem in Marks' analysis is that bodies are assumed to have definite owners and are culturally bounded by custom and personal memory. I do not want to make a claim for the meltdown of cultural specificity per se, but for me the sensations unleashed in the immersive encounter with the moving image exceed personalized frames of reference. (Here I agree with Kennedy's emphasis.) As Deleuze puts it:

[I]t is no longer a motor extension which is established, but rather a dreamlike connection through the intermediary of the liberated sense organs. It is as if the action floats in the situation, rather than bringing it to a conclusion or strengthening it. (*Cinema 2* 4)

However, in terms of my claim for immersive spectatorship, these liberated sensations intercede with personalized frames of reference in their passage through the body, whereas Deleuze's evacuation of agency from this sensational disordering is so absolute that it ends up

reifying the work of art as a form of abstraction without a link to anybody.

Perceptions are no longer perceptions; they are independent of a state of those who experience them ... Sensations, percepts, and affects are beings whose validity lies in themselves and exceeds any lived ... The work of art is a being of sensation and nothing else: it exists in itself.[20]

When Deleuze, with Guattari, says that "sensory becoming is otherness caught in a matter of expression" (*What is Philosophy?* 177), I find myself saying yes, but by whom or what?

glimpses of embodiment

In *The Deleuze Connections*, John Rajchman suggests that habitation and abstract derangement are not mutually exclusive in a Deleuzian framework, as they would not be in Merleau-Ponty's phenomenology where, as we shall see, anonymity and particularity are always interrelated. The following rather lengthy quotations from Rajchman are suggestive, perhaps unwittingly, of some connection between Deleuzian anonymity and the particularity of habitation in these moments of sensory derangement. Rajchman refers to Virginia Woolf's *Mrs. Dalloway*:

When in *What is Philosophy?* Deleuze says that "art is sensation and nothing else," he is trying to capture an idea that runs through his work [...] Affects and percepts are the two basic types of sensation, of which the artwork may be said to be a composite. [...] affects go beyond the subjects that pass through them, and they are impersonal, even inhuman; and percepts are not ways of presenting nature to the eye, but are rather like landscapes, urban as well as natural, in which one must lose oneself so as to see with new eyes, as, for example, with *Mrs. Dalloway*. [...] the aim of art is, through expressive materials, to extract sensations from habitual sensibilia – from habits of perception, memory, recognition, agreement – and cause us to see and feel in new or unforeseen ways. (134–35)

Rajchman also writes:

An hour of a day, a river, a climate, a strange

moment during a concert can be like this – not one of a kind, but the individuation of something that belongs to no kind, but which, though perfectly individuated, yet retains an indefiniteness, as though pointing to something "ineffable." (125)

Rajchman's formulation is useful in that he suggests that the impersonal intuitions in sensory derangement are dependent on the particular bodies they pass through. As he adds:

> A life is in fact composed of many such moments – that is part of what makes it singular. They are the sorts of occurrences that come to us rather like the "waves" of which Virginia Woolf spoke – bits of experience that can't be fitted into a nice narrative unity, and so must be combined or put together in another way. [...] They precede us as subjects or persons, and yet they are always "expressed" in our lives. (85)

While I would want to hold onto Deleuze's notion of sensory derangement and anonymity in considering immersive spectatorship, contextualizing Deleuzian sensory liberation in relation to film history can show why it is desirable to temper his readings of film with a phenomenology of embodiment such as Merleau-Ponty's. In a surprising twist to my argument, an aspect of phenomenology's "transcendental subject" returns in the destruction of the human world that Deleuze associates with cinematic vision. Contrasting Deleuze's writing on Michael Snow's films with Annette Michelson's writing on the same films in the 1970s, using the phenomenological methodology of film analysis available then, delivers the strange proximity of Deleuze's analysis to this aspect of phenomenology.

the return of the "transcendental subject" in deleuze: the disembodied eye

For Deleuze, Snow's films generate a purified vision devoid of human agency. In fact, *The Central Region* (1971), Snow's three-hour film of a remote Canadian landscape, recorded by the pre-programmed choreography of a machine that endlessly turns and swivels like an automaton,

could almost be an answer to Deleuze's rhetorical question: "But how is it possible to speak of images in themselves that are not for anyone and are not addressed to anyone? How is it possible to speak of an Appearing [*Apparaître*], since there is not even an eye?"[21]

In Deleuze's description of the film, we find a succinct example of how cinema is viewed as an Appearing without a seer, external or otherwise. He says:

> Michael Snow's *The Central Region* does not raise perception to the universal variation of a raw and savage matter without also extracting from it a space without reference points where the ground and the sky, the horizontal and the vertical, interchange. Nothingness itself is diverted towards that which comes out of it or falls back on it, the genetic element, the fresh or vanishing perception, which potentialises a space by retaining only the shadow or the account of human events. (*Cinema 1* 122)

There is precedence in Bergson for this kind of purified vision. For Bergson:

> Pure perceptions ... or images are what we should posit at the outset. And sensations, far from being the materials from which the image is wrought, will then appear as the impurity which is introduced into it, being that part of our own body which we project into all others. (*Matter and Memory* 234–35)

The notion that the sensory body is a contaminant is one that Bergson keeps on repeating in the first sections of *Matter and Memory*. Linking affection with sensation, he says that "[a]ffection is, then, that part or aspect of the inside of our body which we mix with the image of external bodies; it is what we must first of all subtract from perception to get to the image in its purity" (ibid. 58). However, there is a productive tension between this desire for a pure perception and Bergson's equal insistence on the body as a special kind of image within the field of images, one which:

> constitutes at every moment, as we have said, a section of the universal becoming. It is then the *place of passage* of the movements received and thrown back, a hyphen, a connecting link between the things which act upon me

and the things upon which I act – the seat, in a word, of the sensori-motor phenomena. (Ibid. 151–52)

The notion of the body as an image within the field of images seems far removed from the situatedness of phenomenology's "perceiving subject," but Bergson's qualification of this as a "place of passage" maintains a dynamic relationship between a screened image and the spectator which can be linked to the Merleau-Ponty of *The Visible and the Invisible*. Bergson's notion of the body (spectator) as a place of passage creates an interval between movements received and movements thrown back. Although body and image are essentially of the same matter, if the body did not act as a differentiating passage, the "universal variation" of movement-images would have the quality of an eternal force or a dreamerless dreamscape, a drugged vision (the latter a motif Deleuze is fond of). By contrast, Bergson insists on the balance between action and recollection for the successful operation of the sensori-motor system. The purity of either the pole of action, i.e., the present divorced from the planes of memory, or the pole of recollection, i.e., immersion in the planes of memory without extension in the present, would result, according to Bergson, in a pathological subjectivity (ibid. 155).

Although taking a direction opposite to that of traditional phenomenology, Deleuze's acentred universe has a strangely similar outcome. In both veins, the embeddedness of a particular body in a scene is eradicated. The proximity of both veins becomes clear when one looks at Annette Michelson's analysis of Michael Snow's films. For Michelson, the spectator Snow engenders is in fact phenomenology's transcendental subject, which she describes as being an eye unfettered by the body. By contrast to Deleuze's celebration of the decentring effects of Snow's camera and the attainment of gaseous perception, Michelson sees Snow as reintroducing, albeit in a questioning way, a sovereignty of the spectator which had been threatened by the "spatial disorientations" of Stan Brakhage's experimental film-making (118). She says:

Wavelength, then, appeared as a celebration of the "apparatus" and a confirmation of the status of the subject, and it is in those terms that we may begin to comprehend the profound effect it had on the broadest spectrum of viewers – especially upon those for whom previous assaults on the spatiotemporality of dominant cinema had obscured that subject's role and place. The spectator for whom that place was obscured – and threatened – by the spatial disorientations of, say, *Dog Star Man* (a space purely optical and a temporality of the perpetual present) could respond, as if in gratitude, to Snow's apparently gratifying confirmation of a threatened sovereignty. (118)

The claims that Michelson makes for Brakhage's *Dog Star Man* are ostensibly closer to Deleuze's analysis of Snow's cinema as engendering a purified, unlocatable, luminous, vision. In fact, Deleuze, in his film historiography, refers to both these film-makers as creating a cinema that attains a pure perception. His description of *Wavelength* exemplifies this viewpoint. He says:

If the experimental cinema tends towards a perception as it was before men (or after), it also tends towards the correlate of this, that is, towards an any-space-whatever released from its human coordinates [...] In *Wavelength* Snow uses a forty-five minute zoom in order to explore a room lengthwise from one end to the other, as far as the wall on which a photograph of the sea is stuck: from this room he extracts a potential space, whose power and quality he progressively exhausts. [...] The space re-enters the empty sea. All the preceding elements of the any-space-whatever, the shadows, the whites, the colours, the inexorable progression, the inexorable reduction, elevation plane [*épure*], the disconnected parts, the empty set: all come into play here in what, according to Sitney, defines the "structural film." (*Cinema 1* 122)

Deleuze's adherence to P. Adams Sitney here (the 1970s film historian who employed a loosely phenomenological approach to film analysis) is telling. Sitney considered *Wavelength* as a metaphor for human consciousness per se, a notion that fits in with Deleuze's emphasis on a cinema of the brain that I have already referred to.[22]

For Michelson, there is also a link between Snow's and Brakhage's ostensibly different styles of film-making, although she reads this differently from Deleuze. Her reading allows me to introduce the possibility that the "transcendental subject" returns in Deleuze's analysis. While Brakhage's emphasis on a vision uncorrupted by language – what Michelson refers to as "the gaze of fascination" – may seem different from Snow's use of filmic signifiers to create spaces of "analytic inspection," Michelson sees these moves in terms of the continuity of American avant-garde film-making rather than the occurrence of a different strain (Michelson 116). "The hallucinated viewer was, so to speak, replaced by the cognitive viewer, but common to them both was the status of *transcendental subject*" (ibid. 116). She claims that, while Snow in *The Central Region* does subject spatio-temporal certainties to questioning, the film's infinitely mobile framing:

> [its] mimesis of and gloss upon spatial exploration offer, most importantly, a fusion of primary scopophilic and epistemophilic impulses in the cinematic rendering of the grand metaphor of the transcendental subject. (Michelson 123)

For her, and I agree, *The Central Region* hyperbolizes the "disembodied mobility of the eye-subject" (121). This corresponds with Snow's assertion that:

> "I wanted the spectator to be the lone center of all these circles. It had to be the place where you can see a long way and you can't see anything man-made. That has something to do with a certain kind of singleness or remoteness that each spectator can have by seeing the film." (Snow quoted in Michelson 120)

That this sense of remoteness occurs from a central position is exemplified in *The Central Region* by the figure X that appears at regular intervals throughout the film, stretching from corner to corner of the frame. Snow discusses this figure X as recentring the viewer: "a reminder of the central region – the whole thing is about being in the middle of this – the camera and the spectator [...] from the ecstatic centre of a complete sphere."[23] The viewer as disembodied eye is continually being recentred in relation to the transcendence of space and time in *The*

Central Region. This is opposed to the kind of immersive spectatorship I am attempting to formulate, where the viewer is not recentred but is continually open and opened by movements (sensations) that pass through him/her and on which s/he is unable to attain the perspective of a disembodied consciousness capable of rational synthesis.

Unlike the subjection of the spectator to replicating the movements of the camera in Snow's *The Central Region*, a mirroring which, while being destabilizing, simultaneously affirms the sovereignty of the subject, the sensations unleashed in the immersive texture of the moving image are not formally recomposed. Rather, they generate a kind of invisible drawing which captures spectator and image in movements that exceed their boundaries. The spectator becomes a point in the vectoral crossing of these sensations, the spectator's body a kind of passive join in a criss-crossing loop, which spatializes duration and temporalizes space. One could say that the viewer is subjected to the construction of space in *Wavelength*, even more so in *The Central Region* where the viewer becomes a kind of involuntary camera, but passivity here is still bound up with the centralized viewpoint from which the viewer follows the camera's movements, "restoring and remapping the space of perspective construction" (Michelson 118). While I am arguing for a sense of location in the state of immersive embodiment that I am attempting to theorize, this sense is not stable and perspectival, but is itself subject to the unhinging force of temporality.

the mutuality of becoming and location

In *The Visible and the Invisible* Merleau-Ponty suggests a way of conceiving of the spectator as both dislocated and located at the same time, where location, as a kind of temporalized spacing, subjects the individual body to the same force of change that occurs via the liberated sense organs. Merleau-Ponty suggests a way of conceiving of the sensibility of being subjected to the unhinging of sensation and of being transported elsewhere in a way that is not beyond the body or that does not position the body in a static frame outside the image. In contrast to the emphasis on a disembodied brain in Deleuze's trajectory, in Merleau-Ponty's phenomenology, communication or "interimplication" between body and world is always occurring.[24] The questions "What time is it?" and "Where am I?" are questions that Merleau-Ponty poses as being continuous motivators of the process of moving across the gaps between time and space (*The Visible and the Invisible* 105). These motivators are to do with *both* location *and* becoming, a notion of location being necessary to obviate the vertigo of becoming which would propel one into "a sidereal time, a system of relativity, where the characters would be not so much human as planetary, and the accents not so much subjective as astronomical, in a plurality of worlds constituting the universe" (*Cinema 2* 102). While Merleau-Ponty discusses mainly "natural objects" attached, as Deleuze would say, to the phenomenological lifeworld, he also discusses a subjectivity constituted by means of a crossing over between the virtual and the visible. This is not dissimilar to aspects of Deleuze's thinking. Indeed, Deleuze goes so far as to credit Merleau-Ponty with following a "Heideggerian inspiration in speaking of 'folds' and 'pleating' (by contrast with Sartrean 'holes' and 'lakes of non-being') from *The Phenomenology of Perception* onwards," and in returning to an ontology of difference and questioning in *The Visible and the Invisible* (*Difference and Repetition* 64). The main difference between them is that Merleau-Ponty locates the body in the intersection between the points of crossover of the virtual and the visible. As Merleau-Ponty puts it:

[I] the seer am also visible. What makes the weight, the thickness, the flesh of each color, of each sound, of each tactile texture, of the present, and of the world is the fact that he who grasps them feels himself emerge from them by a sort of coiling up or redoubling, fundamentally homogenous ... *a whole virtual center.* (*The Visible and the Invisible* 114–15; my emphasis)

In this description of the interrelation between particularity and anonymity, Merleau-Ponty maintains a tension between these two aspects or faces of subjectivity. He says:

we are experiences, that is, thoughts that feel behind themselves the weight of the space, the time, and the very Being they think, and which therefore do not hold under their gaze a serial space and time, not the pure idea of series, but have about themselves a time and a space that exist by piling up, by proliferation, by encroachment, by promiscuity ... ontological vibration. (Ibid. 115)

In *The Visible and the Invisible* Merleau-Ponty alludes to a kind of dynamic passivity that resonates with the scene of immersive spectatorship that I am attempting to articulate, whereby one is captivated by/in an image, yet dynamically moving within that incorporation. In the notion of dynamic passivity that I glean from Merleau-Ponty, the positions of subject and object are superseded by an emphasis on the chiasmic "coiling up of experience over experience" (ibid. 113). Elizabeth Grosz summarizes:

[I]n his last text he [Merleau-Ponty] explores the interrelations of the inside and the outside, the subject and the object, one sense and another in a common flesh – which he describes as the "crisscrossing" of the seer and the visible, of the toucher and the touched, the indeterminacy of the "boundaries" of each of the senses, their inherent transpossibility, their refusal to submit to the exigencies of clear-cut separation or logical identity.[25]

It is this movement of "crisscrossing" that articulates the scenario of a dynamically embodied immersive spectatorship. For Deleuze, cinema's great advantage is that:

because it lacks a centre of anchorage and of horizon, the sections which it makes would not prevent it from going back up the path that natural perception goes down. Instead of going from the acentred state of things to centred perception, it could go back up to the acentred state of things, and get closer to it. (*Cinema 1* 58)

Now while the proximity to an acentred state of things is inspirational for theorizing the scene of immersive spectatorship, it needs to be hybridized with Merleau-Ponty's phenomenological approach to avoid the (film/image) encounter becoming absolutely ungrounded. For Merleau-Ponty, the indeterminate field of the gaze can never be isolated in such a manner. The seer always retains a sense, albeit a shifting one, of her own place and time within the transcendent space of what Merleau-Ponty calls "flesh," or anonymity.

> The superficial pellicle of the visible is only for my vision and for my body. But the depth beneath this surface contains my body and hence contains my vision. My body as a visible thing is contained within the full spectacle. But my seeing body subtends this visible body, and all the visibles with it. There is reciprocal insertion and intertwining of one in the other. Or rather, if, as once again we must, we eschew the thinking by planes and perspectives, there are two circles, or two vortexes, or two spheres, concentric when I live naively, and as soon as I question myself, the one is slightly decentred with respect to the other ... (*The Visible and the Invisible* 138)

However, this notion of two circles or vortexes is not unlike the impetus of subjectivity Deleuze develops in *Difference and Repetition*. In fact, as I have already mentioned, Deleuze credits Merleau-Ponty for theorizing an approach to subjectivity whereby subjectivity is constituted by means of the motion of folds and pleating rather than presence and absence. This is not unlike Deleuze's own model of subjectivity where the subject is constantly and simultaneously forming itself out of two sides that play across the interstices of difference. For Deleuze, the two sides of subjectivity (its splitting) are as follows: "On one side, nothing but an I fractured by that empty form [of time]. On the other, nothing but a passive self always dissolved in that empty form" (*Difference and Repetition* 284). To further develop my notion of immersive spectatorship as both dispersal and embodiment in relation to the image, I want to link Deleuze's notion of passive contraction and what Merleau-Ponty would call "emigration into the outside."

dynamic passivity: beyond the "transcendental subject" and visceral being

> Thus the seer is caught up in what he sees, it is still himself he sees: there is a fundamental narcissism of all vision. And thus, for the same reason, the vision he exercises, he also undergoes from the things, such that, as many painters have said, I feel myself looked at by the things, my activity is equally passivity – which is the second and more profound sense of narcissism: not to see in the outside, as others see it, the contour of a body one inhabits, but especially to be seen by the outside, to exist within it, to emigrate into it, to be seduced, captivated, alienated by the phantom so that the seer and the visible reciprocate one another and we no longer know which sees and which is seen. (*The Visible and the Invisible* 139)

In the above citation, Merleau-Ponty suggests a form of movement which occurs when one is captivated by the outside (an image), a movement where the poles of passivity and activity are continually crossing over and being exchanged with one another due to the embeddedness of the subject in the world. This resonates with Deleuze's account of subjectivity and passivity in *Difference and Repetition*.

For Deleuze, too, the subject is the result of a contemplation of the world. The self contracts itself out of what it contemplates. Deleuze calls this movement "passive synthesis." Deleuze's model is comprised of three passive syntheses. The first passive synthesis initially binds the scattered and diffuse excitations the self is subjected to in its encounter with the outside, reproducing them on a privileged surface of its body (*Difference and Repetition* 96). The self is the result of this contracting of the chaotic energic field in which it is immersed. Rather than this being a once-and-for-all occurrence,

> [a]t the level of each binding, an ego is formed in the Id; a passive, partial, larval, contemplative and contracting ego. The Id is populated by local egos [...] The fact that these egos should be immediately narcissistic is readily explained if we consider narcissism to be not a contemplation of oneself but the fulfillment

of a self-image through the contemplation of something else. (Ibid. 97)

As Deleuze explains: "It (the eye or seeing ego) produces itself or 'draws itself' from what it contemplates (and from what it contracts and invests by contemplation)" (ibid. 97). The first passive synthesis produces passive selves. However, unlike psychoanalytic accounts of the ego where this kind of self-affection would be a turning back of libido on itself and therefore destructive (masochistic), for Deleuze this self-affection produces a play of differences which move in two directions simultaneously. This is the second passive synthesis. One direction moves towards identity, the other direction moves towards a deepening of the first passive synthesis and organizes itself in relation to virtual objects.

> Whereas active synthesis points beyond passive synthesis towards global integrations and the supposition of identical totalisable objects, passive synthesis, as it develops, points beyond itself towards the contemplation of partial objects which remain non-totalisable. (Ibid. 101)

For Deleuze, these (virtual) partial objects are absent in terms of representation, but they are not absolutely absent. They are always folding over and exchanging places with totalizable objects, objects of desire and need, forming a pattern like a Möbius strip. As opposed to a psychoanalytic approach where absence is registered as a limit of representation, for Deleuze absence or the virtual is an unstable category which is continually generating the new, totalizable object. In this dynamic, activity and passivity are not opposite poles on a spectrum, but forces that perform criss-crossing movements, where the "I" is continuously forming versions of itself that are fractured by the empty form of time, which is the third synthesis. In this form of movement, the "I" is both identity and non-identity and thereby can be thought of as a body and as virtuality. The real as sensuous phenomena is not the privileged ground of representation. Rather, the real as virtuality, which splits itself into the interchangeable bifurcation of actual and virtual images, becomes the generator

of representation. The exchange between virtual and actual images, their continual interchange with one another, is how Deleuze characterizes the cinema of the time-image. As he states: "there is no virtual which does not become actual in relation to the actual, the latter becoming virtual through the same relation: it is a place and its obverse which are totally reversible" (*Cinema 2* 69) The spectator is immersed in this circuit of exchange rather than assuming a critical perspective on a real that eludes our grasp except as an idea.

becoming as reversibility

The shifting interrelation between anonymity and particularity is key if one is to avoid falling back onto the notions of a primordial materiality that pre-exists identity or of identity as knowable in terms of its ownership of individual sensations and memories, as we saw in Marks' return to phenomenology in film. The Deleuzian model of subjectivity in *Difference and Repetition* is not incommensurate with Merleau-Ponty when he makes statements such as: "In reality there is neither me nor the other as positive, positive subjectivities. There are two caverns, two openness, two stages where something will take place" (*The Visible and the Invisible* 263). This something that takes place is the crossing of the two movements of what Merleau-Ponty calls "reversibility." The example from Merleau-Ponty that is always taken up to illustrate this notion of reversibility is that of the left hand touching the right hand. Both Luce Irigaray and Elizabeth Grosz take it up, Irigaray to critique Merleau-Ponty's reassertion of mastery, in that the hands are in an asymmetrical relation, one having dominance over the other.[26] However, it must be pointed out that the example of the hands comes from *Phenomenology of Perception* and that, although Merleau-Ponty discusses tactility in *The Visible and the Invisible*, "reversibility" is not necessarily reducible to a commonsense notion of tactility. It is a much more interesting concept, which can profitably be related to the immanently transcendent space of an immersive spectatorship.

In fact, what Merleau-Ponty develops out of this concept of reversibility is a preobjective, anonymous visibility which includes my particular carvings out of vision and those of others, but "extends further than the things I touch and see at present" (ibid. 143). He does discuss the hands, the handshake in terms of a reversibility of touching and being touched; however, he dislocates this mutual touch from a perceiving consciousness. It is rather a general field in which I revolve, displaying an inside and an outside. The only gap between inside and outside is the folding of the body as it coils around the field of visibility.

> The body unites us directly with the things through its own ontogenesis, by welding to one another the two outlines of which it is made, its two laps: the sensible mass it is and the mass of the sensible wherein it is born by segregation and upon which, as seer, it remains open. (Ibid. 136)

The body as seer is propped on the visible.

> What we call a visible is, we said, a quality pregnant with a texture, the surface of a depth, a cross section upon a massive being, a grain or corpuscle borne by a wave of Being. Since the total visible is always behind, or after, or between the aspects we see of it, there is access to it only through an experience which, like it, is wholly outside of itself. (Ibid. 136)

The dehiscence of the body, its two parts, being seen and seeing, is a way of locating what is rather "sometimes wandering and sometimes reassembled," i.e., visibility itself (ibid. 138). The abstract nature of the invisible ground of visibility can be linked to Deleuze's concept of virtuality. In fact, Merleau-Ponty refers to the virtual dimension of invisibility in *The Visible and the Invisible* (112). Both terms are used to replace the notion of an ontological or absolute void or absence that constitutes the subject in metaphysics and which finds its way into film theory via the theories of Jacques Lacan. For Merleau-Ponty "our openness upon 'something'" (ibid. 162) is beyond the oppositional parameters of identity and non-identity, as it is for Deleuze, but the merit of Merleau-Ponty's approach is that invisibility or virtuality is co-dependent on

embodiment. It does not have a life of its own. A rather lengthy citation from *The Visible and the Invisible* makes apparent this interconnection and interdependence between the idea and the sensible:

> But this hiatus between my right hand touched and my right hand touching, between my voice heard and my voice uttered, between one moment of my tactile life and the following one, is not an ontological void, a non-being: it is spanned by the total being of my body, and by that of the world; it is the zero of pressure between two solids that makes them adhere to one another. My flesh and that of the world therefore involve clear zones, clearings, about which pivot their opaque zones, and the primary visibility, that of the *quale* and of the things, does not come without a second visibility, that of the lines of force and dimensions, the massive flesh without a rarefied body, the momentary body without a glorified body. (148–49)

It is not at all necessary to see this emphasis on depth as opposed to Deleuze's emphasis on surface in identity-as-becoming. In fact, Merleau-Ponty, like Deleuze, equally insists that the way things appear is how they mean. The invisible idea, he says, "cannot be detached from the sensible of appearances and be erected into a second positivity" or abstraction (ibid. 149). Ideas appear in sensible disguises, not to reveal a hidden depth but rather to voice an invisible yet transparent depth – a surface depth, the double lining of the sensible to which we are ourselves attached. It is this superficial depth that I wish to appropriate for the sensation of what is happening when the "I" is carried away and moved between the flow of images in a scenario of immersive spectatorship. What is occurring is a double movement, one side of which is always extending beyond itself, the other side of which coils in upon itself, this double movement producing the "interimplication" of states of difference in which the spectator is immersed. Bodily depth is turned inside out, as it were, and dispersed in time as a form of spacing.

Merleau-Ponty's concept of "openness" has similar ramifications to Deleuze's notion of becoming – becoming is not the opposite of being, as openness is not the opposite of closure but a state which allows both being and nothingness to circulate intertwined.

> It has seemed to us that the task was to describe strictly our relation to the world not as an openness of nothingness upon being, but simply as openness: it is through openness that we will be able to understand being and nothingness, not through being and nothingness that we will be able to understand openness. (Ibid. 99)

Merleau-Ponty's notion of an openness that generates both being and nothingness is useful in rethinking the spectatorial relation as one whereby the body is both immersed in, yet informing, the flow of images. Openness or, in Deleuze's terms, virtuality is the condition of a mediation that allows for the reversible exchange between binaries of self and other, space and time, body and mind. An a-personal intervallic mediation which prevents these positions from collapsing into an equivalent sameness. Merleau-Ponty's emphasis on the spatial as well as the temporal dynamic, an emphasis that situates while not stabilizing this exchange, acts as a counterfoil to Deleuze's emphasis on the infinite unfolding of the interval in terms of the empty form of time, what he calls "the outside," a concept heavily influenced by Maurice Blanchot's *The Infinite Conversation*. For Blanchot:

> affliction holds in it the limit from which we should assume a perspective on the human condition – a movement that hinders precisely all perspective – we are not above but beneath time: this is eternity.[27]

For me, this sentiment encapsulates the distinction between Deleuze's Blanchot-inspired "outside" and a sense of embodied time. It is to avoid the static suspension of eternal time that I look to Merleau-Ponty's "hyperdialectics" where that empty intimacy of time is always being dissected by the intervallic spacing of the body that moves *in* time as well as being moved *by* time. Hyperdialectics is a process of reversibility whereby two terms, rather than being synthesized into a whole, each continue to struggle for co-existence in a field of discontinuities in which

the seer/spectator is immersed.[28] Reading Merleau-Ponty's phenomenology via Deleuze and Deleuze via Merleau-Ponty's phenomenology allows for a theoretical configuration of a scene of spectatorship as both immersive and embodied, a space where the body is engaged in a simultaneously fracturing and constituting dynamic passivity. In this scene, "envelopment" and simultaneity, characteristics attributed to virtual technology, do not preclude the gaps and voids of cinema's sequential unfolding in time. Both temporal simultaneity and spatial sequentiality become the bifurcating movements performed by the embodied spectator in relation to the virtual ground of becoming. As Elizabeth Grosz puts it:

> spatiality [is] just as susceptible to the movement of difference as duration [...] Just as time is amenable to both flow and discontinuity [...] so too is space. [...] each is as amenable as the other to being disconcerted by difference, which in any case refuses such a clear-cut distinction between them.[29]

The differential interval that marks the scene of immersive spectatorship that I have elaborated via Deleuze and Merleau-Ponty generates a dynamic of absorption and action, of temporal flow and spatial change. The liberated sensations unleashed by immersion in the flow of images pass through the body as the body punctuates the anonymity of these intensities. The scene of immersive spectatorship thus forms a loop in which the spectator is a willing captive.

notes

1 Gilles Deleuze, *Cinema 2: The Time-Image*, trans. Hugh Tomlinson and Robert Galeta (London: Athlone, 1989) 2.

2 In undertaking this hybridization of Deleuze and Merleau-Ponty, I am deliberately running counter to positions such as Dorothea Olkowski's in *Gilles Deleuze and the Ruin of Representation* (Berkeley: U of California P, 1999), who is at pains to separate them. While there is undoubtedly a case to be made for their differentiation, I am claiming that there is equally a case to be made for reading them in tandem.

3 Margaret Morse, "Body and Screen," *Wide Angle* 21.1 (1999): 64.

4 As well as Morse's "Body and Screen," Yvonne Spielmann's "Aesthetic Features in Digital Imaging: Collage and Morph" in the same issue of *Wide Angle* (special issue, "Digitality and the Memory of Cinema") is also suggestive on this point.

5 Maurice Merleau-Ponty, *The Visible and the Invisible*, trans. Alphonso Lingis (Evanston: Northwestern UP, 1968) 139.

6 Annette Michelson, "About Snow," *October* 8 (spring 1979): 116. Michelson, an influential proponent of a phenomenological approach to film in the 1970s, uses this term to signify the ideal position of the subject from which it reflects on the decentring movements of its operating consciousness. Her usage of the term derives from Jean-Louis Baudry's essay "Ideological Effects of the Basic Cinematographic Apparatus," trans. Alan Williams in *Narrative, Apparatus, Ideology: A Film Theory Reader*, ed. Philip Rosen (New York: Columbia UP, 1986). Originally published in *Cinethique* 7–8 (1970).

7 For a cogent critique of such theorizing in the work of Howard Rheingold and Paul Virilio, see Elizabeth Grosz, *Architecture from the Outside: Essays on Virtual and Real Space* (Cambridge, MA: MIT P, 2001).

8 Henri Bergson, *Matter and Memory*, trans. N.M. Paul and W.S. Palmer (New York: Zone, 1988) 151–52.

9 Barbara Kennedy, "Towards an Aesthetics of Sensation. A Reconsideration of Film Theory through Deleuzian Philosophy and Post-Feminism" (Ph.D. thesis, Staffordshire University, 2000) 50. Although Kennedy's thesis was brought out as a book shortly after submission – *Deleuze and Cinema: The Aesthetics of Sensation* (Edinburgh: Edinburgh UP, 2000) – the detail in the thesis is more useful for my purposes, which is why I refer to it here.

10 Steven Shaviro, in *The Cinematic Body* (Minneapolis: U of Minnesota P, 1993), takes a similar position in his appropriation of Deleuze.

11 Kennedy, *Deleuze and Cinema: The Aesthetics of Sensation* 139.

12 Deleuze, *Difference and Repetition*, trans. Paul Patton (London: Athlone, 1994) 268.

13 John Johnston, "Machinic Vision," *Critical Inquiry* 26 (autumn 1999): 45.

14 Kaja Silverman highlights this notion in Béla Balázs' writings in *The Threshold of the Visible World* (New York and London: Routledge, 1996) 88.

15 As well as Marks' *The Skin of the Film: Intercultural Cinema, Embodiment, and the Senses* (Durham and London: Duke UP, 2000), other recent returns to a traditional use of phenomenology in film theory include: Allan Casebier's *Film and Phenomenology: Toward a Realist Theory of Cinematic Representation* (Cambridge: Cambridge UP, 1991) and Vivian Sobchack's *The Address of the Eye: A Phenomenology of Film Experience* (Princeton: Princeton UP, 1992).

16 Deleuze in Dana Polan, "Francis Bacon: The Logic of Sensation" in *Gilles Deleuze and the Theater of Philosophy*, eds. Constantin V. Boundas and Dorothea Olkowski (New York and London: Routledge, 1994) 252. I am referring to a secondary source here as, at the time of writing this paper, Deleuze's book had not been translated into English. It has since been published by Continuum (London, 2003). Deleuze borrows the term "haptic" from the art historian Alois Reigl, who defined Egyptian art as a haptic aesthetic based on the flattening of space in the bas-relief. For a discussion of the relation of Reigl's notion to the early cinema of George Melies see Antonia Lant's "Haptical Cinema," *October* 74 (fall 1995): 45–73.

17 Proust in Jodi Brooks, "Between Contemplation and Distraction: Cinema, Obsession and Involuntary Memory" in *Kiss Me Deadly: Feminism and Cinema for the Moment*, ed. Laleen Jayamanne (Sydney: Power, 1995) 86.

18 Deleuze, *Proust and Signs: The Complete Text*, trans. Richard Howard (London: Athlone, 2000) 56.

19 Gaylyn Studlar, "De-territorial Imperative" (Review of *Cinema 1: The Movement-Image*), *Quarterly Review of Film & Video* 12.3 (1990): 105; my emphasis.

20 Gilles Deleuze and Félix Guattari, *What is Philosophy?*, trans. Hugh Tomlinson and Graham

Burchill (London and New York: Verso, 1994) 164.

21 Gilles Deleuze, *Cinema 1: The Movement-Image*, trans. Hugh Tomlinson and Barbara Habberjam (London: Athlone, 1992) 59.

22 See James Peterson, *Dreams of Chaos, Visions of Order: Understanding the American Avant-Garde Cinema* (Detroit: Wayne UP, 1994) 74.

23 Snow in William C. Wees, *Light Moving in Time: Studies in the Visual Aesthetics of Avant-Garde Film* (Berkeley: U of California P, 1992) 170. Snow discusses the function of the X extensively in *The Central Region* in an interview with John Du Cane in *Studio International* 186.960 (1973): 179.

24 Elizabeth Grosz, in *Architecture from the Outside: Essays on Virtual and Real Space*, uses the term "interimplication" to describe how the virtual and the real are intertwined and how relations of embeddedness need rethinking (89).

25 Elizabeth Grosz, *Volatile Bodies: Towards a Corporeal Feminism* (Bloomington and Indianapolis: Indiana UP, 1994) 94.

26 See Luce Irigaray, "The Invisible of the Flesh: A Reading of Merleau-Ponty, *The Visible and the Invisible*, 'The Intertwining – The Chiasm'" in her *An Ethics of Sexual Difference*, trans. Carolyn Burke and Gillian C. Gill (Ithaca, NY: Cornell UP, 1993) 151–84; and Grosz, *Volatile Bodies* (100–02).

27 Maurice Blanchot, *The Infinite Conversation*, trans. Susan Hanson (Minneapolis: U of Minnesota P, 1993) 120.

28 See Diana Coole's "Thinking Politically with Merleau-Ponty," *Radical Philosophy* 108 (July/Aug. 2001): 17–28 for a useful account of this dynamic.

29 Elizabeth Grosz, "Thinking the New: Of Futures Yet Unthought" in *Becomings: Explorations in Time, Memory, and Futures*, ed. Elizabeth Grosz (Ithaca and London: Cornell UP, 1999) 22.

Maria Walsh
Chelsea College of Art & Design
Manresa Road
London SW3 6LS
UK
E-mail: maria_walsh@onetel.com

Routledge
Taylor & Francis Group

ANGELAKI
journal of the theoretical humanities
volume 9 number 3 december 2004

> ... images can never be anything but things, and thought is a movement.
>
> *Bergson*, Matter *125*

"it's done i've done the image" 1

A few works have now been dedicated to Deleuze's cinema books and have discussed the relation between Bergson and Deleuze.[2] While there are inevitably points of overlap, this is a complex problem, and my point of focus differs from studies that have appeared so far. That is, nothing has yet been written concerning the pairing of the concepts of representation and presentation in relation to the image in Deleuze, yet this is crucial to my argument here. The purpose of this essay is to look at the role of the image, from a cognitive perspective, as an interaction between notions of "presentation" and "representation," and to use this distinction in order to begin to develop an understanding of how the image might work in art.

In *The Logic of Affect*, Paul Redding traces points of correspondence between eighteenth- and nineteenth-century German idealism and contemporary theories of cognition. Redding underlines how a key distinction, or point of contention, in both nineteenth- and twentieth-century debates about the nature of cognition concerned the problem of whether sensations should be considered "presentations" or "representations." "Direct Realists" consider that sensations are impressed upon us (in the manner of the famous metaphor of the signet ring in wax) and directly perceived by the nervous system. Such presentations are understood to have being in their own right (and therefore one looks to ontology when considering their nature). Others, including idealists such as Fichte and

anthony uhlmann

REPRESENTATION AND PRESENTATION
the deleuzian image

Schelling, argue that what occurs in our experience of the world is the production of "representations." That is, they contend that the immediate process of sensation is always lost and out of reach, and that what remains is the interpretation of the sensation and such interpretations or *re*presentations involve or produce knowledge (and so one looks to epistemology when considering their nature) (Redding 90–123).

bergson's image and deleuze's images

In *Cinema 1*, Deleuze, while acknowledging his debt to Bergson in developing the concept of the movement-image, criticises him for misunderstanding cinema. Bergson, he argues, applies the wrong criteria of the image to cinema, under-

ISSN 0969-725X print/ISSN 1469-2899 online/04/030187–12 © 2004 Taylor & Francis Ltd and the Editors of *Angelaki*
DOI: 10.1080/0969725042000307718

standing it as a succession of frozen states rather than as providing a continuous image of movement (*Cinema 1* 1–2).[3] While it is not possible to fully understand Deleuze's concept of the image, or more specifically the image as sign, through a straightforward comparison with Bergson, certain points of convergence and divergence between them are instructive.

Bergson, as Deleuze points out, is dismissive of cinema. *Matter and Memory*, however, draws heavily upon the concept of the "image," a term which already had a long history in philosophy tying it to inadequate modes of understanding.[4] Yet rather than the "image" being a secondary category, linked to the inferior kinds of understanding derived from the testimony of the senses, the image, in Bergson's system, is given a much more prominent place.

> Matter, in our view, is an aggregate of "images." And by "image" we mean a certain existence which is more than that which the idealists call a representation, but less than that which the realist calls a thing – an existence placed halfway between the "thing" and the "representation." (*Matter* 9)

What Bergson proposes is neither, on the one hand, using the image as a means of displacing terms with a much more aristocratic genealogy such as the "idea" or "thought" – terms which were often set up against the image as superior mental processes and which are both implicit in the term "representation" – nor, on the other hand, as a means of dissolving the reality of "things" external to one who perceives. Rather, he is proposing understanding the "image" as a bridge between those objectively existing things and our thoughts. It is a bridge because the image exists both in the thing which has or projects an image consistent with the nature of its own being, and in our minds which receive the projected images in the manner of a screen. "This is as much to say that there is for images merely a difference of degree, and not of kind, between being and being consciously perceived" (*Matter* 37).

For Bergson, my body too is an image, though different from all others in that it is one that I perceive not only externally through perceptions but internally through my affections (*Matter*

17). The body is an image that acts like all other images, receiving movement and giving back movement, "with, perhaps, this difference only, that my body appears to choose, within certain limits, the manner in which it shall restore what it receives" (*Matter* 19). That is:

> if … all images are posited at the outset, my body will necessarily end by standing out in the midst of them as a distinct thing, since they change unceasingly, and it does not vary. The distinction between the inside and the outside will then be only a distinction between the part and the whole. There is, first of all, the aggregate of images; and, then, in this aggregate, there are "centers of action," from which the interesting images appear to be reflected: thus perceptions are born and actions made ready. (*Matter* 47)

So the brain is more than a screen that passively receives a projection from outside: it is a screen which in turn acts, and acts in two ways. It both analyses the images projected upon it, and itself selects the movements it executes within its body: "the brain appears to us to be an instrument of analysis in regard to the movement received and an instrument of selection with regard to the movement executed" (*Matter* 30). The brain does not produce representations in the manner understood by idealism (bringing the world into being); rather, it receives and acts upon images (*Matter* 19–22, 74).

Representations do occur, but they are not the result of our brain *adding* something to perceptions of images; rather, conscious perception, for Bergson, involves the process of realising representations by *subtracting* what does not interest us from an image (that is, the way in which it is linked to all other images, which comprises its real action) and concentrating on those aspects of it with which we might potentially interact (the virtual action) (*Matter* 35–36). Such a subtraction, focusing only on those elements of the image on which we might act or which might act on us, relates (and Deleuze underlines this point) to the sensori-motor circuit of perceiving and acting. That is, there is a stimulus, and then there is an action or reaction. This involves a selective causal chain, one based on a logic through which the effects one perceives are understood to be first causes.[5] In turn, we isolate these causes in considering what will act on us and what we might act on. This process in turn provides the structure on which narrative (which develops through tracing selected causal chains) is built. The brain, then, is a screen in two senses: in one sense it is the repository for the images of things which it reflects in the manner of a cinema screen; in another it filters or sifts, screening out what is not able to be understood in terms of sensori-motor interest.

> Our [brains, which are] "zones of indetermination" play in some sort the part of the screen. They add nothing to what is there; they effect merely this: that the real action passes through, the virtual action remains. (*Matter* 39)

We begin to see, from what we have selected here, how Bergson's theories should have an effect on notions of representation, and it is worth attempting to trace this effect in Deleuze's work in order to better understand the nature of the "image."

the world and cinema

Deleuze develops the concept of the "image of thought" in *Proust and Signs*, in *Difference and Repetition* and, with Guattari, in *A Thousand Plateaus*, to describe those non-philosophical presuppositions which underlie a thinker's work and allow them to begin creating their system (Deleuze, *Negotiations* 147–49). Using Bergson's presupposition that understanding involves a process of reconstruction, or of attempting step by step to do over again the problem described (*Matter* 116), we might begin by asking what problems might be involved in translating Bergson's concepts, which concern perception per se, perception of the "real world," to processes of perception and affection related to the fabricated worlds of cinema.

The first thing to note is that this apparent difficulty is never noted in Deleuze's cinema books.[6] Nothing is said about it because it does not relate to the action that interests Deleuze in these books; its shadow passes through, however, just as Bergson's real actions (those images of pure perception) pass through us, while the

virtual actions (those representations selected from perception) remain and are absorbed.

What is the effect of this silence? The brain is a screen and the world is a mass of images projected onto that screen. In a sense stronger than merely metaphorical, then, the world is a cinema, though, as we have already seen in the brief overview above, the screen of the brain is not merely a passive instrument of reflection: it not only reflects but selects, analyses, acts, and absorbs action. This stronger than metaphorical link allows Deleuze to make connections, though they are not necessarily those connections we might have come to expect.

The world is a cinema, in which there is cinema, but this does not lead in to a *mise en abîme*; indeed, it is noteworthy that Deleuze avoids this gesture, so common among his French contemporaries. Looking at an image of a reflection (placing a mirror up against a mirror) does not lead to an endless abyss of reflections for Deleuze; rather, when the mirror is brought into play we are given "the crystal-image" where the virtual and real become indistinguishable, crystallising into a new state (*Cinema 2* 68–97). That is, rather than falling into an abyss, we are suspended by a transformative process of crystallisation that offers a strange parity between the real and the virtual: the world is a cinema – the cinema is a world (*Cinema 2* 68–70).

If we assume a critical reading of all this we must retrace these steps. If the world projects onto the screen of the brain, does the film-maker select or screen the real to re-project an already represented world onto the screen of the cinema (which in turn is re-projected onto the brain of the viewer (who in turn screens or filters it further))? If so, how would this process not involve a dissolution or degradation of the image, when Bergson tells us that the representation already involves the subtraction from the image of what does not interest us?

It is worth emphasising this point, which is crucial to my argument. The term "representation" is understood here in the cognitive sense discussed above. For Bergson, as we have seen, the interpretation or cognitive appraisal involved in developing a representation does not involve adding something but, rather, examining what is presented and filtering it, concentrating only on those elements of the presentation which interest us. Conscious perception, then, for Bergson, is a process of selection and this selection is already implicated in processes of interpretation. I see a tiger charging towards me and perceive it by focusing on it, isolating it from the mass of less important information being offered to my senses at that moment. This process is related to the sensori-motor circuit described above: you sense danger, for example, by quickly recognising what you can act upon or what can act upon you, and then you immediately react. In turn, this process can be related to art if the term "representation" is always understood in this sense and not confused with the many other senses it has developed in being used to describe works of art. I understand representation in art, as in cognition, here, to involve this process of selection or screening (in its dual sense), a selection of what is of interest, which already involves interpretation. With cognition this interpretation is single, as the perceiving individual creates a representation from a presentation. In creative forms, when they involve representations, there can be a double process. Some works are representations that already carry clear interpretations with them (which can only be accepted or rejected by an audience). Some are representations of representations (drawing their form and content from previous works of representation rather than offering something new). In each of these cases the interpretations available to an audience will be impoverished.

As I will argue below, however, art (and specifically in this instance film) does not have to represent something that has already been represented or interpret its images to the degree that their meaning is already abundantly clear to an audience. Rather, it can create, and in creating it offers the audience, a new image that they must interpret (with an effort of thought) rather than a pre-interpreted image.

The bad film is one that offers pre-interpreted, pre-digested images, so that the viewer is not called upon to interpret. For Deleuze, however, at least in certain films, films that are not

mediocre, the world is created, not represented. There is no imitation involved in such created images. Such created images do not send us back to the world in order to be authenticated; rather, they immediately form part of our world as we set the screen of our brain against the cinema screen. As Deleuze states:

> Cinema, precisely because it puts the image in motion, or rather endows the image with self-motion, never stops tracing the circuits of the brain. This characteristic can be manifested either positively or negatively. The screen, that is to say ourselves, can be the deficient brain of an idiot as easily as a creative brain ... Bad cinema always travels through circuits created by the lower brain: violence and sexuality in what is represented – a mix of gratuitous cruelty and organized ineptitude. Real cinema achieves another violence, another sexuality, molecular rather than localized. ("The Brain" 366–67)

representation and presentation

Further light might be shed on this problem if we turn to one of the few passages in which Deleuze specifically mentions "representation" in the cinema books. Here we have an example of a submerged system, as Deleuze never seeks to appeal to the concept of representation in order to buttress the concepts related to the image; yet, in looking back to Bergson and in examining one of the few occasions when Deleuze does use the term representation, it becomes clear that there is a distinction between a selected representation (a degraded interpretation of a real image) and the presentation of an image in its fullness (such as is possible in the crystal-image but, perhaps, not only here), which strikes us with its power.

In *Cinema 2*, Deleuze states that the movement-image provides a *representation* of time while the time-image provides a *presentation* of time:

> By raising themselves to the indiscernibility of the real and the imaginary, the signs of the crystal go beyond all psychology of the recollection or dream, and all physics of action. What we see in the crystal is no longer the empirical progression of time as succession of

presents, nor its indirect representation as interval or as whole; it is its direct presentation, its constitutive dividing in two into a present which is passing and a past which is preserved, the strict contemporaneity of the present with the past that it will be, of the past with the present that it has been ... the time-image has arisen through direct or transcendental presentation, as a new element in post-war cinema ... (274–75)

We need to keep in mind how Bergson has defined representation as involving subtraction, as involving a selection from the image rather than the whole image, as being something less than the image. The movement-image *represents* time in that we arrive at an understanding of time not by being shown time directly but by being shown a line of action which necessarily involves the passage of time in its unfolding (an empirical progression). Following Bergson, this is a representation because it involves a process of subtraction from the image. We would be shown a man at the bottom of a staircase, for example, and then, through the techniques of continuity editing, we would be shown the man at the top of the staircase, the passage of time taken to mount the staircase being represented through the subtractions involved in the codes of continuity editing. The time-image, on the other hand, presents the flow of time (which is not simply monodirectional from past to present but involves flux). The cinema of the time-image is the cinema of the seer not the actor. Whereas the movement-image and the narrative form attached to it relate to sensori-motor links (such as those described by Bergson which result from selective perception: that is, the editing out of material from the images received, the subtraction involved in forming representations of the real which in turn allow us to act), the time-image emerges in response to situations "to which one can no longer react" (*Cinema 2* 272).

These are pure optical and sound situations, in which the character does not know how to respond ... But he has gained in an ability to see what he has lost in action or reaction: he SEES so that the viewer's problem becomes "What is there to see in the image?" (and not now "What are we going to see in the next

image?") ... This is no longer a sensory-motor situation, but a purely optical and sound situation, where the seer has replaced the agent ... (Ibid.)

We are given an image that requires us to see with the protagonist, which makes us look and directly experience time. The time-image, then, requires the movement of the viewer into the image in order that that viewer might directly experience seeing and the time involved in seeing. This is described as a "presentation" because there is no process of subtraction involved.

cliché

If the time-image involves the creation of presentations where a real experience of time merges with a virtual experience, what hope is there for the movement-image? We need to remember that the representations we experience in perceiving the real are closely related to the narratives constructed in the cinema of the movement-image. There appears to be a danger in this, which is the danger of habit, the danger of cliché. If there were to be a cinema of the movement-image that would correspond to what Deleuze might term true cinema, it would somehow need to avoid cliché. Our experience of acting, the sensori-motor circuit, is already an understanding through continuity editing: we subtract (or suppress) those perceptions that are not crucial to the action being performed, and link together those perceptions which are crucial to that action in order to better perform that action, just as the narrative film-maker subtracts material extraneous to the action and links those materials considered crucial to the action.

Such an experience of acting includes perceiving, acting, and the experience of emotions related to these perceptions and actions. We can see how this sensori-motor circuit is clearly related to the images of narrative cinema, which Deleuze calls movement-images. He breaks these images into three categories: the perception-image (often associated with the long shot in which an object is seen) is related to real perception, the action-image (often associated with the medium shot in which figures engage in action) is related to real action, and the affection-image (often associated with the close-up in which we register emotion expressed by the face) is related to emotion (see *Cinema 1*). While it might be argued that each of these images involves the selection of items to be shown from an indefinite set of possibilities related to the "real world," and that they therefore correspond to Bergson's definition of representation, following Deleuze's suggestion that, in good films, these images are created rather than subtracted from the real, in a non-clichéd narrative film each might be understood as potentially complete in itself. Such non-clichéd narrative films (these certainly occur prior to the crisis of the action-image Deleuze describes, but the possibility of their re-emergence is never completely closed down) would involve the creation of representations that stand over for, rather than mimic, the representations we create ourselves in the real. In this way, one might speak of such non-clichéd narrative films as being primary representations, working at one remove from or merging with our immediate perceptions, whereas cliché involves the representation of representations, the showing again of the already familiar.

The bad film, then, partakes of cliché. Falling into cliché, for Deleuze, marks the crisis of action-image that is only fully overcome with the emergence of the time-image. With the cliché, that action which occurs is not only an expected action but an action carried by images that complacently refer to earlier images and seek to rely on those images for their (reflected) power. In one sense it is simply a problem of representation within cinema history: the cliché is not a representation of the real; rather, it is a representation of other (cinematic) images. It refers to – in shorthand – and necessarily subtracts from the store of images that has come to make up cinema history. Such a point explains why genres have a life and then pass away or into new forms: the western, the gangster film, the musical ... all these forms have changed markedly over time, and of necessity, as without change the images congeal into cliché. Part of the burden of tradition is the problem of how to escape from cliché, how to avoid the danger of showing again what has been shown too often and has

therefore lost its power to affect or even entertain. The representation of the representation is related to habit, while the image (presentation or non-clichéd representation) eludes habit in forcing the viewer to participate in its understanding (see *Matter* 44–45, 84).

Yet the problem becomes even more pronounced when one considers how cliché emerges not simply through the repetition of images within cinema history but through the imitation of elements of "the real" that have themselves become cliché. It is as if bad cinema has invaded life so that we sometimes (developing our real-life representations with processes of selection already contaminated by common expectations or cliché) play out hackneyed scenarios that are in turn re-represented by bad cinema. The crisis stems from the hardening of the image into a representation, and the hardening of our own perceptions (which, following Bergson, already involve representations) into cliché or habit. One suspects it is not impossible for cinema partaking of the movement-image to avoid this double trap of cliché.[7] The problem now becomes (or becomes again, as it was in literature for Flaubert, Shklovsky, Proust and Beckett among others): how does one overcome cliché in art, how does one overcome habit in life? Deleuze asks:

> if images have become clichés, internally as well as externally, how can an Image be extracted from all these clichés, "just an image", an autonomous mental image? An image *must* emerge from the set of clichés ... With what politics and what consequences? What is an image which would not be a cliché? Where does the cliché end and the image begin? (*Cinema 1* 215)

Deleuze seems to offer an answer that involves two kinds of image. In the cinema, both are kinds of crystal-image, a mutation rather than the completion of the old cinema, which moves from representation to presentation. Firstly, Deleuze describes an "autonomous mental image" which "had not to be content with weaving a set of relations, but had to form a new substance" (ibid. 215). Moving away from the cinema, one might seek to understand this kind of image with reference to Deleuze's essay on Francis Bacon, where he speaks of the process of creating an image through extraction, rather than abstraction, from the real (*Francis Bacon* 9). Such an image is cut from the set of relations commonly offered and presented as an autonomous substance, a pure affect. Secondly, we have seen how Deleuze speaks in the second cinema book of the time-image as presentation. That is, rather than showing us an image which has already passed through the screening process of perception, the time-image offers us an image which makes us see but does not allow us to act, an image in all its fullness. Again moving away from cinema one might mention Proust (who himself knew and drew upon Bergson) and the logic of the madeleine and involuntary memory which casts one back into a previous time, a time which is replete with the image of the memory in all its fullness, prior to the impoverishment brought about through the selections of perception.[8] Such an image is a direct presentation, a non-represented image, a plenitude.

It is apparent, however, that the representation and the presentation can co-exist in a work, just as the image might emerge from cliché. Asked in what sense he means that the cinematic image (the time-image) is not "in the present" Deleuze states:

> it seems obvious to me that the image is not in the present. What the image "represents" is in the present, but not the image itself. The image itself is an ensemble of time relations from the present which merely flows, either as a common multiple, or as the smallest divisor. Relations of time are never seen in ordinary perception, but they are in the image, as long as it is a creative one. ("The Brain" 371)

The presentation can emerge out of the representation in the case of art. On the other hand, there is the representation of the representation alone in the case of non-art. There is, therefore, a need to talk of the actualisation of the virtual in good films or art, that is, the process of drawing out or entering into an image (which always carries with it a set of unrealised or not yet realised possibilities) which is in part undertaken by the viewer.

We find here, then, two interrelated elements towards a general definition of the image in the cinema books. Firstly, the image involves the avoidance of or the escape from clichés, as the creation of the new. Secondly, the image often involves presentation that might be understood as the necessary involvement of the viewer in its interpretation rather than the referral of the viewer to ready-made or habitual responses. Further, the image as presentation has at least two possible forms: (a) the extracted image, the autonomous mental image (in the manner of Francis Bacon) and (b) the direct presentation, the non-represented image (in the manner of Proust). While both of these occur in cinema, one might argue that they are also transportable to other media: indeed, in outlining their nature here we have moved to literature and the visual arts.

In an attempt to clarify these processes further one might, using the terminology of Bergson and Deleuze, represent the processes described above diagrammatically (see Fig. 1).

The order shown in Fig. 1 is determined by Bergson's contention that we always move from the idea to the perception, and not the other way around, in the process of recognition (*Matter* 130–31). The sign, or the idea, then, comes between pure perception and perception, screening the former to produce the latter.

peirce, deleuze, bergson

The reading of Bergson in Deleuze has taken us in a certain direction and we are beginning to see the importance of the interaction between perception and representation. The process is not complete, however. I feel that more light can be shed on the problem and a clearer understanding might be uncovered by linking Bergson with Charles Sanders Peirce.

In developing his theory of the cinematic image in *Cinema 1* and *Cinema 2*, Deleuze turns not only to Bergson but to the founder of semiotics, Charles Sanders Peirce. Deleuze is careful to differentiate between semiotics (the study of signs) and what he calls "semiology" (the study of language-based sign systems). Deleuze consid-

Image 1: projected from "things" to brain			

Image 2: brain as screen			
1. Apprehension (pure perception) Presentation	2. Making sense Idea Interpretation of signs	3. Conscious perception Representation Habit Sensori-motor action Cliché	4. Re-projection of: signs, representations, images
<---Thought--->			

Fig. 1.

ers that the semiologists (those theorists, highly influential in the twentieth-century French intellectual tradition, who built upon theories developed by Saussure) are wrong to use language as the privileged model for all semiotic systems, because this model is limited and unable to do justice to thought which might work through images (or some other means) just as readily as through human language. He prefers Peirce because Peirce does not privilege language, indeed Peirce does not even privilege humans systems of communication; rather, Peirce considers, in effect, that everything is a kind of sign: "[A Sign is] Anything which determines something else (its *interpretant*) to refer to an object to which itself refers (its *object*) in the same way, the interpretant becoming in turn a sign, and so on *ad infinitum*" (Peirce 239). For Peirce this is true of the world as a whole. The human brain is not a prerequisite for thought or for the existence and interaction of semiotic systems:

> Thought is not necessarily connected with a brain. It appears in the work of bees, of crystals, and throughout the purely physical world; and one can no more deny that it is really there, than that the colors, the shapes, etc., of objects are really there. Consistently adhere to that unwarrantable denial, and you will be driven to some form of idealistic nominalism akin to Fichte's. Not only is thought in the organic world, but it develops there. But as there cannot be a General without Instances embodying it, so there cannot be thought without Signs. We must here give "Sign" a very wide sense, no doubt, but not too

wide a sense to come within our definition. (Peirce 252)

We should note that Deleuze criticises Peirce for asserting rather than deducing the nature of the sign (that it does not depend on language). This use of unargued assertion is dangerous, in Deleuze's view, because he considers that it does not provide the sufficiently strong impetus that would allow Peirce's system to resist the gravitational pull of linguistic systems. This is because, for Deleuze, Peirce still tends, from time to time, to privilege "knowledge" or the *interpretation* of signs,[9] which in turn causes Peirce to fall too heavily under the influence of linguistic models of communication. As Deleuze states:

> ... the sign's function must be said to "make relations efficient": not that relations and laws lack actuality *qua* images, but they still lack that efficiency which makes them act "when necessary", and that only knowledge gives them. But, on this basis, Peirce can sometimes find himself as much a linguist as the semiologists. For, if the sign elements still imply no privilege for language, this is no longer the case with the sign, and linguistic signs are perhaps the only ones to constitute a pure knowledge, that is, to absorb and reabsorb the whole content of the image as consciousness or appearance. They do not let any material that cannot be reduced to an utterance survive, and hence reintroduce a subordination of semiotics to a language system. (*Cinema 2* 31)

Deleuze goes on to claim that his own theory of the image in cinema avoids this pitfall because he deduces the three types of images[10] rather than claiming them "as fact" (ibid.).

In order to better understand the nature of the image, it is worth unpacking something of what is at stake here. Peirce develops three categories, the First, Second and Third:

> The First is that whose being is simply in itself, not referring to anything nor lying behind anything. The Second is that which is what it is by force of something to which it is second. The Third is that which is what it is owing to things between which it mediates and which it brings into relation to each other. (188–89)

Although Peirce relates notions of First-, Second- and Thirdness to kinds of signs, the sign, in principle, is an expression of the Third: that is, "A sign is an object [1] which stands for another [2] to some mind [or interpretant, 3]" (Peirce 141) and for Peirce, as we have seen, everything is a sign, and the universe itself is a semiotic system.

How, then, could this be made to fit with the ideas of Bergson? This question is not posed directly by Deleuze, but its outlines can be traced in what we have laid out above. For Bergson, we will remember, an image is "a certain existence which is more than that which the idealists call a representation, but less than that which the realist calls a thing – an existence placed halfway between the 'thing' and the 'representation'" (*Matter* 9). To a certain extent, it is possible to roughly line up these coordinates again with Peirce. The "thing" of the realists would correspond with the First (see Peirce 189), while the "representation" of the idealists would be replaced by Peirce (who breaks definitively with idealist models) with the sign that is the Third. Halfway between the First and the Third is the Second, and I would argue that, at least to an extent, at least on some occasions, the image can correspond with the Second.

That is, moving here in some senses between Peirce and Bergson and in some senses outside their systems, the image can appear in an uninterpreted state. In such a state, it is an image that confronts another (and we are all images for Bergson). As a mind, I may move to understand the image which appears to the image that is my

brain, and, in so far as I succeed in understanding that image, I might be said to interpret it as a representation and convert it into, or recognise it as, a sign. This might occur with some ease or with some difficulty. In so far as the image is already integrated into a semiotic system with which I am familiar, the process will be easy, and the image might immediately be understood as a sign. It is a sign because it stands for something to me.[11] If, however, the image is not easily understood, one of two things will happen. I will either pass over the image as something on which I cannot act, screening it out as being without relevance. Or I will struggle to understand the image (and perhaps fail). The power of the image, then, in part rests in the fact that it is that which I must move towards, that I must actively interpret. Certain signs are understood passively: they belong to systems that have become familiar and to which one can respond through a kind of reflex or habit (*Matter* 44–45, 84). In art, these image-signs can become clichés. The images that are not clichés, then, are those that require the interpretant to actively interpret, to move towards the unfamiliar. These images are not yet signs, but they have already been recognised as significant, and it is the ungrasped significance that gives them their power. They are presentations that we are seeking to grasp as representations. One might bend Peirce's terms here and argue that this involves a movement between Secondness and Thirdness (and even on occasion, where the image is infinite, potentially back to Firstness, which is the apprehension of all being, the presentation in its pure form).

> The First must ... be present and immediate, so as not to be second to a representation ... What the world was to Adam on the day he opened his eyes to it, before he had drawn any distinctions, or had become conscious of his own existence, – that is first, present, immediate, fresh, new, initiative, original, spontaneous, free, vivid, conscious, and evanescent. Only, remember that every description of it must be false to it. (Peirce 189)

Of course, not all images can aspire to dragging us back to this unfallen state (though I would suggest that on certain occasions, such as Proust's endeavour to express spontaneous memory, this is, at least, attempted). In effect, the image, as understood here, largely concerns a Secondness, or the recognition of meaningfulness and the imperative to understand: the recognition of the need to interpret which is not yet complete and possibly impossible to complete.

Such interpretation, in effect, involves an effort to bridge the gap between the Second and the Third (or the First, Second and Third); between presentation and representation. It involves, then, genuine thinking, an active struggle that might even be overwhelming on occasion. It is, I would argue, one way in which one might begin to understand the difference between the affect of art and the affects of kinds of representation. Simple representation does not produce or require thought. Art, in whatever medium it might exist, stimulates thought in the interpretant, and one way in which it does this is by producing images that are on their way to being signs but are not yet or are no longer signs.

bergson and intuition 12

In *Matter and Memory* Bergson states: "images can never be anything but things, and thought is a movement" (125). In developing a description of "intuition" in his *Introduction to Metaphysics* Bergson urges us to develop a kind of thinking that does justice to movement (43–45). There are two kinds of knowledge, he claims. Firstly, there is relative knowledge, which is outside the object it seeks to describe. Such knowledge is relative because I, say, view an object, but I view it from a given position. Another will view it from a different perspective and so the truth of the observations will be relative to the given position from which one observes (the car moves towards me but away from you: "to" is true relative to me, whereas "from" is true relative to you (*Introduction* 43–45)).

The second kind of knowledge, however, is absolute, and it is absolute because the observer

is no longer outside the object; rather, the observer is within the object. The understanding of movement, in such a case, is no longer relative; it is, in respect to the object itself, absolute. Such absolute knowledge is achieved through intuition that involves a being within a given object. In this way I have, at least potentially, in so far as I am able to achieve intuition, an absolute knowledge of my self, as the self is what I inhabit.

> A representation taken from a certain point of view, a translation made with certain symbols, will always remain imperfect in comparison with the object of which a view has been taken, or which the symbols seek to express. But the absolute, which is the object and not its representation, the original and not its translation, is perfect, by being perfectly what it is. (*Introduction* 5–6)

In illustrating this point Bergson turns to art, and specifically to the novel. While claiming that art will always fail to capture the absolute, and while describing the nature of this failure, he also posits an ideal art:

> The author may multiply the traits of his hero's character, may make him speak and act as much as he pleases, but all this can never be equivalent to the simple and indivisible feeling which I should experience if I were able for an instant to identify myself with the person of the hero himself. Out of that indivisible feeling, as from a spring, all the words, gestures, and actions of the man would appear to me to flow naturally ... The character would be given to me all at once, in its entirety ... Description, history, and analysis leave me here in the relative. Coincidence with the person himself would alone give me the absolute. (*Introduction* 3–4)

I would argue, however, that from time to time we do at least get a sense, or the impression, of such identification through works of art, and that this is something we recognise as being part of what affects us when we watch a film that really works, a good film. The "absolute" here is another word for the pure, complete presentation that it is no doubt impossible for any art form to achieve fully. It is the First, and "every description of it must be false to it" (Peirce 189), but, at least, in taking us back to the Second, the image which requires interpretation does bring us as close as possible to this. To cite Bergson one last time:

> Now the image has at least this advantage, that it keeps us in the concrete. No image can replace the intuition of duration, but many diverse images, borrowed from very different orders of things, may, by the convergence of their action, direct consciousness to the precise point where there is a certain intuition to be seized. (*Introduction* 16)

If we are to accept these ideas, we might begin to see how two kinds of understanding differ. In so far as I understand through habit (that is, in so far as I recognise a sign, acknowledge a representation) I am able to achieve only relative understanding. I am external to the object [1] which is a sign of something else [2] to my mind [3]. If, however, the image is recognised as significant but not understood, if it urges me to struggle to understand, I need to move back towards the image in order to understand, and this movement is, at least potentially, one which moves with the image object (that is, it moves towards, while never quite achieving, the absolute). If I ever grasp such an image I will do so through intuition (yet I will fail to represent this understanding when I turn to the kind of critical analysis one must necessarily adopt in discussing an object such as a work of literature).

notes

1 Beckett, *Image* 168.

2 Notably Rodowick (ed.) and Flaxman (ed.).

3 For a discussion of this point see Eric Alliez. On the indivisibility of movement in Bergson (and that there are no instants), see Bergson, *Matter* 188–92.

4 A number of philosophers, however, including Nietzsche, Bergson and Michèle Le Doeuff, have demonstrated how important the image is within philosophical thinking.

5 This complex process, implied in Bergson's theories, is discussed elsewhere in Deleuze's work in relation to Spinoza; see Deleuze, "On the Difference."

6 For discussions of this identification, see Jean-Clet Martin and François Zourabichvili.

7 Though this seems difficult; see Deleuze, *Cinema 1* 214–15.

8 See Uhlmann, chapter 2, on this point.

9 This is apparent in a much earlier (c.1873) definition of the "sign": "A sign is an object which stands for another to some mind" (Peirce 141).

10 The affection-image, the action-image and the relation-image, which correspond to Peirce's categories of Firstness, Secondness and Thirdness (Deleuze, *Cinema 2* 31).

11 This process of reflex recognition is related to systems that are socially determined and belong to groups (such as language), developed through experience, or that work directly through stimulus response as true reflex.

12 Peirce spends a good deal of time critiquing the notion of "intuition" and arguing that it is impossible. It should be noted that he is not directly confronting Bergson here; rather, he is critiquing a notion of intuition as a direct kind of conceptual knowledge, such as Descartes's "clear and distinct" idea which Peirce sees as being put forth as occurring without any prior interpretation. I would argue that Bergson's intuition is a more complex concept, one which does not give one access to clear concepts; rather, the intuition carries with it the imperative that one seeks to express it, but it can never be contained adequately either by concepts or images (see Bergson, "Philosophical"). From this point of view Peirce's critiques might be said to be directed at a different conception of intuition from that found in Bergson. This is not, by any means, to claim they would have been in complete agreement.

bibliography

Alliez, Eric. "Midday, Midnight: The Emergence of Cine-Thinking." *The Brain is the Screen: Deleuze and the Philosophy of Cinema*. Ed. Gregory Flaxman. Minneapolis: U of Minnesota P, 2000.

representation and presentation

Beckett, Samuel. *The Image*. Trans. Edith Fournier. *The Complete Short Prose*. Ed. Stanley Gontarski. New York: Grove, 1995.

Beckett, Samuel. *Proust and Three Dialogues with Georges Duthuit*. London: Calder, 1987.

Bergson, Henri. *Introduction to Metaphysics*. Trans. T.E. Hulme. New York and London: Putnam's, 1912.

Bergson, Henri. *Matter and Memory*. Trans. N.M. Paul and W.S. Palmer. New York: Zone, 1991.

Bergson, Henri. "Philosophical Intuition." *The Creative Mind*. Trans. Mabelle L. Andison. New York: Philosophical Library, 1946.

Deleuze, Gilles. "The Brain is the Screen: An Interview with Gilles Deleuze." Trans. Marie Therese Guirgis. *The Brain is the Screen: Deleuze and the Philosophy of Cinema*. Ed. Gregory Flaxman. Minneapolis: U of Minnesota P, 2000.

Deleuze, Gilles. *Cinema 1: The Movement-Image*. Trans. Hugh Tomlinson and Barbara Habberjam. Minneapolis: U of Minnesota P, 1986.

Deleuze, Gilles. *Cinema 2: The Time-Image*. Trans. Hugh Tomlinson and Robert Galeta. Minneapolis: U of Minnesota P, 1989.

Deleuze, Gilles. *Difference and Repetition*. Trans. Paul Patton. London: Athlone, 1994.

Deleuze, Gilles. *Francis Bacon: Logique de la sensation*. Paris: Éditions de la différence, 1996.

Deleuze, Gilles. *Negotiations, 1972–1990*. Trans. Martin Joughin. New York: Columbia UP, 1995.

Deleuze, Gilles. "On the Difference between *The Ethics* and Morality." *Spinoza: Practical Philosophy*. Trans. Robert Hurley. San Francisco: City Lights, 1988.

Deleuze, Gilles. *Proust and Signs*. Trans. Richard Howard. London: Athlone, 2000.

Deleuze, Gilles and Félix Guattari. *A Thousand Plateaus*. Trans. Brian Massumi. Minneapolis: U of Minnesota P, 1987.

Flaubert, Gustave. *Dictionnaire des idées reçues: Suivi du catalogue des idées chic*. Paris: Aubier, 1978.

Flaxman, Gregory (ed.). *The Brain is the Screen: Deleuze and the Philosophy of Cinema*. Minneapolis: U of Minnesota P, 2000.

Le Doeuff, Michèle. *The Philosophical Imaginary*. Trans. Colin Gordon. London: Athlone, 1989.

Martin, Jean-Clet. "Of Images and Worlds: Toward a Geology of the Cinema." *The Brain is the Screen: Deleuze and the Philosophy of Cinema*. Ed. Gregory Flaxman. Minneapolis: U of Minnesota P, 2000.

Nietzsche, Friedrich. *The Birth of Tragedy: Out of the Spirit of Music*. Ed. Michael Tanner. Trans. Shaun Whiteside. London: Penguin, 1993.

Peirce, Charles Sanders. *Peirce on Signs*. Ed. James Hoopes. Chapel Hill: U of North Carolina P, 1991.

Proust, Marcel. *À la recherche du temps perdu*. Édition publiée sous la direction de Jean-Yves Tadié. Vol. 1. Paris: Gallimard, 1987.

Redding, Paul. *The Logic of Affect*. New York: Cornell UP, 1999.

Rodowick, D.N. *Gilles Deleuze's Time Machine*. Durham, NC: Duke UP, 1997.

Serres, Michel. *Atlas*. Paris: Julliard, 1994.

Shklovsky, Vicktor. "The Resurrection of the Word." Trans. Richard Sherwood. *Russian Formalism: A Collection of Articles and Texts in Translation*. Ed. Stephen Bann and John E. Bowlt. Edinburgh: Scottish Academic P, 1973.

Uhlmann, Anthony. *Beckett and Poststructuralism*. Cambridge: Cambridge UP. 1999.

Zourabichvili, François. "The Eye of Montage: Dziga Vertov and Bergsonian Materialism." *The Brain is the Screen: Deleuze and the Philosophy of Cinema*. Ed. Gregory Flaxman. Minneapolis: U of Minnesota P, 2000.

Anthony Uhlmann
School of Humanities
University of Western Sydney
Locked Bag 1797
Penrith South DC, NSW 1797
Australia
E-mail: a.uhlmann@uws.edu.au

Routledge
Taylor & Francis Group

ANGELAKI
journal of the theoretical humanities
volume 9 number 3 december 2004

In the paper "Math Anxiety," Aden Evens explores the manner by means of which concepts are implicated in the problematic Idea according to the philosophy of Gilles Deleuze. The example that Evens draws from *Difference and Repetition* in order to demonstrate this relation is a mathematics problem, the elements of which are the differentials of the differential calculus. What I would like to offer in the present paper is an historical account of the mathematical problematic that Deleuze deploys in his philosophy, and an introduction to the role that this problematic plays in the development of his philosophy of difference. One of the points of departure that I will take from the Evens paper is the theme of "power series."[2] This will involve a detailed elaboration of the mechanism by means of which power series operate in the differential calculus deployed by Deleuze in *Difference and Repetition*. Deleuze actually constructs an alternative history of mathematics that establishes an historical continuity between the differential point of view of the infinitesimal calculus and modern theories of the differential calculus. It is in relation to the differential point of view of the infinitesimal calculus that Deleuze determines a differential logic which he deploys, in the form of a logic of different/ciation, in the development of his project of constructing a philosophy of difference.

the differential point of view of the infinitesimal calculus

The concept of the differential was introduced by developments in the infinitesimal calculus during the latter part of the seventeenth century. Carl Boyer, in *The History of the Calculus and its Conceptual Development*, describes the early

simon duffy

SCHIZO-MATH[1]
the logic of different/ciation and the philosophy of difference

stages of this development as being "bound up with concepts of geometry [...] and with explanations of [...] the infinitely small."[3] Boyer describes the infinitesimal calculus as dealing with "the infinite sequences [...] obtained by continuing [...] to diminish ad infinitum the intervals between the values of the independent variable. [...] By means of [these] successive subdivisions [...] the smallest possible intervals or differentials" are obtained (CB 12). The differential can therefore be understood to be the infinitesimal difference between consecutive values of a continuously diminishing quantity. Boyer refers to this early form of the infinitesimal calculus as the infinitesimal calculus from "the differential point of view" (CB 12). From the differential point of view of the infinitesimal calculus, Boyer

ISSN 0969-725X print/ISSN 1469-2899 online/04/030199–17 © 2004 Taylor & Francis Ltd and the Editors of *Angelaki*
DOI: 10.1080/0969725042000307727

argues that "the derivative would [...] be defined as the quotient of two such differentials, and the integral would then be the sum of a number (perhaps finite, perhaps infinite) of such differentials" (CB 12).

The infinitesimal calculus consists of two branches which are inverse operations: differential calculus, which is concerned with calculating derivatives, or differential relations; and integral calculus, which is concerned with integration, or the calculation of the infinite sum of the differentials. The derivative, from the differential point of view of the infinitesimal calculus, is the quotient of two differentials, that is, a differential relation, of the type dy/dx. The differential, dy, is an infinitely small quantity, or what Deleuze describes as "a vanishing quantity":[4] a quantity smaller than any given or givable quantity. Therefore, as a vanishing quantity, dy, in relation to y, is, strictly speaking, equal to zero. In the same way dx, in relation to x, is, strictly speaking, equal to zero; that is, dx is the vanishing quantity of x. Given that y is a quantity of the abscissa, and that x is a quantity of the ordinate, $dy = 0$ in relation to the abscissa, and $dx = 0$ in relation to the ordinate. The differential relation can therefore be written as $dy/dx = 0/0$. However, although dy is nothing in relation to y, and dx is nothing in relation to x, dy over dx does not cancel out, that is, dy/dx is not equal to zero. When the differentials are represented as being equal to zero, the relation can no longer be said to exist since the relation between two zeros is zero, that is $0/0 = 0$; there is no relation between two things which do not exist. However, the differentials do actually exist. They exist as vanishing quantities in so far as they continue to vanish as quantities rather than having already vanished as quantities. Therefore, despite the fact that, strictly speaking, they equal zero, they are still not yet, or not quite equal to, zero. The relation between these two differentials, dy/dx, therefore does not equal zero, $dy/dx \neq 0$, despite the fact that $dy/dx = 0/0$. Instead, the differential relation itself, dy/dx, subsists as a relation. "What subsists when dy and dx cancel out under the form of vanishing quantities is the relation dy/dx itself" (DSS). Despite the fact that its terms vanish, the rela-

tion itself is nonetheless real. It is here that Deleuze considers seventeenth-century logic to have made "a fundamental leap," by determining "a logic of relations" (DSS). He argues that "under this form of infinitesimal calculus is discovered a domain where the relations no longer depend on their terms" (DSS). The concept of the infinitely small as vanishing quantities allows the determination of relations independently of their terms. "The differential relation presents itself as the subsistence of the relation when the terms vanish" (DSS). According to Deleuze, "the terms between which the relation establishes itself are neither determined, nor determinable. Only the relation between its terms is determined" (DSS). This is the logic of relations that Deleuze locates in the infinitesimal calculus of the seventeenth century.

The differential relation, which Deleuze characterises as a "pure relation" (DSS) because it is independent of its terms, and which subsists in so far as $dy/dx \neq 0$, has a perfectly expressible finite quantity designated by a third term, z, such that dy/dx equals z. Deleuze argues that "when you have a [differential] relation derived from a circle, this relation doesn't involve the circle at all but refers [rather] to what is called a tangent" (DSS). A tangent is a line that touches a circle or curve at one point. The gradient of a tangent indicates the rate of change of the curve at that point, that is, the rate at which the curve changes on the y-axis relative to the x-axis. The differential relation therefore serves in the determination of this third term, z, the value of which is the gradient of the tangent to the circle or curve.

When referring to the geometrical study of curves in his early mathematical manuscripts, Leibniz writes that "the differential calculus could be employed with diagrams in an even more wonderfully simple manner than it was with numbers."[5] Leibniz presents one such diagram in a paper entitled "Justification of the Infinitesimal Calculus by that of Ordinary Algebra," when he offers an example of what had already been established of the infinitesimal calculus in relation to particular problems before the greater generality of its methods was devel-

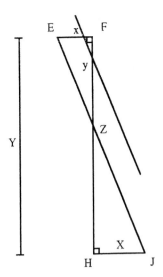

Fig. I.

oped.[6] An outline of the example that Leibniz gives is shown in Fig. 1.

Since the two right triangles, ZFE and ZHJ, that meet at their apex, point Z, are similar, it follows that the ratio y/x is equal to $(Y - y)/X$. As the straight line EJ approaches point F, maintaining the same angle at the variable point Z, the lengths of the straight lines FZ and FE, or y and x, steadily diminish, yet the ratio of y to x remains constant. When the straight line EJ passes through F, the points E and Z coincide with F, and the straight lines, y and x, vanish. Yet y and x will not be absolutely nothing since they preserve the ratio of ZH to HJ, represented by the proportion $(Y - y)/X$, which in this case reduces to Y/X, and obviously does not equal zero. The relation y/x continues to exist even though the terms have vanished since the relation is determinable as equal to Y/X. In this algebraic calculus, the vanished lines x and y are not taken for zeros since they still have an algebraic relation to each other. "And so," Leibniz argues, "they are treated as infinitesimals, exactly as one of the elements which [...] differential calculus recognises in the ordinates of curves for momentary increments and decrements" (PPL 545). That is, the vanished lines x and y are determinable in relation to each other only in so far as they can be replaced by the

infinitesimals dy and dx, by making the supposition that the ratio y/x is equal to the ratio of the infinitesimals, dy/dx. In the first published account of the calculus, Leibniz defines the ratio of infinitesimals as the quotient of first-order differentials, or the differential relation. He says that "the differential dx of the abscissa x is an arbitrary quantity, and that the differential dy of the ordinate y is defined as the quantity which is to dx as the ratio of the ordinate to the subtangent" (CB 210). Leibniz considers differentials to be the fundamental concepts of the infinitesimal calculus, the differential relation being defined in terms of these differentials.

a new theory of relations

Leibniz recognised integration to be a process not only of summation but also of the inverse transformation of differentiation, so the integral is not only the sum of differentials but also the inverse of the differential relation. In the early nineteenth century, the process of integration as a summation was overlooked by most mathematicians in favour of determining integration, instead, as the inverse transformation of differentiation. The main reason for this was that by extending sums to an infinite number of terms, problems began to emerge if the series did not converge. The value or sum of an infinite series is determinable only if the series converges. Divergent series have no sum. It was considered that reckoning with divergent series would therefore lead to false results. The problem of integration as a process of summation from the differential point of view of the infinitesimal calculus did, however, continue to be explored. It was Augustin Cauchy (1789–1857) who first introduced specific tests for the convergence of series, so that divergent series could henceforth be excluded from being used to try to solve problems of integration because of their propensity to lead to false results (CB 287).

The object of the process of integration in general is to determine from the coefficients of the given function of the differential relation the original function from which they were derived. Put simply, given a relation between two differentials, dy/dx, the problem of integration is how to find a relation between the quantities themselves, y and x. This problem corresponds to the geometrical method of finding the function of a curve characterised by a given property of its tangent. The differential relation is thought of as another function which describes, at each point on an original function, the gradient of the line tangent to the curve at that point. The value of this "gradient" indicates a specific quality of the original function; its rate of change at that point. The differential relation therefore indicates the specific qualitative nature of the original function at the different points of the curve.

The inverse process of this method is differentiation, which, in geometrical terms, determines the differential relation as the function of the line tangent to a given curve. Put simply, to determine the tangent of a curve at a specified point, a second point that satisfies the function of the curve is selected, and the gradient of the line that runs through both of these points is calculated. As the second point approaches the point of tangency, the gradient of the line between the two points approaches the gradient of the tangent. The gradient of the tangent is, therefore, the limit of the gradient of the line between the two points.

It was Newton who first came up with this concept of a limit. He conceptualised the tangent geometrically, as the limit of a sequence of lines between two points on a curve, which he called a secant. As the distance between the points approached zero, the secants became progressively smaller; however, they always retained "a real length." The secant therefore approached the tangent without reaching it. When this distance "got arbitrarily small (but remained a real number),"[7] it was considered insignificant for practical purposes, and was ignored. What is different in Lebniz's method is that he "hypothesized infinitely small numbers – infinitesimals – to designate the size of infinitely small intervals" (LN 224). For Newton, on the contrary, these intervals remained only small, and therefore real. When performing calculations, however, both approaches yielded the same results. But they differed ontologically, because Leibniz had hypothesised a new kind of

number, a number Newton did not need, since "his secants always had a real length, while Leibniz's had an infinitesimal length" (LN 224).

For the next two hundred years, various attempts were made to find a rigorous arithmetic foundation for the calculus. One that did not rely on either the mathematical intuition of geometry, with its tangents and secants, which was perceived as imprecise because its conception of limits was not properly understood; or on the vagaries of the infinitesimal, which made many mathematicians wary, so much so that they refused the hypothesis outright, despite the fact that Leibniz "could do calculus using arithmetic without geometry – by using infinitesimal numbers" (LN 224–25). It was not until the late nineteenth century that an adequate solution to this problem of rigour was posed. It was Karl Weierstrass (1815–97) who "developed a pure nongeometric arithmetization for Newtonian calculus" (LN 230), which provided the rigour that had been lacking. "Weierstrass's theory was an updated version of Cauchy's earlier account" (LN 309), which had also had problems conceptualising limits. Cauchy actually begs the question of the concept of limit in his proof.[8] In order to overcome this problem of conceptualising limits, Weierstrass "sought to eliminate all geometry from the study of [...] derivatives and integrals in calculus" (LN 309). In order to characterise calculus purely in terms of arithmetic, it was necessary for the idea of a function, as a curve in the Cartesian plane defined in terms of the motion of a point, to be completely replaced with the idea of a function that is, rather, a set of ordered pairs of real numbers. The geometric idea of "approaching a limit" had to be replaced by an arithmetised concept of limit that relied on static logical constraints on numbers alone. This approach is commonly referred to as the epsilon-delta method. Deleuze argues that:

It is Weierstrass who bypasses all the interpretations of the differential calculus from Leibniz to Lagrange, by saying that it has nothing to do with a process [...] Weierstrass gives an interpretation of the differential and infinitesimal calculus which he himself calls static, where there is no longer fluctuation towards a limit, nor any idea of threshold.[9]

The calculus was thereby reformulated without either geometric secants and tangents or infinitesimals; only the real numbers were used.

Because there is no reference to infinitesimals in this Weierstrassian definition of the calculus, the designation "the infinitesimal calculus" was considered to be "inappropriate" (CB 287). Weierstrass's work not only effectively removed any remnants of geometry from what was now referred to as the differential calculus but it also eliminated the use of Leibniz-inspired infinitesimal arithmetic in doing the calculus for over half a century. It was not until the late 1960s, with the development of the controversial axioms of non-standard analysis by Abraham Robinson (1918–74), that the infinitesimal was given a rigorous foundation,[10] and a formal theory of the infinitesimal calculus was constructed, thus allowing Leibniz's ideas to be "fully vindicated,"[11] as Newtown's had been thanks to Weierstrass.

It is specifically in relation to these developments that Deleuze contends that, when understood from the differential point of view of that infinitesimal calculus, the value of z, which was determined by Leibniz in relation to the differential relation, dy/dx, as the gradient of the tangent, functions as a limit. When the relation establishes itself between infinitely small terms it does not cancel itself out with its terms but rather tends towards a limit. In other words, when the terms of the differential relation vanish, the relation subsists because it tends towards a limit, z. Since the differential relation approaches closer to its limit as the differentials decrease in size, or approach zero, the limit of the relation is represented by the relation between the infinitely small. Of course, despite the geometrical nature of the idea of a variable and a limit, where variables "decrease in size" or "approach zero," and the differential relation "approaches" or "tends towards" a limit, they are not essentially dynamic, but involve purely static considerations, that is, they are rather "to be taken automatically as a kind of shorthand for the corresponding developments of the epsi-

lon-delta approach" (LN 277). It is in this sense that the differential relation between the infinitely small refers to something finite. Or, as Deleuze suggests, it is in the finite itself that there is the "mutual immanence" (DSS) of the relation and the infinitely small.

Given that the method of integration provides a way of working back from the differential relation, the problem of integration is, therefore, how to reverse this process of differentiation. This can be solved by determining the inverse of the given differential relation according to the inverse transformation of differentiation. Or, a solution can be determined from the differential point of view of the infinitesimal calculus by considering integration as a process of summation in the form of a series, according to which, given the specific qualitative nature of a tangent at a point, the problem becomes that of finding not just one other point determinative of the differential relation but a sequence of points, all of which together satisfy, or generate, a curve and therefore a function in the neighbourhood of the given point of tangency, which therefore functions as the limit of the function.

Deleuze considers this to be the base of the infinitesimal calculus as understood or interpreted in the seventeenth century. The formula for the problem of the infinite that Deleuze extracts from this seventeenth-century understanding of the infinitesimal calculus is that "something finite consists of an infinity under a certain relation" (DSS). Deleuze considers this formula to mark "an equilibrium point, for seventeenth-century thought, between the infinite and the finite, by means of a new theory of relations" (DSS). It is the logic of this theory of relations that provides a starting point for the investigation into the logic that Deleuze deploys in *Difference and Repetition* as a part of his project of constructing a philosophy of difference.

the logic of the differential

Having located the logic of the differential from the differential point of view of the infinitesimal calculus in the work of Leibniz, the subsequent developments that this logic undergoes will now be examined in relation to the work of some of the key figures in the history of this branch of the infinitesimal calculus. These figures are implicated in an alternative lineage in the history of mathematics by means of which the differential point of view of the infinitesimal calculus is aligned with the differential calculus of contemporary mathematics. The logic of the differential from the differential point of view of the infinitesimal calculus is then implicated in the development of Deleuze's project of constructing a philosophy of difference. The manner by means of which the figures in the history of the differential point of view of the infinitesimal calculus are implicated in an alternative lineage in the history of mathematics will now be examined.

Ironically, one of the mathematicians who contributed to the development of the differential point of view of the infinitesimal calculus is Karl Weierstrass, who considers the differential relation to be logically prior to the function in the process of determination associated with the infinitesimal calculus; that is, rather than determining the differential relation from a given function, the kinds of mathematical problems that Weierstrass dealt with involved investigating how to generate a function from a given differential relation. Weierstrass develops a theory of integration as the approximation of functions from differential relations according to a process of summation in the form of series. Despite Weierstrass having eliminated both geometry and the infinitesimal from the calculus, Deleuze recovers this theory in order to restore the Leibnizian perspective of the differential, as the genetic force of the differential relation, to the differential point of view of the infinitesimal calculus, by means of the infinitesimal axioms of non-standard analysis.

According to Deleuze's reading of the infinitesimal calculus from the differential point of view, a function does not precede the differential relation, but rather is determined by the differential relation. The differential relation is used to determine the overall shape of the curve of a function primarily by determining the number and distribution of its distinctive points,

which are points of articulation where the nature of the curve changes or the function alters its behaviour. For example, in geometrical terms, when the differential relation is zero, the gradient of the tangent at that point is horizontal, indicating that the curve peaks or dips, therefore determining a maximum or minimum at that point. These distinctive points are known as stationary or turning points. The differential relation characterises or qualifies not only the distinctive points which it determines but also the nature of the regular points in the immediate neighbourhood of these points, that is, the shape of the branches of the curve between each distinctive point. Where the differential relation gives the value of the gradient at the distinctive point, the value of the derivative of the differential relation, that is, the second derivative, indicates the rate at which the gradient is changing at that point, which allows a more accurate approximation of the nature of the function in the neighbourhood of that point. The value of the third derivative indicates the rate at which the second derivative is changing at that point. In fact, the more successive derivatives that can be evaluated at the distinctive point, the more accurate will be the approximation of the function in the immediate neighbourhood of that point.

This method of approximation using successive derivatives is formalised in the calculus according to Weierstrass's theory by a Taylor series or power series expansion. A power series expansion can be written as a polynomial, the coefficients of each of its terms being the successive derivatives evaluated at the distinctive point. The sum of such a series represents the expanded function provided that any remainder approaches zero as the number of terms becomes infinite; the polynomial then becomes an infinite series which converges with the function in the neighbourhood of the distinctive point.[12] This criterion of convergence repeats Cauchy's earlier exclusion of divergent series from the calculus. A power series operates at each distinctive point by successively determining the specific qualitative nature of the function at that point. The power series determines not only the specific qualitative nature of the function at the distinctive point in question but also the specific qualitative nature of all of the regular points in the neighbourhood of that distinctive point, such that the specific qualitative nature of a function in the neighbourhood of a distinctive point insists in that one point. By examining the relation between the differently distributed distinctive points determined by the differential relation, the regular points which are continuous between the distinctive points, that is, in geometrical terms, the branches of the curve, can be determined. In general, the power series converges with a function by generating a continuous branch of a curve in the neighbourhood of a distinctive point. To the extent that all of the regular points are continuous across all of the different branches generated by the power series of the other distinctive points, the entire complex curve or the whole analytic function is generated.

So, according to Deleuze's reading of the infinitesimal calculus, the differential relation is generated by differentials and the power series are generated in a process involving the repeated differentiation of the differential relation. It is due to these processes that a function is generated to begin with. The mathematical elements of this interpretation are most clearly developed by Weierstrassian analysis, according to the theorem on the approximation of analytic functions. An analytic function, being secondary to the differential relation, is differentiable, and therefore continuous, at each point of its domain. According to Weierstrass, for any continuous function on a given interval, or domain, there exists a power series expansion which uniformly converges to this function on the given domain. Given that a power series approximates a function in such a restricted domain, the task is then to determine other power series expansions that approximate the same function in other domains. An analytic function is differentiable at each point of its domain, and is essentially defined for Weierstrass from the neighbourhood of a distinctive point by a power series expansion which is convergent with a "circle of convergence" around that point. A power series expansion that is convergent in such a circle represents a function that is analytic at each point in the circle. By taking a point interior to

the first circle as a new centre, and by determining the values of the coefficients of this new series using the function generated by the first series, a new series and a new centre of convergence is obtained, whose circle of convergence overlaps the first. The new series is continuous with the first if the values of the function coincide in the common part of the two circles. This method of "analytic continuity" allows the gradual construction of a whole domain over which the generated function is continuous. At the points of the new circle of convergence which are exterior to or extend outside of the first, the function represented by the second series is then the analytic continuation of the function defined by the first series – what Weierstrass defines as the analytic continuation of a power series expansion outside its circle of convergence. The domain of the function is extended by the successive adjunction of more and more circles of convergence. Each series expansion which determines a circle of convergence is called an element of the function.[13] In this way, given an element of an analytic function, by analytic continuation one can obtain the entire analytic function over an extended domain. The analytic continuation of power series expansions can be continued in this way in all directions up to the points in the immediate neighbourhood exterior to the circles of convergence where the series obtained diverge.

Power series expansions diverge at specific "singular points" or "singularities" that may arise in the process of analytic continuity. A singular point or singularity of an analytic function is any point which is not a regular or ordinary point of the function. They are points which exhibit distinctive properties and thereby have a dominating and exceptional role in the determination of the characteristics of the function.[14] The distinctive points of a function, which include the turning points, where $dy/dx = 0$, and points of inflection, where $d^2y/dx^2 = 0$, are "removable singular points," since the power series at these points converge with the function. A removable singular point is uniformly determined by the function and therefore redefinable as a distinctive point of the function, such that the function is analytic or continuous at that point. The specific singularities of an analytic function where the series obtained diverge are called "poles." Singularities of this kind are those points where the function no longer satisfies the conditions of regularity which assure its local continuity, such that the rule of analytic continuity breaks down. They are therefore points of discontinuity. A singularity is called a pole of a function when the values of the differential relation, that is, the gradients of the tangents to the points of the function, approach infinity as the function approaches the pole. The function is said to be asymptotic to the pole; it is therefore no longer differentiable at that point but rather remains undefined, or vanishes. A pole is therefore the limit point of a function, and is referred to as an accumulation point or point of condensation. A pole can also be referred to as a jump discontinuity in relation to a finite discontinuous interval both within the same function, for example periodic functions, and between neighbouring analytic functions. Deleuze writes that "a singularity is the point of departure for a series which extends over all the ordinary points of the system, as far as the region of another singularity which itself gives rise to another series which may either converge or diverge from the first" (DR 278). The singularities whose series converge are removable singular points, and those whose series diverge are poles.

The singularities, or poles, that arise in the process of analytic continuity necessarily lie on the boundaries of the circles of convergence of power series. In the neighbourhood of a pole, a circle of convergence extends as far as the pole in order to avoid including it, and the poles of any neighbouring functions, within its domain. The effective domain of an analytic function determined by the process of the analytic continuation of power series expansions is therefore limited to that between its poles. With this method the domain is not circumscribed in advance but results rather from the succession of local operations.

Power series can be used in this way to solve differential relations by determining the analytic function into which they can be expanded. Weierstrass developed his theory alongside the

integral conception of Cauchy, which further developed the inverse relation between the differential and the integral calculus as the fundamental theorem of the calculus. The fundamental theorem maintains that differentiation and integration are inverse operations, such that integrals are computed by finding anti-derivatives, which are otherwise known as primitive functions. There are a number of rules, or algorithms, according to which this reversal is effected.

Deleuze presents Weierstrass's theorem of approximation as an effective method for determining the characteristics of a function from the differential point of view of the infinitesimal calculus. The mathematician Albert Lautman (1908–44) refers to this process as integration from "the local point of view," or simply as "local integration."[15] This form of integration does not involve the determination of the primitive function, which is generated by exercising the inverse operation of integration. The development of a local point of view, rather, requires the analysis of the characteristics of a function at its singular points. The passage from the analytic function defined in the neighbourhood of a singular point to the analytic function defined in each ordinary point is made according to the ideas of Weierstrass, by analytic continuity. This method was eventually deduced from the Cauchy point of view, such that the Weierstrassian approach was no longer emphasised. The unification of both of these points of view, however, was achieved at the beginning of the twentieth century when the rigour of Cauchy's ideas, which were then fused with those of Georg Riemann (1826–66), the other major contributor to the development of the theory of functions, was improved. Deleuze is therefore able to cite the contribution of Weierstrass's theorem of approximation in the development of the differential point of view of the infinitesimal calculus as an alternative point of view of the differential calculus to that developed by Cauchy, and thereby establish an historical continuity between Leibniz's differential point of view of the infinitesimal calculus and the differential calculus of contemporary mathematics, thanks to the axioms of non-standard analysis which allow the inclusion of the infinitesimal in its arithmetisation.

the development of a differential philosophy

While Deleuze draws inspiration and guidance from Salomon Maïmon (1753–1800), who "sought to ground post-Kantianism upon a Leibnizian reinterpretation of the calculus" (DR 170), and "who proposes a fundamental reformation of the *Critique* and an overcoming of the Kantian duality between concept and intuition" (DR 173), it is in the work of Höené Wronski (1778–1853) that Deleuze finds the established expression of the first principle of the differential philosophy. Wronski was "an eager devotee of the differential method of Leibniz and of the transcendental philosophy of Kant" (CB 261). Wronski made a transcendental distinction between the finite and the infinitesimal, determined by the two heterogeneous functions of knowledge, namely understanding and reason. He argued that:

finite quantities bear upon the objects of our knowledge, and infinitesimal quantities on the very generation of this knowledge; such that each of these two classes of knowledge must have laws proper [to them], and it is in the distinction between these laws that the major thesis of the metaphysics of infinitesimal quantities is to be found.[16]

It is imperative not to confuse "the objective laws of finite quantities with the purely subjective laws of infinitesimal quantities" (HW 36, 158). He claims that it is this

confusion that is the source of the inexactitude that is felt to be attached to the infinitesimal Calculus [...] This is also [why] geometers, especially those of the present day, consider the infinitesimal Calculus, which nonetheless they concede always gives true results, to be only an indirect or artificial procedure. (HW 36, 159)

Wronski is referring here to the work of Joseph-Louis Lagrange (1736–1813) and Lazare Carnot (1753–1823), two of the major figures in the history of the differential calculus, whose at-

tempts to provide a rigorous foundation for the differential calculus involved the elimination of the infinitesimal from all calculations, or, as Wronski argued, involved confusing objective and subjective laws in favour of finite quantities (see HW 36, 159). Both of these figures count as precursors to the work of Cauchy and Weierstrass. Wronski argued that the differential calculus constituted "a *primitive algorithm* governing the *generation* of quantities, rather than the laws of quantities *already formed*" (CB 262). According to Wronski, the differential should be interpreted "as having an a priori metaphysical reality associated with the generation of magnitude" (CB 262). The differential is therefore expressed as a pure element of quantitability, in so far as it prepares for the determination of quantity. The work of Wronski represents an extreme example of the differential point of view of the infinitesimal calculus which recurs throughout the nineteenth century.

Another significant figure in this alternative history of mathematics that is constructed by Deleuze is Jean-Baptiste Bordas-Demoulin (1798–1859), who also champions the infinitesimal against those who consider that infinitesimals had to be eliminated in favour of finite quantities. Bordas-Demoulin does not absolve the differential calculus of the accusation of error but rather considers the differential calculus to have this error as its principle. According to Bordas-Demoulin, the minimal error of the infinitesimal "finds itself compensated by reference to an error active in the contrary sense. [...] It is in all necessity that the errors are mutually compensated."[17] The consequence of this mutual compensation "is that one differential is only exact after having been combined with another" (BD 414). Deleuze repeats these arguments of Wronski and Bordas-Demoulin when he maintains that it is in the differential relation that the differential is realised as a pure element of quantitability. Each term of the relation, that is, each differential, each pure element of quantitability, therefore "exists absolutely only in its relation to the other" (DR 172), that is, only in so far as it is reciprocally determined in relation to another.

The question for Deleuze then becomes: "in

what form is the differential relation determinable?" (DR 172). He argues that it is determinable primarily in qualitative form, in so far as it is the reciprocal relation between differentials; and then secondarily, in so far as it is the function of a tangent whose values give the gradient of the line tangent to a curve, or the specific qualitative nature of this curve, at a point. As the function of a tangent, the differential relation "expresses a function which differs in kind from the so-called primitive function" (DR 172). Whereas the primitive function, when differentiated, expresses the whole curve directly,[18] the differential relation, when differentiated, expresses rather the further qualification of the nature of the function at, or in the immediate neighbourhood of, a specific point. The primitive function is the integral of the function determined by the inverse transformation of differentiation, according to the differential calculus. From the differential point of view of the infinitesimal calculus, the differential relation, as the function of the tangent, determines the existence and distribution of the distinctive points of a function, thus preparing for its further qualification. Unlike the primitive function, the differential relation remains tied to the specific qualitative nature of the function at those distinctive points, and, as the function of the tangent, it "is therefore differentiable in turn" (DR 172). When the differential relation is differentiated repeatedly at a distinctive point generating a power series expansion, what is increasingly specified is the qualitative nature of the function in the immediate neighbourhood of that point. Deleuze argues that this convergence of a power series with an analytic function, in its immediate neighbourhood, satisfies "the minimal conditions of an integral" (DR 174), and characterises what is for Deleuze the process of "differen*t*iation" (DR 209).

The differential relation expresses the qualitative relation between not only curves and straight lines but also between linear dimensions and their functions, and plane or surface dimensions and their functions. The domain of the successive adjunction of circles of convergence, as determined by analytic continuity, actually has the structure of a surface. This surface is constituted by the points of the domain and the direction attached to each point in the domain, that is, the tangents to the curve at each point and the direction in which the curve goes at that point. Such a surface can be described as a field of directions or a field of vectors. A vector is a quantity having both magnitude and direction. It is the surface of such a vector field that provides the structure for the local genesis of functions. It is within this context that the example of a jump discontinuity in relation to a finite discontinuous interval between neighbouring analytic or local functions is developed by Deleuze, in order to characterise the generation of another function which extends beyond the points of discontinuity which determine the limits of these local functions. Such a function would characterise the relation between the different domains of different local functions. The genesis of such a function from the local point of view is determined initially by taking any two points on the surface of a vector field, such that each point is a pole of a local function determined independently by the point-wise operations of Weierstrassian analysis. The so determined local functions, which have no common distinctive points or poles in the domain, are discontinuous with each other; each pole being a point of discontinuity, or limit point, for its respective local function. Rather than simply being considered as the unchanging limits of local functions generated by analytic continuity, the limit points of each local function can be considered in relation to each other, within the context of the generation of a new function which encompasses the limit points of each local function and the discontinuity that extends between them. Such a function can be understood initially to be a potential function, which is determined as a line of discontinuity between the poles of the two local functions on the surface of the vector field. The potential function admits these two points as the poles of its domain. However, the domain of the potential function is on a scalar field, which is distinct from the vector field in so far as it is composed of points (scalars) which are non-directional; scalar points are the points onto which a vector field is mapped. The potential function can be defined by the succession of points (scalars) which stretch between the two poles. The scalar field of the potential function is distinct from the vector field of the local functions in so far as, mathematically speaking, it is "cut" from the surface of the vector field. Deleuze argues that "the limit must be conceived not as the limit of a [local] function but as a genuine cut [*coupure*], a border between the changeable and the unchangeable within the function itself [...] the limit no longer presupposes the ideas of a continuous variable and infinite approximation. On the contrary, the concept of limit grounds a new, static and purely ideal definition" (DR 172), that of the potential function. To cut the surface from one of these poles to the next is to generate such a potential function. The poles of the potential function determine the limits of the discontinuous domain, or scalar field, which is cut from the surface of the vector field. The "cut" of the surface in this theory renders the structure of the potential function "apt to a creation" (ALI 8). The precise moment of production, or genesis, resides in the act by which the cut renders the variables of certain functional expressions able to "jump" from pole to pole across the cut. When the variable jumps across this cut, the domain of the potential function is no longer uniformly discontinuous. With each "jump," the poles which determine the domain of discontinuity, represented by the potential function sustained across the cut, seem to have been removed. The more the cut does not separate the potential function on the scalar field from the surface of the vector field, the more the poles seem to have been removed, and the more the potential function seems to be continuous with the local functions across the whole surface of the vectorial field. It is only in so far as this interpretation is conferred on the structure of the potential function that a new function can be understood to have been generated on the surface. A potential function is generated only when there is potential for the creation of a new function between the poles of two local functions. The potential function is therefore always apt to the creation of a new function. This new function, which encompasses the limit points of

each local function and the discontinuity that extends between them, is continuous across this structure of the potential function; it completes the structure of the potential function, in what can be referred to as a "composite function." The connection between the structural completion of the potential function and the generation of the corresponding composite function is the act by which the variable jumps from pole to pole. When the variable jumps across the cut, the value of the composite function sustains a determined increase. Although the increase seems to be sustained by the potential function, it is this increase which actually registers the generation or complete determination of the composite function.

The complete determination of a composite function by the structural completion of the potential function is not determined by Weierstrass's theory of analytic continuity. A function is able to be determined as continuous by analytic continuity across singular points which are removable, but not across singular points which are non-removable. The poles that determine the parameters of the domain of the potential function are non-removable, thus analytic continuity between the two functions, across the cut, is not able to be established. Weierstrass, however, recognised a means of solving this problem by extending his analysis to meromorphic functions.[19] A function is said to be meromorphic in a domain if it is analytic in the domain determined by the poles of analytic functions. A meromorphic function is determined by the quotient of two arbitrary analytic functions, which have been determined independently on the same surface by the point-wise operations of Weierstrassian analysis. Such a function is defined by the differential relation:

$$\frac{dy}{dx} = \frac{Y}{X},$$

where X and Y are the polynomials, or power series, of the two local functions. The meromorphic function, as the function of a differential relation, is just the kind of function which can be understood to have been generated by the structural completion of the potential function. The meromorphic function is therefore the differential relation of the composite function. The expansion of the power series determined by the repeated differentiation of the meromorphic function should generate a function which converges with a composite function. The graph of a composite function, however, consists of curves with infinite branches, because the series generated by the expansion of the meromorphic function is divergent. The representation of such curves posed a problem for Weierstrass, which he was unable to resolve, because divergent series fall outside the parameters of the differential calculus, as determined by the epsilon-delta approach, since they defy the criterion of convergence.

the qualitative theory of differential equations

Henri Poincaré (1854–1912) took up this problem of the representation of composite functions by extending the Weierstrass theory of meromorphic functions to what was called "the qualitative theory of differential equations" (MK 732). In place of studying the properties of complex functions in the neighbourhood of their singularities, Poincaré was occupied primarily with determining the properties of complex functions in the whole plane, that is, the properties of the entire curve. This qualitative method involved the initial investigation of the geometrical form of the curves of functions with infinite branches – only then was the numerical determination of the values of the function able to be made. While such divergent series do not converge, in the Weierstrassian sense, to a function, they may indeed furnish a useful approximation to a function if they can be said to represent the function asymptotically. When such a series is asymptotic to the function, it can represent an analytic or composite function even though the series is divergent.

When this geometrical interpretation was applied to composite functions, Poincaré found the values of the composite function around the singularity produced by the function to be undetermined and irregular. The singularity of a composite function would be the point at which both the numerator and denominator of the quotient of the meromorphic function determinative of the composite function vanish (or equal zero). The peculiarity of the meromorphic function is that the numerator and denominator do not vanish at the same point on the surface of the domain. The points at which the two local functions of the quotient vanish are at their respective poles. The determination of a composite function therefore requires the determination of a new singularity in relation to the poles of the local functions of which it is composed. Poincaré called this new kind of singularity an essential singularity. Observing that the values of a composite function very close to an essential singularity fluctuate through a range of different possibilities without stabilising, Poincaré distinguished four types of essential singularity, which he classified according to the behaviour of the function and the geometrical appearance of the solution curves in the neighbourhood of these points. The first type of singularity is the saddle point or dip (col), through which only two solution curves pass, acting as asymptotes for neighbouring curves. A saddle point is neither a maximum nor a minimum, since it either increases or decreases depending on the direction taken away from it. The second kind of singularity is the node (nœud), which is a point through which an infinite number of curves pass. The third type of singularity is the point of focus (foyer), around which the solution curves turn and towards which they approach in the same way as logarithmic spirals. And the fourth, called a centre, is a point around which the curves are closed, enveloping one another and the centre (see Fig. 2).

The type of essential singularity is determined by the form of the curves constitutive of the meromorphic function. Whereas the potential function remains discontinuous with the other functions on the surface from which it is cut, thereby representing a discontinuous group of functions, the composite function, on the contrary, overcomes this discontinuity in so far as it is continuous in the domain which extends across the whole surface of the discontinuous group of functions. The existence of such a continuous function, however, does not express

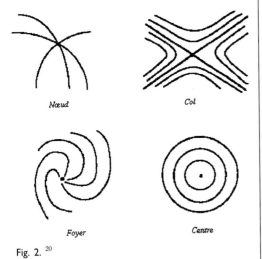

Nœud

Col

Foyer

Centre

Fig. 2. [20]

any less the properties of the domain of discontinuity which serves to define it. The discontinuous group of local functions and the continuous composite function attached to this group exist alongside each other, the transformation from one to the other being determined by the process of the generation and expansion of the meromorphic function. The potential function is actualised in the composite function when the variable jumps from one pole to the other. Its trajectory, in the form of a solution curve, is determined by the type of essential singularity created by the meromorphic function. The essential singularity determines the behaviour of the composite function, or the appearance of the solution curve, in its immediate neighbourhood by acting as an *attractor* for the trajectory of the variable across its domain. It is the value of this function which sustains a determined increase with each jump of the variable. In so far as the trajectory of each variable is attracted to the same final state represented by each of the different essential singularities, these essential singularities can be understood to represent what Manuel DeLanda describes as the "inherent or intrinsic *long-term tendencies* of a system, the states which the system will spontaneously tend to adopt in the long run as long as it is not constrained by other forces."[21]

Deleuze distinguishes this differential point of view of the infinitesimal calculus from the Weierstrassian theory of approximation when he writes that:

> No doubt the specification of the singular points (for example, dips, nodes, focal points, centers) is undertaken by means of the form of integral curves, which refer back to the solutions for the differential equations. There is nevertheless a complete determination with regard to the existence and distribution of these points which depends upon a completely different instance – namely, the field of vectors defined by the equation itself. The complementarity of these two aspects does not obscure their difference in kind – on the contrary. (DR 177)

The equation to which Deleuze refers is the meromorphic function, which is a differential equation or function of a differential relation determined according to the Weierstrassian approach, from which the essential singularity and therefore the composite function are determined according to Poincaré's qualitative approach. This form of integration is again characterised from the local point of view, and is characterised by what Deleuze describes as "an original process of differenciation" (DR 209). Differenciation is the complete determination of the composite function from the reciprocally determined local functions or the structural completion of the potential function. It is the process whereby a potential function is actualised as a composite function.

Deleuze states that "actualisation or differenciation is always a genuine creation," and that to be actualised is "to create divergent lines" (DR 212). The expanded power series of a meromorphic function is actualised in the composite function in so far as it converges with, or creates, the divergent lines of the composite function. Differenciation, therefore, creates an essential singularity, whose divergent lines actualise the specific qualitative nature of the poles of the group of discontinuous local functions, represented by a potential function, in the form of a composite function. These complex functions can be understood to be what Poincaré called "Fuschian functions," which, as Georges Valiron points out, "are more often called automorphic functions."[22] The discontinuous group of local

211

functions can therefore also be understood to be Fuschian groups. Poincaré's pioneering work in this area eventually led to the definitive founding of the geometric theory of analytic functions, the study of which "has not yet been completely carried out" (GV 173) but continues to be developed with the assistance of computers.

Benoit Mandelbrot (b. 1924) considers Poincaré, with his concept of essential singularities, to be "the first student of fractal ('strange') attractors," that is, of the kinds of attractors operative in fractals which occur in mathematics, and cites certain theories of Poincaré as having "led [him] to new lines of research," specifically "the theory of automorphic functions," which made Poincaré and Felix Klein (1849–1925) famous.[23]

Deleuze does not consider this process of differenciation to be arrested with the generation of a composite function, but rather to continue, generating those functions which actualise the relations between different composite functions, and those functions which actualise the relations between these functions, and so on. The conception of differenciation is extended in this way when Deleuze states that "there is a differenciation of differenciation which integrates and welds together the differenciated" (DR 217); each differenciation is simultaneously "a local integration," which then connects with others, according to the same logic, in what is characterised as a "global integration" (DR 211).

The logic of the differential, as determined according to both differentiation and differenciation, designates a process of production, or genesis, which has, for Deleuze, the value of introducing a general theory of relations which unites the Weierstrassian structural considerations of the differential calculus to the concept of "the generation of quantities" (DR 175). "In order to designate the integrity or the integrality of the object," when considered as a composite function from the differential point of view of the infinitesimal calculus, Deleuze argues that "we require the complex concept of different/ciation. The t and the c here are the distinctive feature or the phonological relation of difference in person" (DR 209). Deleuze argues that differenciation is "the second part of difference" (DR 209), the first being expressed by the logic of the differential in differentiation. Where the logic of differentiation characterises a differential philosophy, the complex concept of the logic of different/ciation characterises Deleuze's "philosophy of difference."

The differential point of view of the infinitesimal calculus represents an opening, providing an alternative trajectory for the construction of an alternative history of mathematics; it actually anticipates the return of the infinitesimal in the differential calculus of contemporary mathematics, thanks to the axioms of non-standard analysis. This is the interpretation of the differential calculus to which Deleuze is referring when he appeals to the "barbaric or pre-scientific interpretations of the differential calculus" (DR 171). Deleuze thereby establishes an historical continuity between the differential point of view of the infinitesimal calculus and modern theories of the differential calculus which surpasses the methods of the differential calculus that Weierstrass uses in the epsilon-delta approach to support the development of a rigorous foundation for the calculus. While Weierstrass is interested in making advances in mathematics to secure the development of a rigorous foundation for the differential calculus, Deleuze is interested in using mathematics to problematise the reduction of the differential calculus to set theory, by determining an alternative trajectory in the history of mathematics, one that retrospectively allows the reintroduction of the infinitesimal to an understanding of the operation of the calculus. According to Deleuze, the "finitist interpretations" of the calculus given in modern set-theoretical mathematics – which are congruent with "Cantorian finitism,"[24] that is, "the idea that infinite entities are [...] considered to be finite within set theory"[25] (JS 66) – betray the nature of the differential no less than Weierstrass, since they "both fail to capture the extra-propositional or sub-representative source [...] from which calculus draws its power" (DR 264).

In constructing this theory of relations characteristic of a philosophy of difference, Deleuze draws significantly from the work of Albert Lautman, who refers to this whole process as "the metaphysics of logic" (ALI 3). It is in *Difference and Repetition* that Deleuze formulates a "metaphysics of logic" that corresponds to the logic of the differential from the differential point of view of the infinitesimal calculus. However, he argues that "we should speak of a dialectics of the calculus rather than a metaphysics" (DR 178), since:

> each engendered domain, in which dialectical Ideas of this or that order are incarnated, possesses its own calculus. [...] It is not mathematics which is applied to other domains but the dialectic which establishes [...] the direct differential calculus corresponding or appropriate to the domain under consideration. (DR 181)

Just as he argued that mathematics:

> does not include only solutions to problems; it also includes the expression of problems relative to the field of solvability which they define. [...] That is why the differential calculus belongs to mathematics, even at the very moment when it finds its sense in the revelation of a dialectic which points beyond mathematics. (DR 179)

It is in the differential point of view of the infinitesimal calculus that Deleuze finds a form of the differential calculus appropriate to the determination of a differential logic. This logic is deployed by Deleuze, in the form of the logic of different/ciation, in the development of his project of constructing a philosophy of difference.

The relation between the finite and the infinitesimal is determined according to what Lautman describes as "the logical schemas which preside over the organisation of their edifices."[26] Lautman argues that "it is possible to recover within mathematical theories, logical Ideas incarnated in the same movement of these theories" (ALII 58). The logical Ideas to which Lautman refers include the relations of expression between the finite and the infinitesimal. He argues that these logical Ideas "have no other purpose than to contribute to the illumination of logical schemas within mathematics, which are only knowable through the mathematics themselves" (ALII 58). The project of the present paper has been to locate these "logical Ideas" in the math-

duffy

ematical theory of the infinitesimal calculus from the differential point of view, in order then to determine how Deleuze uses these "logical Ideas" to develop the logical schema of a theory of relations characteristic of a philosophy of difference.

notes

I would like to thank Daniel W. Smith for his generous comments when reviewing an early version of this paper.

1 It is in *Anti-Oedipus* that Deleuze coins the phrase "schizophrenic mathematics" (Gilles Deleuze and Félix Guattari, *Anti-Oedipus: Capitalism and Schizophrenia* 372), which I have borrowed and shortened to "Schizo-Math" in order to expand upon some of the themes introduced in the paper "Math Anxiety" by Aden Evens (*Angelaki* 5:3 (2000): 105).

2 Gilles Deleuze, *Difference and Repetition* 114. Hereafter DR.

3 Carl Benjamin Boyer, *The History of the Calculus and its Conceptual Development* 11. Hereafter CB.

4 Gilles Deleuze, "Sur Spinoza," 17 Feb. 1981. Hereafter DSS.

5 Gottfried Wilhelm Leibniz, *The Early Mathematical Manuscripts* 53.

6 Leibniz, "Letter to Varignon, with a Note on the 'Justification of the Infinitesimal Calculus by that of Ordinary Algebra'" 545. Hereafter PPL.

7 George Lakoff and Rafael E. Nañez, *Where Mathematics Comes From: How the Embodied Mind Brings Mathematics into Being* 224. Hereafter LN.

8 For a thorough analysis of this problem with limits in Cauchy, see CB 281.

9 Deleuze, "Sur Leibniz," 22 Feb. 1972.

10 See J.L. Bell, *A Primer of Infinitesimal Analysis*.

11 Abraham Robinson, *Non-Standard Analysis* 2.

12 Given a function, $f(x)$, having derivatives of all orders, the Taylor series of the function is given by

$$\sum_{k=0}^{\infty} \frac{f^{(k)}(a)}{k!}(x - a)^k,$$

where $f^{(k)}$ is the kth derivative of f at a. A function is equal to its Taylor series if and only if its error term R_n can be made arbitrarily small, where

$$R_n = \left| f(x) - \sum_{k=0}^{\infty} \frac{f^{(k)}(a)}{k!}(x-a)^k \right|.$$

The Taylor series of a function can be represented in the form of a power series, which is given by

$$\sum_{n=0}^{\infty} a_n x^n = a_0 + a_1 x + a_2 x^2 + \cdots + a_n x^n + \cdots,$$

where each a is a distinct constant. It can be shown that any such series either converges at $x = 0$, or for all real x, or for all x with $-R < x < R$ for some positive real R. The interval $(-R, R)$ is called the circle of convergence, or neighbourhood of the distinctive point. This series should be thought of as a function in x for all x in the circle of convergence. Where defined, this function has derivatives of all orders. See H.J. Reinhardt, *Analysis of Approximation Methods for Differential and Integral Equations*.

13 See Morris Kline, *Mathematical Thought from Ancient to Modern Times* 643–44. Hereafter MK.

14 Deleuze argues that "It was a great day for philosophy when […] Leibniz proposed […] that there is no reason for you simply to oppose the singular to the universal. It's much more interesting if you listen to what mathematicians say, who for their own reasons think of 'singular' not in relation to 'universal', but in relation to 'ordinary' or 'regular'" (Deleuze, "Sur Leibniz," 29 Mar. 1980).

15 Albert Lautman, *Essai sur les notions de structure et d'existence en mathématiques* 38; my trans. Hereafter ALI.

16 Höené Wronski, *La Philosophie de l'infini: Contenant des contre-refléxions sur la métaphysique du calcul infinitesimal* 35; large sections of this text, translated by M.B. DeBevoise, appear in Michel Blay (ed.), *Reasoning with the Infinite: From the Closed World to the Mathematical Universe* 158. Hereafter HW. Page references will be given to the French and the English translation respectively.

17 Jean-Baptiste Bordas-Demoulin, *Le Cartésianisme ou la véritable rénovation des sciences, suivi de la théorie de la substance et de celle de l'infini* 414; my trans. Hereafter BD.

18 Note: the primitive function $f(x)dx$, expresses the whole curve $f(x)$.

19 It was Charles A.A. Briot (1817–82) and Jean-Claude Bouquet (1819–85) who introduced the term "meromorphic" for a function which possessed just poles in that domain (MK 642).

20 June Barrow-Green, *Poincaré and the Three Body Problem* 32.

21 Manuel DeLanda, *Intensive Science and Virtual Philosophy* 15.

22 Georges Valiron, "The Origin and the Evolution of the Notion of an Analytic Function of One Variable" 171. Hereafter GV.

23 Benoit B. Mandelbrot, *The Fractal Geometry of Nature* 414. Mandelbrot qualifies these statements when he says of Poincaré that "nothing I know of his work makes him even a distant precursor of the fractal geometry of the visible facets of Nature" (ibid. 414).

24 Penelope Maddy, "Believing the Axioms" 488.

25 Jean-Michel Salanskis, "Idea and Destination" 71.

26 Albert Lautman, *Essai sur l'unité des sciences mathématiques dans leur développement actuel* 58; my trans. Hereafter ALII.

bibliography

Barrow-Green, June. *Poincaré and the Three Body Problem*. Rhode Island: American Mathematical Society, 1997.

Bell, J.L. *A Primer of Infinitesimal Analysis*. New York: Cambridge UP, 1998.

Blay, Michel. *Reasoning with the Infinite: From the Closed World to the Mathematical Universe*. Chicago: U of Chicago P, 1998.

Bordas-Demoulin, Jean-Baptiste. *Le Cartésianisme ou la véritable rénovation des sciences, suivi de la théorie de la substance et de celle de l'infini*. Paris: Gauthier-Villars, 1874.

Boyer, Carl Benjamin. *The History of the Calculus and its Conceptual Development*. New York: Dover, 1959.

DeLanda, Manuel. *Intensive Science and Virtual Philosophy*. Transversals. London and New York: Continuum, 2002.

Deleuze, Gilles. *Difference and Repetition*. Trans. Paul Patton. New York: Columbia UP, 1994.

Deleuze, Gilles. *Expressionism in Philosophy. Spinoza*. Trans. Martin Joughin. New York: Zone, 1992.

Deleuze, Gilles. "Seminars." The seminars on Leibniz and on Spinoza, 1971–87. "Sur Leibniz," 22 Feb. 1972, trans. Simon Duffy; 29 Mar. 1980, trans. Charles J. Stivale. "Sur Spinoza," 17 Feb. 1981, trans. Timothy S. Murphy. Available < http://www.webdeleuze.com >.

Deleuze, Gilles and Félix Guattari. *Anti-Oedipus: Capitalism and Schizophrenia*. Trans. Robert Hurley, Mark Seem and Helen R. Lane. Minneapolis: U of Minnesota P, 1983.

Evens, Aden. "Math Anxiety." *Angelaki* 5.3 (2000): 105–15.

Kline, Morris. *Mathematical Thought from Ancient to Modern Times*. Oxford: Oxford UP, 1972.

Lakoff, George and Rafael E. Nañez. *Where Mathematics Comes From: How the Embodied Mind Brings Mathematics into Being*. New York: Basic Books, 2000.

Lautman, Albert. *Essai sur les notions de structure et d'existence en mathématiques*. Paris: Hermann, 1938.

Lautman, Albert. *Essai sur l'unité des sciences mathématiques dans leur développement actuel*. Paris: Hermann, 1938.

Leibniz, Gottfried Wilhelm. *The Early Mathematical Manuscripts*. Trans. J.M. Childs. Chicago: Open Court, 1920.

Leibniz, Gottfried Wilhelm. "Letter to Varignon, with a Note on the 'Justification of the Infinitesimal Calculus by that of Ordinary Algebra.'" *Philosophical Papers and Letters*. Trans. Leroy E. Loemker. Dordrecht: Reidel, 1969.

Leibniz, Gottfried Wilhelm. *Die Philosophischen Schriften von G. W. Leibniz*. Berlin: Weidmannsche, 1875–90.

Maddy, Penelope. "Believing the Axioms." *Journal of Symbolic Logic* 53.2 (1988): 481–511.

Mandelbrot, Benoit B. *The Fractal Geometry of Nature*. San Francisco: Freeman, 1982.

Reinhardt, H.J. *Analysis of Approximation Methods for Differential and Integral Equations*. New York: Springer, 1985.

Robinson, Abraham. *Non-Standard Analysis*. Revised ed. *Princeton Landmarks in Mathematics and Physics*. Princeton: Princeton UP, 1996.

Salanskis, Jean-Michel. "Idea and Destination." *Deleuze: A Critical Reader*. Ed. Paul Patton. Oxford: Blackwell, 1996.

Valiron, Georges. "The Origin and the Evolution of the Notion of an Analytic Function of One Variable." *Great Currents of Mathematical Thought*. Ed. François Le Lionnais. Vol. I. New York: Dover, 1971.

Wronski, Hoené. *La Philosophie de l'infini: contenant des contre-refléxions sur la métaphysique du calcul infinitesimal*. Paris, 1814.

Simon Duffy
Department of Philosophy
Main Quad A14
University of Sydney
Sydney, NSW 2006
Australia
E-mail: sduffy@usyd.edu.au

notes on the contributors

tammy clewell

is Assistant Professor of English at Kent State University. Her work has appeared in journals including *Modern Fiction Studies*, *Journal of the American Psychoanalytic Association*, and *Literature/Film Quarterly*. She is currently finishing a book-length manuscript on the politics of mourning in the twentieth-century British novel.

steven corcoran (translator)

is a Ph.D. candidate at the University of New South Wales, Australia. He is working on political ontology in the work of Badiou and Rancière.

simon duffy

teaches in the Department of Philosophy at the University of Sydney (Australia). His publications include "The Logic of Expression in Deleuze's *Expressionism in Philosophy: Spinoza*. A Strategy of Engagement," *International Journal of Philosophical Studies* 12.1 (2004); and he is the editor of *Virtual Mathematics: The Logic of Difference*, a collection on the theme of Deleuze and mathematics forthcoming from Clinamen Press.

alexander garcía düttmann

lives in London and teaches at Goldsmiths College. Recent publications include *Philosophy of Exaggeration* (Suhrkamp, 2004), *Thus It Is. A Philosophical Commentary on Adorno's* Minima Moralia (Suhrkamp, 2004) and *Erase the Traces* (Diaphanes, 2004).

karen s. feldman

is author of *Binding Words: Conscience and Rhetoric in Hobbes, Hegel and Heidegger* (Northwestern UP, forthcoming in 2005) and co-editor of *Continental Philosophy: An Anthology* (Blackwell, 1998). She teaches in the Departments of Rhetoric and German at the University of California at Berkeley.

sean gaston (translator)

is a Research Fellow of the Department of English, University of Melbourne. His forthcoming book is entitled *Derrida and Disinterest* (New York: Continuum, 2005).

kristin gjesdal

is a postdoctoral research fellow in the Department of Philosophy at the University of Oslo, Norway. For the past couple of years she has also been teaching in the Department of Philosophy at the University of Essex. She has written a number of forthcoming articles on issues in hermeneutics, phenomenology, and the philosophy of art.

pelagia goulimari (editor)

teaches part-time at the University of Oxford. She is the General Editor of *Angelaki: Journal of the Theoretical Humanities*. She has published articles in *Angelaki*, *Textual Practice*, *Hypatia: Journal of Feminist Philosophy*, *Postmodern Culture* and elsewhere. She is currently editing *Postmodernism. What Moment?* (Manchester UP, 2005) and *Event Gilles Deleuze* (Manchester UP, 2005).

david huddart

is Lecturer in Cultural Studies at Bath Spa University College. Books on Homi Bhabha and postcolonial autobiography are forthcoming from Routledge.

dominique lecourt

is Professor of Philosophy at the Université Denis Diderot – Paris VII. His publications include *Marx and Epistemology: Bachelard, Canguilhem, Foucault* (1975); *Proletarian Science? The Case of Lysenko* (1977); and, more recently, the *Dictionnaire d'histoire et philosophie des sciences* (1999), which received an award from the Institut de France; the "Que sais je?" edition on *La Philosophie des sciences* (2001); and *The Mediocracy: French Philosophy since the Mid-1970s* (2001).

alan lopez

is a Ph.D. candidate in English at SUNY Buffalo. He received his MA at Syracuse University and BA at Indiana University South Bend. He is currently working on a project on Gilles Deleuze's thought in the context of romantic and Continental narratives on the aporias of alterity and representation.

ethan h. macadam

is a lecturer in the Department of English at the University of Miami. He is currently working on a study of the idea of the state of nature, as this idea runs through political and literary discourse from the seventeenth century to the present day.

jacques rancière

is Emeritus Professor of Aesthetics and Politics at the University of Paris VIII (Saint-Denis). His books in English include: *The Nights of Labor* (1989); *The Ignorant Schoolmaster* (1991); *The Names of History* (1994); *On the Shores of Politics* (1995); *Disagreement* (1999); and *Short Voyages to the Land of the People* (2003).

gabriel riera

is Assistant Professor of Comparative Literature at Princeton University. He is the editor of *Alain Badiou, Philosophy and its Conditions* (SUNY Press, forthcoming in 2004). He completed a book called *Intrigues of the Other. Ethics and Literary Writing in Levinas and Blanchot* and has published essays on such subjects as twentieth-century literature, philosophy and psychoanalysis, Heidegger, Lacan and Badiou. He is currently working on two book projects: *Fidelity to the Event: Of Narration in Saer* and *Singularities: Ethics of Narration*.

anthony uhlmann

teaches literature and film in the School of Humanities at the University of Western Sydney, Australia. He is the author of *Beckett and Poststructuralism* (Cambridge UP, 1999). He is currently completing a new study concerning the nature of the "image" in modernist aesthetics and the use of images drawn from philosophy in Beckett's works.

elizabeth walden

is Assistant Professor of Philosophy and Cultural Studies at Bryant College, Smithfield, Rhode Island. Her writing on philosophy, film and media includes "Subjects after New Media" forthcoming in the *Quarterly Review of Film and Video* 23.1 and "Vision, Touch and Feminist Epistemology" in *Tessera* 32.

isabelle loring wallace

is Assistant Professor of Contemporary Art at the University of Georgia in Athens. A regular contributor to *artUS*, she has published several articles in the fields of modern and contemporary art and is currently at work on a book entitled *Signification and the Subject: The Art of Jasper Johns*.

maria walsh

is a Senior Lecturer in Art History and Theory at Chelsea College of Art & Design. She has written on artists' film and video for a number of magazines such as *COIL*, *Senses of Cinema*, and *filmwaves*.

ANGELAKI
journal of the theoretical humanities

BEST NEW JOURNAL
Council of Editors of
Learned Journals 1996 Awards

Modern Language Association Convention,
Washington, D.C.

Transcript of the presentation

This year's Best New Journal is *Angelaki*.

One judge called *Angelaki* "A strong and surprising publication that is interested in a wide range of cultural studies issues from harder-theory perspectives," while another praised its "speaking-to-the-moment stance." *Angelaki*'s "position papers" and "substantial essays, addressing current concerns in cultural theory" zero in on "interesting and problematical topics and fields," with results that are "resourceful," "rigorous," and "lively."

Another judge remarked on *Angelaki*'s physical strengths: "The covers and small format are attractive, and the two-column layout is readable, the paper good." The following remark, however, sums things up best: "I put *Angelaki* at the top because I find it refreshingly alive, buzzing with critical energy."

Angelaki 36A Norham Rd
Oxford OX2 6SQ UK

E-mail: editorial@angelaki.demon.co.uk
http://www.tandf.co.uk/journals/
routledge/0969725x.html

back issues

vol. 1, no. 1
the uses of theory

Publication: September 1993. Pages: 144.
ISBN: 1 899567 00 3

Editors: Pelagia Goulimari
Oxford
and Gerard Greenway
Oxford

vol. 1, no. 2
narratives of forgery

Publication: April 1994. Pages: 176.

Editor: Nick Groom
University of Exeter

vol. 1, no. 3
reconsidering the political

Publication: January 1995. Pages: 200.
ISBN: 1 899567 02 X

Editors: David Howarth
University of Essex
and Aletta J. Norval
University of Essex

vol. 2, no. 1
home and family

Publication: November 1995. Pages: 208.
ISBN: 1 899567 03 8

Editor: Sarah Wood
Oxford

vol. 2, no. 2
authorizing culture

Publication: March 1996. Pages: 168.
ISBN: 1 899567 04 6

Editors: Gary Hall
University of Middlesex
and Simon Wortham
University of Portsmouth

vol. 5, no. 2
rhizomatics, genealogy, deconstruction

Publication: August 2000. Pages: 239.
ISBN: 0 902879 41 3

Editor: Constantin V. Boundas
Trent University

vol. 5, no. 3
general issue 2000

Publication: December 2000. Pages: 160.
ISBN: 0 902879 46 4

Editor: Pelagia Goulimari
Oxford

vol. 6, no. 1
subaltern affect

Publication: April 2001. Pages: 206.
ISBN: 0415 27109 6

Editors: Jon Beasley-Murray
University of Manchester
and Alberto Moreiras
Duke University

Contents

vol. 6, no. 2
gift, theft, apology

Publication: August 2001. Pages: 206.
ISBN: 0415 27110 X

Editor: Constantin V. Boundas
Trent University

Contents

vol. 6, no. 3
general issue 2001

Publication: December 2001. Pages: 238.
ISBN: 0415 27111 8

Editor: Pelagia Goulimari
Oxford

Contents

vol. 7, no. I
aesthetics and the ends of art

Publication: April 2002. Pages: 262.
ISBN: 1 899567 06 02

Editor: Gary Banham
         Manchester Metropolitan University
Curator: Sharon Kivland

Contents

vol. 7, no. 2
inventions of death: literature, philosophy, psychoanalysis

Publication: August 2002. Pages: 214.
ISBN: 1 899567 07 0

Editor: Roger Starling
        University of Warwick

Contents

vol. 7, no. 3
general issue 2002

Publication: December 2002. Pages: 190
ISBN: 1-899567-08-9

Editor: Pelagia Goulimari
Oxford

Contents

vol. 8, no. 1
general issue 2003 1

Publication: April 2003. Pages: 180
ISBN: 1-899567-09-7

Editor: Pelagia Goulimari
Oxford

Contents

vol. 8, no. 2
the one or the other
french philosophy today

Publication: August 2003. Pages: 248
ISBN: 1-899567-10-0

Editor: Peter Hallward
King's College London

Contents

Editorial Introduction, *Peter Hallward*. Some Comments on the Question of the One, *Christian Jambet*. "Our World": An Interview, *Jean-Luc Nancy & Peter Hallward*. Stagings of Mimesis: An Interview, *Philippe Lacoue-Labarthe & Peter Hallward*. Despite Everything, Happiness is Still Happiness: An Interview, *Clément Rosset & Nicolas Truong*. The Problem of Great Politics in the Light of Obviously Deficient Modes of Subjectivation, *Guy Lardreau*. Phenomenology of Life, *Michel Henry*. Beyond Formalisation: An Interview, *Alain Badiou & Peter Hallward/Bruno Bosteels*. Sexual Alterity and the Alterity of the Real for Thought, *Monique David-Ménard*. Technics of Decision: An Interview, *Bernard Stiegler & Peter Hallward*. What Can Non-Philosophy Do?, *François Laruelle*. Politics and Aesthetics: An Interview, *Jacques Rancière & Peter Hallward*. The Mole and the Locomotive, *Daniel Bensaïd*. The Science of Relations: An Interview, *Michel Serres & Peter Hallward*.

vol. 8, no. 3
general issue 2003 II

Publication: December 2003. Pages: 210
ISBN: 1-899567-11-9

Editor: Pelagia Goulimari
Oxford

Contents

Editorial Introduction, *Pelagia Goulimari*. Non-violence and the Other: A Composite Theory of Multiplism, Heterology and Heteronomy Drawn from Jainism and Gandhi, *Chakravarthi Ram-Prasad*. Infinite Spaces: Walter Benjamin and the Spurious Creations of Capitalism, *Mark Cauchi*. Übermenschen, Mestizas, Nomads: The Ontology of Becoming and the Scene of Transnational Citizenship in Anzaldúa and Nietzsche, *Salah el Moncef*. Cavaillès, Husserl and the Historicity of Science, *David Webb*. The Theatre of Phenomenology, *Andrew Haas*. Statements and Profiles, *Gilles Deleuze*. Her Voiceless Voice: Reviewing Sappho's Poetics, *Cornelia Tsakiridou*. Lacanians and the Fate of Critical Theory, *Filip Kovacevic*. Bataille and the Erotics of Hegelian Geist, *Kane X. Faucher*. The Problem of a Material Element in the Cinematic Sign: Deleuze, Metz and Peirce, *Roger Dawkins*. Amidst the Plurality of Voices: Philosophy of Music after Adorno, *Nikolas Kompridis*. A Harmless Suggestion, *Robert Smith*.

vol. 9, no. 1
hotel psychoanalysis

Publication: July 2004. Pages: 222
ISBN: 1-899567-12-7

Editor: Sarah Wood
University of Kent

Contents

Call for Papers, *Sarah Wood*. Hotel Psychoanalysis: Some Remarks on Mark Twain and Sigmund Freud, *Nicholas Royle*. [Last Year \, *Sharon Kivland*. Light without Glimmer, *Timothy Bahti*. Reservations ... Concerning Libido Theory and the Afterlife of Psychoanalysis, *Caroline Rooney*. Did Women Threaten the Oedipus Complex between 1922 and 1933? Freud's Battle with Universality and its Aftermath in the Work of K. Horney and M. Torok, *Nicholas Rand*. The Schizoanalytic Protest: *Homosexual Desire* Revisited, *James Penney*. Having Words, *Suzy Gordon*. Pasolini in the Desert, *Cesare Casarino*. Freudian Idiom – A Hotel Chain, *Forbes Morlock*. From Sacher-Masoch to Masochism, *Gilles Deleuze*. Rebirth through Incest: On Deleuze's Early Jungianism, *Christian Kerslake*. The Girl with the Open Mouth: Through the Looking Glass, *Sara Guyer*. Caresses, Excesses, Intimacies and Estrangements, *Mark Paterson*. On Cixous's Tongue (Beyond Scopic Desire), *Frédéric Regard*. The Punning of Reason: On the Strange Case of Dr Jacques L ..., *Dany Nobus*. Free Association Revisted: Freud, Adorno and the Gift of the Gab, *Roy Sellars*.

vol. 9, no. 2
the politics of place

Publication: December 2004. Pages: 236
ISBN: 1-899567-13-5

Editors: Andrew Benjamin
Monash University
Dimitris Vardoulakis
Monash University

Contents

Editorial Introduction: The Politics of Place, *Andrew Benjamin & Dimitris Vardoulakis*. On Cultural Survival, *Gil Anidjar*. Thinking Love *with* Drawn in the Process of Becoming Australian, *Louise Gray*. Banks, Edges, Limits (of Singularity), *Jean-Luc Nancy*. Placing Speaking: Notes on the First Stasimon of Sophocles' *Antigone*, *Andrew Benjamin*. Spaces of Hospitality, *Heidrun Friese*. The Critique of Loneliness: Towards the Political Motives of the Doppelgänger, *Dimitris Vardoulakis*. Territory, Landscape, Garden: Toward Geoaesthetics, *Gary Shapiro*. Ecstatic Dwelling: Perspectives on Place in European Romanticism, *Kate Rigby*. Keeping Art to its Edge, *Edward S. Casey*. "I Don't Think they Invented the Wheel": The Case for Aboriginal Modernity, *Stephen Muecke*. Colonizing the Ideal: Neoclassical Articulations and European Modernities, *Neni Panourgiá*. Mapping: The Locus of the Project, *Teresa Stoppani*. Factory, Territory, Metropolis, Empire, *Alberto Toscano*. Architecture at War: A Report from Ground Zero, *Reinhold Martin*.

ANGELAKI

journal of the theoretical humanities

annual index
volume 9, 2004

(author, title, issue no., page no.)